DR. MARTIN LUTHER KING JR. AND THE POOR PEOPLE'S CAMPAIGN OF 1968

DR. MARTIN LUTHER KING JR. AND THE POOR PEOPLE'S CAMPAIGN OF 1968

ROBERT HAMILTON

THE UNIVERSITY OF GEORGIA PRESS ATHENS

A Sarah Mills Hodge Fund Publication
This publication is made possible in part through a grant from the
Hodge Foundation in memory of its founder, Sarah Mills Hodge,
who devoted her life to the relief and education of African Americans
in Savannah, Georgia.

Set in 9.5/13.5 Utopia Std by Kaelin Chappell Broaddus

Most University of Georgia Press titles are
available from popular e-book vendors.

Printed digitally

Library of Congress Cataloging-in-Publication Data

Names: Hamilton, Robert (Senior Lecturer), author.
Title: Dr. Martin Luther King Jr. and the Poor People's Campaign of 1968 / Robert Hamilton.
Description: Athens : The University of Georgia Press, [2020] | Series: The Morehouse College King
    collection series on civil & human rights | Includes bibliographical references and index.
Identifiers: LCCN 2020028086 (print) | LCCN 2020028087 (ebook) | ISBN 9780820358284
    (hardback) | ISBN 9780820358277 (paperback) | ISBN 9780820358291 (ebook)
Subjects: LCSH: King, Martin Luther, Jr., 1929-1968. | Poor People's Campaign—History. | Civil rights
    movements—Washington (D.C.)—History—20th century. | Minorities—United States—Economic
    conditions—20th century. | Poor—United States—Social conditions—20th century. | Minorities—Civil
    rights—United States—History—20th century. | United States—Race relations—History—20th century.
Classification: LCC E185.97.K5 H259 2020 (print) | LCC E185.97.K5 (ebook) | DDC 323.09753/0904—dc23
LC record available at https://lccn.loc.gov/2020028086
LC ebook record available at https://lccn.loc.gov/2020028087

For Dr. Bernard Lafayette Jr.
and for my twin brother, Craig Hamilton;
my mother, Marjory;
and May and Douglas

Resurrection City cannot be seen as a mudhole in Washington, but it is rather an idea unleashed in history. . . . The idea has taken root and is growing across the country.

—JESSE JACKSON

CONTENTS

ACKNOWLEDGMENTS

First of all, I would like to thank my editors: Walter Biggins, executive editor of the University of Georgia Press, and Vicki Crawford, director of the Martin Luther King Jr. Collection and an associate professor of African-American Studies at Morehouse College. Both were patient and encouraging from the outset, and I am grateful for their professionalism and their support. Thanks also to project editor Thomas Roche.

I owe a great deal to the staffs in various archives in the United States who were so helpful and generous with their time, support, and advice. Primary source material for the book was drawn from the following archives: the Martin Luther King Jr. Collection, Atlanta University Center, Robert W. Woodruff Library, Morehouse College, Atlanta; the King Library and Archives, King Center, Atlanta; the Schomburg Center for Research in Black Culture (including the Catherine Clarke Civil Rights Collection and the Albert E. Gollin Collection), New York; the Hosea Williams Collection, Auburn Avenue Research Library on African American Culture and History, Atlanta; the Ralph J. Bunche Oral History Collection, Moorland-Spingarn Research Center, Manuscript Division, Howard University, Washington, D.C.; and the Dr. Martin Luther King Jr. Papers at the Howard Gotlieb Archival Research Center, Boston University.

Many individuals offered crucial advice and support, including Bernard Lafayette, who was appointed by King as the national director of the PPC in 1968. From our first meeting in 2014, when I began working on scholarly articles on the PPC, Bernard offered invaluable support and guidance. As the founding director of the University of Rhode Island's Center for Nonviolence and Peace Studies, Lafayette continues to lead education and training programs in Kingian nonviolence (strategies of nonviolent social change) on state, national, and international levels. In our various meetings over the years, he has been unfailingly gracious and has offered many unique insights. I also express my appreciation to Charles Lewis, president of the SCLC, who kindly met with me in his office with Lafayette to discuss the Poor People's Campaign. Tyrone Brooks of the SCLC provided important information on both the Mule Train and Resurrection City. I would also like to thank Lalage Bown, whose zeal for adult education and the difference it can make in people's lives is undiminished more than twenty-five years after her retirement as a professor of adult and continuing education at the University of Glasgow. She read drafts of the book, and her insights were invaluable. I also appreciate Claire Gilmour, whose work on the endnotes and general formatting of the book was so important.

Portions of the book previously appeared as "Did the Dream End There? Adult Education and Resurrection City, 1968," *Studies in the Education of Adults* 45, no. 1 (2013): 4–26, and "The Mule Train: Adult Learning and the Poor People's Campaign, 1968," *Studies in the Education of Adults* 48, no. 1 (2016): 38–64. I would like to thank Jim Crowther, former editor of *Studies in the Education of Adults*, for his advice and support.

This book could not have been completed without the support of colleagues. My appreciation to Stella Heath, director of Short Courses at the University of Glasgow, and all of my colleagues past and present. My gratitude to friends who provided encouragement and insights into civil rights and social justice issues. Finally, I offer thanks to all members of my extended family for their support during the writing of this book. Special thanks to my twin brother and best friend, Craig Hamilton; to my mother, Marjory Hamilton; and to May and Douglas.

DR. MARTIN LUTHER KING JR.
AND THE POOR PEOPLE'S
CAMPAIGN OF 1968

This book is about the last days of Dr. Martin Luther King Jr. and one of King's major projects, which was carried forward by his successors—the Poor People's Campaign (PPC) of 1968. This campaign has often been undervalued and misunderstood, and my main aim here is to revalue and reflect on that initiative. I look at it in part as an educational exercise: the campaign was planned and worked out not only to develop a new form of social protest but also as an instrument for the participants to expand their social knowledge and understanding. With that focus, the importance of the campaign is considerably more obvious.

In August 1967, National Association for the Advancement of Colored People (NAACP) Legal Defense and Educational Fund attorney Marian Wright (she married in 1968 and is best known as Marian Wright Edelman, which is the name I use in this book) met with Senator Robert F. Kennedy at his home in Hickory Hill, Virginia. An impressive figure, Edelman was the first black woman admitted to the Mississippi bar. She was counsel to the Child Development Group of Mississippi (CDGM), which served thirteen thousand children and created three thousand jobs free of the plantation system in the South.[1] Her encounter with Robert Kennedy that day would have profound implications for the civil rights movement and for Southern Christian Leadership Conference (SCLC) leader Dr. Martin Luther King Jr. in particular. Edelman recalled it was a "gorgeous day" with everyone lounging about the pool.[2] The contrast between their pleasant surroundings at Hickory Hill and the focus of some of their discussions could not have been starker. Amid their "small chat" on what was going on across America, Edelman and Kennedy focused on the issue of poverty and how "everybody" was being distracted by the Vietnam War.[3]

One brief exchange defined their meeting and helped to set in motion a series of events leading to what became the Poor People's Campaign of 1968. On hearing that Edelman was due to call on King in Atlanta, Robert Kennedy suggested she encourage him to bring poor people to Washington. Kennedy believed Congress would be willing to make concessions by enacting legislation against poverty in order to make the poor go away again. He undoubtedly also had broader political objectives in mind. Kennedy advised Edelman to "get in President Lyndon Johnson's face, bring them [the poor] and make them visible."[4] In the weeks and months prior to their discussion, Kennedy had established himself as one of the Democratic Party's leading critics of the domestic and foreign policies of President Johnson. He had grown increasingly unhappy with Johnson's approaches to urban unrest, poverty, and the war in Vietnam. Kennedy was also aware that Dr. King had intensified his own pressure on the federal government to take decisive action against poverty. Robert Kennedy anticipated that the presence of poor people in Washington, D.C., would expose the limitations of Johnson's War on Poverty and thereby embarrass the president.

Marian Wright Edelman was close to both Dr. King and Senator Kennedy. She was grateful for King's assistance in late 1965 in support of the efforts in Mississippi to continue funding for the CDGM, the largest multicounty Head Start program in America. Conservative politicians in Mississippi were keen to close the CDGM, viewing it as radical and as a Trojan horse designed to help bring about equality of the races in the South. Edelman later observed that Dr. King's "presence and support [were] invaluable" during a challenging period for her.[5] The Johnson administration, wary of offending white sensibilities in the South, regarded King as an "outside agitator" for getting involved in Mississippi on Edelman's behalf.[6] Edelman was also instrumental in helping Robert Kennedy to understand how poverty and its various manifestations, such as low-quality education, inadequate housing, unemployment, and an unfair welfare system, had blighted lives in the United States. At her request, Kennedy had visited Mississippi in April 1967 just a few months before their meeting at Hickory Hill. In the company of fellow members of the Senate Subcommittee on Employment, Manpower and Poverty, Robert Kennedy came to the Mississippi Delta to investigate the impact of Johnson's War on Poverty programs. The Economic Opportunity Act (EOA) was up for reauthorization during this period. In a hostile political climate, in which spending associated with the War on Poverty was falling out of favor in Washington and with the public generally, everything was potentially up for grabs.

Kennedy attracted significant media attention as the star of the delegation to Mississippi, which helped to shine a light on the work of the committee as it uncovered the realities of life for the poorest of the poor in the richest nation on earth. The evidence presented to the subcommittee in Mississippi personalized the plight of poverty-stricken children, mothers, and families. Testimony from Edelman and impoverished people from the Delta placed America and its social policies on trial. In support of a campaign against poverty, the SCLC later cited evidence from the government field hearings conducted by Kennedy and others and claimed that this revealed poverty to be no less than "a national disgrace" with "chronic hunger and malnutrition" to be found in every part of the United States.[7]

Marian Wright Edelman was receptive to Robert Kennedy's idea of a campaign in Washington led by the poor and agreed to raise it with Dr. King in Atlanta. She met with King soon after her discussion with Kennedy. Four unemployed men from the Mississippi Delta accompanied Edelman to the meeting in Atlanta.[8] Their presence set the tone for the campaign against poverty to come. Each of these family men were unemployed due to well-off farmers leaving their lands fallow in order to claim government subsidies. Their authentic voices were representative of thousands of others who would soon answer the call from Dr. King to set up camp in Washington for the PPC in 1968. Marian Wright Edelman herself would act as counsel and congressional liaison officer for the campaign.

Edelman recalled that Dr. King at first seemed depressed.[9] A number of factors could explain his state of mind in the summer of 1967, including his despair over the urban riots, which had increasingly become a feature of American life. There were also the threats to both his hopes for full integration of the races and his advocacy of nonviolence from the more strident voices of Black Power. The urban riots and the rise of Black Power had helped to intensify a political and public backlash against the civil rights movement. In addition, King was by now aware of the limitations of the landmark civil rights legislation of 1964 and 1965 and the failure of the movement to achieve equality for all in America. The political fallout from King's public opposition to the Vietnam War had taken its toll on his resolve and on his spirit as well. With so many different problems weighing on his mind, King seemed unsure as to where he might turn next.[10] Given his apparent demeanor as the meeting began, Edelman could not have anticipated how enthusiastically Dr. King would embrace the Kennedy proposal. On hearing about the suggestion to organize a campaign in Washington, King seemed transformed. Edelman wrote that "Dr. King's eyes lit up and he called me an angel sent by God, thus, the idea of a Poor People's Campaign, for which I was honored to serve as a messenger, was born."[11]

King was convinced that this was the way forward and committed himself to a plan to hold nonviolent protests in Washington against poverty. Within months, he began to put together a multiracial coalition of the poor, including blacks, whites, Puerto Ricans, Mexican Americans, and Native Americans, to go to the nation's capital. This became the Poor People's Campaign of 1968. Coretta Scott King later said of her husband, "The prospect of establishing a rainbow coalition that could eventually see beyond racism and challenge the systems that demeaned all persons, excited Martin."[12] Unlike previous civil rights campaigns, which often sought a single piece of legislation, the PPC's demands were for the development by the federal government of new costly economic and social policies.[13]

The demands eventually covered a range of civil rights and human rights issues. Housing, education, welfare, and jobs were all included in the requests to Congress. More specific demands were also made on a range of issues, reflecting both the particular and shared needs of the various racial and cultural groups of poor people involved in the campaign. Native Americans, for example, were concerned with fishing rights, land rights, and better education and called in particular for compliance with the legal treaties between tribes and the U.S. government, observing that "citizenship is not something you sell for trinkets, blankets and beads."[14] Mexican Americans were interested in economic questions and land issues. The main PPC demand was for an Economic Bill of Rights to apply to every citizen. It included calls for a meaningful guaranteed job with a livable wage, a secure income, the ability to access land for economic reasons, access to capital for the less well-off, and citizens to have a larger role in government.

Tragedy was around the corner, however. In early 1968, with planning for the Washington campaign under way, King's attention was directed to a black sanitation worker strike for better pay, union recognition, and decent working conditions in Memphis, Tennessee. Many in King's SCLC inner circle were opposed to his involvement in Memphis, viewing it as a distraction from the main PPC event. King maintained that Memphis was about poor people and therefore represented the Washington campaign in microcosm. If he did not help the low-paid sanitation workers, there was no point in continuing with plans for the PPC. The SCLC leader was committed to the cause of the most vulnerable in society and gave his full support to the Memphis struggle. His assassination in Memphis on April 4, the day after he delivered a memorable speech, robbed Dr. King of the chance to lead the poor to the nation's capital. His loss was felt across the globe yet at the same time strengthened the resolve of PPC organizers and participants to continue with his initiative. Just over one month later, a multiracial group of around six thousand poor people made final preparations to travel to Washington, D.C., from across the United States. They came to fulfill King's dream to end poverty in America.

On May 13, 1968, King's successor as president of the SCLC, the Reverend Ralph Abernathy, officially opened the temporary encampment, which was called Resurrection City and was intended to house thousands of poor people while they were demonstrating against poverty across Washington. In the spirit of nonviolence, the residents of the camp came armed only with a series of demands for the federal government. Decades before the modern Occupy movement similarly set up camps to protest global poverty and inequality, the PPC participants constructed wooden huts and tents on the Mall, a traditional site of protest and a center of democracy. Resurrection City was situated at the heart of the great Washington landmarks and in the symbolic shadow of the Lincoln Memorial. The camp had a basic infrastructure, and attempts were made to incorporate many of the facilities found in larger permanent urban centers. It provided the normal city functions of maintenance, sanitation, supplies, information (scheduling, communications, and mail), security (police, fire protection), transportation, health services, food services, childcare, and recreation. The city was divided into communities, neighborhoods, and blocks. It also had a city hall, a healthcare center, and, in recognition of the importance given to learning, a Poor People's University (PPU), Freedom Schools, and a library.

Resurrection City was a short-lived experiment. It was forcibly evacuated and torn down by D.C. authorities beginning on June 24, 1968, just six weeks after it was declared open.[15] Since then, the PPC has been dismissed by the majority of historians as "an almost perfect failure," which was "poorly timed, poorly organized and poorly led."[16] Frady, for example, argued that Resurrection City's problem as a strategy for continuing the movement after King's death was that "it was not movement but emblem, static and so passive."[17] Elements in the press at the time presented an image of the campaign as chaotic and disorganized. *U.S. News and World Report* described the camp as a place from which "nothing but further virulence and infection can issue."[18] This image has endured. The PPC has invariably been regarded as a footnote in the story of the civil rights movement.

Yet there is another side to the story, which deserves to be heard. Compared to other social movements before 1968 and arguably since, the national and racial reach of the PPC was unique. It can be contrasted, for example, with the lack of racial diversity at the Seattle protests against the World Trade Organization in 1999.[19] The temporary community of Resurrection City was particularly important in that it afforded the pedagogical space for poor people of different races and cultural backgrounds to come together in ways unparalleled in U.S. history until this point. Although there were some problems with its organization, Resurrection City was still viewed as "a useful model of community development in action," and "there was, in some areas, a sense of place and participation seldom seen in slums or public housing."[20] One PPC activist maintained that its best achievement was to bring together different races and religions under one tent.[21] Although tensions and conflict were in evidence within and between the various groups in Resurrection City, many of the residents worked and learned together in a spirit of solidarity.

Impoverished people came to Resurrection City in May 1968 from different points in the nation by means of nine caravans, dubbed "Freedom Roads." Some traveled by bus and train, and others even in carts pulled by mules, a universal symbol of poverty. For many of them this was the first time they had left their own counties. Their journeys to Washington were long and taxing, but they were filled with hope that they might effect change. They were part of something both historic and significant, and their unique contributions to the enduring struggles of low-income people against poverty and inequality should be acknowledged. Those who traveled to Washington included Native Americans from reservations where the life expectancy, according to the SCLC, was only forty-three and a half years and who were six times more likely to die from tuberculosis and more than forty thousand times more likely to catch severe pneumonia than other citizens were. Also in Resurrection City were white families from mill towns who were now unemployed after twenty years of work as well as those regarded as "white trash," who scrounged in garbage cans. Black people—who made up over a quarter of the Americans living in poverty but constituted just over 10 percent of the population—came from the South, North, and West to demand jobs, decent housing, and education.[22] Mexican Americans who came to Washington charged that "poverty and city living under the Anglos' colonial system" had "castrated their culture, consciousness of heritage, and language."[23] They demanded decent living accommodations, quality education, recognition of Spanish as a first language in schools, a school curriculum reflecting their cultural heritage, and the return of all stolen "property," including minerals, water, and timber and grazing rights.[24]

The people who traveled to Washington in May–June 1968 included in their ranks 101-year-old Mrs. Mattie Grinnell (Mandan). Her participation in the occupation of space in the nation's capital showed that even the oldest people were motivated by Dr. King to try to make a difference in the life conditions of the poor. Although late in life, she was determined to turn things around for herself and for others. Grinnell explained to a Senate hearing in Washington that she had made the journey from her reservation in North Dakota to tell President Johnson that she received no help back home. She reflected on a past when things had been better, when her people could live off the land. Mrs. Grinnell alleged that Native American people were starving on the reservation. They received only scraps to eat such as cornmeal, oats, and rice, often infested with worms.

Mrs. Myrtle Brown, an unemployed mother of five from Marks, Mississippi, the poorest town in the poorest state in America, told the same Senate hearing that she joined the campaign on the day Dr. King visited her community to promote the initiative. Another woman from Mississippi said she came to Washington to put right her situation: she had worked all her life, yet her family was "starving to death." She had no home fit to live in, and she stayed up all night holding a light over her children to keep the roaches away while they slept.[25]

Peggy, a white grandmother from Alabama, described in the press as a "hillbilly," came to Resurrection City with her children and grandchildren. She bonded in the camp with Ray, a young black man who had lived with his wife and children in ghettos in the North, the South, and Washington, D.C. Ray had a simple but evocative sign hanging outside his hut: "We have lived in many houses. This is our first home. Welcome."[26]

The people who came to Washington in 1968 deserve better from history than to have the PPC dismissed as being of little consequence. Many of them worked together in solidarity during the preparations for the PPC in their home communities, on the road to Washington, and in Resurrection City itself. They learned about the causes of poverty and how they might change their root condition. Some of them took part in various forms of protest and in workshops, informal discussions, Freedom Schools, and cultural activities. Regularly, hundreds set off for government departments and Congress to lobby and demonstrate in support of their demands for legislation to end poverty. All who came were making a statement about the unacceptability of poverty in America. Some of the poor stayed for only a few days before leaving for home. But in remarkable displays of fortitude and resilience, other residents of Resurrection City remained and endured incessant rain and attempts by the forces of the state to make them go away again. And we are reminded, "something wonderful happens to people when they are somehow determining their own destiny and beginning to control and change their real conditions."[27]

One of the greatest injustices in failing to recognize the merits of the PPC is that this neglect also does a disservice to Dr. King's legacy. The PPC would not have been possible without his leadership, his vision to end economic injustice, and his determination to hold America to account for its treatment of the poor of all races. He devoted the last few months of his life to drive the idea forward, worked intensively to recruit leaders and poor people from a variety of racial groups, and provided the inspiration for large numbers of the participants even after his death. The campaign represents the best example of his career-long affinity with the most marginalized people in society. Although Dr. King did not live to see the realization of his plan to unite the poor across racial, gender, age, ethnic, and regional differences, his spirit was with many of those who made the journey to the nation's capital.

King's vision for the PPC was radical and expansive. He referred to the campaign not in terms of civil rights, but as a "human rights struggle." He had argued from 1966 that the civil rights movement now needed to grapple with "basic class issues between the privileged and the underprivileged." This required no less than the "restructuring of the architecture of American society," a phrase he uttered repeatedly in the final years of his life.[28] The campaign offered an alternative to the dominant politics of the state and a rejection of the postwar liberal consensus.

King's stance on economic injustice and the immorality of the Vietnam conflict attracted the feverish attention of the FBI under the leadership of Director J. Edgar Hoover, as well as of the police. Amid the Cold War, urban unrest, black militancy, a polarized political climate, a backlash against the civil rights movement and the poor people whose interests it represented, and opposition to the Vietnam War and to the counterculture movement, King's rhetoric on economic injustice, including references to the need for a redistribution of the nation's wealth, saw him denounced as a communist.[29] In a political and social context hostile to the "great unwashed" arriving in Washington, Senator John Stennis of Mississippi spoke for many political elites in calling for the poor to be blockaded.[30] Even liberal allies of the SCLC leader cut King loose, especially after his public condemnations of the Vietnam War.

My examination of the PPC reveals Dr. King to be revolutionary in his aspirations for America. Yet many still think of him in a "narrow sense as a civil rights rather than a human rights leader."[31] Attempts have even been made to "dilute and sanitize much of what King represented."[32] Some scholars have argued, for example, that many on the Left have a false idea of King, "portraying him as a well-meaning if naïve liberal . . . finally coming to see . . . that some variant of socialism might be necessary."[33] The relative absence in civil rights literature of the PPC and King's commitment to the issues it represented can be compared, for example, to the iconic status accorded to his speech in August 1963 during the March on Washington. Ironically, that was an event, in common with the PPC, concerned with demands for jobs and economic justice.

In this book I show that Dr. King's journey toward a campaign against poverty did not begin at his meeting with Marian Wright Edelman in 1967. The idea marked a logical development in his career and in his thinking; in addition, it fit the needs of the time when Robert Kennedy suggested it. Social justice and economic justice had long been central to King's ministry.[34] His educational background highlights some of the early forces that helped to shape him as a civil rights and human rights leader who would throw his lot in with the poor. In 1944, King followed the example of his grandfather and father in enrolling at Morehouse College in Atlanta; he was only fifteen years old. Morehouse has deep roots in the black Baptist tradition. Inherent in this mission is the "belief that alumni will become leaders and help deliver those who are oppressed."[35] The intellectual influences he encountered at Morehouse remained with King throughout his life. He read Thoreau's essay "Civil Disobedience," an experience he described as his first intellectual contact with the theory of nonviolent resistance. Civil disobedience, a refusal to cooperate with an evil system, fascinated him and came to characterize his career, including plans for the Poor People's Campaign beginning in 1967. King became convinced that noncooperation with evil was as much a moral obligation as cooperation with good.[36] He learned during the Montgomery Bus Boycott in 1955–1956 from Bayard Rustin, an authority on Gandhian methods of nonviolence, to see clearly that the philosophy, strategy, and tactics of nonviolence could fashion a transformative revolutionary movement.[37] Gandhi's struggle in India against British imperialism provided an example for King on how to confront the power of "those who resisted progress."[38]

While Gandhi provided the methods, King's religious beliefs gave him the spirit and motivation.[39] Social Gospel thinkers, including Walter Rauschenbusch, provided King with the theological basis for his social concerns. Morehouse College professor George Kelsey encouraged King to bridge the gap between religious and secular ideas by emphasizing the "Christian gospel as the basis for social reform."[40] King learned this lesson well; he later wrote that "the church must develop a social action program and take a stand wherever economic and social injustice exists."[41] The opportunity at Morehouse to learn about the ideas of the Social Gospel laid the groundwork for further reflections in King's own "intellectual quest for a method to eliminate social evil."[42] In his penultimate year at Morehouse, King realized that he wanted to join the ministry and to follow the examples of his father and grandfather. In 1960, he observed, "Any religion that professes to be concerned about the souls of men and is not concerned about the slums that damn them, the economic conditions that strangle them and the social conditions that cripple them, is a spiritually moribund religion awaiting burial."[43]

I argue that Dr. King was consciously working toward the concept of the Poor People's Campaign from at least 1964 and more intensively from 1966. Although the suggestion to mount such an effort came from Senator Robert Kennedy in 1967, King could claim ownership of the idea. In a prophetic article published in 1964, Dr. King called for a multiracial effort to tackle unemployment, a "grand alliance" of black and white, which should consist of the vast majority of each group.[44] He claimed that the need for such an effort was becoming more urgent because of societal changes pushing people into "permanent uselessness and hopeless impoverishment."[45] King's concerns were expressed during a period of intensive reform in the United States. The civil rights movement achieved two major pieces of legislation: the Civil Rights Act of 1964 and the Voting Rights Act of 1965. In addition to the progress made possible by this legislation, President Lyndon Johnson's War on Poverty, announced in January 1964, encouraged many civil rights leaders to hope that full equality, including economic justice for all American citizens, was within reach. While King had reservations about the scope of the War on Poverty, he remained cautiously optimistic from 1964 to 1965 that the Johnson initiatives would improve the condition of poor people.

Although Johnson's roots were in the segregated South, the new president's commitment to tackling poverty seemed sincere. Johnson's upbringing in poverty-stricken rural Texas, his personal insights into the role of government in tackling unemployment during the New Deal, and the fact he now enjoyed the power he had worked for all his life—all motivated the president to try to address the issue of poverty in America. The seeds of the War on Poverty can arguably be found in the New Frontier agendas of Johnson's predecessor, President John F. Kennedy. However, Johnson deserves great credit for his abilities to overcome opposition to his plans in Congress. Demonstrating the renowned "Johnson treatment," he took the case to elected representatives, cajoling, persuading, threatening, and promising in equal measure to win the support of those sympathetic to his cause as well as those implacably opposed to progressive legislation.

Spending on fighting poverty by 1964 was made possible by low unemployment levels and increasing productivity. While many benefited from economic expansion, it is estimated that at the dawn of the 1960s 20 percent of Americans lived below the poverty line.[46] Two books, John Kenneth Galbraith's *The Affluent Society* and Michael Harrington's *The Other America*, revealed that millions had missed out during a period of assumed general prosperity for America.

Harrington later served on King's research committee that provided much of the data underpinning arguments in favor of a national campaign against poverty. King asked him to write an overview plan for the PPC. Both Harrington and King agreed on the necessity to change the income structure of U.S. society through a redistribution of wealth.[47] The rediscovery of poverty amid assumed abundance provoked much debate and controversy among politicians and academics. The War on Poverty initiative brought the issue of economic injustice firmly onto the national agenda and incorporated civil rights and tax cuts into an overall plan of action. President Johnson believed his ideas would provide social justice, tackle urban conditions including inadequate housing and education, further deliver on the goals of the civil rights movement, and show the world, in the context of the Cold War, that capitalism was a superior system to communism.

The Johnson poverty plans initially scored well with King and more broadly with eastern liberals. Johnson brought business on board, cultivated industry, and argued that all could benefit from his initiatives. To win over middle-class Americans to his ideas and overcome the stereotype of the "unworthy poor," the president aspired to end dependence on welfare and bring poor people into the fold by making them taxpayers rather than tax eaters, providing a hand up, not a handout. In May 1964, Johnson introduced the notion of the Great Society, a phrase inspired in part by Walter Lippmann's book *The Good Society*. The goals expressed in the Great Society speech, crafted by Richard Goodwin, were far-reaching, expansive, and ambitious. President Johnson aspired to promote the quality as well as the quantity of American life, rejecting crass materialism and national wealth as ends in themselves. Johnson also viewed the War on Poverty and the Great Society as part of a broader solution to civil rights issues with the aim of racial harmony.[48]

The buoyant economy and his landslide presidential election win in 1964 over right-wing Republican Barry Goldwater made all things possible in President Johnson's estimation. The Johnson election mandate also encouraged King to believe that the federal government would now lead the way in tackling poverty and inequality. He shared with many others in the movement a belief that government could act as an agent of positive change. Eighty-three percent of black people polled in 1963 believed the federal government was helpful to them, although they did not express the same confidence in state and local governments.[49] High points of the War on Poverty included Medicare, Medicaid, and the Elementary and Secondary Education Act, all in 1965. Head Start provided education, hot meals, and medical care for disadvantaged preschool children; it passed despite conservative resistance in Congress, which labeled it as a socialist attempt to take control away from parents. Marian Wright Edelman, of course, felt the brunt of this conservative onslaught in her work with the Child Development Group of Mississippi. Also in 1965, Johnson signed the Higher Education Act into law at his old teacher training college, a symbolic act of great significance for the president. He also tried to address the negative impacts of rapid urbanization, an issue soon to vex Dr. King as the shortfalls of the War on Poverty became more evident. In urban affairs, various housing acts began the process of slum clearance, and the Demonstration Cities Act of 1966 promoted better coordination of public facility construction projects in cities. Other pieces of legislation tackled the nationalization of commercial power and provided protection for the environment, consumers, and workers. Although King pointed to the limitations of the War on Poverty, the initiative achieved some success. Unemployment for nonwhite people decreased from 12 percent to 6 percent between 1961 and 1969; black poverty fell between 1959 and 1974 from 55 percent to 30 percent.[50]

No sooner was the ink dry at the official signing of the Voting Rights Act in August 1965 than riots broke out in the poor, mainly black community of Watts in Los Angeles. In the wake of the disturbances, President Johnson felt let down that his efforts to resolve race and poverty issues had not prevented urban unrest. A shocked King visited Watts to see the devastation for himself and to hear firsthand accounts from the residents on what had occurred and why. Watts set King on the path to the Poor People's Campaign. All the evidence suggested to the SCLC leader that conditions in housing, unemployment, and education were, if anything, worsening despite the War on Poverty initiatives. His initial confidence in the possibilities offered by the Johnson legislative program gradually dissipated. King became increasingly concerned that the War on Poverty did not include policies to bring about wealth redistribution. Johnson believed instead that a growing economy would allow everyone to rise up and improve their condition in life. King's relationship with the president became fraught, and they were keeping each other at arm's length by mid-1966.

Continuing urban unrest during 1965 helped Dr. King to see ever more clearly that poverty was a class issue that transcended race. He placed jobs, housing, and education at the center of a new ambitious urban agenda. In January 1966, King began an effort to establish his own nonviolent movement in the North, in the Chicago slums. He aspired to create an "open city" in Chicago. He planned to use direct action and nonviolence, to mobilize both black and white people to end the situation of slum tenements, to enforce open housing policies, and to provide effective access to job opportunities.[51] He believed that through organized protest he could move poor black people from being "passive" subjects to "active" citizens. With public opinion turning against the movement in part due to urban uprisings, King's presence was antagonistic to whites in Chicago, who responded to the protests with a backlash of noncooperation, violence, and intimidation. He described racism in that city as the worst he had ever experienced. He surmised that the powerlessness of poor people in ghetto areas explained their plight. What turned out to be an inconclusive campaign in Chicago to end the slums merely encouraged King to intensify his efforts to end economic injustice.

In an article for *Ebony* magazine in October 1966, more than one year after the passage of the Voting Rights Act, King reflected on the journey traveled and the road ahead. He warned that the movement was now approaching areas where "the voice of the Constitution" was not clear, noting that activists had "left the realm of constitutional rights and were entering the arena of human rights."[52] King appreciated that legislation had brought down segregation signs and in theory had assured the right to vote. However, there remained no "such assurance of the right to adequate housing, or the right to an adequate income."[53] He wrote in the same article of the moral right of every citizen to decent housing, an adequate education, and enough money to provide for one's family.

Dr. King became ever more radical in his rhetoric against economic injustice from 1966 through 1968. He was uncompromising; his words were far-reaching in their implications for the administration of President Johnson and for the nation. He also focused his fire on the escalating Vietnam War. King attacked the war economy and the immorality of U.S. domestic and foreign policy. He argued that America would never invest the necessary funds or energies to address poverty as long as Vietnam continued to draw men, skills, and money like "some demoniacal suction tube."[54] The slums and Vietnam became one in his thinking. He called for human rights for all; opposed poverty, racism, and imperialism; and viewed inequality not only in American but also in global terms. King now realized that the war was an enemy of poor people, and he had no choice other than to speak out and "tell the truth."[55]

In May 1967, just a few months before his meeting with Edelman, Dr. King told the SCLC staff that "we have moved from the era of civil rights to the era of human rights, an era where we are called upon to raise certain basic questions about the whole society."[56] One month later, King began a punishing schedule to publicize his new book, *Where Do We Go from Here: Chaos or Community?* The book provided a useful summary of his reflections on what had been a tumultuous and exhausting few years with many facets. He outlined his deep-rooted concerns about America and the challenges faced by the civil rights movement in the new phase beyond the Voting Rights Act of 1965. These included an increasing white backlash against the movement fueled by sentiment that social programs rewarded rioters and looters. King regretted also the fractures and divisions within the civil rights movement itself. This included the rise of Black Power, which saw some established leaders "cast aside," for example, John Lewis of the Student Nonviolent Coordinating Committee, symbolizing a radical change of tactics, including a rejection of nonviolence. Black militancy threatened the already crumbling alliance between the civil rights movement and its white liberal supporters. The media portrayed supporters of Black Power as violent and antiwhite. As a slogan, it evoked whites' fears of a race war and re-ignited the flames still smoldering in the public memory of the 1959 television documentary by Mike Wallace and Louis Lomax on the Nation of Islam called *The Hate That Hate Produced*. The emergence of black militants Stokely Carmichael and H. Rap Brown in 1966 had far-reaching consequences. They represented change in the makeup of civil rights activism and undermined coalitions that President Kennedy and President Johnson had worked on for years.[57] It became impossible to speak of one civil rights movement because different objectives and different methodologies came to the fore.

King's decision to take up the proposal from Robert Kennedy's emissary Marian Wright Edelman—to organize a campaign of the poor in Washington—was in part motivated by his determination to offer young people an alternative to Black Power. He shared the concerns of black militants about conditions in urban centers and their analysis of a racist capitalist system in America. In June 1967, the Justice Department reported disturbances in 110 cities.[58] The nation was divided, and a race war seemed possible to some. On July 25, 1967, only one month before Edelman came to see him carrying the message from Kennedy, King sent a telegram to President Johnson outlining his grave concerns about the response of the federal government to yet another summer of urban uprisings. He informed Johnson that "only drastic changes in the life of the poor will provide the kind of order and stability you desire." King cited recent legislation and cuts in the War on Poverty programs as examples of how the "moral degradation" of Congress had hastened the "destruction of the lives of blacks in the ghettos." He called on Johnson to use the full powers of his office and follow the example of the New Deal in the 1930s to take radical steps to end the scourge of unemployment. Only substantive measures, he suggested, would end the "turmoil of the ghetto," which itself represented the "externalization of the black's inner torment and rage."[59] The measures he demanded would take real form in his plans for the Poor People's Campaign.

Dr. King became increasingly dissatisfied with the Johnson administration's responses to the crisis in urban centers. King sympathized with the alienation and frustration felt by many young black people caught in the cycle of poverty, which was the root of the anger being expressed in such dramatic form in the ghettos. He wrote that the limitations of the War on Poverty in terms of ever-reduced funding, the absence of policies to redistribute wealth, and top-down management merely accentuated the disaffection felt by young people. In the belief that continuing disorder in the cities would further erode the diminishing support for the nonviolent civil rights movement, King observed that young black people "in an irrational burst of rage had sought to say something, but the flames had blackened both themselves and their oppressors."[60] His book *Where Do We Go from Here?* called for a renewed focus on economic agendas as a response to Black Power and the endemic nature of poverty across the nation. Dr. King shared the view of black militants that power could change conditions for people. He noted, however, that "Power for Poor People" was a much more appropriate slogan than "Black Power."[61] King advised poor people to organize and gain power in three main areas: electoral politics, labor union activism, and economic boycotts. With reference to electoral politics, he urged black people to play their part by voting and by building political alliances. In this way, they might counter the white backlash and political candidates whose "magic" was "achieved with a witches' brew of bigotry, prejudice, half-truths and whole lies."[62] King argued that a united black vote would deliver quality education, good well-paid jobs, and decent comfortable homes.

In an indication of the destination King was rapidly moving toward, he also more directly set out the case for a national campaign against poverty to involve all races. Looking ahead to what would become the Poor People's Campaign of 1968, Dr. King prophetically wrote that the future of the "deep structural changes we seek will not be found in the decaying political machines, it lies in new alliances of blacks, Puerto Ricans, labor, liberals, certain church and middle-class elements."[63] Finally, King wrote that he regretted that Black Power gave priority to the race question to the detriment of the crucial economic issues facing the poor, who included both black and white. He concluded that little had in fact changed in America. The impulses leading to what amounted to a time of profound crisis in the United States had deep roots. He argued that "White America" did not act in good faith. It was willing to treat black people with a "degree of decency" but not "equality." Whites may have been horrified by the violence against blacks in the South during the campaigns in Birmingham in 1963 and Selma in 1965, but King argued that they were not prepared to take the final steps. Economic injustice lay at the heart of the matter. He surmised America had "never been truly committed to helping him [the black person] out of poverty, exploitation or all forms of discrimination."[64] In another reference to a key demand that would underpin the Poor People's Campaign of 1968, King calculated that federal programs involving billions of dollars could solve the economic problems facing poor people.[65]

The various events and challenges documented in *Where Do We Go from Here?* highlighted the cumulative stress on King brought about by many struggles. Faced with criticism from all sides, the period 1965–1967 tested his energies and resolve as never before. In the summer of 1967, when he met with Edelman, some of those closest to Dr. King were concerned about his well-being, including his mental health. The second phase of the movement's struggle for freedom, the "realization of equality," remained elusive. The high-water mark of civil rights reform, which began with President Kennedy's public commitment in June 1963 to bring forward a civil rights bill, had passed. King observed that white allies were disappearing, and in a hostile social and political climate whites felt that blacks were greedy in asking for more so soon. Meanwhile, he concluded, black people, especially those in the North, felt cheated.[66] King now understood that the War on Poverty was unlikely to end the cycle of poverty experienced by generation after generation in the areas of housing, health, welfare, education, and employment. It was evident to him that poverty was a structural issue. For King, the movement had changed from a struggle for human dignity to a struggle for rights and opportunities.[67] America stood at a crossroads; it was time to push forward beyond the gains of the Civil Rights Act of 1964 and the Voting Rights Act of 1965.

King announced the launch of the Poor People's Campaign in December 1967. He described the campaign as a "Satyagraha," a nonviolent mass movement whose name meant "truth force."[68] In the Cold War context, the PPC's demands for a redistribution of America's wealth led to yet a further loss of support for the movement from politicians and many citizens, who believed it challenged fundamental American values and perceived it as an attack on capitalism.[69] The flagging of the economy due to spending on the war in Vietnam also increased opposition to King's demands for massive expenditures to defeat poverty on the grounds they were unaffordable. For King, it was a matter of priorities. The adverse reaction to the campaign arguably further polarized opinions on race, war, and poverty across the nation. King's campaign planning in early 1968 took place amid a backlash against "uppity blacks," antiwar demonstrators, the New Left of radical politics, and "welfare bums."[70] In addition, 1968 was a presidential election year, and race became a preeminent issue in the campaign.[71] There was a sense that the PPC had further alienated the white majority and that things were moving too far and too fast on poverty.

Dr. Martin Luther King Jr. was a leader who committed himself to the poorest in the land who had no voice, no power, and no influence in American society. To help them he called for structural change, not mere reform. King referred to the need for "democratic socialism" in America.[72] Some scholars now view him as part of a long tradition of black dissenters, including the formerly enslaved Frederick Douglass, who stressed class and structural forces in relation to the struggle for equality.[73] King observed that racial inequality was embedded in class.[74] His idea of the Poor People's Campaign was for a "class-based" confrontation to force real change.[75] Prominent SCLC leader and Resurrection City manager Jesse Jackson agreed that the focus of the PPC was on "class, primarily, and race, secondarily."[76] King's rhetoric on the haves and the have-nots provoked accusations in the Cold War environment that he was in league with communists.

King maintained his commitment to taking poor people to Washington, D.C., in 1968 in the face of increasing social and political hostility from right-wing Republicans, conservative Democrats, and a general backlash against the movement. Opponents of the PPC told poor people to call off their planned occupation of the nation's capital. Thousands of poor people defied this message and rallied to King's cause. In the final months of his life, he had refused to be intimidated by regular death threats and a concerted attack by the FBI and other forces of the state to discredit him by exposing alleged failings in his private life. In the end, racism, hatred, and perhaps even fear of what he proposed for America killed him. But his death only further inspired impoverished people and their leaders to continue with their plans to come to Washington in May 1968 to dramatize the issue of poverty. This is the story of Dr. King's final campaign.

PART I
DREAMING

CHAPTER 1

THE CHICAGO CAMPAIGN
FROM CIVIL RIGHTS TO HUMAN RIGHTS

I n August 1965, the leader of the Southern Christian Leadership Conference (SCLC), Dr. Martin Luther King Jr., stood at the forefront of the civil rights movement. Two major pieces of legislation had been achieved, the Civil Rights Act of 1964 and the Voting Rights Act of 1965. In theory, these addressed social and political discrimination, respectively. Further progress seemed possible. Taken together with President Lyndon Johnson's War on Poverty, announced in January 1964, and the administration's expansive plans for the Great Society, announced later the same year, the legislation encouraged many in the civil rights movement to hope that full equality for all American citizens, including economic justice, was within reach.

Much remained to be achieved. The depth and scope of poverty in the United States presented monumental challenges. Michael Harrington's book *The Other America*, published in 1962, argued that between forty and fifty million Americans, up to 25 percent of the population, were in need. The poverty line in 1964 was $3,130 annual income for a family of four and $1,500 for an individual. The gap between the richest and poorest in society highlighted the scale of inequality in America during the period. A family in the top 1 percent in the early 1960s was 125 times better off than an average family.[1] Some groups suffered more than others. More than half of black people, nearly half of people living in female-headed families, and a third of those over sixty-five were deemed to be below the poverty line.[2] Racial economic inequality increased in the early to mid-sixties. Black men earned on average 55 percent of the income of white men in 1962 and were mainly working as unskilled labor. Black women worked largely in low-paid and unskilled occupations. Three times as many blacks as whites earned low wages and were unemployed in 1964.[3]

Even as Dr. King and President Johnson savored the passage of the Voting Rights Act in 1965, forces were converging that would derail plans for the

Great Society. Both leaders were devastated by riots in Watts in August 1965 in which thirty-four people, mainly black, lost their lives. America had already experienced urban unrest in 1964 in several cities, including New York and Chicago. However, coming so soon after the euphoria of the Voting Rights legislation, Watts demonstrated ever more clearly that the problems in urban centers went far beyond the issues of racial integration and the ballot, two issues being addressed by the civil rights movement in the South. Johnson's hopes that his domestic policies would achieve racial harmony were dashed. King rushed to southern California to see for himself what had unfolded. Many in Watts felt almost liberated in destroying the area. A young black man told King that "we won," meaning the people trapped in Watts had drawn the attention of the world to them.[4] Watts demonstrated to King that those living in urban ghettos were effectively invisible and forgotten, unlike the situation in the South where in previous campaigns the virulent responses of segregationists to the civil rights movement had revealed racism and discrimination to the wider public.

While most politicians closed ranks to condemn the Watts riots, King regarded the unrest as the actions of those in "despair," who could not see a way out of their "economic dilemma." He rejected the racial significance of the disturbances, claiming the disorder was much more about the have-nots who had not shared in the achievements of the civil rights movement. Significantly, King said that the main issue in Watts was economic, prophetically adding that unless work could be found for the unemployed and underemployed, the United States would face further outbreaks of violence in its cities. The potential for further unrest, he conceded, was also a threat to his nonviolent movement.[5] A government commission set up to investigate Watts largely echoed King's analysis when its findings were published in December 1965. Headed by the former director of the CIA, John McCone, the commission report concluded that the riots were caused by unemployment, poor housing, poor educational opportunities, and other issues. Young people in urban centers like Watts were particularly badly affected and had few prospects for the future. In 1965, black teenage unemployment in America stood at 23 percent, whereas the figure for white teenagers was 10.8 percent.[6]

From King's perspective, the evidence in Watts suggested that at a time when aspirations to fight poverty were at a peak due to the War on Poverty, conditions in housing, employment, and education were, if anything, worsening. He concluded that the situation was not peculiar to Los Angeles but was a national problem. His initial cautious confidence in liberal politics and the possibilities offered by the Johnson legislative program gradually dissipated from this point. King maintained that the civil rights campaigns beginning with Montgomery in

1955–1956 through Selma in 1965 represented a struggle for "decency" whereas the new phase was about trying to achieve full and genuine equality. He argued that the years between 1955 and 1965 had changed the psyche of black Americans and given them a new sense of dignity and self-respect. The edifice of segregation was beginning to break down in the South, but that was not enough.[7] Previous successes were therefore only steps toward true equality. The destination on this road for King turned out to be the Poor People's Campaign (PPC) in 1968 to end poverty and all its manifestations in America.

King's determination to secure economic justice for every citizen in the wake of Watts presented him with perhaps his greatest career challenge to date. Conservative politicians blamed Lyndon Johnson's War on Poverty for the unrest in Watts; the president stood accused of indulging the rioters and looters. In August 1965 political opinion and public sentiment was already split on both race and the War on Poverty. The Civil Rights Act had been particularly contentious for southern Democrats and conservative Republicans in Congress. On becoming president following the assassination of John F. Kennedy, Johnson had reached out to southerners in his own party, arguing that unless they fell in behind him on the civil rights bill there was a risk there would never be another southern president. He also courted the Republican Senate minority leader, Everett Dirksen, arguing that it was important for the country to take the historic step of approving a civil rights bill. As a result of a mixture of threats, persuasion, flattery, and bribes (for example, Senator Carl Hayden was promised a water dam project in Arizona), Congress approved the civil rights legislation, and Johnson signed it into law on July 2, 1964.[8]

The passage of the Civil Rights Act masked deep fissures in the country across race, class, and political party lines. Johnson's social engineering plans, including his hopes to build the Great Society, were quickly condemned by both Republicans and Democrats. Both parties were ideologically diverse in the 1960s. The liberal wing of the Democrats in the Northeast contrasted sharply with the southern wing's advocacy of states' rights, nullification, and defense of the status quo in race relations. Ideologically driven, conservative, laissez-faire Republicans maintained that the federal government should not intervene in state-level policy issues. They had taken over the machinery of their deeply divided party by 1964.[9] The Republican presidential nominee in 1964, Arizona senator Barry Goldwater, had emerged as a prominent spokesperson for the conservative Right and was an early opponent of Johnson's social programs. He had forged his right-wing credentials in the 1950s by attacking Republican president Dwight D. Eisenhower on tax rates and public spending. Goldwater's manifesto *The Conscience of a Conservative*, published in 1960, cemented his reputation as a conservative who stood for individual liberty and against big government. Goldwater supported the free market, constitutional government, and political freedom and stood against communism. He voted against Johnson's civil rights bill on the grounds that he believed aspects of it relating to public accommodations and fair employment were unconstitutional. He cited states' rights to justify his position on the bill. Southern Democrats and conservative Republicans also condemned what they believed to be the erosion of states' rights in other Johnson social policy programs.

Having won the nomination with the support of conservative groups such as William Buckley's Young Americans for Freedom, Goldwater called on delegates at the 1964 Republican Party convention to oppose "collectivism and communism," a direct attack on the encroachment of the state into the lives of individuals as represented in both the civil rights bill and the War on Poverty. Moderate voices were shouted down as the 1964 convention rejected amendments on ending extremism, a demand for nuclear responsibility, and a call to penalize states that denied the right to vote on the grounds of race. In 1964 Goldwater adopted many of the themes that would work well four years later for the Republicans in the 1968 presidential election. He pursued a southern strategy, argued that the Democrats were soft on communism, attacked the excesses of President Johnson's social programs, and talked about crime and the need for law and order. On a visit to Appalachia during the 1964 presidential campaign, Goldwater attacked the "phony" War on Poverty.[10]

The landslide win for Lyndon Johnson in 1964 encouraged Dr. King to believe that the way was now clear for the federal government to address poverty. The Democratic Party also strengthened its hold on both the House of Representatives and the Senate in that election. However, although the Democrats achieved a record 61 percent of the popular vote, green shoots were appearing for the Republicans in the South. President Johnson had correctly predicted he would lose the support of southern Democrats through his determination to push forward with his civil rights bill in the summer of 1964. Johnson lost several southern states to the Republicans in the 1964 presidential election: Mississippi, Alabama, South Carolina, Louisiana, and Georgia. In addition, Arizona, Goldwater's home state, went Republican that year. Segregationist, anti-progressive Democrats in the South were also opposed to other Johnson domestic policies. The backlash against the gains of the civil rights movement and against social programs to combat poverty included the national emergence of populist George Wallace, who was inaugurated governor of Alabama in 1963 and then challenged Johnson for the Democratic presidential nomination. Wallace performed well in a few Democratic Party primaries in 1964. His message of "segregation now and segregation forever" represented a hardening of resolve among anti-progressive southern Democrats against the civil rights movement and what it was seen to stand for in terms of social changes in race relations. This growing sentiment reached its peak in 1968 just as King was planning to take the poor to Washington for his Poor People's Campaign. The backlash against the movement and against the poor helped to position Wallace as a national candidate for northern blue-collar workers and rural southerners in the presidential campaign in 1968.

In the wake of the unrest in Watts, King feared that the backlash against both urban riots and initiatives to combat poverty would put the brakes on further legislation associated with President Johnson's ambitions for the Great Society. The War on Poverty had been a political football almost from its inception. How America should respond to the rediscovery of poverty remained one of the most contentious political issues in the nation throughout the 1960s. Johnson's plans to end poverty were under fire from the moment they were first announced in January 1964. He faced an anti-reform voting bloc of conservative Republicans and conservative Democrats in Congress. Republican minority leader Everett Dirksen described the War on Poverty as the "greatest boondoggle since bread and circuses in the days of the Roman Empire."[11] Johnson was accused of "bleeding-heart liberalism." The idea of "maximum feasible participation," which involved poor people in the running of programs, also rapidly fell out of favor with elements in both political parties. It was alleged that radicals had taken over some programs. Other reasons were advanced to stop Johnson's initiatives in their tracks. Some Republicans in Congress were opposed to his proposed tax cuts to boost the economy and make possible the War on Poverty, claiming that federal deficits were bad for the country. By contrast, other Republicans viewed tax cuts as favorable to free enterprise. The Head Start program, which helped disadvantaged preschool children, was labeled by conservative Republicans as a socialist attempt to take control of children away from their parents.

Arguably, the War on Poverty suffered from fundamental flaws from the outset, not least the inflated rhetoric used by Lyndon Johnson to talk up his great initiative. He made high-profile visits to Appalachia and other impoverished regions to go over the heads of Congress and win support from the public for his legislation. His Poverty Tour converted some but alienated others. Johnson's lofty rhetoric inevitably led to raised expectations, which were followed by anger and frustration on the part of the poor. Social policy in the United States had generally focused, with some exceptions (for example, during the Depression in the 1930s), on the notion that income assistance should protect the most vulnerable in society, including the elderly, disabled people, and other such groups. In addition, social policies traditionally provided a hand up for other citizens to help make them self-sufficient through private employment and not having to rely on government handouts.[12] Both Johnson and his predecessor, John F. Kennedy, took steps to assist entry into the private economy for those who were less well-off. These included increases in the minimum wage, job training, civil rights legislation to address job discrimination, federal aid to education (including Head Start for young children), and steps to provide healthcare for the poor and elderly.[13] But these steps did not go far enough; President Johnson's goal to end poverty could not be achieved without significant spending and redistributive policies. However, both the president and the head of the War on Poverty, Sargent Shriver, were opposed to massively increased spending and welfare dependency. The president aspired to provide what he described as a hand up and not a handout.

Concerned about the political fallout from a white backlash, Johnson gave assurances to conservatives opposed to his plans that he would not increase spending but would instead focus his attention on education programs and training.[14] This included the Jobs Corps and Neighborhood Youth Corps initiatives, yet neither training guaranteed a job at the end of it. President Johnson assumed that the jobs were there for everyone who wanted to work; in his eyes the problem was largely one of a skills deficit.[15] In targeting urban youth, especially black teens in the ghettos, the spending on job training programs also added to the resentments of whites in both the North and South. Stories appeared of disruptive young black men in the residential camps, which played into the idea they were not worth the effort nor the investment of tax dollars. Many of Johnson's opponents believed in a black pathology: that blacks were responsible for their own problems and were incapable of doing any better in life.

Dr. King criticized aspects of both the Civil Rights Act and the War on Poverty from at least mid-1964. He argued that the antidiscrimination Title VII policies in the act could not properly address structural issues in relation to unemployment and housing.[16] He called for a massive public works program to help end poverty. From 1965 King continually referenced the issues of unemployment and underemployment, arguing that the War on Poverty failed to provide enough public jobs. He also became disillusioned by the budgets allocated to the War on Poverty initiative. It was underfunded throughout and became increasingly squeezed by other budget imperatives, especially the war in Vietnam. Even before the Watts riots in August 1965, King thought that President Johnson's plans did not go far enough if poverty were to end in America. He brought forward his own ambitious remedy to tackle the shortfalls of the War on Poverty in 1964. He proposed an Economic Bill of Rights for the disadvantaged that included a guarantee of full employment plus a minimum income for everyone as a right of citizenship. This would apply to poor people of all races. But King failed to persuade the 1964 Democratic Party convention to adopt these proposals for the presidential election that year.[17] The Johnson administration was apparently unwilling to recognize economic opportunity as a basic civil right.[18] King never deviated from his proposal for an Economic Bill of Rights, including a guaranteed minimum income, and carried this idea forward into the Poor People's Campaign of 1968.

King's goal for the civil rights movement to redeem the "soul of America" presented ever more complex challenges in the period beyond Watts. His SCLC colleague Andrew Young echoed King in recognizing that the civil rights movement had yet to provide answers for those who were victims of poverty, including addressing the problem of inadequate education.[19] Having lost faith in the capacity of Johnson's War on Poverty programs to address the issues of economic injustice, King was determined to move beyond civil rights reforms. He refuted accusations that black people had made "too much" progress in recent years. Poor whites were also in his thoughts as King began to view poverty more strongly as a class issue that transcended race. Following the riots in Watts in 1965, he was astonished to read data suggesting that the majority of the poor in America were white.[20] In 1965–1966 and beyond, Dr. King began to focus more directly on the urban underclasses and the poverty that blighted their lives. He placed jobs, housing, and education at the center of a new ambitious urban agenda. In a radical move, he proposed taking the Southern Christian Leadership Conference to Chicago in the North to address the slum conditions he held responsible for urban unrest. His objective was to bring national reform in relation to poverty through a successful localized campaign.[21] The SCLC at this point was an organization with national contacts but was not a national organization. Some black leaders in northern cities resisted King's overtures to come to their patches. His proposed shift in focus for the SCLC was viewed as interference in their own backyards. Congressman Adam Clayton Powell, for example, advised him to stay away from Harlem in New York.

Although the northern states represented new territory for King and the SCLC, he understood that racial injustice existed there. In 1960 he had observed that racism was not a sectional but a national problem, adding that "injustice anywhere is a threat to justice everywhere."[22] Countless nonviolent campaigns in the North led by others had previously targeted black poverty and inequality.[23] Black people in the North experienced economic, political, and legal discrimination just like those in the South.[24] Groups such as the National Urban

League, for example, were seasoned nonviolent campaigners against economic injustice in the North. King also recognized that his own southern campaigns integrally related the issues of racism and economics. The southern movement under King's leadership from the Montgomery Bus Boycott in 1955–1956 had reached out to the poorest in society, including low-paid black women domestic workers. The SCLC leader consistently located the civil rights struggle in a broader context, viewing discrimination as part of a desire by whites to maintain "economic enslavement."[25]

King's determination to right the wrongs of Watts and other urban centers therefore took him to Chicago in 1966 and ultimately led to the Poor People's Campaign in 1968. He described 1966 as a "year of vital education" for him on the issue of economic injustice.[26] Much of his education that year took place in a nonviolent campaign to end the slums. His Chicago Plan, announced in January 1966, consisted of a "multi-faceted assault" directed against public and private institutions that "created slums responsible for the involuntary enslavement of black men, women and children."[27] King aspired to make Chicago an "open city." He planned to mobilize both black and white using nonviolent direct action to enforce open housing policies, open up job opportunities, and make the resources of social institutions available to all.[28] The first phase focused on welfare rights, tenants' rights, exploitative practices, and a lack of jobs. The second phase addressed open housing.[29] The Reverend Al Raby of the Coordinating Council of Community Organizations (CCCO) invited King to join the Chicago Freedom Movement in the belief that the SCLC leader's presence in the city would revitalize stalled local campaign efforts to target housing conditions and residential segregation. In addition to Raby, many other leaders and grassroots activists were involved in organizing in Chicago as part of the umbrella CCCO, a coalition of civil rights, labor, and leftist organizations that included the Urban League, the National Association for the Advancement of Colored People (NAACP), the Congress of Racial Equality (CORE), and other white and biracial groups.[30] Dr. King eagerly accepted the invitation, viewing the CCCO efforts in Chicago as the "foundation stones upon which any movement must build."[31]

King thought that if he could break the system in Chicago, he could break it across the nation in other urban centers.[32] He had faith that nonviolent marches, demonstrations, and other forms of protest would harness the rage and frustration in the ghettos caused by economic deprivation. He reflected that if peaceful marches had been organized in Watts, the violence and unrest would never have occurred. Dr. King's commitment to nonviolence was lifelong and unequivocal. He rejected violence as both impractical and immoral, arguing that even if they chose to do so black people did not have the firepower to defeat the forces stacked against them. He had explored the "potency [of nonviolence] in the area of social reform" from a young age.[33] Chicago was a crossroads for the SCLC leader; it shaped his final years and pointed him inexorably in the direction of a campaign against poverty and all its manifestations. The issues identified by King and his partner organizations in Chicago, including squalid and segregated housing, poor-quality education, underemployment, and unemployment, later served as a blueprint for many of the demands of the Poor People's Campaign.

The Chicago campaign also came at a pivotal period for the civil rights movement and the United States more generally. It took place in a context of increasing threat to King's ideas from advocates of Black Power in urban centers across the North. King viewed black militancy as a response to the reluctance of white power to make the necessary changes in society to ensure justice for all. He argued that northern injustice was a consequence of "economic exploitation." He regarded urban riots as the language of the unheard and believed they would continue summer after summer unless action were taken to alleviate the plight of those living in the ghettos. The SCLC thought of Chicago as a symbol of things happening elsewhere in cities like Newark and Detroit.[34] Riots in major urban centers from 1964 also put the movement at a disadvantage as the tide of political and public opinion began to turn against those working for justice. This backlash continued to grow.

The proposal to go to Chicago caused consternation among some of Dr. King's closest advisors. The SCLC leadership often failed to find unanimity on the big issues, and King's style was to allow everyone to have their say before settling on a course of action. A "kitchen cabinet" meeting of the SCLC discussed the Chicago invitation at the Atlanta Hilton Inn in September 1965. All of the leaders in the SCLC attended. Andrew Young thought they could best change the nation as a whole by concentrating their limited resources on voter registration in the South.[35] Bayard Rustin also argued that much unfinished business remained in the South. The narrow interests of some key figures may have played a part in the discussions. Young claimed that personal issues encouraged Hosea Williams to support the Chicago initiative, since it would remove his potential rival James Bevel from involvement in the South. Young also suggested that Rustin was unwilling to risk labor union support for the movement in a city where Mayor Richard Daley wielded significant influence with the backing of northern labor Democrats.[36] Yet the support of labor was key to success in Chicago.[37] At the end of the spirited debate in Atlanta, King announced that if the SCLC wished to be a serious national organization, it should go to Chicago.

The Chicago Freedom Movement campaign began on a freezing day in January 1966, when King, with his wife, Coretta Scott, and their family, moved into a Chicago West Side fourth-floor railroad flat at Sixteenth Street and Hamlin Avenue. King's assistant Bernard Lee and a secretary, Diana Smith, had earlier posed as a young couple looking for a home and managed to sign the lease for the flat before the property owner realized who the real occupant would be. King's motive for living in the apartment was a genuine and sincere attempt to understand the life conditions of the poor and to demonstrate solidarity with them. The act typified his lifetime commitment to the dispossessed. Although the SCLC leader spent limited time there due to the many demands on him, the apartment sometimes served as an alternative to the official campaign headquarters in the Blue Room at Warren Avenue Congregational Church in East Garfield Park. The flat had a tiny kitchen, a broken refrigerator, and a stove that barely worked.[38] It was located in a mainly black community where whites owned many of the businesses. Mary Lou Finley, a white woman from the area and later a coeditor of a book on the Chicago campaign, maintained that the ghetto was "a dumping ground" in 1966. The food sold in shops was often of poor quality and had been rejected for sale in more prosperous areas.[39]

Both Bayard Rustin and SCLC staffer Tom Kahn warned King not to underestimate Chicago mayor Richard Daley. He ran the city as his personal fiefdom yet, ironically, this was one of the factors that attracted King to the idea of a campaign there. The SCLC leader clung to the belief that someone holding so much power and authority could work to the movement's advantage.[40] He was confident that with Daley's support, both open housing and integrated education were within reach. But Daley and King inhabited different worlds. Whereas King was offended by the separation of the races in Chicago, Daley saw merely a "city of neighborhoods," where "free people" could "stick together with their own kind."[41] Andrew Young reminded King that Daley was "no Bull Connor," the ruthless opponent whom the SCLC had taken on during the Birmingham campaign in 1963. In Birmingham and Selma, white opponents had "made" the campaigns in the sense that their brutality won sympathy for the movement. Daley, however, was not ready to play the villain in a play staged by King. He operated in a subtler way, often appearing conciliatory in his public actions and pronouncements. Some scholars have warned against simply viewing the Chicago campaign as a battle of resolve between King and Daley.[42] King rejected such a narrow interpretation of the campaign: "we are not anti-Daley; we are anti-economic and -political injustice."[43]

The fears engendered by urban uprisings in other cities put white Chicago on alert in anticipation of King's arrival. Historically, the ethnically and economically diverse city had a reputation for racism. Thirty-eight people died in the infamous "race riot" of 1919. The Great Migration between 1910 and 1970 saw six and a half million black Americans move from the South to northern cities, five million of them after 1940.[44] In the 1950s, the black population of Chicago grew to 813,000.[45] Seasoned activist James Bevel maintained that black communities in Chicago were simply "Mississippi moved north" and that many migrants had a personal affinity for King. An estimated 42 percent of black people in Chicago were first or second generation from Mississippi.[46] In 1959, the U.S. Commission on Civil Rights called Chicago "the most residentially segregated large city in the nation."[47] While the city had provided some better prospects for black people from the South, in 1966 it remained highly divided. King's closest SCLC colleague, Ralph Abernathy, described the city as "a segregated society without the stigma of the Jim Crow laws."[48] Segregation was maintained through racial steering by real estate brokers, white covenants on house sales, and the threat of violence and other forms of retaliation.[49] Twenty percent of black people in the city lived below the poverty level.[50]

King drew on a network of friends and trusted associates in Chicago, including attorney Chauncey Eskridge and gospel singer and activist Mahalia Jackson.[51] Jackson captivated audiences with her inspirational singing at campaign events, leading King to comment on one memorable occasion that no one could now doubt he had a movement in Chicago.[52] The SCLC's Chicago campaign staff included James Orange, James Bevel, Diane Nash Bevel (James's wife), Dorothy Wright (later Tillman), and Lynn Adler. Jesse Jackson, a young local activist, liaised with the Coordinating Council of Community Organizations during the campaign. Dorothy Wright, age seventeen, had arrived from Alabama to join the advance team. She recalled her shock at the sight of the housing conditions for black people in Chicago. At first, she thought the dwellings were factories.[53] King relied especially on Bernard Lafayette in Chicago and later appointed him as the national director of the Poor People's Campaign. Lafayette's future wife, Kate, would work in Resurrection City, the camp built to accommodate the demonstrators during the PPC occupation of Washington in May–June 1968. Lafayette had impeccable credentials, including an unwavering commitment to nonviolence. He was involved in the Nashville lunch-counter movement, was a founding member of the Student Nonviolent Coordinating

Committee, and was a driving force in the Freedom Rides in 1961. He worked with James Bevel and Diane Nash to organize the Jackson Nonviolent Movement. In a national campaign for voting rights, King had adopted Lafayette's local voting rights movement in Selma. Raymond Arsenault heaped praise on Lafayette and others in Selma for having "exposed the violent underpinnings of white supremacist politics, cracked the mystique of Jim Crow in the Deep South, and prompted federal legislation that changed the character of American democracy."[54] Lafayette later revealed that fear of what he might find in Chicago led him to take out an extra life insurance policy.[55]

Lafayette, whom King "respected a great deal," was among the strongest advocates in favor of an SCLC campaign in Chicago because he believed that nonviolence would work in the North.[56] Lafayette offered important strategic links for King during both the Chicago campaign and the PPC through his work on behalf of the American Friends Service Committee (AFSC), the Quakers. Unlike the AFSC, the SCLC had limited links with and little presence in the grassroots communities of the urban North. Kale Williams of the AFSC had invited Lafayette to Chicago for the summer of 1964 because he wanted someone with experience to experiment with nonviolence in the North.[57] Williams asked Lafayette to address slum-housing issues on the West Side. The collaboration between King and the AFSC in Chicago brought a "flood of energy" into the city.[58] The AFSC's Chicago regional office was already actively engaged in nonviolent efforts to integrate housing and had developed a program to help black people find houses in the suburbs. Bill Moyer, director of HOME (Home Opportunities Made Equal), had oversight of the AFSC initiative on suburban fair housing and became a pivotal figure during the Chicago campaign's open housing demonstrations. The AFSC tactics of marches, organizing tenant unions, and "tent-ins" to house the unemployed were familiar to King's SCLC.

Since he was schooled in the ideas of the Social Gospel and the possibilities for building the "kingdom of God" on earth, King's primary objective under the Chicago Plan was to bring about the "unconditional surrender" of forces dedicated to the creation and maintenance of slums.[59] He denounced structural wealth inequality in all of its forms in Chicago. He maintained that exploitation in the city led to poor-quality housing, segregation in housing, inadequate education, unemployment, and underemployment. The problem was that unlike the high-profile sheriffs and white vigilante mobs in the South during the struggle against segregation, the forces exploiting the slums in Chicago were largely invisible, certainly to those in the ghettos. In the absence of such villains and in a city with no legal segregation in place, King appreciated that it was difficult for those in the slums to understand where they might direct their frustrations.

However, he believed that through SCLC organizing, people could get to a point where they could see that something was badly wrong with their economic situation and would be prepared to nonviolently do something about it.

King pointed an accusing finger at some of the powerful and influential forces that he claimed profited from the slums. The alleged perpetrators included labor unions that barred black people from certain occupations and employers who looked on black people as sources of cheap labor. Several of the old American Federation of Labor (AFL) craft unions representing white workers were reluctant to get involved in the Chicago effort for fear their support might lead to a loss of jobs for members.[60] Some of the industrial union leaders, however, came on board, including Ralph Helstein of the United Packinghouse Workers of America and Norman Hill, the legislative and civil rights representative of the Industrial Union Department of the American Federation of Labor–Congress of Industrial Organizations (AFL-CIO). Two other King targets in Chicago were real estate boards that restricted the housing supply for blacks so that they would pay more in rent and receive less services than whites, and the banks that charged black people higher interest rates yet often refused to finance real estate in poor communities, leaving people prey to loan sharks. King argued it was time to ensure that the resources of social institutions in the city were available to all. He savaged Chicago authorities for their failure to provide adequate services in black communities and for operating a political system that denied a "democratic voice" through the use of "patronage and pressure." Black communities were abandoned in effect: streets were not swept regularly, and parks were neglected. Finally, according to King, the police, often viewed as the enemy by black people, functioned only to control black communities and keep them in line.[61] Policing in urban centers was a contentious issue throughout the turmoil of the 1960s. The white backlash against urban riots fostered demands for law and order and for the police to crack down on the troublemakers. Many of the uprisings during the period broke out in response to allegations of police brutality.

King's rapidly developing analysis of economic injustice placed conditions in Chicago within both a national and a broader global context. He viewed the nature and problems of the ghetto as comparable to the colonialist exploitation of underdeveloped nations, for example, the treatment of Congo by Belgium. He argued that the inequities of capitalism worked against the interests of the poor trapped in slum areas, leading to a form of "internal colonialism." King insisted, "Every condition exists simply because someone profits from its existence," and added that the Chicago problem was another matter of economic exploitation.[62] He claimed that the overall situation contributed to a "cycle of poverty" passing from generation to generation. According to this analysis, the life chances of those born in the slums were inevitably limited. They had restricted opportunities in the job market, education, welfare, healthcare, and housing. They had neither power nor influence in the political arena. King declared, "When you deprive a man of his job . . . you place him in a situation which controls his political life and denies his children an adequate education and health services while forcing his wife to live on welfare in a dilapidated dwelling and you have a systematic pattern of humiliation which is as immoral as slavery and a lot more crippling than southern segregation."[63]

The Chicago campaign focused particular attention on open housing and on slum landlords who let properties run down so that they paid lower taxes and who encouraged overcrowding while failing to comply with city codes regarding housing standards. The CCCO adopted a range of tactics and strategies. Campaign leaders organized and educated people through neighborhood rallies, workshops, and demonstrations and encouraged them to participate in protests and to collectively bargain with property owners and the city authorities. King insisted that demonstrations must be thought of as educational and organizational tools, should reveal the agents of exploitation, and should "paint a portrait of the evils which beset us" by exposing the nature of slums. The belief that oppressed people learn through participation in social movements also underpinned the Poor People's Campaign in 1968. King wanted people to learn how to dramatize the problems affecting their lives. He was confident he had the recipe for success, maintaining that "from the bases of power, encompassed in a viable nonviolent movement, we will have forces which can be mobilized to dramatize issues as they occur."[64]

As in previous campaigns, King aspired to create drama and sympathy for his nonviolent approaches. Ever aware of the need for dramatic effect, he dressed in ordinary work clothes and took along reporters to record him cleaning up a neglected, rat-infested tenement. Sometimes there was no need to put on a show as real life intervened. Local resident Jim Keck recalled holding a community meeting in one apartment to persuade reluctant tenants to withhold their rents until essential repairs were undertaken. Things were not going well until a rat decided to hop onto the coffee table to help himself to the snacks provided for those at the meeting. Everyone quickly forgot about possible reprisals from the landlord and signed up on the spot for the rent strike.[65] King, Young, Al Raby, James Bevel, and Bernard Lafayette organized the rent strikes and collected the money due to landlords directly from residents, a process known as "trusteeship." Some of the houses were subsequently bought from the owners, grants were secured to renovate them, and finally the houses were resold to those renting them. *Time* magazine was unimpressed, arguing that flouting laws by with-holding rents from landlords was tantamount to theft and was unacceptable in the "North," the inference being of course that lower standards of behavior were to be expected in the South.[66]

Away from the spotlight, Mayor Richard Daley exploited the system of po-litical patronage by offering local preachers local services and some funding for projects in neighborhoods where the Chicago Freedom Movement was ac-tive. Andrew Young noted that many black people had more access to the po-litical machinery in Chicago than they did in New York or Los Angeles.[67] Some ministers and black political representatives organized a stance of noncompli-ance with King's campaign.[68] Abernathy grasped that King was up against it in the absence of real black unity.[69] Splits between Christian denominations were common: no black Congregational church invited Young to speak, although he spoke in more than fifty Baptist churches in Chicago.[70] Activist Dorothy Wright (Tillman) recalled how several of Chicago's black ministers rebuffed King and told him to go home, even in front of television cameras. She quoted King say-ing the "Daley plantation" was worse than the Mississippi plantation, and some black people were "in deep."[71] Things got so bad that she thought about packing up and going back to Alabama.

In reaching out to create black unity, King courted controversy by meet-ing with the head of the Nation of Islam, Elijah Muhammad, in Chicago.[72] The SCLC leader also had to come to terms with the opposition to his philosophy of nonviolence posed by black militancy, especially in the North. The shoot-ing and wounding of James Meredith on June 6, 1966, just after the start of his March against Fear in Mississippi to protest the denial of voting rights, signaled widening splits in the civil rights movement. Stokely Carmichael of the Student Nonviolent Coordinating Committee seized the limelight and dominated head-lines across the nation with his call for Black Power. The black militant mes-sage of self-determination, self-defense, and separation from whites appealed to lower-class blacks in urban centers, the very people King worked for in Chi-cago. The SCLC leader was concerned that no matter how much the press por-trayed Carmichael of SNCC and other young militants as extreme and even de-ranged, the Black Power message appealed to those who had few prospects in relation to education, jobs, and housing and who lived in communities where the police were regarded as an occupying force. Carmichael was articulate, per-suasive, and charismatic and, more important, presented a clear and coherent denunciation of a system stacked against black people.

King understood that Black Power was born out of the alienation, rage, and despair of people living in the slums. He agreed with black militants on the need for jobs, housing, education, and justice. The Chicago Freedom Movement sought to mobilize young people against the racist practices and inadequate facilities in the city's education system.[73] King highlighted similarities between education in Chicago and one of the most oppressive systems in the world, South African apartheid, alleging that the education system was "designed to perpetuate the inferior status of slum children." Many black children in Chicago attended underresourced segregated schools, which provided them with limited prospects for their futures. They also often had poor health. King spoke of their "emotional and environmental deprivation." The runny noses of ghetto children became a "graphic symbol" for him of "medical neglect in a society which had mastered most of the diseases from which they would soon die."[74] The problems of poor education and inadequate healthcare were compounded, he alleged, because the children's parents were usually unemployed or underemployed. In another indication of how Chicago shaped King, both education and healthcare became key demands during the Poor People's Campaign two years later.

Vice Lords, Cobras, and Roman Saints gang members were among the first to visit King in his Chicago apartment, where they debated the issue of nonviolence.[75] According to the SCLC's Citizenship Education Program organizer Dorothy Cotton, young people were motivated by their desire to experience a better future.[76] They learned what was "meant by nonviolent protest and why it was important."[77] King wanted children and young adults to be active agents in constructing their own futures, another strategy he adopted for those who joined the PPC in 1968. By being prepared to sit down on an equal basis alongside them, he hoped to move gang members away from violence and criminality. Ralph Abernathy observed that through various interactions with angry young black people in Chicago, King saw "the myriad faces of the Black Power movement."[78] Lawrence Johnson, leader of the conservative Vice Lords gang, agreed with King's analysis on the need to tackle economic injustice but spoke of seizing the trade of the neighborhood to make sure money stayed in the community.[79] Johnson described the discussions on the best methods to address problems in the community as "respectful."[80] The Blackstone Rangers gang displayed a banner with an image of a machine gun at a King nonviolent rally; the less than subtle message was "count us in or cut us out."[81]

Black militancy was only one factor in King's thinking about the welfare of those starting out in life. He identified with young people and strove to improve their life opportunities. The respect was mutual, and the number of young people who traveled to set up camp in Washington for the Poor People's Campaign in May 1968 testifies to this. King aspired to involve gang members in the Chicago campaign, and he hoped to give them a sense of belonging while working to open new possibilities for their futures in education and employment. NAACP Legal Defense attorney Marian Wright Edelman observed that the SCLC leader was a listener who was unbelievably patient in his dealings with young people.[82] King's basic humanity and empathy shone through, and Lawrence Johnson claimed that young people admired King for his compassion and sincerity; they wanted to protect him, and they grew to love him.[83] Another young man admiringly described King as a "heavy stud."[84] Billy Hollins, who was homeless in 1965, fell under King's spell during the Chicago campaign and became a field staffer with the SCLC and later a coordinator in the Poor People's Campaign.[85] Assistant attorney general John Doar and community relations service director Roger Wilkins visited King in his West Side apartment. They were amazed to find him leading a seminar on nonviolence and surrounded by "notorious" black gangs. Wilkins commented on the "reverence" King showed for the humanity of the young people around him, and he was confident that the civil rights leader had persuaded many of them to turn away from violence.[86] King took great pride in the commitment of gang members from Chicago to nonviolence when they protected women and children during the Meredith march in Mississippi in 1966.[87]

The SCLC engagement with gangs and other young people also benefited during the campaign from the work already undertaken by Bernard Lafayette and the American Friends Service Committee on the West Side of Chicago. Lafayette, brethren service volunteer David Jehnsen, and Tony Henry of the AFSC organized students in an investigation of childhood lead poisoning in the neighborhood. From his experiences on the West Side, Lafayette regarded gangs that turned to nonviolence as a potential resource. He felt that with good leadership, gangs could become involved in a bigger movement.[88] Throughout the Chicago campaign, James Bevel and others trained young people, including gang members, in nonviolence and movement history to prepare them to participate in peaceful and dramatic protests. Bevel asked young people to be on standby to close Chicago down by keeping protests going even in the face of mass arrests.[89] The Blackstone Rangers and other gangs worked as marshals at marches and demonstrations in Chicago, a role requiring a commitment to nonviolence. Lafayette observed that marches in Chicago were organized in the same way as those in the Deep South in that marshals gave structure, kept people in line, and provided a wall of protection.[90] He praised gang members for their discipline and courage on the marches into white neighborhoods in Chicago. Lafayette believed that involvement in the campaign gave gang members a sense of pride that they were helping to protect the community. In another link between the Chicago campaign and the PPC, the Blackstone Rangers and Egyptian Cobras later went to Resurrection City to work as marshals. King and his colleagues played a part therefore in turning at least some gang members away from violence.

The seeds of King's multiracial coalition, which went to Washington, D.C., in May 1968 for the Poor People's Campaign, can be found in the 1966 Chicago Freedom Movement. On June 12, 1966, disturbances broke out in the Chicago Puerto Rican community following a police shooting of a young man, Aracelis Cruz, yet another episode in an already turbulent summer in urban centers. Al Raby commented that this was the first—yet predictable—revolt of an "oppressed Latin American community."[91] Puerto Ricans shared many of the injustices experienced by black communities in the areas of employment, education, and housing. Yet much of the attention of the press and city authorities had tended to focus on what was a primarily black civil rights movement until this point. King made a personal appeal for Puerto Ricans to join him in a common struggle against the "power structure."[92] The Chicago Freedom Movement announced it was seeking ways to join in a united effort with its "Latin American brothers."[93] However, the evidence suggests that at this stage the proposal to work together did not go beyond rhetorical cooperation with Mexican Americans and Puerto Ricans.[94] Collaboration between the SCLC and Latin Americans was minimal and would wait until King reached out again during planning for the PPC.

By midsummer 1966, the Chicago initiative could point to modest success only through the rent strikes, support for tenant unions, and work with local gangs. Mayor Daley continued to play a benevolent role in his public pronouncements and in his refusal to jail protesters.[95] Pressure was growing on King; he needed a victory in Chicago to demonstrate that his nonviolent methods still had resonance. Campaign funds were short, and the specter of Black Power was never far from his thoughts. A rally at Soldier Field on July 10 began the direct-action phase of the Chicago Plan. Black Muslims boycotted the event in another indication of the changing direction of the movement. King tried to steal some of the black militants' thunder by punctuating his speech with references to "black heritage" and "pride" in his race. He also made clear there would be no compromise on nonviolence. At the same event, Raby referred to the "grievances of our Spanish speaking amigos," which mirrored the problems experienced by black people.[96] King and his close colleagues now more clearly recognized that black people were not alone in their desperate need for services, jobs, housing, and education.

On Tuesday, July 12, following another police incident, burning and looting in Chicago spread to 140 blocks; it lasted for two days. The SCLC used its influence to persuade city gangs not to respond and not to inflame the situation further. With the American economy already slowing down due to spending on the Vietnam War, the disturbances threatened the loss of some support in Congress and among the public for the civil rights movement. Riots also occurred in Cleveland that summer. President Johnson advised a group of businesspeople on July 23 that riots would never bring lasting reform and would turn away those who should and could support reform.[97] The unrest was a huge blow to King's desire to channel frustration in the slums in nonviolent ways. On the other hand, historian Thomas F. Jackson has argued that the riots helped to radicalize King.[98] King and Young listened intently to young black men on the final day of the unrest and heard about their lack of opportunities in housing, education, and employment. King was able to see that society ignored violence in the slums and only condemned it when unrest spilled out of the ghettos.

With the Chicago campaign at an impasse, the SCLC leader needed a tangible and visible success to justify his decision to move north. On July 28, 1966, the Chicago Freedom Movement reached a turning point.[99] The focus was the issue of open housing and the evident apartheid in Chicago. King addressed supporters at New Friendship Baptist Church in Englewood in sweltering heat and announced they would march into white neighborhoods. He hoped to achieve a legally enforceable, comprehensive housing ordinance.[100] White neighborhoods symbolized some of the very power structures the campaign was struggling against. The SCLC saw the potential for marches into white communities to "empower" those who took part. Bernard Lafayette said this was the first time the SCLC had planned protest demonstrations as opposed to the sympathy marches previously held in the South.[101] Training and mobilization were critical in preparing participants to undertake such dangerous ventures. Andrew Young hoped the act of entering into "no go" territory would break the physical and psychological barriers of the mental and legal restrictions placed on the citizens of the ghetto.[102] Young later reflected that the PPC set out to challenge those same barriers on the national stage, only that time "in a new social movement that transcended race."[103]

Whites were determined not to buckle against the "invaders," who were now demanding integration in the North. At each march through white ethnic districts, ever-growing mobs shouted Nazi-like slogans and pelted the marchers with various objects. Activist Dorothy Tillman reflected on the irony that those throwing things were first- or second-generation immigrants who had not been in the country as long as the black demonstrators and their ancestors.[104] King and the other marchers experienced a white working-class backlash firsthand. At a march on August 5, 1966, ten thousand counterprotesters heckled and abused the marchers, threw various objects, including cherry bombs, and threatened to lynch King and his supporters. A rock struck King on the head. The old civil rights adage, "adversaries make the movement," played out in front of the television cameras. These events led the SCLC leader to declare that racism in Chicago was worse than in the Deep South.

Court injunctions halted SCLC plans to step up the marches through white areas. Ralph Abernathy later reflected that the decision to quit marching in the face of injunctions was a grave error: "the future either belonged to Christian nonviolence or to Black Power, and Black Power in 1966 meant something akin to civil war."[105] King got around the injunctions by leading marches in suburban Chicago Heights, Evergreen Park, and South Deering.[106] The effective end of the Chicago campaign came when Daley and King signed a summit agreement at the Palmer House hotel on August 26, 1966. The city agreed to enforce existing laws on open housing. Daley also promised both to support state-level open occupancy legislation and to empower those at the sharp end of discrimination in housing by establishing procedures to investigate complaints. The Chicago Real Estate Board urged its members to observe the law and to apply open housing policies in their daily practices. Finally, the Mortgage Bankers Association agreed to make mortgages available regardless of the race of the applicants. Initially, King welcomed the housing agreement as significant, but in March 1967 he conceded that the public agencies had failed to keep their word and the housing agreement was a sham.

The fallout for King from the unsatisfactory outcome in Chicago was predictable. Criticism intensified from those who regarded him and his nonviolent methods as relics from the past. Activist Chester Robinson complained that "blacks were sold out."[107] Abernathy acknowledged that the "broken pledge of Chicago became a key arguing point in the rhetoric of Black Power advocates."[108] The hope of salvaging a significant victory from the dying embers of the Chicago campaign in the form of a fair housing bill slipped from King's grasp during the summer of 1966. King had hoped the vicious, hateful attacks on nonviolent marchers in Chicago would win public sympathy and the support of Washington. The bill would have allowed King to maintain credibility and momentum for the nonviolent movement. With his hold on Congress now weakening due to the backlash against his policies, President Lyndon Johnson failed in his attempt to push through a broad civil rights bill in 1966. Among other measures, it would have made illegal any discrimination in the sale or rental of housing. Johnson did his best to persuade Congress to support the bill, arguing in language King would have recognized and approved of: "As long as the color of a man's skin determines his choice of housing, no investment in the physical rebuilding of our cities will free the men and women living there."[109]

Housing remained a controversial issue as it had been since the 1964 Civil Rights Act was first under consideration in Congress. The issue became a proxy war in the struggles between the movement for justice and the white backlash from 1964 through the Poor People's Campaign in 1968. Senate minority leader Everett Dirksen from Illinois, whose support Johnson needed to pass the 1964 civil rights bill, personified northern hostility to fair housing legislation. The National Association of Real Estate Boards also consistently opposed civil rights in housing.[110] The Senate filibustered the fair housing bill in 1966 in a context in which the public was losing patience with civil rights. King condemned the hypocrisy of politicians who voted for civil rights legislation to end segregation and to ensure the right to vote yet refused to support the housing issue because the resulting changes would apply in the North. Johnson aide Joseph Califano later said that middle-class white constituents who wanted to keep black people out of their neighborhoods had besieged urban representatives in Congress.[111] Public opinion had turned against the movement. For King, this backlash was simply a continuation of the white vacillation that black people had always experienced. He observed that whites reacted against the viciousness of Bull Connor in Birmingham, Alabama, in 1963, but they had not acted in good faith in the North on other issues. As demonstrated in Chicago, many northern voters were content to see integration take place in the South, but not in their own backyards. Far from winning support for fair housing, marches through white neighborhoods stiffened the resistance of those opposed to change. In the end, a mix of indifference, prejudice, and resentment among the public and legislators sank the housing bill.

Despite the unsatisfactory conclusion to the campaign, Chicago set King on the path to the Poor People's Campaign. His experiences in the city led him to denounce Chicago authorities and the federal government on several counts. He slammed an immoral welfare system that discriminated against family life in the slums, attacked the shortfalls of the War on Poverty (which meant little money was available to finance low-cost housing or renovation), highlighted the failure to address inner-city areas, and condemned centuries of segregation and discrimination. All of these issues—welfare, housing, the inadequacies of the War on Poverty, conditions in the slums—became part of his agenda for the PPC two years later.

CHAPTER 2

A YEAR OF EDUCATION FOR DR. KING

By late 1966, President Lyndon Johnson's political influence was on the wane, and the high hopes for the War on Poverty and the Great Society were slowly evaporating. Rising costs of the war in Vietnam demonstrated that spending on both "guns and butter" was no longer sustainable. The buoyant economy that had underpinned the spending on social programs was beginning to give way to rising inflation and budget deficits. A white backlash against Johnson's policies was fueled by a summer of violence and unrest in the cities. Midterm elections loomed in November 1966, and the president carefully kept some degree of distance from King for fear of paying a high price at the polls because of resistance from white supporters. The Southern Christian Leadership Conference convention in August 1966 had discussed King's reflections about the connections between the slums and the Vietnam War. In a significant move, the SCLC delegates passed a resolution against the recent escalation of the conflict in Vietnam. King and Johnson were moving in different directions. Johnson's confidence in the capacity of the existing system to deal with the issues of poverty, particularly his continued failure to initiate policies to redistribute wealth, now seemed naïve to the SCLC leader.

In this rapidly changing political context, the Chicago campaign represented a major turning point for the SCLC in relation to economic injustice. Andrew Young argued that the campaign was a success in that they had managed to draw national attention to deprivation, discrimination, and institutional racism in urban areas. Having ventured north, the SCLC had focused the unwilling eyes of America on poverty. The same tactic—to make poverty visible—would become one of the main objectives of the Poor People's Campaign in 1968. Bernard Lafayette reflected that King dramatized the issues by his very presence in Chicago and had been able to "articulate them in a way that everything became obvious."[1] Lafayette also maintained that the campaign had brought issues to a head in Chicago and had given people hope that they could effect change. King's experiences in Chicago further clarified his own thinking on economic injustice and defined his activism for the remainder of his life. It led him to a "new analysis of urban political economy."[2] Young wrote that from Chicago on, the SCLC concerned itself more directly with the multifaceted implications of urban poverty and looked at its underlying causes. Mirroring King's analysis as outlined in the Chicago Plan, now vindicated by the harsh experiences throughout the campaign, Young observed, "We knew that poverty, abetted and supported by a history of oppression and discrimination, equaled powerlessness."[3] King similarly reflected in August 1966 that powerless people in society were unable to participate in decision-making, adding that the "cries of warning and the shouts of desperation of our ghettos now fall on deaf ears."[4]

Coretta Scott King noted that her husband was haunted by the faces of poverty he had seen in the ghettos of Chicago and later in rural Mississippi, and he wanted to make the "plight of those in the lower classes visible to the world."[5] King's essential humanity and his genuine empathy for the poor found true expression in the Chicago slums. The Chicago campaign was significant in helping him to understand more clearly the nature of daily life in the slums and the causes of economic injustice. Having challenged the forces opposing progress in Chicago and having met and worked alongside alienated young people in the slums and experienced poverty firsthand, he rejected suggestions of a black pathology. King argued that poor people were not responsible for their own plight; in reality, the white power structure exploited them and kept families down. He now thought more deeply about possible remedies. It seemed to him that "empowerment" of those living in the slums was the solution to the structural problem.[6] Economic development was key to his thinking. In order to bring wealth and businesses and create employment, King argued, it was essential for black people to control the economy of their communities. He continued to reflect on this issue as he planned the PPC. He maintained, "Poor people are kept in poverty because they are kept from power. . . . we must create poor people's power."[7]

Al Raby of the Coordinating Council of Community Organizations later observed that Chicago had prepared them for the Poor People's Campaign, not least because it had provided "an education in terms of the conquerability of poverty in northern areas."[8] Several key leaders in the Chicago campaign would use their experiences to help shape the PPC. Al Sampson, for example, worked for the PPC in Newark, New Jersey.[9] Anthony Henry of the American Friends Service Committee became associate director of the PPC and headed the Washington, D.C., office. Henry brought a wealth of experience having worked on a variety of projects in Chicago, including a $200,000 War on Poverty program concerned with the cultural enrichment of young people. He also previously worked in community development in Tanzania.[10] Henry credited key Chicago campaign figures James Bevel and Bernard Lafayette for constructing many of the ideas that eventually came out during the planning period for the PPC from late 1967. Bevel became coordinator of nonviolent training and action for the Poor People's Campaign and director of the Marks, Mississippi, to Washington Freedom Train, one of nine caravans that took the poor to the nation's capital in May 1968. Lafayette particularly impressed King in Chicago and received further plaudits from the civil rights leader for his management of nonviolent anti–Vietnam War marches in 1967, leading to his appointment as national director of the PPC.

Others also gained valuable experience during the Chicago campaign and became prominent figures in the PPC two years later. Jesse Jackson was the director of Operation Breadbasket in Chicago, which aimed to begin capital turnover in poor black communities by boycotting and pressuring merchants to employ black people and to make use of black businesses, services, and products. The initiative helped ministers involved in the Chicago campaign to develop their "sense of ethics around social issues, it introduced them to a little bit of Social Gospel theology."[11] Churches, or at least those prepared to support the campaign, represented a "power factor" in Chicago.[12] Both Jesse Jackson and Herman Jenkins later served for short periods as mayor of Resurrection City, the temporary encampment built by the SCLC to house the demonstrators in Washington during the Poor People's Campaign in May–June 1968. Jackson took on the role of mayor of Resurrection City in part to ensure that the Chicago gang members who had accompanied him to Washington for the PPC adhered to nonviolence.[13] His ability to move and excite people was a factor also. Jackson proved to be an effective organizer in Resurrection City, but he was often away from the camp leading demonstrations, which in the view of some others in the SCLC leadership left a void.[14]

The education brought about by the Chicago campaign not only affected King and his close associates, it was felt at the grassroots. Scholars have suggested that in addition to "inspired leadership," a broad community fed up with decades of discrimination drove the Chicago campaign. Some have claimed in hindsight that the Chicago Freedom Movement both built on what was already there and started new initiatives, which came to fruition over subsequent years.[15] King was keen to broaden the base of the civil rights movement beyond its middle-class orientation to include working-class and poor communities.[16] He was particularly encouraged by the capacity of ordinary people to stand tall against injustice. Perhaps of greatest significance for the Poor People's Campaign to come, he sought to involve poor people living in the slums as partners in the Chicago effort. Workshops on nonviolence, direct actions, protests outside real estate offices, and dangerous and risky strategies, including marches through white neighborhoods, all helped to lay the groundwork for a national campaign against poverty. The same focus on learning and on building a politicized force of people working in solidarity would characterize the Poor People's Campaign. King wanted poor people to take their futures into their own hands. He spoke of the need to strengthen community organizations and to recruit local people to engage in dramatic protest against the forces that maintained the slums. He believed that through organizing efforts, he could move poor people from being passive subjects stuck in their lives to being active citizens able to take control of their own futures. This same philosophy applied to the PPC.

Chicago also played a small role in ensuring that a future campaign against poverty would be multiracial. It was already evident to King that poverty existed beyond black communities, especially among other minority groups. As early as 1959, he compared the appalling gap between the living conditions of blacks and whites: 43 percent of black families earned less than $2,000 a year, while just 17 percent of white families earned less than $2,000 a year. He added that "similar statistics can be quoted for other minority groups."[17] Chicago saw the first real stirrings of King's determination to mobilize a broad multiracial coalition against economic injustice. It was the first time the SCLC had attempted to engage with Latinos as part of a wider operation in slum communities. This came about because of the growing Puerto Rican and Mexican American presence in black neighborhoods and because the SCLC needed every ally in the struggle against oppression.[18] Young people from different racial groups and ethnic backgrounds attended King's "gang convention" in June 1966 in the East Room of the Blackstone Sheraton Hotel.[19] Eighteen gangs—black, white, Native American, Latino, male, female—all participated. Their diverse backgrounds visibly demonstrated how King was moving in the direction of a multiracial initiative. Asking the gang members to turn away from the dead end of violence, King reminded them that real "power" lay in pressuring the Chicago political machine to "say yes when it wants to say no."[20] This event, together with his other interactions with poor people in Chicago, was an education for King and helped him to more clearly understand that poverty transcended race and was, in fact, a class issue.

In a reflection of public sentiment across the North, whites in Chicago viewed the demands of the movement as a risk to their jobs, houses, and schools. The SCLC leader felt that it had been easier to integrate lunch counters in the South. King continued to look for a strategy to deal with the multifaceted problems of northern ghettos. More work and more sacrifices were required if poverty were to be defeated. Grappling with the challenges posed by unrest in urban communities, he wrote, "We have not devised the tactics for urban slum reform. We spent ten years in the South using new tactics of nonviolence that were successful. However, in the northern cities, with time running out, we failed to achieve creative methods of work. As a result, a desperate essentially leaderless mass of people acted with violence and without a program."[21] The Chicago Freedom Movement offered the beginnings of a solution to urban riots and to the problems faced by the poor. The intractable nature of the discrimination and racism he found in Chicago led King to support civil disobedience, for example, as a strategy to force the pace of change.

In the final months of 1966, the plan to build a rainbow coalition of the poor to work in solidarity and campaign against economic injustice was already forming in King's mind. The experience of Chicago, the need to provide an alternative to black militant separatism for those living in urban centers, the growing backlash against the demands of the civil rights movement and against urban unrest, and his increasing concerns about the war in Vietnam were all factors in his thinking. The Poor People's Campaign began to take shape. King first showed his hand after Chicago at a news conference in October 1966 where he provided a hint of his direction. He called for the organizing of the poor in a "crusade to reform society to realize economic and social justice."[22] This would include a demand for a national guaranteed income. He also delivered a speech to the Atlanta Junior Chamber of Commerce that same month, where he repeated his call for a guaranteed annual income of $4,000. Frustrated by a line of questioning from the audience suggesting that black people should stand on their own feet and stop relying on government handouts, a common view during the period as sentiment turned against the movement, King discussed the matter with aides after the meeting. He insisted that the only way to overcome such prejudice and ignorance was to make poverty visible in the nation's capital. Only then would America understand the true nature and scale of poverty in its midst. Showing remarkable foresight, King recommended to his advisors that the SCLC take a large number of poor people to Washington; they should travel there in old mule carts and other similar forms of transport, and if necessary, the poor should sit down in the street and refuse to leave until the government took action in their favor.[23] All of these suggestions became central planks of the Poor People's Campaign in 1968.

Dr. King reflected further on the dramatic events of 1966 in two key speeches in November of that year. They revealed his stances on several pressing issues, including poverty and the Vietnam War. He also offered significant insights into his evolving ideas for a national mass nonviolent campaign to end poverty. The first of these events was the annual Gandhi Memorial Lecture at the historically black Howard University in Washington, D.C., on November 6, 1966. Before addressing the range of challenges in the period beyond civil rights and voting rights legislation, King looked back to acknowledge the significant strides made by the movement in weakening the barriers of segregation. He paid tribute to those who had suffered so much in the fight for the ballot, describing the Voting Rights Act as written with the "pen and ink of human sacrifice."[24] He then moved on to discuss the work that remained and the issue now consuming much of his energy: economic injustice. Drawing on the experience of Chicago, King condemned conditions in the slums. He noted that little had changed over time: "The black person still finds himself perishing on the lonely island of poverty amid a vast ocean of prosperity, and that economic problem is more critical today than it has ever been."[25] The problems were made worse, he alleged, by unemployment and underemployment. Turning to urban unrest, King reiterated that riots created more social problems than they solved because they intensified the fears of white communities and relieved their guilt.[26] The uprisings gave whites an excuse for inaction. His sympathies, however, were with those in the slums, and he stated that a riot is "the language of the unheard."[27]

The SCLC leader questioned the priorities of the Johnson administration, which took money from the War on Poverty to fund the war in Vietnam. The reference to Vietnam represented a public shift in his thinking. The commitment of ground troops by President Johnson to Vietnam in 1965 had escalated U.S. involvement in the conflict and dramatically increased the cost of the engagement. King's comments were an opening salvo in an analysis that later fused the slums and Vietnam as one problem. Warming to the main theme of his address, King suggested to the Howard University audience the potential outline of a campaign to fight poverty. He called for a "massive action program by people of good will" and demanded that America stop spending billions in Vietnam and on the space race and spend money instead on winning the war against poverty. He insisted, "We must develop a program to keep this issue before the conscience of the nation, making it palpably clear that this economic problem must be solved."[28] Reflecting another change of emphasis in his thinking, King referred to his expansive vision for change not in terms of civil rights, but as a "human rights struggle." The movement now needed to grapple, he asserted, with "basic class issues between the privileged and the underprivileged." This required no less than the "restructuring of the architecture of American society," a phrase he would repeat during the planning for the PPC in 1968.[29] King stressed the multiracial nature of a potential ambitious effort against economic injustice, including his conviction that "black and white are inextricably bound together, no man is an island."[30] The challenge ahead was to bring people together who were different in identity and background and who thought they had little in common. The die was cast; King had set the course for a campaign against poverty in all its forms. Only the timetable and specific shape of it remained to be determined.

The Howard University speech was two days before the U.S. midterm elections on November 8, 1966. The electoral setbacks in the elections for the Democrats in the House, Senate, and gubernatorial races suggested that the public was turning against Lyndon Johnson and his War on Poverty in part due to urban unrest and alarm over the rise of Black Power. King's second important speech on economic injustice came less than a week later, at the SCLC retreat in Frogmore, South Carolina, on November 14. He revisited many of the themes outlined at Howard University. On this occasion, however, he put his staff on alert for a possible campaign to come. His address once again captured the lessons of the Chicago campaign. King acknowledged that the people living in the "teeming ghettos" had gained little from the legislative achievements in 1964 and 1965.[31] King declared that while Chicago had demonstrated the enduring, deep-rooted, endemic, and apparently intractable nature of racism in America, everyone at the meeting should take heart since all movements encounter periods when things do not go well. Using the phrase he had included in his speech a week earlier, King reiterated that the white backlash now evidenced in the midterm elections was a predictable response to demands for a "restructuring of the very architecture of American society." Hinting at the need for a redistribution of wealth in the United States, he argued that the haves were not prepared to give up something to help the have-nots.

Frogmore also saw King attempt to counter the challenges to his methods from advocates of Black Power. The developing fissures in the civil rights movement and the evolving nature of black protest forced him to take a stance. Stokely Carmichael of the Student Nonviolent Coordinating Committee with his slogan of Black Power personified much of the radical politics in the 1960s and represented a change in the public face of SNCC.[32] Carmichael had replaced John Lewis as the SNCC chair in 1966, and he advocated that the organization be exclusively black. He embodied the emergence of young black people who believed that nonviolence and cooperation with white power structures had taken them as far as they could go. Carmichael urged black people to organize themselves and seize control of their own lives. He viewed the old ways of mobilizing whites in support of civil rights as no longer relevant. His relation-

ship with King went back to the early 1960s; they had met at a seminar on nonviolence. NAACP Legal Defense attorney Marian Wright Edelman later described
how a "saddened" King would shake his head and repeatedly ask Stokely if it
was "really that bad."[33] Despite their differences, ultimately King and Carmichael developed "a deeper friendship."[34]

Black Power could be seen as a vague concept, but it represented a different response to white violence, unfulfilled promises, and the limitations of
recent race legislation. Edelman attributed its appeal to a lack of progress in
economic and political life in Mississippi, which was "resented by impatient
young black people eager to loosen the noose of bondage."[35] The War on Poverty had done little to alleviate the circumstances of many young black people.
The Black Power advocacy of self-defense and self-determination also exacer-
bated white fears of black insurrection and the so-called red peril of communism in the 1960s. Director of the FBI J. Edgar Hoover helped to fan the flames
of a white backlash against moderate and militant black people throughout
this period. Hoover attributed riots, looting, and deaths during the urban disturbances from 1964 through 1968 to a sinister partnership between the American Communist Party and black militants.[36] He regarded black nationalists
generally as a threat to national stability and accordingly instructed the Coun-
terintelligence Program (COINTELPRO) to neutralize their activities. Carmichael drew inspiration from some radical groups in the North, including the
Revolutionary Action Movement (RAM), which came out of Cleveland in 1961.
RAM worked alongside SNCC in the South from 1964 and drew support for
their advocacy of self-defense and their anti-imperialism rhetoric.[37] Carmichael's race and his politics offended Hoover.

King found himself increasingly at a disadvantage after the Meredith march
in June 1966, and he was grasping for a public position to satisfy all sides of the
debate. At the time of his Frogmore address, he was apparently worried he had
not taken a more negative position on Black Power.[38] His advisors were divided
on the issue; Bayard Rustin, for example, demanded that King denounce the slogan and the explicit idea of black separatism. Rustin spoke out against Stokely
Carmichael and Floyd McKissick of the Congress of Racial Equality (CORE) for
their support of something that "would destroy them and their movement."[39]
Roy Wilkins of the NAACP bluntly alleged that SNCC had chosen a racist course.
King viewed the controversy around Black Power as a distraction from the main
issue of economic injustice. To provide a reasonably definitive position and put
the matter to rest, he asserted at the SCLC Frogmore retreat that urban riots and
the appeal of black militancy could be explained by "lost hope" and the realiza-

tion of those in the slums that their conditions had not changed. He observed that Black Power "was born from the wounds of despair and disappointment.... it is in fact a reaction to the failure of 'White Power'" to deliver."[40]

King understood the importance of maintaining a united front and was aware that white opponents would use the specter of Black Power to undermine his agenda. He later would ask Stokely Carmichael and others to stand by him in solidarity during the PPC. He acknowledged there was some merit in Black Power, if one recognized it as the "amassing of economic and political power." Commenting on his own methods, he maintained that love without power was weak and agreed with Carmichael and others that black people had to organize for power. However, King cautioned that power should involve "the right use of strength."[41] Perhaps with an eye to a future multiracial campaign against poverty, he also urged unity and togetherness among the poor of all races and dismissed the idea that whites no longer had a role to play in the movement. The SCLC leader revealed his growing awareness that poverty was not simply about race in calling for an end to "class systems."[42] He reaffirmed his belief in the need for interracial cooperation, stating that the SCLC must be "the lamp of hope, that light in a very dark difficult situation." He maintained, "There is no separate black path to power and fulfillment that does not intersect white roots."[43]

King's rhetoric on the issue of poverty at the Frogmore retreat echoed his Howard University speech yet at the same time clearly outlined a new, more radical path for the SCLC. He pointed directly toward the concept of a future campaign "of" the poor and "for" the poor. From this point on, King insisted, the SCLC would deal with "substantive" rather than "surface" issues. He conceded that these issues would cost the nation because they related to "class" and involved the "privileged" and the "underprivileged." President Johnson's attempts to placate conservatives by restricting spending on War on Poverty programs had begun to irk King. The SCLC leader appreciated that the gains of the civil rights movement thus far, including the Voting Rights Act of 1965, were achieved at bargain rates for America; they did not cost the nation anything whereas his new agenda would require massive spending. King called directly for a "redistribution" of wealth and placed capitalism in question by pointing out the inequities of the economic system. He condemned the current government spending to combat poverty as no more than a "skirmish." Demanding that the federal government commit significant funds to fighting poverty and take other actions to end discrimination, he summarized what he had taken from the experience of the Chicago campaign. He said, "You cannot talk about solving the economic problem of black people without talking about billions of dollars. You cannot talk about ending slums without first saying profit must be taken out of slums."[44]

In highlighting capitalism as the problem, King was playing into the hands of his enemies, who had long denounced him as a communist, especially Hoover. The director of the FBI believed that communist agitators were directing the civil rights movement. Allegations that King was, at least, a communist sympathizer came from elements within the black churches also. Pastor Vernon Charles Lyons typified such sentiment when he condemned King's demand for social revolution as contrary to the Bible, and he taught "spiritual rebirth" as a solution to the nation's ills.[45] The accusation that King was a communist was in part a case of guilt by association. His adversaries were aware that the SCLC leader had spent a great deal of time in the company of left-leaning activists. They included the Brotherhood of Sleeping Car Porters official Edgar Daniel Nixon and leader A. Philip Randolph, activist and lawyer Stanley Levison from the American Jewish Congress, radical activist Jack O'Dell, and Bayard Rustin. All of them played a part in shaping King's views on economic justice and the importance of alliances with labor unions. The Montgomery Bus Boycott took place against a backdrop of fear engendered by both racism and the "red peril." The Poor People's Campaign took place in a similarly hostile environment.

No direct link between King and communism has ever been uncovered.[46] King swatted away such accusations, declaring that he "loved God too much" to believe in an atheist system of government. While he admired the great passion of Marx for social justice, he rejected the materialistic interpretations of history by Marxists because this left no place for God.[47] King also abhorred the "deprecation of individual freedom" under communist systems.[48] He accepted, however, that deep historical structures shaped the black and poor experience.[49] Robert Kennedy observed in the early 1960s that communist infiltration of black organizations was feeble and posed little threat.[50] Aware of the certain fallout from his Frogmore speech, King couched his goals in terms of "democratic socialism," holding up Sweden and other nations in Scandinavia as models of systems where there was a more equitable distribution of wealth.[51] He said that this stance did not make him a communist or a Marxist. Drawing from the example of the Social Gospel, King maintained, "Truth is found neither in the rugged individualism of capitalism nor in the impersonal collectivism of communism. The Kingdom of God is found in a synthesis that combines the truth of these two opposites."[52]

The SCLC decided at the November 1966 Frogmore meeting on an "as you were" agenda for the immediate future, reaffirming support for a campaign already under way against school segregation in Grenada, Mississippi, and for a voter registration drive as part of the continuing effort in Chicago. However, King had charted a more radical course for the future. On December 15, 1966, he took the opportunity to express his developing views on poverty to members of Congress and the public at large. He appeared before a hearing of Democrat Abraham Ribicoff's Government Operations Committee on Urban Affairs, whose membership included Democratic senator Robert Kennedy. The committee also heard testimony from Washington residents on the impact of the War on Poverty on their communities.

The hearings had several undercurrents. Floyd McKissick presented evidence on the plight of young people, including the "social violence" perpetrated by school conditions in the slums, which impressed Senator Kennedy although the CORE leader was moving toward advocacy of Black Power. Whitney Young of the National Urban League, Bayard Rustin, and A. Philip Randolph also all testified before the Ribicoff Committee in support of the Freedom Budget for all Americans. King had written the foreword earlier in 1966 for the ambitious and radical book *Freedom Budget*, which envisaged the elimination of poverty within ten years.[53] This plan would in effect begin the War on Poverty all over again to include redistributive aspects. Many of the ideas contained in the Freedom Budget would find their way into the demands articulated under the banner of the Poor People's Campaign, including job creation, improvements in schools, an end to slums, and investment in public works programs. Rustin argued that the Freedom Budget plans would benefit everyone who was poor, regardless of race.[54] In targeting poor people of all races, the proposals rejected the cultural deficit explanation of poverty so often directed at black people by white conservatives.

Senator Robert F. Kennedy shared an interest with King in the problems faced by alienated young people, especially those living in urban centers. As attorney general, Kennedy chaired the President's Committee on Juvenile Delinquency, which came to view poverty as the root cause of delinquency.[55] Kennedy delivered three speeches in 1966 on the topic of cities, which taken together show his deep dissatisfaction with the impact of the War on Poverty and with President Johnson. Just five days before King appeared in front of the Ribicoff Committee, Kennedy spoke in the Senate of the shortcomings of the Johnson administration's strategies to combat poverty in cities, evidenced by unemployment, lack of education, rats, disease, and hopelessness.[56] In common with King, Kennedy saw that government programs had not brought fundamental change, and he organized his own initiative, the Bedford-Stuyvesant Restoration Corporation in New York, a self-help project in a predominantly black community.

Among other remedies, Kennedy encouraged more private investment in the slums, an idea he shared with former Republican vice president Richard Nixon. Kennedy encouraged community residents to work out their own programs for jobs, housing rehabilitation, and educational advancement with financial help furnished by some of America's largest corporations. This idea of citizen participation in government programs became a key demand of the Poor People's Campaign.

The Ribicoff hearings were part of Robert Kennedy's education and pushed him closer to a complete break with Lyndon Johnson on the way forward for America on poverty. Throughout the summer of 1966 and into the fall, the press excitedly had reported every Kennedy word and action, which was dubbed "Bobby watching." A Gallup Poll in August 1966 had showed that 40 percent favored Kennedy for president compared to 38 percent for Johnson.[57] In time Senator Robert Kennedy became one of the strongest supporters of the PPC; he had been the first to suggest that King bring the poor to Washington, D.C.

In advance of the Ribicoff hearings, King had advised Stanley Levison that he intended to blame the costs of the Vietnam War for the recent budget cuts in the War on Poverty. This was only the latest of his increasingly assertive statements against the escalating conflict. He had expressed similar sentiments about government spending on the war in the Howard University speech in early November. In his Frogmore speech later in November, King had attacked the "immorality" of U.S. domestic and foreign policy, arguing that it was impossible to separate the "brutalization" by America of the Vietnamese from the situation at home.[58] Levison was wary of King becoming further embroiled in such a divisive issue but assisted him to prepare the statement for the Ribicoff Committee.[59] Aides from the Ford Foundation also contributed to King's statement.

In his comments to the Senate committee, King came straight to the point. He asserted that as a black man in America, he was concerned with the racial slums, arguing that the "ghetto exists at the very core of and is both a part and a cause of our cities' sickness."[60] Fresh from firsthand experiences in Chicago, King outlined his recent thinking on the connections between conditions in the slums and the war in Vietnam. His eloquent words resounded across the room. He highlighted a situation in which powerless poor black people were denied basic human rights. Condemning neglect of the needs of the poor, King referred to America's distorted values, which spent billions on Vietnam yet financed merely a "skirmish against poverty."[61] Alluding to urban riots, he warned of increasing social tensions and further unrest. He stressed the structural nature of poverty in that urban squalor affected both black and white, although he also acknowledged the average income gaps between the two groups.

King then contrasted the lives of the poor with the crass materialism of the affluent. He called for a rebalancing of government priorities to include less spending on the "striking absurdity" of sending a man to the moon and giving more resources instead to helping men on earth.[62] The attack on President John Kennedy's "shooting for the moon" flagship New Frontier policy went down badly with his brother Robert. However, as Stanley Levison had feared, the issue of Vietnam proved more controversial. King suggested that to ignore conditions in the slums in favor of spending on an immoral war was potentially calamitous. He challenged the premise of the war, Cold War thinking, and the fear of making concessions to supposedly dangerous regimes. One key phrase he uttered has lived long in memory. He declared, "The bombs in Vietnam explode at home; and destroy the hopes and possibilities for a decent America."[63] The phrase became the headline grabber of his presentation and brilliantly framed King's position on the war.

King revealed to the Ribicoff Committee how far his thinking had come in the relatively short time since the struggles to end segregation and to win the vote. In acknowledging that the movement had reached a new stage, he used his favored phrase, asserting that the focus was now on the "economic restructuring of the architecture of American society."[64] This included requirements for radical change in "human rights" areas, such as housing and education. Having described the problems and choices facing the United States, King prescribed a coherent and coordinated response to poverty and all its manifestations. One of his remedies was a guaranteed annual minimum income, which would signal, in his words, a "shift from exclusive attention to putting people to work to enabling people to consume."[65] He concluded with an admission of his failings as a leader of the movement and, in so doing, pointed to the potential shape of a mass campaign against poverty. Not for the first time, he admitted shortcomings in that the movement until now had been mainly middle class, and there was a pressing need to go into ghetto areas to mobilize among working-class and poor people.[66] His aim was to unite in solidarity those who shared the common bond of poverty in order to take forward the struggle against economic injustice. Chicago had been a starting point for something more democratic, more fundamental, and more expansive. With an aside to the lure of Black Power, which threatened to put the brakes on further progress by the nonviolent movement, he claimed that a renewed effort would help to offset some of the ground lost to those opposed to his methods. Robert Kennedy agreed with King that Black Power had set back the movement and blamed it in part for the election losses by the Democratic Party in the most recent elections.[67] King left the senators with a warning. Time was running out for America, he said, and the nation needed to deal with the issues of racism and poverty.

King had a great deal to ponder during the final months of 1966. As the year ended, a rapidly changing social and political climate brought little encouragement for his agenda on tackling economic injustice. From his perspective, the toxic mix included the continuing urban unrest and associated challenges to his methods from Black Power, his growing concerns about escalation of the war in Vietnam, including its impact on spending at home on the War on Poverty, and even SCLC financial worries as the organization struggled to cope with competing demands. The various challenges threatened to halt, and perhaps even reverse, any progress already made toward ending poverty.

The unpredictable political climate and the growing hostility from the public toward the poor were especially troublesome to King. Republican congressman Gerald R. Ford spoke for many others in 1966 in calling for an end to the abdication of law and order in the cities. He condemned the Democrats for indulging rioters.[68] A proposed program to get rid of slum rats had been defeated by conservatives in Congress following riots in Newark in the summer of 1966. While the Democrats retained control of both the House and the Senate in the midterm elections in November 1966, a resurgent Republican Party cost the Democrats forty-seven seats in the House and three Senate seats. For example, Illinois Democrat Paul Douglas, a prominent member of the liberal coalition and an ally of the SCLC in Congress, lost his seat in the Senate. Democratic governors from the North and South lambasted President Johnson for his civil rights policies, which they argued were leading to ruin for their party.[69]

The bruising events of 1966 took their toll on Dr. King, but he learned from the experiences of Chicago in particular. By the close of the year, economic injustice, which had previously trailed in his actions, writings, and speeches, took center stage, and it absorbed his attention for the remainder of his life. The demands for a guaranteed annual income, decent housing for all, and quality education for young people consumed his thinking. King also understood there were no easy solutions to the human rights issues he increasingly referenced. He was not naïve about the challenges ahead, observing that the "achievement of these goals will be a lot more difficult and require much more discipline, understanding, organization and sacrifice."[70] For the SCLC leader, complex economic exploitation lay at the heart of urban riots, which from his perspective represented the frustration and anger of those living in poverty. He viewed police brutality as a major factor in the riots and explained the looting that characterized the unrest as a form of social protest. His analysis of urban America fused unemployment, underemployment, inadequate housing, poor-quality education, and police treatment of black people living in slums. King's critique foreshadowed some of the findings of the government's Kerner Commission more than one year later, which investigated the causes of urban unrest and highlighted structural racism as a significant contributory factor. Others in Congress and in communities across America did not share King's analysis, however, preferring to blame the rioters themselves.

Historian David Garrow maintained that by late 1966 King was more relaxed and more accepting of the challenges yet to be addressed.[71] The clock, however, was ticking. The countdown would continue to the moment when King would go for broke by announcing an ambitious effort to end poverty in the United States. He would plan a movement where people from different races and backgrounds would come together to learn in a shared space, set aside their differences, and mount a nonviolent mass campaign against poverty. Momentum would soon build within the SCLC to take forward the fight against economic injustice and to oppose the related issue of the war in Vietnam.

CHAPTER 3

THE WAR AT HOME AND ABROAD

With the Chicago campaign behind him, King was looking forward in early 1967 to beginning writing a new book to document his thoughts and reflections on the challenges facing the movement and America in this crucial period. It proved impossible, however, to escape the many forces closing in on him. Urban uprisings throughout the summer of 1966, including in Chicago, Cleveland, and Philadelphia, had strengthened public and political sentiment against "rewarding" looters and rioters. A congressional survey in July 1966 of twelve thousand constituents had indicated that a majority were in favor of cuts to spending on poverty, welfare, and the cities. Ninety percent were against further civil rights legislation.[1]

Support for reform had waned by 1967. The issue of crime and the associated demands for law and order became part of the national narrative. President Lyndon Johnson felt compelled to act; otherwise, he left himself open to accusations of being soft on crime. The president had given gradual support for a war on crime from the first urban riots in 1964. The threat of a resurgent Republican Party brought a further hardening of his resolve to stamp down the looters and rioters. By early 1967, electoral setbacks forced Johnson to identify with the new political realities, and he more assertively joined the crusade against crime.[2] At the same time, support diminished in Congress for further legislation to combat poverty. In June 1968, during the Poor People's Campaign (PPC) in Washington, D.C., in yet another manifestation of a backlash against protesters, Congress would pass the Omnibus Crime Control and Safe Streets Act, which among other law enforcement measures allowed increased wiretapping and bugging.[3]

The midterm election losses for the liberal wing of the Democratic Party in November 1966 had provided another ominous sign for King's plans for economic justice. The elections included victories for the staunch segregationist and populist Democrat Lester Maddox as governor of Georgia and Republican Ronald Reagan as governor of California. Reagan first made his name on the national political stage by endorsing Republican Barry Goldwater in the 1964 presidential election. His speech, "A Time for Choosing," delivered just before the Republican convention that year captured the growing resentment against the liberal consensus, the War on Poverty, and civil rights.[4] Reagan's politics offered a conservative alternative to the Great Society. In support of the Goldwater candidacy and for the remainder of his political career, he argued for self-government and against the encroachment of the "intellectual elite" into the lives of ordinary citizens. His rejection of big government found favor with anti-progressive Democrats in the South and with right-wing radicals in his own Republican Party.

Reflecting what would become an increasingly powerful sentiment against "handouts" to the poor, Reagan stood against the expansion of the welfare state, for example, writing in December 1964 that "there ain't no such thing as a free lunch."[5] The right to welfare support became a key PPC demand in 1968. Reagan claimed that his sympathies were with workers forced to pay high taxes to finance the lifestyles of those happy to live off welfare programs. In 1965, Ronald Reagan opposed Johnson's Medicare bill, which would provide medical care for the elderly, on the grounds it represented "the advance wave of socialism which would invade every area of life in the country."[6] California proved to be fertile territory in 1966 for a Reagan campaign against the forces of change and the perceived excesses of the Johnson administration. Many working-class Democrats also shared his concerns about urban riots and university campus disorder.[7] Reagan's opponent for governor in November 1966 was the incumbent, Democrat Edmund G. "Pat" Brown, who attributed his loss in the election to race.[8] Brown had supported Johnson's War on Poverty and the civil rights revolution, both of which provoked a backlash from working-class whites.[9] Reagan capitalized on the political fallout of the Watt riots in August 1965 to position himself as a candidate for governor the following year. He took a hard-line law-and-order stance and described city streets as "jungle paths after dark."[10] He also attacked campus unrest, which began in the state with student protests at the Berkeley campus of the University of California against the alleged suppression of free speech by university administrators. In 1967–1968 student demonstrations against the war in Vietnam became a feature of a divided nation.

King rejected Reagan's philosophy that the United States was a level playing field where everyone enjoyed equality of opportunity. However, the white backlash as represented in populist and right-wing politicians posed a major threat to the SCLC leader's hopes for legislation to tackle economic injustice.

At the beginning of 1967, King's gloom also deepened over both the immorality of the war in Vietnam and its impact on spending to fight poverty. The costs of Vietnam were spinning out of control and threatened to undermine domestic social programs. In his State of the Union address one year earlier, in January 1966, President Lyndon Johnson had expressed confidence that he could win the war in Vietnam and the War on Poverty. He had announced that America was "mighty enough, its society healthy enough, its people strong enough to pursue our goals in the rest of the world while building a Great Society here at home."[11] Johnson's optimism now seemed badly misplaced. The influential Republican minority leader, Senator Everett Dirksen, voiced his opposition to the billions spent on social programs, especially if it meant raising taxes to sustain them.

President Johnson in October 1966 had told a group of black candidates for political office that funding both "guns and butter" was no longer sustainable, and he did not intend to deny anything to the boys fighting in the rice paddies in Vietnam.[12] By January 1967, spending by the Office of Economic Opportunity, the engine room of the War on Poverty, had leveled at $1.5 billion whereas the projected bill for Vietnam had dramatically increased to $10 billion.[13] King would soon argue that poverty was one of the major casualties of the war. Economic growth and a buoyant economy that Johnson had hoped would lift up the poor now gave way to rising inflation and cuts in social program spending. The years of progress for the civil rights movement since the Montgomery Bus Boycott were firmly at an end. While remaining optimistic that he could arouse the conscience of the nation about issues other than the war, King now tempered his hopes for the future with a large degree of realism. The war made it increasingly difficult for the country to focus on economic injustice; by the summer of 1967 King believed America had lost its social perspective. He surmised that the war had strengthened the forces of reaction; the conflict had desensitized people to social issues, making less likely the passage of new programs to combat poverty.

There appeared to be no end in sight to the war. Johnson believed he was in an impossible situation: to be branded soft on communism was a dangerous label in the Cold War climate. He had inherited the "unavoidable commitment" of Vietnam from his predecessors in the Oval Office. President John F. Kennedy had successfully portrayed the Cold War in idealistic terms, using Vietnam to justify public policies. Kennedy even mentioned the issue in his June 1963 civil rights speech. President Johnson privately discussed his concerns about the escalation of the war in Vietnam with southern Democratic senator Richard Russell as early as May 1964. Russell and Johnson had agreed that involvement in the region could potentially draw the United States into a war with China. However, the Cold War climate led Johnson to believe he had no alternative but to stand up to communist insurgency. Reflecting his belief in the domino theory of the period, the president observed, "If we let them take Asia, they're going to try to take us. I think aggression must be deterred."[14] Thus, the steady escalation of the war in Vietnam from 1965 undermined his quest to achieve the Great Society. There were two hundred thousand troops in Vietnam by the end of 1966. Secretary of Defense Robert McNamara advised the president that the war would need six hundred thousand by 1968.[15] As the backlash against his policies gathered strength, Johnson acknowledged that the increasing cost of the war in Vietnam inevitably had reduced the spending available for the War on Poverty.

President Johnson's approval rating on Vietnam had fallen steadily throughout 1966. It dropped from 59 percent in January to 50 percent in March and to 41 percent in September. Democratic senator William Fulbright expressed the thoughts of many in saying America was losing the war at home and abroad.[16] The nation was dividing into hawks and doves, and an estimated one-third of senators were opposed to the conflict as early as mid-1966.[17] The divisive nature of the conflict inevitably meant that King could not remain neutral. Opponents of the war coveted his voice and influence. As a Nobel Peace Prize winner, his views were respected on the international stage. Delivering his formal Nobel lecture at Oslo University in 1964, King had heightened future expectations of him by stressing the global significance of his freedom movement in spreading "the widest liberation in human history."[18] He also had mentioned the problems of racial injustice, poverty, and war. Some among the New Left, including Allard Lowenstein and Norman Thomas, tried to persuade King to come out more assertively against the war in Vietnam. The organization Clergy and Laity Concerned about Vietnam believed that in speaking out King could make a difference. It thus became increasingly difficult for him to stand aside as the war threatened to tear the nation apart.

King had much to ponder about Vietnam during a vacation in Jamaica in January 1967. According to his aide Bernard Lee, perhaps the most crucial factor that pushed the leader of the Southern Christian Leadership Conference to take a stand were graphic images of injured Vietnamese children in the January issue of *Ramparts* magazine. Lee reported that on seeing the photographs, King became physically ill and overcome with rage.[19] King thought it was outrageous that the civil rights movement was praised for its use of nonviolence against Jim Crow, yet America seemed to condone violence against the children of Vietnam. Returning from vacation, King told key associates, including Andrew Young and Stanley Levison, that the civil rights movement should join forces with the peace movement. The unsatisfactory end to the Chicago campaign was part of his analysis. King observed, "We are marking time in the battle in the ghetto with the war in Vietnam going on."[20]

The *Ramparts* article may have been the catalyst, but King had already been moving toward a position where he would overtly denounce the war. In early March 1965, King had called for a negotiated settlement following President Johnson's decision to launch concerted bombing of North Vietnam under Operation Rolling Thunder.[21] The United States was soon engaged in a full-scale ground war. Johnson justified his escalation of the conflict by claiming that opponents in Congress would have denounced him for a failure to act in the face of attacks on U.S. personnel. Ironically, given the later threats from political opponents to the War on Poverty, the president argued that doing nothing in Vietnam would have led to criticism from Congress and less support for his domestic programs.[22] Amid an increasingly polarized situation across the country, the SCLC board of directors had expressed opposition to King making further statements on the war, although at the national convention in August 1965 they would be supportive. In May 1965, King proposed peaceful anti–Vietnam War protests while on a tour of poor communities in Alabama.[23] His various pronouncements raised the hackles of the White House. However, for the moment, King drew back from breaking his ties with Johnson over the issue. In July 1965, just before Congress passed the Voting Rights Act, the SCLC leader apologized to the president for comments he had made on Vietnam, stating that the press had taken them out of context.[24]

King then refrained from making public statements on the conflict for the majority of 1966. His priority was to keep President Johnson on the side of the civil rights movement and to protect the War on Poverty agenda. King was also wary of dividing the SCLC and the movement. Colleagues warned him against taking any actions likely to reduce donations to the SCLC.[25] By the close of 1966, King believed that the War on Poverty had become one of the major casualties of the Vietnam conflict. Vietnam drove an increasing wedge between him and the White House as King realized that his conscience would no longer allow for prolonged silence on the issue. The midterm election losses for the Democrats in November 1966 were a sign of what was to come on the political front as the tide turned against President Johnson in Congress.

By 1967, some of King's closest associates advised it was folly to conflate civil rights with the movement against the war. While Jim Bevel was in favor of King speaking out more forcefully, Bayard Rustin urged the SCLC leader to dodge the issue in order not to lose support from the White House for antipoverty measures. Levison thought it would be a mistake for King to take a public stance.[26]

Clarence Jones, King's attorney and one of his speechwriters, feared the potential damage to federal government support for the movement should King
speak out. Similarly, Whitney Young of the National Urban League thought it
unwise to alienate Johnson in case his patronage for the movement was lost.[27]
Both Whitney Young and Roy Wilkins of the NAACP correctly predicted that
black organizations would stand accused of communist infiltration if they took
an unpopular position on the war.[28]

As a black man and someone unelected to political office, King was aware
he would court serious criticism should he speak out on an issue already dividing the nation. Coupled with the resistance he had faced in the North during the
Chicago campaign, the criticism that he should only express views on "black"
issues depressed him.[29] However, by late 1966, he had come to a point where it
was "increasingly clear his compassion for humanity would not be contained
to calls for justice on a single front."[30] His moral conscience was decisive in the
stand he eventually took against the war. As mentioned in the previous chapter, Dr. King first broke serious cover on Vietnam at Howard University. He then
went on to fuse the evils of racism, excessive materialism, and militarism at the
Frogmore SCLC convention in November 1966.[31] King's attack on U.S. policy in
Vietnam at the Ribicoff urban affairs hearing in December 1966 was his most
detailed public critique of the war thus far. He denounced the conflict as one
that would have serious consequences for stability and peace on the domestic front. His warning was prophetic. Within eighteen months, dissent on the
streets and college campuses over Vietnam split the country on race, class, and
generational grounds. King described the conflict as symptomatic of a broader
malaise in America. His opposition to the war became a political movement
against various injustices, including poverty.[32]

In a speech on February 25, 1967, in Los Angeles entitled "The Casualties
of the War in Vietnam," King made his most damning criticism of the conflict
thus far. Highlighting the foreign and domestic damage caused by the war, he
said, "We see grief-stricken mothers with crying babies clutched in their arms
as they watch their little huts burst forth into flames, we see young men, being sent home half-men, physically handicapped and mentally deranged."[33] In
a move bound to enrage his opponents and alienate many of his supporters, the
Los Angeles speech included condemnation of a war whose casualties included
American principles and values. King accused the United States of breaching
international law and undermining the United Nations. In his estimation, an ar-
rogant America had lost its position of moral leadership in the world through
policies that amounted to "white colonialism." King's argument that flawed foreign policy decisions damaged U.S. prestige and influence echoed several of his

earlier career pronouncements on the impact of domestic policies on the world stage. One month after President Kennedy took office, the SCLC leader had observed that America was not so strong nor the final triumph of the democratic ideal so inevitable that it could ignore what the world thought of the United States and its record.[34] He also had warned in 1962 that America was in danger of losing its moral and political voice in the world community of nations over the issue of racial segregation.[35] In 1967, now bringing together conditions in the slums and foreign policy, King slammed U.S. priorities. He drew parallels between the situation of the oppressed in Vietnam and the oppressed on the domestic front.

The Los Angeles speech contained colorful and powerful language. King denounced Vietnam as the most blatant example of American economic imperialism. The real casualties, in his view, were the poor. He called for a radical shift in government policy away from waging a war of aggression overseas in favor of a renewed effort to achieve domestic harmony and economic justice at home. He linked "economic revitalization to demilitarization."[36] His supporting evidence for such a controversial view was the "$322,000 for each enemy we kill, while we spend in the so-called War on Poverty in America only about $53.00 for each person classified as poor."[37] Attacking the self-appointed world policeman role inherent in U.S. foreign policy, King questioned why his nation ignored apartheid in South Africa while it also supported dictatorships across the globe under the guise of fighting communism.

Still smarting from the fallout of the Chicago campaign, King seared senators who opposed a fair housing bill, denying black people decent housing, yet at the same time, the Congress armed black soldiers to kill on the battlefield. He reeled off some damning statistics intended to shame America into getting its priorities in order. In one telling phrase, King observed that America made a black person a 100 percent citizen in warfare yet reduced him to 50 percent of a citizen on U.S. soil. Vietnam, he suggested, encapsulated a broader situation in which black people had twice the share of the negative things in life. They were twice as likely to be both unemployed and live in inadequate accommodations. Yet, he revealed, there were twice as many black people in combat in Vietnam at the beginning of 1967, and twice as many died in action (20.6 percent) in proportion to their numbers in the population compared to whites.[38]

King had now moved even closer toward outright opposition to the war. In pushing himself forward as a potential leader of this effort, he was aware of the consequences. He referred in the Los Angeles speech to those vilified as traitors and fools for dissenting against the war. Anticipating the criticism that would inevitably come his way in a polarized nation, King made it clear that he opposed the war in Vietnam because he loved America. Precisely because he loved his country, he saw the need to castigate it. Throughout this period, King consistently called for a revolution in values in America. The SCLC leader seemed determined to go for broke to end both the war in Vietnam and poverty at home. He called for organizing against the war, arguing for activists to demonstrate, teach, and preach until the very foundations of the United States were shaken. Groups such as Students for a Democratic Society had become increasingly active in their opposition to the war. On April 17, 1967, SDS organized an antiwar demonstration in Washington; many other demonstrations would take place through 1968 and beyond as opposition to the conflict gained increasing momentum. The activism of young people against the war inspired King in part because they asked legitimate questions about the direction of their country.

In March 1967, in a speech at the Chicago Coliseum, King called for the peace and civil rights movements to come together.[39] Also in March, at a meeting of the SCLC board, he argued that the evils of capitalism were as real as the evils of militarism and the evils of racism.[40] Andrew Young supported his leader's proposition that the SCLC stand up against the war. Many board members, on the other hand, opposed King's intention to speak out more assertively on the issue. Aaron Henry, for example, wondered what exactly they were getting into by campaigning against the conflict.[41] Some sensed it would be folly for the movement to alienate President Lyndon Johnson further. King understood that his decision was not politically expedient. King's last private call with Johnson had been in November 1966, the same month as his speeches at Howard University and Frogmore.[42] He showed little interest in rebuilding bridges with the president.

Opposition to the war increased as 1967 progressed, and King was challenged to offer his voice in support of the thousands demonstrating against the conflict on campuses and on the streets. By April 1967, he concluded it was time to "tell the truth." He was prepared to risk splits in the civil rights movement, dismissing those who he thought preferred to preserve their invitations to high-profile conferences at the White House. King confided in other civil rights leaders that he had communed with himself and prayed before speaking out.[43] He was under no illusions and assumed that his stance would bring problems for the SCLC and other civil rights organizations. But he did not believe he had "the strategic option of silence."[44]

King's silence was well and truly broken at Riverside Church, New York, on April 4, 1967. He delivered a resolute and uncompromising speech, "A Time to Break Silence: Beyond Vietnam." Andrew Young wrote the final draft from material provided by historian and civil rights activist Vincent Harding and John

Maguire, a white scholar at Wesleyan University. King aligned himself with the oppressed peasants of Vietnam and put himself in their shoes, alleging that America had created a hell for the poor in that country. He declared, "We have destroyed their two most cherished institutions: the family and the village. We have destroyed their land and their crops."[45] The SCLC leader framed the war as an enemy of the poor in both the United States and Vietnam. He spoke sadly of the lost promises of the War on Poverty programs, which had now given way to spending on an escalating and immoral war in Vietnam. He claimed that his Nobel Peace Prize was a commission to work harder for the "brotherhood of man," a calling that took him beyond national allegiances.

King felt almost a sense of release in being true to his conscience since he believed that his country no longer had a moral conscience. King linked the barbarity of U.S. policy in Vietnam with the treatment of the oppressed at home. The Chicago slums had played their part in leading him to this juncture. He condemned the double standards of an administration that denounced violence in the slums yet supported the worst kind of violence in Vietnam. King described his feelings on meeting young black people in American urban ghettos in the wake of riots and disturbances: he knew he could never again raise his voice against the violence of the oppressed without having first spoken clearly to the "greatest purveyor of violence in the world today," the United States. These words echoed across America and around the globe. It is worth remembering the risks King took in speaking out. To describe U.S. foreign policy in such scathing terms opened him up to accusations of disloyalty to his country. King compounded an alleged lack of patriotism through his call for young men to become conscientious objectors. For King, his patriotism justified a stance against the war. The following year, in March 1968, in his response to the Kerner Commission's report on urban riots, he wrote, "We believe the highest patriotism demands the ending of that war and the opening of a bloodless war to fund victory over racism and poverty."[46] Bernard Lafayette observed that, if anything, black people in the public eye had to appear "extra patriotic"; otherwise, they became targets for attack in the media and from the forces of the state.[47]

The Riverside speech provoked a crescendo of criticism. Any possibility of reconciliation with President Johnson was now out of the question. In an age of regular red scares, J. Edgar Hoover viewed the speech as proof of King's complicity with a radical left-wing ideology. Hoover updated his "King monograph" alleging communist influence over the civil rights leader.[48] The FBI later would hold a "racial conference" to discuss ways to disrupt the Poor People's Campaign. Techniques included spreading lies and rumors.[49] King, of course, was not the only individual to attract intense scrutiny from the forces of the state.

The FBI also infiltrated antiwar and New Left organizations during this period. An institution in his own right, Hoover used his power to attack various groups and organizations that offended his view of what America should be. Black columnist Carl Rowan joined the red-baiting by suggesting that sinister left-wing forces were guiding King.[50] A poll revealed that 73 percent of the public disagreed with King's stand.[51] The dismay from elements within the civil rights movement was no less powerful; both the NAACP and the National Urban League distanced themselves from his position on the war.

The "Beyond Vietnam" speech also provoked feverish debate in the press. The *Washington Post* suggested King had demonstrated that his best years were behind him; in short, he was no longer relevant. Its editorial wistfully noted that "he has diminished his usefulness to his cause, to his country and to his people and that is a great tragedy."[52] The SCLC fought back against the press criticism and compiled a list of rebuttals to accusations that its leader was unpatriotic, meddlesome, and out of step. The organization's response included reference to a letter from an academic published in the *New York Times*, which defended King's right to speak out. The letter claimed King stood in a solid historical tradition of dissent from civil rights leaders in relation to U.S. foreign policy. It cited the example of the first president of the NAACP, Moorfield Storey, who was anti-imperialist and had condemned U.S. intervention in the Dominican Republic, Haiti, and Nicaragua. The SCLC stressed that King had taken a moral stance against the war, and this was a perfectly consistent position for him to take as a man of peace. The organization also highlighted Ralph Bunche's satisfaction with King's public position not to formally merge the civil rights movement with the peace movement.[53] There was talk that King might run as a peace candidate in what was certain to be a fiercely contested and divisive presidential election in 1968.

King's antiwar stance brought other problems for him in a polarized nation. Vietnam made it easier for opponents to tie him to black militants, such as Stokely Carmichael. The Black Power leader viewed the war in Vietnam as "an example of American racism that defined the nation as an empire whose imperial ambitions threatened humanity's future."[54] In the summer of 1966, Carmichael had described black people fighting in Vietnam as American "mercenaries."[55] He had delivered his own key speech on Vietnam just one month before King's Riverside address.[56] While Black Power was one of many forces pushing King to the left, it would be a disservice to King to argue that Carmichael led the way on the issue of Vietnam. Carmichael did urge the SCLC leader to come out publicly against the war, yet King's personal opposition to the conflict had deep roots, although he had chosen to be less outspoken on the issue for much of the preceding three years. The Riverside speech was useful in setting aside accusations from radical black youths who regarded him as an "Uncle Tom."[57] He was on their side, and for the SCLC leader it was a great tragedy that class and race inequalities meant that military service was often the only escape out of poverty for young black men.[58] In late April 1967, King invited Carmichael to hear him preach a sermon on Vietnam at Ebenezer Baptist Church in Atlanta. They agreed to refrain from public criticism of each other and to advocate for shared objectives wherever possible.

In May 1967, King joined his SCLC colleagues at another retreat at Frogmore. He dealt with both the changing nature of the civil rights movement and the war in Vietnam, attacking the war as the most significant obstacle to the struggle against poverty. On the broad issue of the movement, he confirmed what many in the SCLC already understood from his numerous previous statements and actions: from his perspective, they had moved from a period of "civil rights" to one of "human rights." He emphasized that this change brought certain responsibilities, including the necessity for the SCLC to shift focus. The organization could no longer be content with being a "reform" movement but needed to move forward to meet new imposing challenges in this "era of revolution."[59] The battle to sit down at lunch counters had been won; however, real integration meant shared power. He maintained that the problems of America could only be solved by a "radical redistribution of economic and political power."[60]

King appealed to his colleagues to examine their consciences, to look beyond their individual projects and aspirations, and to join him in working for a better America and for a better world. He acknowledged that he personally had vacillated for a long period before being true to his own conscience. He now felt he had to align himself with poor people; otherwise, he was not a true follower of Christ. Reaching deep into the Social Gospel, King asserted, "The ultimate measure of a man is not where he stands in moments of convenience, but where he stands in moments of challenge, moments of great crisis and controversy. There may be others who want to go another way, but when I took up the cross, I recognized its meaning. The cross may mean the death of your popularity. It may mean the death of your bridge to the White House. It may cut your budget down a little but take up your cross and just bear it. And that is the way I have decided to go."[61] Having issued a challenge to the SCLC and the nation at large, King understood that an inevitable confrontation was ahead. He concluded his address with a defiant note, "I will be heard."[62]

The tumultuous summer of 1967, including continued urban unrest, black militancy, backlash against the liberal consensus, and escalation of the war in Vietnam, propelled King inevitably toward the idea of a campaign against poverty. In his own words, events led him to a realization that the problems of poor black people were "inextricably bound up in the problems of the overall materialism and militarism of the nation."[63] While some politicians and members of the public thought that the War on Poverty had already given too much to the poor, many in the urban slums in the North saw things from a different perspective. The summer of 1967 brought disturbances in 125 cities, which provoked a national political conversation. In Detroit, for example, forty people lost their lives in the general mayhem of rioting and looting, and more than seven thousand were arrested. The property damage bill in Detroit alone was $50 million. Army troops and National Guardsmen restored and maintained order.[64] President Johnson felt that the rioters were ungrateful after all he had done for the poor. James Farmer of the Congress of Racial Equality observed that Johnson simply did not understand the angry, raucous, and desperate folks in the ghettos.[65]

The idea for a campaign against economic injustice received added resonance in 1967 due to what amounted to a rediscovery of poverty in the United States earlier that year. Attorney Marian Wright Edelman was fighting against attempts by powerful white political elites to defund the Head Start program called the Child Development Group of Mississippi (CDGM). The organization provided early education, health screening, meals, and other services to people who were among the most impoverished in America. The CDGM offended white interests in Mississippi by promoting "black" community action, including voter registration. From 1965 Edelman not only had battled to convince officialdom in Washington, D.C., that the CDGM was good value for the money, but had also been fighting against political opponents determined to discredit the organization and what they claimed it represented. Hard-line Mississippi senators John Stennis and James Eastland charged the CDGM with ineffective management and misuse of funds. Their stand was in large measure ideological and political. Stennis argued that the CDGM was in the hands of dangerous radicals.[66] Both senators were steadfast supporters of the status quo in social and racial matters and viewed the CDGM as a Trojan horse intent on helping to bring about equality of the races in a state widely known as a "closed society." Eastland had vowed not to obey the "political" Supreme Court following the *Brown v. Board of Education* ruling against segregation in 1954.

In March 1967, Democrat Joseph Clark of Pennsylvania, chair of the Senate Subcommittee on Employment, Manpower and Poverty, asked Edelman to testify before a hearing of his committee on the reauthorization of funding for programs, including Head Start. Edelman painted a picture of starvation and abject poverty in Mississippi resulting from a number of factors. Automated methods of picking cotton and the use of herbicides had reduced the demand for farm labor, a traditional area of employment for poor black people in Mississippi.[67] One estimate stated that in 1959, there were sixty-five thousand jobs for hand-picking cotton in the Mississippi Delta fields, yet there were fewer than three thousand hand-picking jobs in 1966.[68] Compounding the problem of poverty, the enactment of an agricultural minimum wage had seen a decline in employment figures as growers in the state looked to cut costs. Many families could not afford the $2.00 per person for food stamps. Regulations meant that welfare was only available to one-parent families. Finally, farmers received subsidies as an incentive *not* to grow crops to avoid overproduction. Remarkably, Senator Eastland in Mississippi received more than $157,000 from the scheme in 1967.[69] In sum, as Senator Robert Kennedy aide Peter Edelman observed, "Rural poverty was highly politicized, intimately connected to race and rooted in the nature of the local economy."[70]

Marian Wright Edelman took the opportunity during her testimony to request that the committee members come and see for themselves the suffering and hunger in the Delta. Senators, including Democrats Joseph Clark and Robert Kennedy and Republicans Jacob Javits and George Murphy, took up the invitation. Edelman advised the subcommittee that helpless families were starving and desperate.[71] It also heard testimony from poor people in Mississippi about widespread malnutrition, inadequate housing and sanitation, hunger, limited access to healthcare, and children with growth retardation.[72]

Senators Kennedy and Clark created two teams to visit poor people in their homes in the Mississippi Delta towns of Greenville, Cleveland, and Clarksdale. People were living in shacks, and some families were starving. Kennedy was shocked at what they found in the squalid dwellings and confided to aide Peter Edelman that conditions were worse than in third world countries he had visited. Kennedy reached out to those he met, including malnourished and barefoot children. His empathy impressed Marian Wright Edelman. She later confided she had been skeptical about the intentions of the members of the subcommittee, including Robert Kennedy. Edelman reported she had thought "it was just a bunch of guys coming down for publicity. He [Kennedy] did things that I had not done. He went into the dirtiest, filthiest, poorest, black homes, places with barely any floor, and only potbellied stoves; and he would sit with a baby who had open sores and whose belly was bloated from malnutrition."[73] Robert Kennedy was moved to tears at the sight of a "listless baby with bloated stomach lying on the floor with a few grains of rice."[74] Edelman concluded that

Kennedy always understood that the "real culprit of hunger was poverty and a lack of good jobs."[75] She sensed from this point that he would be a major force in trying to deal with hunger in Mississippi.[76]

Senator Kennedy returned to Washington from Mississippi and quickly put words into action. He met with Secretary of Agriculture Orville Freeman to request a softening of food stamp rules. Poverty in Mississippi was becoming visible to the nation. Press and television reports prompted a group of physicians under the auspices of the Field Foundation of Chicago to lead an evaluation of the health of eight hundred children in Head Start in Mississippi. They presented their findings, "Hungry Children: Special Report," which was supported by photographs taken by Al Clayton, in July 1967 to Clark's subcommittee. They had found rickets and general evidence of what they described as a "national disaster." The physicians reported that children were "living under insanitary conditions, without proper food, without access to doctors or dentists, under crowded conditions and in flimsy shacks."[77]

America could no longer be under any illusions about the poverty in its midst. The question remained: What were politicians and the public prepared to do about it? Although opinion was divided on how to respond or if at all, King intended to play his part. The need to address hunger, inadequate housing, and zero healthcare for the poor would become central demands of the Poor People's Campaign. At the SCLC convention in August 1967, King outlined his plan for future action against poverty, discrimination, and racism, and he provided his analysis of the recent social disorder in urban areas. He acknowledged the intense pressure on him from the movement to come up with a plan to end poverty and in the process win over those young people in urban centers falling under the spell of Black Power separatism. His experiences in Chicago had taught King that "true equality" would be "resisted to the death." He conceded Chicago demonstrated that the movement had thus far failed to devise tactics for urban slum reform.[78] Dr. King used the title of his book *Where Do We Go from Here?* to frame his presentation. The recently published book had received mixed reviews from critics. Journalist Andrew Kopkind had described the work in the *New York Times Book Review* as further evidence that King was a man of the past who had "arrived at the wrong conclusions about the world."[79] Kopkind argued that King had no real strategy to tackle the structural issues highlighted in the book. King's main message emphasized that government could not have racial harmony when there was white affluence amid black poverty.[80]

King set out the shape of a campaign against poverty and all its manifestations. He gave approval to delegates for a national effort that would require new ways of thinking and new methodologies to address the interconnected prob-

lems of white backlash, unemployment (especially among urban youth), discrimination, war, and conditions in the slums. In the context of a fourth year
of urban unrest, most recently in Detroit and Newark, he aligned himself with
those trapped in the slums with the observation "if the soul is left in darkness,
sins will be committed."[81] His analysis of the causes of urban riots provoked little sympathy in a divided nation. Former president Dwight D. Eisenhower reflected an intense backlash against the rioters in suggesting a communist conspiracy was at the root of the problem. A poll of whites indicated that 45 percent
blamed outside agitators.[82] Conspiracy theories were a convenient way to ignore more plausible reasons for the outbreaks of violence in the slums. As urban unrest continued to polarize public opinion, the newly elected governor of
California, Ronald Reagan, helped to politicize the religious Right's concerns
about an alleged lack of respect for law and order.[83] King took the opposite view.
Dramatic action was required, he suggested, to harness the legitimate rage of
the powerless in nonviolent directions as an alternative to riots. These would include disciplined disruption in the form of civil disobedience. He argued that to
dislocate the functioning of a city without destroying it could be more effective
than a riot.[84] Refusing to compromise on nonviolence and to ensure such tactics would be effective, he observed, "We will have to develop mass disciplined
forces that can remain excited and determined without dramatic conflagra-
tions."[85] Once again, he was calling for the development of a nonviolent mass
movement of poor people who would learn and work together in solidarity to
combat poverty. The delegates at the SCLC convention agreed on a resolution
denouncing the inadequacies of the War on Poverty in relation to job creation,
housing, and economic development.[86]

As already described, King met with NAACP Legal Defense attorney Marian
Wright Edelman in late August 1967, during which she communicated advice
from Senator Robert Kennedy to bring the poor to Washington, D.C., to protest
poverty. This was the final piece in the puzzle, which led to the Poor People's
Campaign. In September 1967, although still worn down by the many pressures
on him, King took the idea to an SCLC retreat at Airlie House in Warrenton, Virginia. The proposal later received cautious approval during a retreat at Frogmore in November 1967, when he also announced that nonviolence now had to
adapt to urban conditions and urban moods.[87] But King's intention to launch
a campaign in Washington did not sit well with many of his colleagues. Hosea Williams maintained that much work remained on voter registration in the
South, and he regarded the proposed Poor People's Campaign as a distraction.
SCLC board member Marian Logan thought it would harden opinion against
the movement and would result in a political backlash in the form of a resur-

gent Republican Party. She argued that some whites in America looked down on poor black people in the slums and condemned their behavior. In her opinion, bringing poor people to the seat of government was therefore like "throwing it in their faces."[88] William Rutherford, executive director of the SCLC, acknowledged that almost no one on the staff thought the next priority should be such a "vast and amorphous issue" as poverty.[89] Requests for a "handout" in the form of a guaranteed annual income and/or government jobs were felt to be unrealistic and would not play well with Congress in an economic climate not conducive to massive spending.[90] King countered by pointing out that opinion polls suggested that the public supported a guaranteed annual income or a negative income tax.[91]

With others in the SCLC leadership, James Bevel supported a "stop the draft" movement instead of a campaign against poverty.[92] For King, Vietnam and poverty were fused together, meaning there was no conflict of interest. Jesse Jackson fretted about the impact of the PPC on what remained of President Johnson's support for the movement. Jackson was also concerned there was no "plan B" for the PPC. "Going for broke," as King described the objective of the campaign, brought risks should the government fail to make concessions by way of legislation. Jackson also had his own priorities to take care of, including Operation Breadbasket. Rather than go to Washington, Jackson preferred to expand the Operation Breadbasket focus on black economic exclusion through, for example, a national boycott of General Motors.[93] Bernard Lafayette, who would become national director of the PPC, pressured SCLC staff leaders to support the initiative. He insisted that they allocate a portion of their budgets to the campaign against poverty; the challenge for them was to work out how to steer their projects to meet the needs of the PPC since SCLC project budgets were set one year in advance.[94]

In the end, the decision on whether to go ahead with a campaign against poverty was down to King himself. He decided to press on and prepared to announce that he would bring the poor to Washington, D.C.

PART II
CONVERGING

CHAPTER 4

PLANNING THE POOR PEOPLE'S CAMPAIGN

On December 4, 1967, King finally confirmed at a press conference that he would lead thousands of the nation's poor people to Washington, D.C. He had reached a point where nothing less than an all-out assault on poverty would address the shortfalls of the previous civil rights and voting rights legislation. He informed an expectant press that waves of the nation's poor and disinherited would go to Washington, D.C., in the spring of 1968 to demand redress of their grievances by the U.S. government and to secure at least jobs or a guaranteed income for all.[1] Close SCLC colleague Andrew Young described the plan for the Poor People's Campaign as part of a great American tradition of nonviolent dissent.[2] King's Washington campaign had several precursors in U.S. history. Previous examples of protesters occupying space in the nation's capital included Coxey's Army of the Unemployed in 1894 and the Bonus Army marchers of 1932. Both challenged the government and claimed the capital as a political space where citizens could voice their concerns.[3] In terms of scale and ambition and the multiracial nature of the proposed campaign, however, the Poor People's Campaign could rightly claim to be unique in American history until this point in time.

King demanded no less than a "reconstruction of the entire society, a revolution of values."[4] His call for universal economic rights to end poverty in America was radical and ambitious. Myles Horton, head of the Highlander Folk School in Tennessee, wrote, "King evidently judged that the time had come for a major societal change and that massive nonviolent, transforming action was called for. He had labored with the idea of reforming the existing institutions, a little change here, a little change there, but now he felt quite differently."[5] The SCLC leader promised that poor people would remain in the nation's capital until the government responded to their demands and would stand their ground come what may. He was undoubtedly aware of the fate of the Bonus Army, who were characterized at the time as communist sympathizers and then forcibly removed from their camps and kicked out of Washington.[6] He confirmed that he and others were prepared to go to jail on behalf of the millions of poor already "imprisoned by exploitation and discrimination." He took solace from the fact that dramatic and direct confrontation had secured significant concessions from the government in the past, citing the campaigns in Birmingham and Selma as recent examples. He reminded the press that the focus of his attention had moved from segregation and the ballot to the economic plight of people across the nation. Summarizing the essence of the proposed campaign, King declared his intention to "channel the smoldering rage and frustration of black people into an effective, militant and nonviolent movement of massive proportions in Washington and other areas."[7]

Sensing the historical significance of his great effort, King informed the press that the United States was at a crossroads and needed to choose new paths in domestic and foreign policies. His multiracial coalition against economic injustice would assist America to fulfill its true destiny. King's choice of language was almost apocalyptic; he argued that the very "stability of a civilization, the potential of free government, and the simple honor of men" were all at stake.[8] He described America as fraught by bitterness, despair, and frustration, which threatened the worst chaos, hatred, and violence any nation had ever encountered. In the context of a divided nation, King predicted that inaction would lead to class conflict and national ruin. The only way to avoid this, he counseled, was to take the necessary steps to stop the divisions between the affluent Americans "locked in the suburbs of physical comfort and mental insecurity" and the poor Americans "locked inside ghettos of material privation and spiritual debilitation."[9]

King now called on America to radically reevaluate its priorities. He fused conditions in the slums with the immoral costly war in Vietnam and lambasted the bombardment of that nation while "political brokers" disarmed action against poverty. The United States, he declared was "a nation gorged on money," which at the same time denied millions of its citizens a good education, adequate health services, decent housing, meaningful employment, and even respect. Turning to the rationale for a projected campaign in the heart of political power in Washington, King put the federal government in the spotlight, declaring it had caused the problems but could also provide the solutions.[10] He called for America to reorder its economic and power arrangements, the values and terms on which the nation worked.[11] From his perspective and within the nonviolent movement generally, there was a consensus that justice should reside at the heart of American political power.[12] In my interview with the national director of the PPC, Bernard Lafayette, he reflected, "Our presence was a powerful form of protest. The Federal Government regulates in terms of the distribution of wealth, it is the overseer. We asked who is in control of the resources of the nation and who has the power to bring forward legislation."[13]

Throughout his career, King regularly highlighted the central role of the federal government as the prime regulator of resources with the capacity to make life better for the poor. He had learned from Benjamin Mays at Morehouse that the federal government was responsible for ensuring economic and social equality for all. In 1959, King demanded that President Eisenhower enact federal and state fair employment practices laws on the basis that "the government alone had the power to establish the legal undergirding that can ensure progress."[14] Two years later, in 1961, King targeted the fledgling Kennedy presidency in a similar vein, arguing that only the federal government had sufficient power at its disposal to guide America through the changes ahead.[15] He drew from the lessons of history to support the case for Kennedy to intervene to address areas of economic injustice. King observed that the New Deal under Franklin D. Roosevelt had changed fundamental economic relationships in the United States. He wrote, "The nation which five years earlier viewed federal intervention on any level as collectivism or socialism, in amazingly swift transition, supported the new role of government as appropriate and justified."[16] The Poor People's Campaign, as envisaged by King, would equal the scale of both the New Deal and the Marshall Plan to reconstruct Europe in the aftermath of World War II.

The federal government and the nation's capital city were already indelibly linked with King through the March on Washington for Jobs and Freedom in 1963. That march was arguably conducted in a more favorable political context for the movement, while the 1968 campaign was hampered by the increasing threat of federal budget cuts and a hostile political climate.[17] Public sentiment had turned against the movement by 1967. Although the media largely had ignored arguments from the event platform in 1963 on the economic condition of the poor, the March on Washington and the PPC had the issue in common. The March on Washington had brought many poor farmers and sharecroppers from the Deep South to Washington for the first time in their lives. Other low-income people would replicate these journeys in 1968 for the PPC. The abiding memory of the 1963 event had become the King speech, "I Have a Dream," but the media had neglected to highlight the potentially more controversial messages in his speech. For example, in an early indication of his travel toward what would become the PPC five years later, King spoke at the March on Washington of how America had given black people a bad check that had been "returned, unpaid, due to insufficient funds." His powerful speech in 1963 included references to those who lived on a "lonely island of poverty . . . in the corners of American society."[18]

The press corps was keen to find out what form the occupation of the nation's capital might take and what the demonstrators might get up to in Washington. With few details to impart at this point, King promised there would a "tent-in" of sorts. Stanley Levison was credited with the idea of establishing a camp in Washington, similar to the Bonus Army's tent city.[19] The SCLC leader speculated that a core group of around three thousand people from across America would travel to Washington. The participants would be enlightened on everything the SCLC was seeking to do on jobs and income. They would be trained and educated and would work together in solidarity in the shared space of their camp in Washington. King conceded that protests could potentially take place around the White House. He confirmed the proposition put to him that the campaign would be more militant than ever before. He stood his ground in declaring he would bring "massive dislocation without destroying life or property." From his perspective, there was no alternative but to mount a "strong, dramatic and attention getting" campaign to achieve the grand objective of ending poverty in America.

With an eye on the divisive Vietnam War, King dismissed press suggestions that the civil rights movement and antiwar forces had now fully coalesced. In October 1967, the peace movement had organized its biggest protest in Washington to date in a demonstration at the Pentagon under the umbrella of the National Mobilization Committee to End the War in Vietnam. David Dellinger, one of the architects of the National Mobilization Committee, wrote in terms familiar to King's own movement that the peace movement was forging a "creative synthesis of Gandhi and guerrilla."[20] But King stated that even those in favor of continuing the war in Vietnam were welcome to join the struggle for jobs and income. He denied that the campaign was intended to embarrass Lyndon Johnson. King stressed that the urban coalition in support of the PPC included the president's own constituents and people from both major political parties.

At the announcement launching the PPC in December 1967, journalists raised an issue worrying even those close to King, that is, the extent to which the campaign and its methods of civil disobedience might further erode already diminishing support for civil rights. The SCLC planned to undertake militant nonviolent actions until legislators moved against poverty. King maintained that the government and the people of Washington had nothing to fear from a campaign of nonviolence, and, on the contrary, he predicted certain chaos and social disruption in America should the initiative *not* take place. The perceived threat to law and order posed by the arrival of thousands of poor people in Washington was very much in the forefront of journalists' minds. The SCLC leader confirmed that he aspired to mobilize demonstrators in different regions across the United States. The scope and ambition of the campaign were like nothing seen before. It would involve "suffering and outraged citizens" who would remain in Washington until some definite and positive action was taken to provide jobs and income for the poor.[21] Questions directed at King on this issue reflected broader public and political anxieties at the prospect of an invasion of the "great unwashed." He acknowledged there were some risks but confirmed the SCLC would train participants in the discipline of nonviolence and the whole idea of "jail without bail." King planned to recruit and train core groups of around two hundred in each location, who would then lead and guide other people as they assembled in larger numbers. He drew from recent experiences to assert that people, however angry and bitter they might be, responded to nonviolence if it was militant enough and if it was really doing something. He cited the example of the Chicago campaign when the Blackstone Rangers responded positively to nonviolence and marched with the SCLC every day, despite being the "worst gang in Chicago."

In a bid to reassure the public and politicians, King emphasized the requirement for all participants to adhere to the discipline of nonviolence as a strategy for social change. The subsequent discussions with Stokely Carmichael, H. Rap Brown, and SNCC brought agreement that black militants would not interfere with the campaign, but there was no commitment from them to get involved either. King met twice with Carmichael in February 1968.[22] Carmichael insisted that the organizational autonomy of both his newly formed cross-class militant Black United Front and SNCC should be preserved.[23] Carmichael and King showed their mutual respect throughout the campaign, a fact their enemies, including the FBI, thought was suggestive of close collaboration. In a television appearance, King was accused of joining forces with Carmichael and Brown, who were described in the broadcast as "two of the most extreme agitators in the whole civil rights movement" who "have attained a reputation for promoting violence." The recent urban riots were uppermost in the minds of people across the nation. King was urged on camera to drop his plans for a Washington campaign; otherwise, "our nation may see a new high in violence resulting from a so-called peaceful demonstration."[24] The relationship between King and Carmichael on the issue of the PPC provoked much speculation in the press. A walkout by Stokely Carmichael and the Black United Front from the February 1968 SCLC board meeting captured headlines.[25] King remained on alert. He reportedly said Carmichael was as "sweet as pie" at a meeting in Pitts Motor Hotel in Washington, but suspected the black militant of a "power play" in trying to alter the focus of the PPC.[26] King was ultimately unmoved by advocates of Black Power; during the final months of his life he held fast to his dream of integration of the races, which included an opportunity for everyone to share in the wealth of the nation.

Opposition from a range of other quarters to plans for the Poor People's Campaign was immediate and persisted through May 1968, when the first demonstrators arrived to begin their occupation of the Mall in Washington. The NAACP leader Roy Wilkins was initially opposed to major disruption in D.C. for fear it would scupper the remaining support from the Johnson administration. A poll in December 1967 provided much less than a resounding endorsement for King. It seemed to suggest that most black people were not in favor of the campaign to "dislocate" Washington and could no longer be counted on to react nonviolently when harassed and intimidated. The poll also indicated that black people were worried President Johnson's reelection prospects in 1968 would be jeopardized. It further revealed that blacks were aware of increasing resistance by whites to civil rights demonstrations and thought King had run out of ideas; he should step aside and let someone else take over.[27]

More broadly, the critique that America should pay its debts to the poorest in society seemed to many among the political elites to be no less than an assault on capitalist values and a threat to social order. At the height of Cold War tensions and with a country divided over the war in Vietnam, King was usually careful to temper his language for fear of being the object of red-baiting. For a long period, he felt unable to speak out strongly on his socialist beliefs.[28] Some scholars have argued that during the decade after 1955, King downplayed his more controversial views regarding economic justice and that his Social Gospel perspective only came to the fore again after the award of the Nobel Prize in 1964.[29] That said, as early as 1957, King had made it clear he never intended to adjust himself to the "tragic inequalities of an economic system which takes necessities from the many to give luxuries to the few."[30] Tackling economic injustice would become the central plank of the Poor People's Campaign in 1968. King's increasingly radical rhetoric from 1966 brought yet more attention from the FBI.[31] Hoover shaped the response of the White House to the campaign.[32] The negative reaction to plans for the PPC reflected fear of a campaign that could be seen as an example of the kind of social movement that offers "an important alternative to the politics of the state."[33] Andrew Young noted that plans for the PPC led to the campaigners—not poverty—becoming the "enemy" from the perspective of Congress.[34] Similarly, Coretta Scott King observed that "we had become the enemy" by daring to unify protesters across a broad spectrum of ethnic and economic groups.[35]

An ever-worsening social and political climate in early 1968 brought additional urgency to King's plans for the Poor People's Campaign. Campaign planning took place amid a backlash against the so-called agitators and radicals. The backlash targets included "uppity blacks" perceived to be getting above their station, antiwar demonstrators, the New Left of radical politics, and those allegedly content to live off welfare and the sweat and taxes of others.[36] The State of the Union address delivered by President Lyndon Johnson in January 1968 was particularly disappointing for the SCLC leader in its vision and hopes for America. The president confirmed that the United States would persevere in Vietnam so that "aggression" would not prevail. Johnson refused to agree to an unconditional end to the bombing of North Vietnam.[37] Although the president promised more jobs, housing programs, and the regeneration of the cities, King heard nothing that dissuaded him from carrying on with his plans for the PPC.

The backlash against civil rights and poor people intensified. President Johnson remained concerned the PPC might further alienate white support for the Democrats in the swirling politics of 1968 and diminish his chances in the November presidential election. On February 2, 1968, he called on King to use more productive means of protest than those envisaged for the PPC.[38] Johnson eventually agreed, however, with the assessment of Attorney General Ramsey Clark that cooperation with the PPC was the best way to keep things under control and peaceful.[39] Clark took the view that it was unjust to hide poor people away and thought they deserved to be visible at least. The attorney general thought the president showed courage in allowing the campaign to go ahead, but he later revealed Johnson never really came to terms with the idea of an occupation of the city he loved. Clark claimed that "to see these pitiful poor people with their psychotics and their ugliness and misery sprawled on the monument grounds really hurt Johnson."[40] This was King's idea, of course: to make poverty visible, to open the wounds of social class in America, and to force the government to do something about the ugliness of poverty in the nation.

Just as King had predicted in his testimony before the Ribicoff Committee in December 1966 and in other forums, events in early 1968 saw America fall further into the mire. Only weeks after President Johnson claimed in his State of the Union address that the enemy had been defeated in "battle after battle," South Vietnam was invaded on several fronts in January–February 1968 during the Tet Offensive. Television coverage exposed America's flawed foreign policy in Vietnam. Johnson's legislative achievements seemed to count for little in the face of opposition even from within his own party. He rarely referred to his beloved Great Society in 1968. Engulfed by the counterculture, Johnson felt betrayed by those whom he had assisted: poor people, black people, and young people. Vietnam peace talks in Paris dragged on through the summer of 1968, and student demonstrations on the streets promised a further law-and-order backlash against the unrest.

Johnson's Democratic Party began to fragment. Senator Eugene McCarthy from Minnesota almost defeated the president in the party's New Hampshire primary in March 1968, and the closeness of the vote count showed that Johnson was vulnerable. First elected to the Senate in 1958 following ten years as a congressional representative, the former college professor McCarthy took up the invitation of antiwar Democrats in late 1967 to run for the presidency. King offered a few words of encouragement for McCarthy at the launch of the PPC in December 1967, recognizing him as a man of social conscience who understood that domestic problems were related to the "tragically unjust war in Vietnam." He later expressed support for Senator McCarthy and Senator Robert F. Kennedy on the grounds that both were preferable to President Johnson. McCarthy surprised everyone with his showing in New Hampshire. Some of his fellow senators regarded him as aloof and detached. Senator Edward Kennedy, for example, thought McCarthy had little interest in any of the great issues facing the United States other than the war in Vietnam.[41] However, McCarthy's stance for peace in the 1968 election made him a credible candidate and played well in particular with college students who were looking for a standard-bearer against the war.

Appalled by the moral bankruptcy of U.S. foreign policy in Vietnam and the shortfalls of the War on Poverty, Senator Robert Kennedy announced on March 16 that he was entering the race to challenge Lyndon Johnson for the Democratic Party nomination for president. His delayed entry after Eugene McCarthy's bold attempt to unseat Johnson in the New Hampshire primary proved controversial. The timing of Kennedy's decision to run provoked anger and derision from political opponents who had long regarded him as a ruthless opportunist. Some evidence suggests, however, that Kennedy had already decided to run even before the New Hampshire primary weakened Johnson's hold over the Democratic Party and the country.[42]

As the year unfolded, former vice president Richard Nixon emerged as the frontrunner for the Republican presidential nomination. He managed to block a challenge from Ronald Reagan for the nomination by building up his southern support with the help of segregationist senator Strom Thurmond. Nixon carefully crafted his campaign messages in favor of law and order while blaming the Democrats for the excesses of 1967–1968: university campus unrest, antiwar demonstrations, and urban riots. In March 1968, he condemned the newly released report of the Kerner Commission for blaming the urban riots on ev-

erybody except the perpetrators. In a nationwide radio broadcast, Nixon promised to "meet force with force" in the cities.[43] The student, peace, and civil rights
movements attracted adverse publicity, which promised danger for the Democrats at the polls in November 1968. Republicans promoted a vote for Nixon as a
vote for a return to normality and the traditional standards of hard work, respect
for the flag, no drugs, and family values. Rejecting much of what King stood for,
Nixon said that the role of poverty as a cause of crime had been "grossly exaggerated" by the Democrats. He also claimed that the 1968 economic crisis ruled
out allocating additional funds to fight poverty.[44] After King's assassination,
Nixon bolstered his conservative credentials later that summer by choosing
Maryland governor Spiro Agnew as his running mate for the election. Agnew's
lack of empathy with the poor and his scorn for the counterculture endeared
him to elements of the white backlash. Moderate Republicans were outraged
at the selection of a candidate who had ruthlessly crushed the Baltimore uprisings following King's assassination. James Reston argued that his choice of running mate demonstrated that Richard Nixon was going with the conservative
minority and defying the liberal majority, and in the process would help to re-
unite the Democrats and divide the Republicans.[45]

The visible and raucous presence of a third-party candidate, the populist
governor George Wallace, added to what became a bitter and highly polarized presidential election campaign in 1968. Wallace caused alarm in both the
Democratic and Republican camps. Riding high in the polls in 1968, his success threatened to undermine Nixon's southern strategy to capture voters in
the old Confederacy concerned about the changing nature of race relations, urban unrest, and the War on Poverty initiatives. His message, which scapegoated
hippies, radical left-wing agitators, antiwar demonstrators, and militant black
people, played well in conservative white communities where people believed
things had gone too far. Television amplified both the actions of "pampered"
college students occupying administration buildings and the "rioting and looting" by black Americans.[46] Wallace threatened to run over any demonstrator who lay down in front of his car when he was elected president. Blue-collar
white voters identified with his anger about the excesses of the 1960s, some
believing that black progress was achieved at their expense. The Wallace slogan "Send Them a Message" struck a chord with those fed up with both political parties. Wallace eventually won 13.5 percent of the popular vote in the 1968
presidential election.

In this challenging social and political environment, King was hard at work
planning his Poor People's Campaign. To rally his supporters, he organized a
special SCLC three-day retreat at Ebenezer Baptist Church in mid-January 1968.

Due to the "many unforeseen problems," including organizational challenges that were emerging, attendance was compulsory. Only "grave sickness" was an acceptable reason for not turning up. Staff members were instructed to bring their personal belongings and be prepared to leave Atlanta on January 16, 1968, to report to their designated project areas to begin work on the Poor People's Campaign. King reminded delegates that the forthcoming campaign was about the underclasses, the poorest in society, who continued to miss out on prosperity in America.

The SCLC produced an economic fact sheet with statistics showing the depth of poverty in the country. It provided a rationale for the campaign by pointing to the unequal distribution of power and resources. King urged delegates to give their all and to bring on board various groups in society, including the middle classes and ministers, who he felt were vital for the campaign's success. He sensed that better-off black people might think their own continued progress would be hindered should they advance the cause of the poor.[47] The broader political and public sentiment against his plans and the polarized state of the nation were on his mind also. King informed reporters on January 16 that he hoped America was not heading for fascism as a justification to move against the campaign.[48]

King visited Washington, D.C., in the first week of February 1968 on a public relations exercise to sell the idea of the PPC. He met with a whole range of potential campaign stakeholders, including the SCLC executive board, local civil rights leaders, and black ministers.[49] He also met with the press to update them on plans for the initiative. Aware of the need to avoid negative headlines concerning the potential for civil disobedience, he carefully focused on the campaign's goals and played down the issue of tactics.[50] King informed reporters that the overall PPC goal was a $30 billion government investment to eliminate poverty, and the minimum he would accept were measures to assure full employment, construction of low-cost housing, and an annual guaranteed income.[51]

Planning for the campaign thus began in earnest in January 1968 and lasted until May when Resurrection City, the camp in Washington built to house the poor, opened. The scale of the task facing King and the SCLC in organizing such an ambitious and bold national campaign in a relatively short few months was enormous. Logistical challenges were daunting. The PPC was put together long before personal computers, mobile phones, social media, and other forms of modern communication came into being. Bernard Lafayette, in his role as PPC national director, stressed the need to think through the detailed plans and campaign demands.[52] The mobilization of thousands of poor people necessitated hard work, including the support of other organizations at the grassroots. It is to the great credit of King, the SCLC, their partners, and the poorest people of all races from across America that thousands eventually traveled to Washington, where they built Resurrection City.

King's leadership was bound to be a crucial factor in how successful the campaign turned out to be. Only he had the reputation, standing, and arguably the vision regarding economic justice to pull off such an audacious effort. He could not do it on his own, however. The projected reach of the campaign demanded that the SCLC engage with organizations and individuals in every corner of the nation, including with leaders of other racial groups. A private document circulated in January 1968 for the consideration of SCLC staff members set out the proposed tone and approach of the campaign against poverty.[53] The content bore the stamp of King's thoughts as to the way forward and included, for example, his call for the reform of the capitalist system. Civil disobedience was justified on the basis that "all dissenters from Socrates to Gandhi felt the evil of injustice confronting them was greater than the potential evil of widespread lawlessness."[54] A "dislocation" of Washington was called for to counter the kind of "disruption" affecting poor people's lives every day. The SCLC asserted, "We want to put a stop to this poverty, racism and discrimination that causes families to be kept apart, men to become desperate, women to live in fear and children to starve."[55] Finally, an authentic campaign would be both for and by poor people. The SCLC declared, "This is the poor people's fight, they will use their right to lay their burdens at the door of the government and make government, and all the people, face the problems of poverty, racism, exploitation and the military machine."[56]

The Washington campaign strategy envisaged poor people of all races taking their demands to the government after Easter in April 1968 when Congress was in session, which would be followed by a camp-in and demonstrations in May in the nation's capital. Gandhi's policy of nonviolent action underpinned what became King's final mass movement campaign.[57] King observed that "the more nonviolent we are, the more we will arouse the conscience of the nation. Then the Federal Government will turn out to be the villain."[58] He regarded nonviolent resistance as the only morally and practically sound method open to oppressed people in their struggle for freedom.[59] To King and his SCLC colleagues, nonviolence was integrally related to their philosophy of life and was neither passivism nor cowardice.[60] The scope of the PPC presented King with his biggest challenge thus far for his methods.

The marches and demonstrations used successfully in the South were seemingly no longer enough on their own. King maintained that the different circumstances called for the lobbying of Congress and protests outside government buildings. He demanded "massive, energetic protest tactics."[61] The escalation to civil disobedience would depend on the response of the government to the campaign's demands. Possible tactics included a camp-in of thousands of unemployed youth, which was inspired by the example of the veterans Bonus Army of 1932.[62] Suggestions were made to occupy government buildings, hold factory sit-ins, jam the White House switchboard, and generally bring normal life in Washington, D.C., to a standstill. King argued that for nonviolence to be effective, it had to be disruptive.[63] He appreciated that nonviolence would face more severe tests in the Washington campaign than it had encountered in the past. The tactics needed to appeal to those who might otherwise be tempted to express their frustration in urban riots and to many others who no longer believed that things would ever change for the better.

Dr. King's commitment to civil disobedience and confrontation proved to be particularly controversial even within his own organization. Very few of the SCLC leaders relished the prospect of jail sentences for civil disobedience.[64] Both Bayard Rustin and Michael Harrington opposed its use. Rustin favored conciliation with President Johnson and feared that the political climate was not conducive to tactics of civil disobedience because it was already shaping up to be a polarized national election year.[65] Sensitive to a growing mood in America against the counterculture, Rustin wrote to Marian Logan, an SCLC board member, stating he doubted that disruptive actions would move the conscience of Congress. If anything, civil disobedience, he argued, would harden resolve against the demonstrators and lead to a victory of reactionary candidates in the 1968 elections.[66] Rustin believed that successive summers of unrest had made the country nervous, and hordes of poor people bringing Washington to a standstill would be counterproductive.[67] He also maintained there was the danger that civil disobedience would appeal to disruptive elements who would join the campaign effort and who could not be controlled.[68]

In place of dramatic protests, Rustin favored building coalitions of the willing, as expressed in the Freedom Budget of 1966. This would bring together labor unions, civil rights organizations, and sympathetic supporters to demand structural reforms and link "racial justice for African Americans and economic justice for all."[69] He was especially anxious to maintain the old alliances with the Democratic Party and viewed disruptive strategies on the streets as likely to alienate the Johnson administration and lead to further erosion of liberal support for movement goals. Stanley Levison dismissed Rustin's stand as his old rival "showing his true colors."[70] King appeared to take notice of some of the concerns; he advised staff to avoid frequent use of the phrase "civil disobedience."[71]

After King's assassination in Memphis, the SCLC leadership put aside the idea of "going for broke" by way of civil disobedience. The tactic of civil disobedience did come to characterize the campaign, however, during the last days of the PPC occupation of Washington as organizers looked to intensify pressure on Congress to make concessions.

In early 1968, with King at the helm, the SCLC provided local PPC organizers with a checklist of likely questions and recommended answers to justify civil disobedience and breaking the law.[72] The National Association of Social Workers, strong supporters of the PPC, devised a similar crib list of questions and recommended responses for staff members participating in the campaign.[73] The document made a robust defense of the right of poor people to demonstrate and camp in Washington and to engage in civil disobedience.[74] Some of the organizations and groups with which the SCLC hoped to cooperate in Washington during the campaign were not so convinced. For example, Mr. Bruce Beaudin of the Legal Aid Agency, a civic and educational organization, thought the strategy of civil disobedience "used" people.[75]

Many tasks lay ahead for the campaign organizers, including mobilizing the poor and nonpoor, raising funds for the campaign, and establishing effective organizational structures. The evidence suggests the SCLC was efficient and thorough in its approach to the various tasks as far as the resources and tools at its disposal allowed. There was a critical need to recruit staff in regions where there was little or no SCLC presence, to develop ways and means to enhance awareness of the campaign, and to assign responsibilities to different individuals to spread out the work burden. Finally, all stakeholder groups had to try to reach agreement on a set of demands to be presented in Washington, D.C.[76] From the outset, the PPC leaders were keen to counter the misinterpretation that they were looking for increased welfare handouts. Their goal was to make sure people could participate on an equal footing in the economy. They wanted a guarantee of effective access to jobs and training and to good health. All citizens were to have a guaranteed minimum annual income as a civil right. The importance of providing a safety net for the most vulnerable in society was also stressed; for example, people who could not work due to disability or other circumstance should be supported to "live" and thus must be entitled to a decent annual income.[77]

King planned to hold the president and Congress responsible for low minimum wages, a degrading and inadequate welfare system, subsidies for the rich, and unemployment and underemployment.[78] He aimed to make the poor visible to the nation at large and prove that nonviolence would work.[79] He declared, "We're going to let the whole world know how America is treating its citizens."[80] This treatment of the poor was highlighted in an SCLC document indicting America as a nation that denied many of its citizens basic human rights. The United States was graphically described as "the dazzling affluent society of two-car-fur-coat families, yet millions of Americans, blacks, whites, Mexicans, Puerto Ricans, Indians, retire each evening with pangs of hunger. They suffer from crowded and insanitary housing in Northern tenements, Southern shacks; they grow up with unattended diseases and abnormalities, they live a life of underdeveloped intellect due to the wasted years of a poor, negative education."[81]

The SCLC put essential building blocks in place from the outset. The Poor People's Action Committee first met in September 1967, three months before King officially launched the campaign. Ralph Abernathy chaired the group, whose members were all officers or staff members of the SCLC.[82] The exclusive composition of the committee left the SCLC open to criticism from other racial groups and organizations that joined the campaign effort. Apart from Dorothy Cotton (director, Citizenship Education Program), all of the members were male, black, and middle class. The committee included most of the leading lights in the SCLC: the Reverend Andrew Young (executive vice president), the Reverend Bernard Lafayette (national director of the PPC), Hosea L. Williams (PPC field director), and the Reverend Jesse Jackson (national director, Operation Breadbasket). As the campaign evolved and developed, the SCLC increasingly drew from a broader range of stakeholders beyond the SCLC inner circle. Representatives from different racial and ethnic groups joined the PPC national steering committee, for example, and were able to influence many of the major decisions, especially around the campaign demands.

The tentacles of the PPC reached into every region in the United States. Organizers mobilized in approximately a dozen big cities in the North and West and half a dozen southern states.[83] Major areas of activity included Illinois, Ohio, Michigan, Massachusetts, New York, New Jersey, Pennsylvania, Maryland, D.C., Virginia, North Carolina, South Carolina, Georgia, Alabama, Mississippi, California, and Tennessee. PPC national area offices were in different regions and included D.C., Mississippi, Alabama, Georgia, South Carolina, North Carolina, Virginia, Tennessee, Maryland, Pennsylvania, New Jersey, New York, Rhode Island, and Massachusetts.[84] By late March 1968, the target quota was being met to recruit two hundred volunteers in each city to go to Washington.[85]

The civil rights movement did not exist in a vacuum, and the wider social and political culture was influential in providing support. Previous civil rights campaigns, like the Montgomery Bus Boycott in 1955–1956, had benefited from the foundations laid by individual activists and the contributions of civic organizations, including women's groups, churches, and labor unions, all of which came together in a coalition against racism and discrimination.[86] In a similar vein, the SCLC gained support for the PPC from organizations concerned with poverty and civil rights across America.[87] Bernard Lafayette was a key figure in building the necessary progressive alliances. His background in the American Friends Service Committee, his contacts over at least ten years of movement activism, and his leadership experience in the mobilization against the Vietnam War in the spring of 1967 all made him a good fit to deliver King's vision for a multiracial campaign. Lafayette invited two white men—Coretta Scott King's ex-chauffeur and SCLC member Tom Houk and Ernie Austin of the Appalachian Volunteers—to join the effort.[88] Both had extensive contacts and assisted in compiling a list of interested individuals and organizations.[89]

Many challenges lay ahead, and even the prospect of involving poor whites was daunting. Lafayette had broached the subject of white participation in the early stages of planning. King had leaned back, smiled, and said, "They are poor, aren't they?"[90] In view of the racial crisis in the United States, including white concerns about the rise of black militancy, King wanted to engage with as many poor and middle-class whites as possible. This did not imply merely "detached" support for the campaign but "parallel participation."[91] Houk sent out a summary of the campaign to around four thousand nonblack groups and organizations striving for social justice and change.[92] Poor whites were successfully integrated into the campaign effort. The Highlander Folk School in Tennessee, for example, provided access to networks of whites in Kentucky and West Virginia.

Primary efforts for the PPC in each locality involved the mobilization of poor communities, churches, business and professional people, youth and young adults, militants, conservatives, and radicals. Scores of "sponsoring organizations" were recruited, and they helped with mobilization of the poor to go to Washington. These included groups as diverse as the Alliance for Black Unity, Berkeley, California; American People Together, Ithaca, New York; Black Congress, Los Angeles, California; Chicago Community Welfare, Chicago, Illinois; Committee for Poor People, Kentucky; Concerned Citizens for Migrants, Lansing, Michigan; Freedom and Peace Committee, Buffalo, New York; Highlander Research and Education Center, Knoxville, Tennessee; Mexican American Youth Organization, San Antonio, Texas; National Catholic Conference for Interracial Justice, New Orleans, Louisiana; Peace and Freedom Party, New York; Welfare Recipients in Action, New York; United Farm Workers, Dunkirk, New York; and the War Resisters League.[93]

The sponsoring organizations reflected the diversity and complexity of activism in every corner of the nation. All of those who signed up for the campaign shared the broad aim of tackling poverty. It would have been naïve, however, to assume that all the groups would find consensus on all the issues. For example, not all were in sympathy with the religious dimension of the SCLC nor with its proposed leadership role. While some groups and organizations across the nation gave enthusiastic support, others regarded the days of mass demonstrations as over and refused to cooperate. Thomas Payne of the Washington Metropolitan Citizens Advisory Council, for example, helped with the campaign when it eventually came to the nation's capital but thought "politicking" was preferable to an extended stay in D.C. with an emphasis on demonstrations.[94] Some groups preferred to be self-reliant, having lost faith in the promises made by whites and regarding the days of mass demonstrations as over. Black Muslims in Washington predictably refused to take any position on the PPC, stating they were against "begging and integration"; they would not ask for what was rightfully theirs already.[95] Mr. U. Robinson of the Phoenix Society in Washington, a nonprofit, nonpolitical organization working with young black people to change their outlooks and provide them with salable skills, thought the campaign would only lead to frustration. He argued that marching was the direct road to defeatism and would produce no positive results.[96]

Some scholars have suggested that black militants "nixed" the efforts to mobilize in parts of New York City, and generally the initial response in some districts there was poor. The National Committee of Black Churchmen appealed for unity to fight the "real exploiter" of poverty, arguing in Dr. King's terms that people needed "real power." The group called for the mobilization of poor people to "seek their right to live" by means of mass demonstrations.[97] In a challenging environment, the SCLC continued its efforts "to pull New York."[98] Various organizations were wary because it was felt the SCLC wanted to dominate and give direction to people. The New York City Coordinating Council for the PPC was established independently of the SCLC efforts. It included peace groups, antipoverty groups, unaffiliated poor people, and welfare mothers.[99]

Churches and their networks were particularly significant for the campaign. King relied on middle-class ministers to mobilize some of the poor people at the grassroots. He suspected that some ministers did not wish to get their hands dirty by engaging directly with the poorest in society, and he decided to speak to them at the SCLC conference in the Sheraton Four Ambassadors in Miami in mid-February. The delegates included 150 ministers from cities with the largest black populations, including Detroit, Chicago, and New York. King asked them to demonstrate "political" commitment and not merely preach to the less fortunate. He urged them to minister to the social and economic needs of congregations in some of the poorest communities. The SCLC leader invoked the Social Gospel mission by citing the example of Jesus, "a far more potent leader than

Karl Marx," to inspire them to force America to pay its "promissory note" of economic justice.[100] Churches became key partners for the PPC during the planning period and in Washington, D.C., itself when thousands of poor converged on the nation's capital to begin their protests.

King stressed the need to win the hearts and minds of the public, including the middle classes, which might be reluctant to support massive government spending against poverty. The Educational Task Force (ETF) was an integral part of that charm offensive. One hundred and fifty volunteers who constituted the Speakers Bureau (the ETF) worked to educate and involve the nonpoor on the issue of poverty.[101] Their focus was on "changing attitudes in that area of society which has the greatest potential for effective response."[102] The ETF goals included some of the long-range measures suggested by the Kerner Commission report in March 1968. The Speakers Bureau took steps to increase communication across racial lines, sought to destroy stereotypes of the poor, and tried to create common ground for efforts toward public order and social justice.[103] Stretched and understaffed due to the unprecedented pressures of the PPC, the SCLC asked the Peace Corps Speakers Bureau to take over the ETF in April 1968.[104] Around five thousand people were contacted in one weekend in Washington just days before the poor were due to arrive in town. A snapshot of activity on April 30 included ETF presentations to the South East Young Democrats, the Cub Scouts at Fairlington Methodist Church, and a neighborhood group in Lee, Virginia.[105]

Impressive work was undertaken behind the scenes to organize people in diverse communities all over the United States. Local PPC field reports from the time give the flavor of what was going on. In North Carolina, four full-time paid organizers worked with local groups, distributed posters and copies of the SCLC publication *Soul Force*, and organized a workshop on nonviolence.[106] Similarly, in Georgia in February and March, the Savannah–Chatham County Crusade for Voters distributed ten thousand posters, leaflets, and copies of *Soul Force*. It also held a workshop on nonviolence.[107] Cook County in Illinois successfully recruited twenty-two office workers to assist in the campaign; eighteen of them came from a meeting with the Independent League of Catholic Aid Employees. The Cook County organizers also were hoping to recruit participants through grassroots organizing and workshops on nonviolence.[108]

PPC-related events often brought additional benefits to communities beyond the goals set out for the campaign. In Alabama, for example, local organizing resulted in the formation of a state-wide group, the Alabama Poor People's Crusade, which linked activists across the state to foster local activity during and after the PPC.[109] An upbeat Albert Turner in Alabama reported on the success of his PPC recruitment attempts. Twenty-five people were signed up on the streets of Selma. Turner wrote of the positive reception he received from fifty white students at Auburn University who expressed interest in the Washington campaign and requested Dr. King come to speak to them. On February 18, a "great" meeting was held in Marion, Alabama: up to a thousand were present, support for the PPC was reported to be strong, and more than $1,000 was collected for a headstone for a victim of racism, Jimmie Lee Jackson, who had been murdered.[110] On April 3, Albert Turner reported he had recruited 233 volunteers from Selma, Birmingham, and Greensboro.[111]

The SCLC Department of Voter Registration and Political Education had responsibility for the mobilization of PPC participants in Kentucky, Tennessee, Mississippi, Alabama, Georgia, the Carolinas, and Virginia. Key campaign leaders in this vast region included the PPC national field director, Hosea Williams; the assistant director, Tina Lewis; and Laura Hammonds and Terrie Randolph.[112] Fulfilling King's wish, Williams and his colleagues trained poor people in nonviolence to prepare them for the demonstrations and protests in Washington. They recruited fifty marshals per state, all of whom attended workshops on nonviolence. Marshals then returned to their areas to sign up and train at least ten people each to go to Washington. It was emphasized that those brought on board by the marshals needed to be really "hard-core poor people" able to articulate the campaign's demands in Washington.[113] All participants intending to go to D.C. needed to be "on message"; any violence or ill-disciplined behavior would play into the hands of campaign opponents.[114]

Cleveland, Ohio, provides a window into the typical kinds of activities that took place in every corner of America as preparations continued. Strenuous efforts were undertaken to raise funds for a person to work full time on the campaign. Having exhausted all options for support in black communities, local whites were approached. The Council of Churches agreed to fund half the salary of Hilbert Perry, and the SCLC provided some financial support. The Reverend Robert Gillespie of the Garden Valley Neighborhood House provided meeting rooms for the PPC, office stationery, the use of minibuses, and some babysitting services for meetings. Meetings took place throughout February 1968 with various organizations, including Americans for Democratic Action, American Friends Service Committee, Western Reserve Faculty, the Domestic Workers of America, the Welfare Rights Movement, the Council of Churches, and Hough Community Council Unitarian Society. At a press conference on February 23, 1968, representatives of the Bruce Klunder Freedom House, the Domestic Workers of America, and the Cleveland Welfare Rights Movement all endorsed the PPC. A mass rally planned for the end of March hoped to raise money and to recruit for the campaign. Dick Gregory, James Bevel, Stokely Carmichael, Eartha Kitt, and other well-known individuals were among those expected to appear.[115] The rally involved much time and effort, and many were motivated to get involved because of what they learned during the session about unfair welfare laws. After the meeting, fifteen attendees joined the Welfare Rights Movement, and twenty joined the PPC. The Reverend Al Sampson was praised for the "magnificent job" he did on the panel.[116]

The SCLC explored every avenue to raise funds for the most ambitious campaign in its history. Strict instructions on handling funds were provided for all project leaders and field staff involved in the mobilization of "field troops."[117] Hosea Williams observed that some local leaders did a fine job in raising funds; others did not do so well. The finances of the Southern Christian Leadership Conference almost buckled under the strain as the campaign progressed. Transportation was one of the most expensive items. The cost to the SCLC of $11,000 for the bus journey from Marks, Mississippi, to Washington was only one of countless examples of how coffers were emptied by the campaign. The group from Marks traveled a thousand miles by bus with stops in Memphis, Nashville, Knoxville, and Danville. Churches often took the lead in fundraising, but not exclusively. Many regional and local groups struggled to raise the necessary funds to mobilize support for the program. Billy Hollins wrote to Hosea Williams stating that he had gone to Chicago with "only a letterhead and an idea, [and] the people wanted more."[118] Herbert V. Coulton of the Virginia unit communicated his concerns to Hosea Williams on March 20, 1968. He informed Williams he was unable to pay for "basic needs," including office rental, lighting, telephone, and postage. Coulton cited the case of an unemployed father of three children, Nathaniel Hawthorne, whose only source of income was a meager disability check yet who spent his own money driving around Virginia mobilizing others to go to Washington. Coulton felt he had no option but to reimburse Hawthorne for his expenses out of his own pocket unless Williams could send money to support the campaign.[119] Ironically, King's assassination on April 4 and the sympathy it engendered led to an upsurge in campaign donations.

The SCLC left few stones unturned in mobilizing the poor to go to Washington. A personal visit from King was highly prized. But because of the geographical reach of the Poor People's Campaign, he could not be everywhere. Volunteers in New Jersey and elsewhere received the next best thing to a visit, a personal message from King for distribution in the community. It said, "We have opened up an office in your community to recruit poor people for the Washington campaign this spring. We need your help in a time of grave national crisis, please contribute in whatever way you can to this effort."[120] Radio stations carried campaign messages across the country. SCLC staffer William Ruther-ford argued that radio could reach ghetto communities and sought advice on its potential from Milton Moskowitz, a journalist and broadcaster.[121] KNOK in Fort Worth, KATZ in St. Louis, WYLD in New Orleans, and other broadcasters carried regular campaign bulletins from King entitled *MLK Speaks*.[122]

Given the scope of the PPC, it is not surprising that things did not always go according to plan. Local squabbles sometimes broke out as disparate groups and individuals came together, often for the first time. In Trenton, New Jersey, Edith Savage selected chairs to undertake preliminary preparations for the northeastern leg of the journey to Washington. "Power plays" and other forms of dissension, including between young people and older participants, threatened the campaign there. A visit by an SCLC central office staff member, the Reverend Charles Kenzie Steele, on April 25 failed to quell the unrest. Local interest and sentiment in favor of the campaign decreased. Press relations worsened, and key rallies and meetings in Trenton were canceled. On June 21, local organizers requested that the SCLC National Office investigate and bring an end to the alleged misconduct, misuse of funds, and abuse of public trust.[123]

The sheer reach of the campaign was impressive; it extended into every region and into countless communities in America. The SCLC relied on a small group of key national partners to assist with mobilization efforts. They included the American Friends Service Committee (AFSC) the National Welfare Rights Organization (NWRO), labor unions, religious organizations including the United Church of Christ, and the anti–Vietnam War National Mobilization Committee. The AFSC was a natural ally and shared many of the SCLC values, including a commitment to nonviolence. As previously mentioned, the SCLC Chicago campaign in 1966 had drawn from the experience and community roots of long-standing AFSC activism in the slums. Two AFSC staffers from Chicago, Anthony Henry and William Moyer, headed the PPC office in Washington.[124] The AFSC was a main player in the campaign at every level from PPC committees to grassroots recruiting.[125] Among numerous other examples, Bernard Lafayette reported that a professor at American University in Washington was active with the Quakers and established a support committee in D.C.[126] The AFSC had long supported civil rights and human rights issues, including projects to promote school integration in the South.[127] It already enjoyed a close association with Dr. King, having arranged publication of his "Letter from a Birmingham Jail" in 1963 and nominating him for the Nobel Peace Prize one year later.[128] In common with countless other civil rights activists, AFSC staff and volunteers were willing to put themselves in harm's way to forward the cause of justice. For example, Unitarian Universalist pastor James Reeb had paid the highest price for his social activism: he was brutally murdered during the Selma campaign in 1965.

The AFSC commitment to ending the war in Vietnam was particularly appealing to King. The Quakers' organized opposition predated his own public position on the conflict and included domestic activities and involvement in Vietnam itself.[129] The AFSC staff shared an increasing concern with King about the steady escalation of the war and its impact on the civilian population in Vietnam. They helped the SCLC stay the course on Vietnam so that opposition to the war became part of the DNA of the Washington campaign against poverty. The AFSC also fought to ensure that nonblacks were included in PPC decision-making, and it was crucial in connecting the campaign at the grassroots with Native Americans and Mexican Americans.[130] In December 1967, King had asked Colin Bell if the AFSC would become the organization partner for the SCLC in the upcoming Washington campaign against poverty. King wrote of his deep gratitude for "the devotion, cooperation and help accorded to us in the past by [the AFSC] in many of the areas we have worked. Specifically, I would like to ask if you could assign some of your highly qualified, skilled staff to work with us on this project for a period of perhaps six months."[131] AFSC regional offices helped to organize poor people to travel to Washington thanks to the work of staff members Barbara Moffett, Pam Coe, and Eleanor Eaton and the efforts of Warren Witte in Colorado, who recruited Hispanics and Native Americans.[132]

The National Welfare Rights Organization was another potential prize catch. The NWRO advocated for improvements in the lives of welfare recipients. It supported larger welfare budgets and the dignified treatment of those in need. It challenged, for example, the increasing scrutiny and surveillance of those claiming what were often very modest welfare payments. Its predecessor, the Poverty Rights Action Center, had sponsored a one-day poor people's campaign in Washington, D.C., in 1966. The organization typified the challenges King faced in trying to build a coalition of disparate groups with their own proud history of activism and their own agendas. NWRO founder George Wiley, chair Johnnie Tillmon, and others, such as Beulah Sanders, already worked with thousands of volunteers across the nation and reached into communities where the SCLC had no real local influence. The NWRO also provided another crucial building block in King's coalition in that it addressed the issue of gender discrimination in the American capitalist society. Alongside other partners in the welfare rights movement more generally, it stressed the empowerment of women with an emphasis on maintaining their dignity and ensuring adequate state assistance and support for their children.[133] King hoped to get the ten thousand "welfare mothers"—the members of the NWRO—on board and to maximize their potential to organize at the local level. However, as head of a patriarchal organization where men made almost all the decisions, he had much to learn from women's activism.

King met with Tillmon, Wiley, and other leaders of the organization on February 3, 1968.[134] Tillmon was a vastly experienced community and labor organizer. She was not intimidated in King's presence, and the meeting turned out to be one of the most bruising of his career. King seemed hopelessly ill informed on the most pressing welfare issues, including NWRO attempts to fight legislation forcing people to work for less than the minimum wage. Welfare programs were under attack in Congress in part because of whites' sentiment that welfare rewarded idle black people. Attacks on welfare represented only part of the toxic opposition to antipoverty programs during the period. Congress was considering legislation to cut welfare for mothers whose children were born outside of marriage or children whose fathers had left home. Just as he had done in Chicago when meeting young people angry at their lack of opportunities for employment and education, King listened and learned. The meeting was effectively a seminar with the SCLC leader playing the role of student. The SCLC and the NWRO then agreed to collaborate on the PPC.

The collaboration was conditional on the NWRO preserving its grassroots identity during the campaign. The NWRO also wanted to lead on setting the campaign's goals in relation to welfare. It wanted the prime responsibility for policy, negotiations with government agencies, and public statements on welfare issues, including Public Law 90-248 (an anti-welfare law).[135] Finally, NWRO leaders were opposed to their members taking part in civil disobedience because they had children to care for and could not risk imprisonment. King included all he had learned from the NWRO about welfare in the list of campaign demands.[136] He now better understood the complexities of the welfare system and how it discriminated against some of the most vulnerable people in society. The opportunities for King to meet people operating at the grassroots during the planning period for the PPC helped him to grow as an individual. The NWRO partnership also significantly assisted with campaign recruitment. Geraldine Smith of the NWRO organized King's speeches in Mississippi as he traveled around to boost the campaign. The PPC eventually kicked off in Washington with an NWRO-sponsored march of welfare mothers led by Coretta Scott King on May 12, one day before the official opening of Resurrection City.

Black people were likely to be in the majority of those traveling to D.C. On February 15, 1968, King delivered a rousing address to the Alabama Christian Movement for Human Rights at St. Thomas AME Church in Birmingham. He aimed his fire directly at the black middle classes that had "made it" in America; some middle-class black people were not inclined to support the PPC for fear of damaging their own prospects for the future. King also reached out during the campaign to northern "angry black youths" in a bid to steer them away from the lure of Black Power. Without such "gutsy, sweaty organizers," some argued, the campaign would "run in tandem with ghetto uprisings" but "would not re-place them."[137] Some Black Panthers supported the campaign, contributing to the portrayal of King by campaign opponents as someone who was in league with the most militant elements in the country.

Significantly, the SCLC leader called for blacks and whites to work together to tackle poverty, and in a swipe at both the advocates and detractors of Black Power reminded America that the PPC was about the poor of all races and that everyone had a legitimate place in the movement. King's next task was to build a genuine multiracial coalition to go to Washington. Events, however, were about to take a sinister turn.

CHAPTER 5
THE MEMPHIS CAMPAIGN

The early months of 1968 brought no letup as Dr. Martin Luther King Jr. moved forward the idea to build a multiracial coalition of the poor to end poverty in America. Based on his experiences in Chicago and after, he planned to develop a new form of social protest and to use the Poor People's Campaign as an instrument for the participants to expand their social knowledge and understanding of their situation as poor people.

In his book *Where Do We Go from Here?* King had observed that no group could go it alone in a multiracial society that was racist and discriminatory. Unity among the different racial groups therefore was the key to progress for those shut out of society. Just as he hoped, the PPC would become a broad coalition of the poor and not exclusively a protest movement of African Americans.[1] The plans and organizing efforts in early 1968 were directed toward creating a populist wave of poor people of all races and backgrounds coming together to press their demands.[2] The overall objective was to recruit thousands of the "powerless poor" of all races to go to Washington, D.C.[3] A coalition of the poor of many races also challenged a dominant narrative about black pathology, that is, the stereotype of lazy and inadequate black people who are incapable of taking advantage of the opportunities available to them. The campaign would show instead that poor people of all backgrounds are victims of structural inequalities. A government report in 1965 by Daniel Patrick Moynihan, an assistant secretary of labor under Lyndon Johnson, *The Negro Family: The Case for National Action*, had suggested that cultural deficits are responsible for poverty and black family breakups. Ironically, Moynihan was a supporter of King's idea of a guaranteed annual income. However, *The Negro Family* helped to lead to the Law Enforcement Assistance Act of 1965, which cracked down on crime in poor communities.

The PPC set out to challenge the blame-the-victim narrative. King hoped to establish alliances with organized groups of Mexican Americans, Appalachian whites, Native Americans, Puerto Ricans, and others, in addition to black people, in order to dramatize the many faces of poverty. In devising this strategy, King drew on the 1930s examples of the Southern Tenant Farmers Union, a group of cotton pickers who united across race lines, and the black and white veterans of the Bonus Army march in Washington.[4] However, he aspired to a much grander scale than anything seen before.

The press announcement launching the Washington campaign in December 1967 gave King his first real opportunity to reach out to request the participation of the poor of all races. All Americans of "goodwill" who favored moving the government to a new path of social, economic, and political reform were also welcomed. The Southern Christian Leadership Conference faced significant ideological and logistical challenges in building a broad multiracial coalition in such a short period of time.[5] Each potential racial partner had its own identities, needs, world views, aspirations, and ideas on how to achieve its goals. Different racial groups historically often looked on each other with suspicion. There was also bound to be inevitable tension between the leader-centered approach favored by the SCLC and the group-centered approaches adopted by many grassroots organizations. In addition, although the SCLC was a leading light in civil rights activism, it lacked solid links at the grassroots with other racial and ethnic groups. The reality for King was that he had limited influence among the other racial groups he aspired to attract to the campaign.

The major factor in building a successful multiracial coalition, however, turned out to be King himself. He remained a giant figure in social justice circles and as a Nobel Prize winner was widely respected. His charisma, standing, sincerity, and personality played a crucial role in bringing influential leaders of other racial groups together. King convened an unprecedented multiracial gathering to discuss participation in the PPC, the Minority Group Conference, at the historic Paschal's Motor Hotel in Atlanta on March 14, 1968. The meeting was a turning point for the campaign. Until then he had struggled to recruit enough numbers of "hard-core" poor people from different racial and ethnic groups. The way to reach them was through their leaders. The diversity of those in attendance at Paschal's was remarkable and represented the kind of class and racial solidarity the SCLC leader was seeking to build. Representatives of every kind of social movement attended. Coretta Scott King recalled the presence of seventy nonblack individuals, including Puerto Ricans, Mexican Americans, Native Americans, and poor Appalachian whites, thereby "countering the criticism we were planning an all-black crusade against the economic power structures of America."[6]

The eclectic mix of attendees included Richard Boone of the interracial Citizens Crusade against Poverty; Eddie Bariego (Colorado) of the Crusade for Justice; George Bross (California) of Vocations for Social Change; and Cecil Corbett (Arizona) of the United Presbyterian American Indian Ministries.[7] Peggy Terry, reportedly raised by a KKK family in Kentucky, attended in her capacity as a member of the Congress of Racial Equality (CORE) and the SCLC.[8] Several prominent Indigenous people also turned up.[9] Mad Bear Anderson (Tuscarora) represented the poor Iroquois Confederacy from upstate New York; John Belindo (Kiowa/Navajo) attended on behalf of the National Congress of American Indians; Hank Adams and Mel Thom represented the National Indian Youth Council; and Alfred J. Elgin Jr. came on behalf of the Intertribal Friendship House in California. Finally, Tillie Walker represented the interests of the United Scholarship Service in Denver.[10] Tom Houk had recruited her.[11]

Tillie Walker proved to be an invaluable asset for the PPC. She drew on her extensive networks of contacts to boost the campaign's reach. She believed passionately that the poor of every race were fighting the same battle.[12] The visible presence of so many Native Americans was indicative of the vibrant nature of activism in their communities by 1968 and the rise of identity politics more generally in the 1960s. The PPC provided burgeoning movements, including those of Native Americans and Chicanos, "an opportunity to coordinate their many local, grassroots campaigns into national cohesive movements."[13] The historic American Indian Chicago Conference in 1961 promoted the idea of community action and concluded with the "Declaration of Purpose," which demanded self-determination for Indigenous people.[14] Hundreds of Native Americans of all ages and backgrounds eventually participated in the PPC, and many went to Resurrection City. They included Mandans and Hidatsas from Fort Berthold, North Dakota; Cherokees and Poncas from Oklahoma; Puyallups and Nisquallys from Washington state; Pomos from Oakland, California; Pimas from Tucson, Arizona; and Senecas and Tuscaroras from the Haudenosaunee.[15]

Native Americans who expressed support at the Minority Group Conference included Rose Crow Flies High (Hidatsa), Myra Snow (Hidatsa), Louella Young Bear (Mandan), Naomi Foolish Bear (Hidatsa), Agnes Yellow Wolf (Hidatsa), and Mattie Grinnell, a 101-year-old Mandan woman who later traveled to Washington, D.C., for the campaign.[16] Clyde Warrior of the National Indian Youth Council shared King's perspective on the need for power to be located in the hands of communities. He perhaps went even further than King in demanding that the campaign seek to destroy the social, economic, and political structures of the United States in order to start again to build a new nation. Warrior contended that "blacks, Mexican Americans, and Puerto Ricans can only take colonialism, exploitation, and abuse for so long; then they [do] something about it."[17] That "something" was the Poor People's Campaign. Warrior tragically died in July 1968 just weeks after Resurrection City closed. His stance in favor of the PPC had typified the consensus arrived at by most Native American delegates attending the Paschal's event. Indigenous people enthusiastically mobilized in different regions for the Washington campaign, for example, Andrew Dreadfulwater and George Groundhog in Oklahoma, Hank Adams and Charles McEvers in the Pacific Northwest, and Alfred Elgin Jr. and Mel Thom in urban areas and the far West. Robert Dumont (Assiniboine) from Montana traveled all over the country to muster support.[18]

Not everyone was persuaded. Some Native Americans were opposed to the PPC. The National Congress of American Indians announced on March 31 that it would not endorse the campaign.[19] One factor in that group's thinking was a desire to maintain the broad political support already coming its way from the highest levels in the nation. President Lyndon Johnson and Senator Robert F. Kennedy were both strong advocates of Native American social and educational programs. The relationship between King and Johnson was already broken in March 1968, and for some Native Americans it was a matter of going wherever power could be found. Perhaps to take the wind out of King's sails, Johnson reached out to Indigenous people, referring to them as the "Forgotten Americans" just one week before the Paschal's meeting. The National Congress of American Indians was keen not to be dragged down as the tide of public and political opinion turned against civil rights campaigns.

Chicano representatives at Paschal's included Jose Angel Gutiérrez of the Mexican American Youth Organization; Bert Corona of the Mexican American Political Association; Baldemar Velásquez, founder of the Ohio-based Farm Labor Organizing Committee; and Corky Gonzales of the Denver-based civil rights group Crusade for Justice.[20] Gonzales was a significant figure in the growing Chicano movement in 1968. A strong advocate of land rights, he referred to the Southwest as "Aztlan," the ancestral home for Mexicans.[21] He would play a pivotal role in the PPC occupation of Washington in May–June 1968.

Reies Lopez Tijerina, a New Mexico–based Pentecostal preacher and Mexican American leader, also accepted King's invitation to participate in the Paschal's event. A remarkable figure, Tijerina organized Spanish-speaking families across the southwestern United States to seek the repatriation of lands obtained by North American Anglos in violation of the 1848 Treaty of Guadalupe Hidalgo, which ended the U.S.–Mexican War. In 1967, members of Tijerina's Alianza Federal de Mercedes (Federal Alliance of Land Grants) had forcibly taken over a courthouse in New Mexico to highlight the issue of land rights. The armed take-over captured headlines and focused national attention on Tijerina's group. Like King, he viewed the plight of oppressed peoples in the United States in a global context. Tijerina connected the experiences of Mexican Americans to poor people in Africa, Asia, and Latin America, all of whom had been exploited by "Anglo-Saxons."[22]

In recognition of their shared history of exploitation, Tijerina built alliances from the early 1960s with Native Americans across the United States. He publicly denounced America for its theft and colonization of land in the Southwest, which belonged to both Native Americans and Mexican Americans. His efforts helped to forge a "politicized Indo-Hispano identity" in the 1960s.[23] Bringing together groups that had previously been divided seemed to mirror King's own hopes for the PPC. By contrast with some other Mexican American leaders, Tijerina also sought to reach out to black people because they were also oppressed by whites. The annual convention in October 1967 of the Alianza Federal de Pueblos Libres (formerly the Alianza Federal de Mercedes) even had attracted advocates of Black Power. The SCLC was aware that Tijerina was involved in "guerrilla warfare" with the police and federal agents.[24] This checkered history did not deter King. The SCLC leader had met with Tijerina in September 1967 in Chicago, where they discussed a possible alliance between the SCLC and Chicanos to obtain justice for both of their peoples.[25] Tijerina reportedly was thrilled to meet him.[26] The Chicano leader was honored with a seat at King's right-hand side during the meal at Paschal's, and he was unanimously elected by the Chicanos in attendance as their PPC representative.[27] King chose Tijerina as the leader of the PPC Southwest contingent.

Some scholars have argued that the charismatic paternalism of the SCLC leadership saw nonblack leaders relegated to the status of junior partners in the PPC.[28] However, King was sincere in his intent to bring everyone into the fold as equal partners. Reies Tijerina was not an individual who could be pushed around in any case. He stood his ground and set his own terms as the price for his participation and cooperation. King needed Tijerina more than the Chicano leader needed him. The SCLC leader's reputation carried little weight in grassroots Chicano communities. When King first approached him, Tijerina declared that he wanted "neither scraps nor charity, only justice."[29] Tijerina's main demand on behalf of the Indo-Hispanos, which was written into the list of PPC demands and approved by King, was for the U.S. government to abide by the Treaty of Guadalupe Hidalgo and return the stolen land. King also agreed to support a demand for Indo-Hispano children to be educated in the Spanish language. SCLC staffer Tom Houk described Tijerina's contribution as "elegant and dynamic"; Tijerina was very much in favor of the entire coalition campaign.[30]

Tijerina faced criminal charges in 1968 because of the previous year's court-house raid. He claimed that the charges were trumped up to prevent a Mexican American from sitting beside the nonviolent King. Ralph Abernathy offered his support by suggesting that the arrest was part of a conspiracy against the poor.[31] He invited Tijerina to join him in Memphis after King's death. With Tijerina's support, many hundreds of Chicanos would later make the trip to Washington for the PPC. During the occupation, Tijerina complained that some in the SCLC had conspired to exclude the Chicano political and cultural demands from the list presented to Congress. However, both the Treaty of Guadalupe Hidalgo and the demand for Spanish-language instruction were included in presentations to Congress at different stages during the PPC occupation of Washington. Tijerina exempted Abernathy and Andrew Young from his criticism of the SCLC and placed the blame on other SCLC leaders. Tijerina used his raised profile, made possible by the PPC, to run for the governorship of New Mexico in late 1968. Although unsuccessful in his election bid, he used the opportunity to highlight some PPC demands, including a call for the curriculum in schools to cover more Mexican history.[32]

King had hoped to attract Cesar Chavez, leader of the migrant farm workers in California, to the Paschal's event. While concerned about the close links Chavez enjoyed with the AFL-CIO labor union, which unequivocally supported the Vietnam War, King reached out to him before the Minority Group Conference. It was imperative for the SCLC leader to achieve black-brown cooperation against economic injustice wherever it was possible to do so. For his part, Chavez was inspired by the successes of the black struggle in the South and described his own movement as "having the spirit of Zapata and the tactics of Martin Luther King."[33] Just like King, he had adopted Gandhi as his role model.[34] King had written to him before the Paschal's event, stressing solidarity and stating that they were engaged in a common struggle. But Chavez was on a hunger strike to draw attention to his cause of better working conditions for migrant farm workers. He sent a telephone message of support and a representative to King's conference at Paschal's.[35] An associate of Chavez later commented that the farm workers' leader was reluctant for King to come to his side during the fast because the SCLC president was "someone on the way down trying to attach himself to someone on the way up."[36] Regardless of the truth of this alleged statement, Chavez admired King. He kept photographs of Gandhi and King in his office, and in 1977 he would confide to a group of students that like Dr. Martin Luther King Jr., he had a dream: to build a Poor People's Union, a union of the unemployed in cities.[37]

At different points during the PPC, concerns were expressed about the insen-

sitive attitudes of black leaders toward other racial groups involved in the great
effort to defeat poverty. Even King himself sometimes ignored the other groups'
needs and demands in his speeches and writings.[38] In fairness, the SCLC leaders were entering new territory for them in trying to build a multiracial coalition, which brought new agendas, new leadership, and new grassroots activists.
King understood that the Minority Group Conference represented his best opportunity to convince other racial and ethnic groups they could play a meaningful role as partners in the PPC. He sensed the historic nature of the Paschal's
event and ensured that all representatives enjoyed equal status at the meeting.
Everyone was encouraged to speak freely. The participants at one point broke
into workshops described as the Spanish American Caucus, the Poor White
Caucus, and the Black Caucus although anyone could join any of them.

The Paschal's event was supposed to finish at 5 p.m., but the majority stayed
for dinner and beyond. Father Miguel Barragan sang some Spanish folk songs,
"hillbilly" songs roused the audience, and some Native Americans delivered
what they called a "tongue talk."[39] Dr. King described the event to participants
as the "beginning of a new cooperation, understanding, and a determination by
poor people of all colors and backgrounds to assert and win their right to a decent life and respect for their culture and dignity."[40] The SCLC leader used the
forum to reiterate his commitment to the radical redistribution of political and
economic power; this idea had been shaped in the black slums of Chicago. He
advised the delegates that they had it in their hands to set the United States on
the right path again.

The SCLC justifiably hailed the meeting at Paschal's as "historic." The organization announced that representatives of Native Americans, poor whites, and
Mexican Americans had given their support to the campaign. Tom Hayden of
Students for a Democratic Society (SDS), although previously skeptical about
the merits of the PPC, signed up for the campaign.[41] Hayden was a long-time
supporter of increased public spending, and he demanded an immediate end
to the war in Vietnam. Before King arrived in Chicago to join the 1966 Chicago
Freedom Movement, SDS was already there working alongside SNCC to improve jobs and income for local people.[42] Students for a Democratic Society had
moved into the slum areas of Chicago in 1964 to try to build an interracial movement known as the Economic Research and Action Project.[43] Hayden's participation in the PPC provided a way for the SCLC to involve students, young people from the radical Left, and others unhappy with the plight of the poor in a
land of plenty.

The Minority Group Conference helped to shape the demands presented to
Congress in Washington, D.C. The Paschal's event also saw poor people elected

to join the other leaders on the national PPC steering committee. They included Reies Tijerina; Hank Adams from the Indian Committee for Fishing Rights; Rodolfo "Corky" Gonzales of the Crusade for Justice; and Tillie Walker representing the United Scholarship Service. The Puerto Ricans elected Grace Moore Newman and Haleong Valentine; the whites elected Peggy Terry and Bob Fulcher.[44] Cornelius Givens was chosen to represent the interests of black people. Other representatives during the campaign included Dionicie Paden for Puerto Ricans and Ted Wulpert for whites. Hulbert James of the National Welfare Rights Organization was one of the key drivers in the decision to establish a national steering committee.[45] In agreeing to work together, the delegates committed themselves to organizing a powerful, militant coalition for social, political, and economic reform. They issued a statement of intent alleging that the "established powers" of rich America had exploited poor people by isolating them in ethnic, nationality, religious, and racial groups. These divide-and-rule policies had kept poor people down, but "we will no longer permit them to divide us."[46]

The great majority of those attending the Minority Group Conference regarded the event as a success. Ernest Austin of the Appalachian group representing poor whites acknowledged that he now recognized through his interaction with others that poverty was color-blind; it could be found everywhere.[47] Historian Daniel Cobb has argued that the PPC from the perspective of many of the groups there represented "a reckoning with colonialism."[48] Myles Horton of the Highlander Folk School perhaps best summed up the event. Horton wrote to Andrew Young:

> I believe we caught a glimpse of the future at the March 14, 1968, meeting called by the SCLC. We had there in Atlanta, authentic spokespersons for poor Mexican Americans, American Indians, blacks, and whites, the making of a bottom-up coalition. Martin, and those of you close to him, will have to spearhead the putting together of grassroots coalitions for the Washington demonstrations. This could lay the groundwork for something tremendously exciting and significant. Just as it is fitting for the SCLC to make ending the war in Vietnam a basic part of the program, it would be fitting now, it seems to me, for SCLC to provide leadership for a bona fide coalition. No other organization has this opportunity and therefore, this responsibility.[49]

As the May deadline came ever nearer to take the campaign to Washington, an exhausted and stressed King became increasingly concerned that the PPC was failing to recruit enough authentic poor people. This added to a sense of melancholy he found difficult to shake off. Despite his best efforts in working with key partner organizations and other groups in every region in the United States, he despaired the campaign was not reaching those he referred to as the "hard-core poor people." The successful Minority Group Conference had helped to turn things around, but additional efforts were required. Events across the nation made it even more imperative that the campaign reach out to the poorest in the nation. In March 1968, the National Advisory Commission on Civil Disorders, set up by President Johnson to investigate the causes of urban riots, issued its report. King had contributed to the commission hearings and had seized the opportunity to put forward his analysis that the problems in the slums could be explained by economic factors. Known as the Kerner Commission after its chair, Governor Otto Kerner of Illinois, the group delivered a devastating indictment of a nation with "two societies, one black, one white, separate and unequal."[50] The report referred to what amounted to a "system of apartheid" in American cities.[51] As part of the solution, it called for significant investments in the slums and raised the possibility of a guaranteed minimum income. Just as King had argued from Watts in 1965, Kerner said that the police had come to symbolize white power in black communities.[52] The SCLC welcomed the recommendations but in view of previous similar warnings of a racial crisis dismissed the Kerner group as the "commission of repetition."[53]

Although the Kerner Commission did not go as far as King might have, the SCLC leader felt vindicated in his own condemnations of the slums. King responded to the report by repeating his analysis: "The ghetto is looted by outside profit-makers. No wonder then men who see their poor communities raped by this society sometimes turn to violence."[54] The Kerner Commission had confirmed to King what he already knew. However, he feared the findings would be filed away and lost in a dark drawer alongside previous commissions' reports, which similarly had "warned of the growing darkness" in America. He noted that discrimination, segregation, poverty, and violence had not disappeared, but instead continued to grow in the "prejudice-soaked soil of racism until the roots split the foundation of the social order."[55] King's pessimism had some validity: the Permanent Senate Subcommittee on Investigations under John L. McClellan countered the Kerner report by alleging that the War on Poverty programs had fomented urban riots.[56]

The Kerner Commission strengthened King's view of the need to take drastic action against inequality; otherwise, the country was doomed to suffer increasing chaos. The report was published in early 1968, when President Johnson renewed his call for a 10 percent tax surcharge to pay for Vietnam and the cost of social programs. Further budget reductions on social programs were now on the horizon. Congress would agree to the surcharge in June 1968 although it was conditional on $6 billion of cuts in domestic spending.[57] The prospects looked bleak for King's demands for massive spending to end poverty. Encouraged, however, by the lessons of previous campaigns, he observed that the federal government, especially Congress, never moved meaningfully against social ills until the nation was confronted directly and massively.[58] The time for decisive action had arrived. The deepening crisis in America had convinced King he was right to intensify his struggle for economic justice for all citizens and in his advocacy against the war. He viewed the Poor People's Campaign as an opportunity for the government to "unite with its people and open a new age for America. All those who now speak of goodwill and who praise the work of such groups as the President's Commission now have the gravest responsibility to stand up and act for the social changes that are necessary to conquer racism in America. If we as a society fail, I fear that we will learn very shortly racism is a sickness until death."[59]

In March, the SCLC announced that King was planning a nationwide tour ahead of the campaign in Washington. The SCLC hoped this would rouse America to face up to poverty and racism and would motivate poor people to join the campaign for the right to "a decent life."[60] His self-styled "people-to-people" visits to different communities across the United States were intended to be "informative and educational, for the haves, but much more so for the have nots."[61] The threefold purpose of going directly to where people lived was to meet impoverished citizens in their homes and communities, expose the plight of the poor to wider audiences, and garner support for the PPC. King planned to meet with poor families in their "rural shanties and slum tenements, walk the streets of America's ghettos, visit disadvantaged school children, and speak at mass rallies where poor people will present their grievances in hearings" during his nationwide tour.[62]

King traveled in a small charter plane accompanied by two aides and two reporters. Andrew Young, Bernard Lee, Fred Bennett, Ralph Abernathy, and others joined him at various points. At his first stop, in Grosse Pointe, Michigan, in a sign of the polarized climate of the times, he was heckled and called a communist.[63] In advance of his visits, the SCLC reminded local organizers that grassroots leaders and the poor were the most important people in the area. They were informed, "Dr. King is not coming to organize; his job is not to mobilize, but to stimulate that which you have already organized and mobilized."[64] It was emphasized that King was of no service or value to an area unless the groundwork was undertaken for his visit. Arrangements were made for him to meet poor people in their own neighborhoods and homes so that he could observe poverty firsthand.[65] Hosea Williams stressed that the "grassroots leaders and poor people are the most important for Dr. King to talk to. I would make this the most important and longest meeting; it should take place in a poor area or poor neighborhood."[66]

King set himself an exhausting and hectic schedule in early 1968, which included his other responsibilities as president of the SCLC and his role as effective leader of the nonviolent civil rights movement. His sons, Marty and Dexter, accompanied him on a tour of Georgia. Throughout this period, inevitable delays meant that he sometimes arrived at his final destination after midnight. He invariably found crowds waiting patiently for his arrival even at such late hours. In Mississippi, for example, King toured ten cities, each day beginning at 10 a.m. and concluding at 10 p.m.[67] On one occasion, he endured a twenty-one-hour day, arriving at his motel in Jackson, Mississippi, at 4 a.m.[68] In addition to D.C., King visited cities in New Jersey, Maryland, Virginia, South Carolina, North Carolina, Ohio, Michigan, and Illinois. King relished walking from house to house when visiting poor communities. The visits were part of his continuing education about the true nature of poverty at the grassroots level. He met poor families in their rural shanties and slum tenements and listened to their testimonies at rallies and events.[69] He requested that people be given no warning of his visits; he wanted to understand their real living conditions. The SCLC cautioned local organizers that if people knew Dr. King was coming, they would try to clean up and dress up—but he wanted to "catch them in their natural habitat."[70] He also welcomed invitations to eat lunch, usually a simple "soul food" meal, in at least one house on a tour and shaking hands and meeting children.[71]

On March 20, King delivered a memorable speech at a rally for a mainly black audience in Eutaw, Alabama. The speech laid bare his blueprint to build a temporary camp to house the poor who would travel to Washington, D.C., so that the world could see "how the poor lived back home." He looked forward to a campaign of civil disobedience and promised to "tie up" Washington through the sheer weight of the protesters' numbers. His expansive vision for the campaign included some of the tenets of Black Power, demonstrating yet again that his relationship with black militants was more complex than what is often portrayed in the media. King said the campaign in Washington would provide the opportunity for participants to celebrate their black culture and to learn together in Freedom Schools. His aspiration in this regard would be met: workshops on black history and black culture and access to Freedom Schools were provided for many of those preparing for the trip as well as later in Resurrection City itself. In the powerful conclusion to his Eutaw speech, King called on poor people to "put on your walking shoes, and walk together, pray together, struggle together, believe together, have faith together, and come on to Washington. And there will be a great camp meeting in the Promised Land."[72] Two days later King requested that his colleagues, including Bernard Lafayette, Andrew Young, Hosea Williams, and Ralph Abernathy, report on their progress with mobilization efforts across the country.[73]

Events, however, were to take a tragic turn as King looked to finalize plans for the PPC. He received a telephone call in March 1968 from his friend the Reverend James Lawson, leader of the Memphis group Community on the Move for Equality. Lawson and his group were engaged in a bitter strike in Memphis in support of the right of black sanitation workers to unionize, to have meaningful grievance procedures, and to have decent wages and better working conditions. Lawson hoped that King would lend his presence to the sanitation workers campaign and help bring a resolution to what had become a volatile and entrenched struggle between powerless low-income individuals and unyielding white power structures. Black people invariably found low pay, few employment opportunities, racism, and discrimination in all areas of life. Politically, working-class black people had no power or influence in 1960s Memphis. Attempts to get the city's recognition of a black sanitation workers union were unsuccessful. Public opinion split along racial lines, and white opposition to black union organizing became a proxy war against the civil rights movement more generally. Black people, in contrast, viewed union recognition as a basic human right not denied to others.

The deaths of two workers, Echol Cole and Robert Walker, in an accident caused by faulty equipment on February 1, 1968, had been the catalyst leading to the strike. Angry and frustrated by years of discrimination and racism, 1,300 black men from the Memphis Department of Public Works withdrew their labor. Black Mississippian and labor union official Thomas O. Jones led the dispute and was supported by Jerry Wurf, president of the American Federation of State, County, and Municipal Employees, part of the American Federation of Labor–Congress of Industrial Organizations (AFL-CIO). The CIO had long pledged to organize workers regardless of race, gender, nationality, or political beliefs; in 1939 it was described in Tennessee as "n——r unionism and communism."[74] In Memphis King would try to align a cross-section of the population, including women, black workers, young people, ministers, and other activists.[75] An uncompromising Mayor Henry Loeb, who had taken office in January 1968, added fuel to the flames following the decision of workers to go on strike on February 11. With tensions at a new high, a nonviolent march by the sanitation workers on February 23 was brutally attacked by the police. Local ministers had seen enough, and they came together to form Community on the Move for Equality with the goal of using nonviolent protest to bring attention to the striking low-income workers.

To several of King's closest colleagues, the idea of going to Memphis was at best a distraction from the PPC and at worst a dangerous interference in an already tense situation. Bernard Lafayette and Andrew Young pleaded with him not to go.[76] Young appreciated that campaigns for justice were rarely short endeavors and sapped energies. In his view, the PPC demanded King's full attention. Clarence Jones and Stanley Levison also said they were not in favor because Memphis would focus attention away from the bigger picture of the PPC.[77] Jesse Jackson's wife, Jackie, claimed that her husband told King to ignore Memphis because it was too small and urged him to focus on Chicago instead, where he would be dealing with economic conditions that would be the issue of the next century.[78]

From King's perspective, the Memphis strike represented the Poor People's Campaign in microcosm. He saw an opportunity to establish a beachhead for social and economic justice in the city, which would serve as an exemplar for the imminent national campaign in Washington. By helping powerless low-paid workers to win bargaining rights, decent wages, and better working conditions, Memphis would be for King a more limited, nonviolent proxy war against poverty. The striking sanitation workers were precisely the kind of poor and oppressed people he identified with. Significantly, Memphis offered King an opportunity to dramatize the conditions of the poor and to work more closely with labor unions to address economic injustice.[79] Throughout his career, he had tried to forge close relationships with labor unions supportive of his agendas.[80] He had struggled to persuade many labor unions to get behind the PPC initiative. Bayard Rustin, for example, expressed concern at the absence of labor during the planning period for the Washington campaign.[81] The response from labor unions to the PPC had been mixed at best. Rustin and A. Philip Randolph's Freedom Budget in 1966 had envisaged a crucial role for sympathetic labor unions in a broad coalition for change. Throughout his career, King consistently praised the labor movement as the best vehicle to raise the economic and cultural status of workers. He celebrated the birth of labor unions and the foothold they had given to the working classes as the day when "economic democracy was born."[82] In 1961, King had vowed to support labor's demands, to attack "hard-core unemployment," and to fight laws that curbed union activities.[83]

Throughout the 1960s, culminating with the Memphis strike and the PPC, King looked to strengthen his ties with progressive labor unions, fighting in particular for the right of powerless low-income workers to unionize.[84] This was consistent with his long-held position that "our needs are identified with labor's needs—decent wages, fair working conditions, liveable housing, and old age security, health and welfare measures."[85] He looked on labor unions as effective agents of change in making economic justice a reality.[86] He wrote of his hopes for a revitalized labor movement since black people "were placing economic issues on the highest agenda."[87] As he prepared to enter the dispute in Memphis, King was aware that his support for the peace movement and his attempts to find common ground with advocates of Black Power were troublesome to some union leaders, including George Meany, president of the AFL-CIO. Although the AFL-CIO had supported the passage of the Civil Rights Act of 1964, it now disagreed with King on the crucial issue of the war in Vietnam.

Some in the labor movement rejected King's proposal for a guaranteed minimum annual income as an encouragement to welfare dependency and a potential threat to workers' wages. Walter Reuther of the United Auto Workers, for example, supported a minimum income entitlement for factory workers who were temporarily idle due to a shortage of orders but was not supportive of an expansive national minimum income program. Reuther was also anxious about the potential involvement of both black militants and the peace movement in the PPC but remained supportive of the campaign.[88] Reuther sympathized with the plight of poor people across the nation and demanded that the federal government close tax loopholes and fund programs for the poor and the cities.[89] The United Steelworkers voiced approval of the PPC's demands for job creation. Much of the support for the PPC came from small local unions. Teamster vice president Harold Gibbons raised funds from unions in the St. Louis area; the Washington Retail Clerks donated funds; and Chicago area locals of the Packinghouse Workers union would attend the Solidarity Day rally in Resurrection City.[90] The American Federation of Teachers and Local 1199 of the Drug and Hospital Workers Union provided support from New York.[91]

The local nonviolent protest in Memphis for living wages and improved working conditions provided King with a prelude to the national campaign in Washington, D.C. He delivered a rousing speech on March 18 in Memphis at the Charles Mason Temple. An estimated twenty-five thousand supporters packed into the building. King returned to the theme of powerlessness, asserting that black poverty did not result because of inherent faults in any individual, but was a consequence of the powerlessness inflicted by unjust structures in society. He informed his audience, "Power is the ability to achieve purpose; power is the ability to effect change."[92] He proclaimed, "Freedom is not something that is voluntarily given by the oppressor. It is something that must be demanded by the oppressed."[93] He also suggested that black people could not go it alone. King stressed the importance of uniting beyond class lines. He commended the audience, whose participation highlighted that "we are all tied in a single garment of destiny, and that if one black person suffers, if one black person is down, we are all down."[94] The composition of the audience, which included the poorest in society as well as the better-off middle classes, was a visible demonstration to King of the cross-class strike coalition in Memphis. This encouraged the SCLC leader to believe that the same outcome might be achieved for the PPC.

As King became more committed to the unfolding drama in Memphis, his closest aides continued to urge him to take a step back. His response to their advice was clear and unequivocal; the underpaid black sanitation workers represented the plight of the underemployed and unemployed of all races across the nation. King declared, "These are poor folks; if we don't stop for them then we don't need to go to Washington."[95] However, both his resolve and his methods of nonviolence were tested by the course of events in Memphis. King led a march in support of the sanitation workers on March 28, 1968. The march ended in widespread disruption and with police attacks on the demonstrators. A local group called the Invaders, known for wearing military jackets and berets in a style reminiscent of the Black Panthers, was blamed for smashing windows on the route, sparking disorder and chaos. A leader of the Invaders, Charles Cabbage, apparently admitted they had deliberately disrupted the march to discredit the philosophy of nonviolence.[96] However, several other young people may have contributed to the violent scenes. King seemed in imminent danger from a volatile situation and was driven to safety in a nearby hotel, only to receive criticism that he was a chicken who had fled the debacle he was responsible for creating in the first place. The FBI, implacable opponents of the PPC and its goals, blamed the disorder on King, claiming that violence followed him around. King stood accused of introducing violence into an already volatile situation in Memphis. The chaos around the march even led some white allies to claim that he could no longer hold the line on nonviolence.

King saw "black unity as the first prerequisite for further change and division as the way to failure."[97] The violence suggested that he had lost ground to those who rejected turning the other cheek as a slave mentality. His morale was possibly at its lowest point ever, not least because those opposed to the PPC thought they saw an opportunity to use the disturbances as a stick with which to beat him. The events were viewed as a grim warning of what was to come in the Washington campaign.[98] The national media set the tone: the PPC was expected to fail—if it even went ahead.[99] The Memphis *Commercial Appeal*, a newspaper unsympathetic to the strike, stated that King's pose as the leader of a nonviolent movement had been shattered.[100] King's associates and friends were shaken by the impact of the chaos on him. The Reverend Walter Fauntroy observed that King was "terribly depressed" following the violence. Abernathy wrote that he personally could not shake off a sense of foreboding about the SCLC leader at this point; he observed that King seemed to be "preoccupied and depressed."[101] Young noted that he saw in King a kind of despair he had never seen before.[102] All of their concerns seemed justified. King felt so upset that he reportedly said to Levison that he wanted to call off the PPC.[103]

The SCLC leader resolved to put things right by planning to return to Memphis for a nonviolent march on April 5. King agreed to raise funds for the Invaders if they acted as nonviolent marshals at the march.[104] The Invaders eventually would work as marshals in Resurrection City. One SCLC official in Resurrection City would report that a leading Invader, Lance "Sweet Willie" Watson, "had to be tamed" to accept nonviolence. For his part, Watson later said, "After Dr. King's death, we felt more committed to him personally."[105]

King met with his closest SCLC colleagues in his study at Ebenezer Baptist Church. He rarely lost his cool but was furious to discover that several of his inner circle continued to oppose his decision to intercede in the labor union dispute and throw in his lot with the sanitation workers. Andrew Young joined James Bevel, Jesse Jackson, and Hosea Williams in advising King to concentrate on the PPC. According to Ralph Abernathy, King listened to them with "barely constrained anger."[106] Opposition to his plans from within was nothing new for King, however. As discussed above, the proposal to mount the Chicago campaign in 1966 had brought tensions, egos, and rivalries to the surface even among those closest to him. But Memphis was a step too far for some, and opposition to King's plans simmered within the SCLC. C. T. Vivian, Randolph Blackwell, and Bernard Lafayette supported their leader.[107] Jesse Jackson came in for particular hostility as King finally lost patience with those who did not share his analysis of the interconnectedness of the Memphis strike and the planned campaign in Washington. Jackson argued that King needed an exit strategy for the PPC if things did not go as planned.

Since he had first proposed the idea for the PPC, King had tried to bring everyone together in an uneasy coalition; however, competing visions and different agendas continued to overshadow his leadership. The pressure from all sides brought on migraine headaches as he struggled to cope.[108] During what was one of the most difficult periods of his life, King confided in Stanley Levison that other black leaders, including Roy Wilkins, Bayard Rustin, and Congressman Adam Clayton Powell, were no longer listening to him, and they regarded him as "dead and finished."[109] King left the SCLC meeting to cool down at Dorothy Cotton's home. He returned to find that his colleagues were beginning to come together in support of both the Memphis campaign and the PPC. Andrew Young thought that King's outburst was a call for unity in the belief the SCLC was one of the few organizations that could save the country.[110]

Under siege as perhaps never before, the opposition from close associates and from others in the movement was almost unbearable for King. He confided to Abernathy that the opposition from black militants and others in a divided black community "broke his heart": "we need to prove to the nation [that] violence is wrong."[111] King considered going on a three-day fast to demonstrate his commitment for the campaign and thereby bring everyone in the SCLC into line.[112] A fast was associated with self-purification and would help sustain commitment.[113] Resistance to his ideas only strengthened King's belief in the justice of the cause and stiffened his resolve to craft and shape a bold and radical campaign against poverty.

At the National Cathedral in Washington, D.C., on March 31, 1968, Dr. King delivered what would be the final sermon of his life. Once again, he denounced racism, poverty, and war and called on America to fulfill its obligations to the poor. He referred to those who were with him as dedicated individuals willing to be co-workers with God. He drew attention to poverty in places as far apart as India and Newark, New Jersey. In his estimation, the PPC was a unique opportunity for the United States to "help bridge the gulf between the haves and the have-nots. The question is whether America will do it. There is nothing new about poverty. What is new is that we now have the techniques and the resources to get rid of poverty. The real question is whether we have the will."[114] He elaborated his thoughts at a press conference after the sermon, warning as on previous occasions that America was in danger of becoming a fascist state unless it mended its ways in both foreign and domestic policy arenas. King speculated that either Robert F. Kennedy or Eugene McCarthy would be better candidates than Lyndon Johnson for the Democratic Party nomination for president in the November election. He had little or no faith left in the capacity of Johnson to be the leader the country needed in a time of great crisis. That same evening, events took a dramatic turn. Lyndon Johnson made the unexpected announcement that he did not intend to seek reelection. King was dumbfounded but hoped the prospect of a new president would bring about a sea change in public policy and help him realize his dream to end poverty.

Although many of his closest aides feared for his safety, King returned to Memphis on April 3, 1968, to offer further support to the striking sanitation workers. In what could be seen as an omen of what was to come, the departure of his plane to Memphis was delayed due to a bomb threat. King moved into the modest Lorraine Motel and invited some of the Invaders to join him. Although he was not scheduled to speak at the rally in Charles Mason Temple on the evening of April 3, King was contacted from the hall by Ralph Abernathy, who said the crowd was expecting him to address them. Jesse Jackson was already at the auditorium and offered to stand in, but it was clear the audience wanted Dr. King.[115] Unable to disappoint his people, the poor of Memphis, King agreed to join Abernathy at the event. In what would be his final speech, King outlined the power of nonviolence, called for black unity in the face of oppressive forces, and praised the determination thus far of the oppressed to effect social change. He reflected some of the tenets of Black Power by alluding to the racist nature of U.S. capitalism.

His speech captured the essential reasons for mounting the Poor People's Campaign. In declaring there was no other time in history that he would rather be living, King pointed to the possibilities that lay ahead in Memphis and for the PPC to come. Striking an optimistic note, he declared that something was happening in Memphis: oppressed people were standing up for their rights. Not for the first time, he also seemed to speak like a prophet, predicting that the dark, hate-filled forces gathering against him would put an end to his life. Dr. King delivered his own eulogy on that stormy evening in Memphis.[116] He was shot and killed the next day while standing on the balcony of his room in the Lorraine Motel. His murder remains mired in controversy to this day. After initially pleading guilty to avoid a death sentence, convicted assassin James Earl Ray proclaimed his innocence of the crime until the day he died.

Irrespective of the specific circumstances of his death in Memphis, racism and hate killed Dr. King. He never abandoned his nonviolent beliefs despite the most severe provocations, including regular threats against his life and the lives of his family. He was committed to nonviolence and warned that self-defense could turn into aggressive violence.[117] Violence appalled King, be it in Vietnam or in the racism and other injustices inherent in the treatment of poor people in America and across the globe. Andrew Young claimed to be "strangely relieved when Martin died." It was the only way King could find peace, he said: "he was so tormented by the violence in this country."[118]

The events in Memphis remained etched in the memories of those who were there and rippled across the entire country. Rage about the assassination brought riots in more than a hundred American cities. J. Edgar Hoover moved to expand his plan to undermine the PPC, known as Operation POCAM, to every FBI field office in the United States.[119] The FBI would do everything in its power to destroy the campaign. The various caravans traveling to Washington, D.C., were infiltrated, and rumors and misinformation were spread, including about interracial sex among the campaigners. King's death was felt in all corners of the world. He was accorded the equivalent of a state funeral, and many of the candidates for the 1968 presidential election attended, including Democratic senators Robert F. Kennedy and Eugene McCarthy, Vice President Hubert Humphrey, Republican governor George Romney, and former vice president Richard Nixon. Reflecting the tensions around race in 1968, Nixon was aware that his decision to attend the funeral might prove controversial among some of the southern politicians who supported his candidacy for the presidency. He confided to aides that in going to the funeral he would be a "prisoner of the civil rights movement."[120] King's coffin was carried in a mule-drawn wagon to the burial site. A national day of mourning was held on Sunday, April 7.

President Johnson finally signed the Fair Housing Act (Title VIII of the Civil Rights Act of 1968) into law on April 11, 1968, just one week after the assassination. Supporters of the bill in Congress had previously feared that negative attitudes toward the PPC would doom it to failure. But Johnson used the tragedy to build a consensus to get the bill through Congress. He announced at the signing that the "bell of freedom rings out a little louder."[121] King had achieved in death what he had been unable to do in life. The passage of the bill was pure Lyndon Johnson, the consummate politician. In the Senate, Walter Mondale alleged that Alaska senator Edward Bartlett had agreed to provide a crucial vote in favor of the bill after Johnson approved $18 million for public housing in Alaska.[122] Republican Everett Dirksen supported the passage of the bill, thinking it might help to end urban violence. In a sign of the times, the bill contained some compromises reflecting conservative fears about crime and the potential influx of black people into their communities. It included provisions against people who crossed state lines with intent to "incite riots."[123] It was also left up to individuals to file a suit alleging any discrimination in housing.

The voice of Black Power was heard in the wake of the tragedy of the assassination. Stokely Carmichael reportedly strode along Pennsylvania Avenue in Washington, D.C., carrying a pistol and said that others should follow suit. Riots raged in Washington, which almost immediately led to widespread rumors among whites that a conspiracy of militant black people was behind the unrest.[124] Carmichael added further fuel to the burning flames by announcing at a press conference that King's death represented a loss of hope for black people in that the man everybody listened to was dead, killed by "white America."[125] Carmichael declared that black men were going to "stand up on their feet and die like men."[126] The press interpreted his comments to mean the gloves were off now that the man in the middle, Dr. King, was gone. In common with everyone else in King's inner circle, Bayard Rustin was devastated at the loss of his friend and colleague. Getting to the heart of King's true contribution to history, he said the slain leader understood that "political and social justice could not exist without economic justice." Arguing that the SCLC leader's death was not in vain, Rustin summarized the sanitation workers strike as no less than the "beginning of the entry into economic justice" for people of all races.[127] Rustin asserted that it was incumbent on everyone who shared King's dream of the "beloved community," including racial reconciliation, peace, and economic justice, to carry on with the struggle.[128]

King's leadership was crucial for the success of the Poor People's Campaign, especially as he crisscrossed the country to mobilize poor communities during his people-to-people tours in March 1968. Billy Hollins, who served as the PPC's Midwest regional coordinator, related how he went to Michigan to recruit Native Americans, to Indiana for "white folks," and to churches and organizations to talk about the PPC. He continually stressed to those he met, "This is Martin Luther King's movement—we always used Martin Luther King's name—you need to get on this bus—you need to be part of this thing."[129] One of the most poignant PPC field reports focused on Dr. King's proposed visit to North Carolina on April 4, the day he was killed in Memphis. Before the sanitation workers strike led him to Tennessee, King had been scheduled to meet in North Carolina with "poor families in voter registration lines and in their urban and rural shanties and slum tenements." Arrangements were in place for him to be met at the airport by students and local leaders, to walk the streets of Greensboro, to preside over a mock trial against poverty in Durham, and to deliver a major address at a local high school on the evening of April 4. Everyone had been looking forward to his visit. Golden A. Frinks, SCLC field secretary for North Carolina, said that the "people had received the message of Dr. King's proposed tour with enthusiasm."[130] They would never have the opportunity to meet him in person.

King's death could conceivably have brought a halt to the PPC planning; so much of the campaign was apparently invested in him and vice versa. However, his loss stiffened the resolve of the SCLC, the leaders of other racial groups, supporters in other organizations, and the poor people of America to continue his legacy. Jackie Jackson, the wife of Jesse, later recalled, "We could not let the enemies of peace and enemies of our movement win like that, our time stopped in Memphis and it began in Memphis."[131] The Memphis strike ended in agreement following King's death. Other public worker strikes followed, inspired by the example of Memphis.

Despite their sense of loss and the great void left by Dr. King's death, the leaders of the different racial groups and many of the thousands of poor people who had already signed up to go to Washington vowed to carry on with the Poor People's Campaign. The PPC steering group met in Atlanta a month after King's assassination. They found solace in coming together again. Ernest Austin, co-ordinator of the Appalachian PPC group, later recalled that the staff retreat in Atlanta after King's death "provided basic therapy for a lot of people."[132] In the aftermath of the assassination, Cesar Chavez comforted King's widow, Coretta Scott King, assuring her that the "courage which we have found in our struggle for justice in the fields has had its roots in the example set by your husband."[133]

Activist Lee Dora Collins stated that before the assassination, it had been difficult to get people to go to Washington, but after Memphis "people came from everywhere."[134] PPC activist Tyrone Brooks reflected that "we had no option but to continue as a tribute to Dr. King."[135] King's name was synonymous with the campaign even after his death. It is a paradox that his spirit was present to the many demonstrators in Resurrection City, yet his absence was sorely felt. Even some of those he had only briefly touched for the first time through the vehicle of the PPC were traumatized by his loss. Dolores Huerta, who helped Cesar Chavez organize migrant workers in California, surely spoke for countless thousands across America and the world. She wrote in moving terms to Bayard Rustin, "I do not believe there can be any recovery from the loss of a life as great as Martin Luther King."[136] King's supporters in the PPC, including the leaders of the other racial groups, would carry on.

CHAPTER SIX
THE MULE TRAIN

Following Martin Luther King Jr.'s death, the Southern Christian Leadership Conference distributed a flyer for the Poor People's Campaign containing a prophetic quote from the Bible. It read, "Behold the Dreamer cometh. Come now, therefore, and let us slay him . . . and we shall see what will become of his dream" (Genesis 37:19-20).[1] With King gone, the story of the PPC might have ended. However, his own chosen successor as president of the SCLC, Ralph Abernathy, announced on April 19 that the campaign would continue.

His closest friend's premature death placed a reluctant Abernathy in the spotlight. Abernathy had been with King since they were young Baptist ministers in Montgomery during the bus boycott in 1955-1956. Raised on an Alabama farm, he understood poverty. Andrew Young said that because of his humble origins, Ralph Abernathy could "talk the language" of the poor.[2] How would he now respond in the most difficult of situations? Abernathy later reflected that he took over after the movement had peaked and the SCLC had begun to decline in influence.[3] He also had to face up to the fact that the philosophy of nonviolence was under threat from the uprisings that broke out in cities across the nation in response to the assassination. On a personal level, Abernathy advised the press that no one person could fill King's shoes. He acknowledged he did not have as many academic qualifications as King, and Young warned that the press would treat him differently because his skin was darker than King's.[4] Abernathy was not as good a speaker as King was, but then few could match his slain friend's oratory and delivery. King also seemed more acceptable to white elite audiences. Abernathy was reported to have performed badly when speaking at a Boston fundraiser just after King's death.[5]

Despite his personal grief, Abernathy took the reins and tried to look to the future. He told those heading for Washington, D.C., not to tarry around King's gravesite because they had business on the road to freedom.[6] Campaign leaders intensified their efforts in the weeks after King's death. Stanley Levison reported that additional donations flowed in to boost campaign coffers. A *New York Times* advertisement signed by Harry Belafonte raised more than $300,000.[7] Donations of tiny sums of money came from people who had virtually nothing. One thousand denim jackets sewn by black women in Crawfordville, Georgia, were donated.[8] Thousands of new volunteers came forward. King's death had galvanized the campaign; the question was whether this impetus could be sustained to take the poor to Washington. Some claimed that King's assassination muted criticism of the PPC.[9] Politicians backed off on the grounds it was unseemly to condemn King's final campaign in the immediate period after his murder. It was soon business as usual, however. The riots in the wake of the assassination heightened concerns in Congress and among the public at the prospect of the arrival in D.C. of thousands of demonstrators. On May 3, one month after the assassination, President Lyndon Johnson voiced the fears of many by saying there were "inherent dangers in the SCLC enterprise."[10]

Refusing to be intimidated by the strength of the opposition against them, thousands of poor people signed up for the PPC to make themselves and their plight visible to the nation. Eventually, nine caravans came from different regions across the country, bringing poor people of all races to Washington. They were ordinary people inspired by King and by their own leaders, including Corky Gonzales and Reies Tijerina, to make the long trek to Washington to make life better for themselves, for their families, and for people they had never met. Criticism that the Poor People's Campaign was of limited significance does no justice to those who in 1968 made the challenging journey to Washington, D.C., to occupy space and to make their case directly to the government. One of the most significant groups was the southeastern caravan contingent, which traveled from Marks, Quitman County, Mississippi. In what is known to history as the Mule Train, part of their journey from Marks to Washington was undertaken on wagons pulled by mules. The iconic Mule Train from Marks provides an important case study for understanding the human side of the PPC.

Coretta Scott King, among others, credited her husband with the idea of using mules for at least part of the journey to Washington.[11] The "Queen of the Mule Train," Quitman County resident Bertha Burres Johnson, said that King wanted to evoke the idea of the "West" to symbolize a new beginning.[12] As previously mentioned, King had floated the idea of the poor traveling to D.C. on wagons pulled by mules as early as October 1966. The association of the mule with the cause of black equality has some of its origin in the unfulfilled promise of "forty acres and a mule" made to formerly enslaved people. In the modern civil rights era, King and other SCLC leaders looked on mules and their en-during association with the impoverished dirt farmer as a "valuable metaphor for the economic changes and the resulting impacts on employment on which the PPC would focus."[13] In 1968, the image of the mule found a niche as atten-tion moved to the issue of poverty. The use of the mules sent a powerful mes-sage. Their historical symbolic significance along with their quiet, timeless dignity represented universal poverty, and they traveled slowly through Missis-sippi, Alabama, and Georgia before being loaded onto a train in Atlanta for the final leg to Washington. Perhaps a measure of the social and political climate of the period in America, Bernard Lafayette, national director of the PPC, ob-served that "through the attention of the Humane Society more concern was ex-pressed about the condition of the mules than the people, but we got our mes-sage across."[14]

The inspirational tactic to have the poor travel from Marks at least part of the way on the Mule Train also had a pedagogical purpose. The Mule Train was a means of educating the American public about the realities of poverty. Lafay-ette said the purpose was "to put a face on poverty," and he explained that "the Mule Train was a publicity arm. It would take a long time to get to Washington and would attract press and media interest."[15] Activist Myrna Copeland further reflected this perspective in observing, "perhaps this can be looked on as an ed-ucation for the people of America. I think a lot of Americans just do not realize, are ignorant, of how many poor people live in the United States."[16]

According to the 1960 U.S. Census figures for average income, Marks, Missis-sippi, was officially the poorest town in the poorest state in America.[17] In 1968 cotton remained the main source of income for the majority of the 21,000 peo-ple who lived in Quitman County, including the 2,402 residents of Marks.[18] Mul-tiple indicators of poverty were in evidence. Despite the best efforts of civil rights activists in Mississippi over several decades, it seemed that Marks remained largely untouched by the changes affecting race relations elsewhere. In some respects, Marks provided a window into the past. The small town was described as "still Confederate," a place where "time has stood still."[19] Very few black peo-ple owned land. People worshipped on segregated lines. Whites were Southern Baptists, blacks were Missionary Baptists, and those black people lucky enough to be educated attended the African Methodist Episcopal Church.[20] Schools re-mained segregated. Marian Wright Edelman observed that the pavement began where "white folks lived and ended where blacks lived."[21] Racism and discrimi-nation in all areas of life meant that black people in Quitman County had never even dared to "invade white social life at any level."[22] Community facilities were badly lacking. There was no swimming pool or movie theater, although there were pool halls.[23] Black people sat in the doctor's waiting room until whites were seen first.[24]

Although King was killed more than one month before the Mule Train departed for Washington, D.C., his influence on the campaign in Marks was profound. Conditions in Marks in March 1968 had led him to decide that the PPC would begin there so that poverty would be placed firmly in the national spotlight. The small community became a focal point of the campaign. Because of the poverty and the history of discrimination in the Mississippi Delta, the SCLC regarded Quitman as the most important county of the whole campaign: "it could come to define the national effort as a whole."[25] Black people in Quitman County were "near starvation," SCLC staff reported.[26] The SCLC faced huge challenges in Marks. Was it possible to mobilize, train, and motivate the poorest community in the United States to go to Washington? The task was daunting. Some low-income individuals in Quitman County had never left their own communities. Many had little or no education.

King's visit to Marks on one of his people-to-people tours on March 19, 1968, was his second trip to the small community.[27] On each occasion, King felt the pain of those he identified with. He wept on observing the abject poverty of local people. On his first visit in 1966, to preach at the funeral of a local activist, Armstead Phipps, King broke down at the sight of a teacher with only a meager supply of apples and crackers trying to provide lunch to a whole class of hungry children. His basic humanity and empathy for those at the margins of society came to the fore again during his second visit in March 1968. He cried again while visiting families living in run-down shacks. Several of the dwellings stood in water. One black youth declared to King that his life was so miserable he wished he had been born white.[28] The personal testimonies of impoverished mothers in Marks in March 1968 led Dr. King to relate, "I wept with them as I heard numerous women stand up on their feet. I heard them talking about the fact that they did not even have any blankets to cover their children up on a cold night."[29]

As King reached out to people in their own homes, churches, and communities, they reached back to him. He told the people in Marks that their living conditions were criminal, adding, "God does not want you to live like you are living."[30] The sense of loss many ordinary people felt on his death cannot be measured. Mule Train participant Lee Dora Collins recalled the experience of sharing the same space with him in 1968. Throughout her life, she had moved from plantation to plantation. She remembered how "Dr. King and his people came right here to Marks. First, he came to my church, the Silent Grove Baptist

Church. When he walked down the aisle, something came over me. You see, a Christian can feel a Christian, and this day, his presence touched my spirit like he was God-sent. I just knew our time had come. We were bound for freedom."[31]

For PPC planning purposes, the SCLC divided Mississippi into north and south. Two caravans eventually left from Mississippi for Washington: the Freedom Trail from Memphis and the Mule Train from Marks. The goal was to involve masses of poor people and to do things in the poor way. A busy schedule from late January 1968 included a series of meetings between SCLC staff and local leaders and groups. SCLC staff canvassed in high schools and elementary schools in places like Memphis. They stood on cafeteria tables and told people that Dr. King had "switched his agenda, we want you to switch yours."[32] Many young women dropped out of high school in Memphis and worked as volunteers for the campaign. Events included a mass meeting of the Grenada County Freedom Movement on January 30 and a discussion with Charles Evers (NAACP) and attorneys from the Lawyers Committee in Jackson, Mississippi, on February 2.[33] King met with state-wide political, religious, and civil rights leaders at Mount Beulah in Edwards, Mississippi, on February 14 and 15. The SCLC paid the bills for food, transportation, and housing for all who attended.[34] Leon Hall reported there was the expected amount of dissent from leaders of various organizations, but generally the idea for a Washington campaign was well received.[35] The leaders agreed to go back to their own areas to meet with groups not represented at the meeting to gather ideas and support for the program.

Workshops were organized to train those recruited to the campaign. The discussions throughout January and February helped to frame the issues and demands that would be presented to legislators in Washington, D.C. These included unemployment and underemployment, the lack of housing, an inadequate and flawed welfare system, low-quality education, and cuts in federal programs. It was recognized that local people needed to be educated about King's idea for a guaranteed annual income program so that they would understand the point of making the demand in Washington and how they could benefit from it.[36]

King's personality and presence were crucial throughout February and March 1968 as the campaign in Mississippi gained momentum. Everyone was expected to do their best and not let their leader down. The PPC national field director, Hosea Williams, tried to keep the pressure on local organizers to deliver. Weekly report forms required them to detail the numbers of paid field staff, paid office workers, volunteer field staff, television and radio appearances, posters and leaflets distributed, copies distributed of the SCLC magazine, and planned mass meetings, as well as the amount of money spent. Local ministers, businesses, professional people, and, most crucially, poor people were mobilized. Local organizers were reminded, "Dr. King must be sure we are up tight. Our future is inextricably bound; each brother must do his job well."[37]

In the early months of 1968, King made approaches to leaders in the state. The SCLC was keen to avoid stepping on the toes of groups and organizations with deep roots in communities in Mississippi. Acting as the coordinator only, the SCLC was wary of rekindling old grudges and organizational and personality clashes. Individuals and groups were asked to set aside personal differences for the greater good and to work hard to recruit poor people.[38] The SCLC tapped into the richness of the local activism that had characterized the state for decades. Representatives of nearly every civil rights organization in Mississippi attended meetings led by King in March 1968.[39] Dittmer noted in his groundbreaking work on civil rights in Mississippi that the PPC helped to foster closer cooperation between groups that previously had felt they had little in common.[40] In April 1968, a variety of organizations in Mississippi came together to discuss strategy. These included state-wide welfare rights groups, the Grenada County Freedom Movement, the National Association for the Advancement of Colored People, and the Mississippi Freedom Democratic Party.[41] The NAACP in Mississippi was cautious initially because its staff believed that the PPC was unlikely to succeed and would drain resources from other campaigns.[42] It eventually endorsed the campaign.

At different points, Dr. King, Ralph Abernathy, Andrew Young, James Bevel, Andrew Marrisett, and Willie Bolden all played important roles in the organizing of the PPC in Marks. J. T. Johnson came from Washington, D.C., to Quitman County to help develop the Mule Train.[43] The SCLC had resolved to build a campaign in Marks from the bottom up, and R. B. Cottonreader was appointed director of the Quitman County Project of the PPC with the brief to recruit "hardcore poor people."[44] He was a seasoned activist who had been trying to run a Head Start program for five hundred children with no federal funding. Cottonreader organized a mass meeting for the campaign on March 15 and undertook some of the preparatory work in advance of King's visit to Marks on March 19. He wrote to Hosea Williams on March 14 requesting office facilities and a car to get him around the state to organize the campaign.[45] The shortage of money was acutely felt by grassroots organizers struggling to operate in already challenging circumstances. Twenty-eight-year-old Willie Bolden went to Marks on behalf of the SCLC to help mobilize poor people and became the wagon master of the Mule Train. Bolden was assisted by twenty-seven-year-old Andrew Marrisett, twenty-one-year-old Jimmie L. Wells, and twenty-one-year-old Margie

Hyatt.[46] They relied for support on a number of local leaders, including the Reverend L. C. Coleman and Leon Hall.

Numerous local citizens in Mississippi contributed to what turned out to be one of the most iconic and enduring aspects of the Poor People's Campaign. They included James Taper, James Figgs, Azra Towner, Madison Shannon Palmer, Ned Gathwright, Lydia McKinnon, Manuel Killebrew, Jimmy Holman, and Johnny and Margaret McGlown.[47] Television reporter Jean Smith recalled that a mother of thirteen, Lee Dora Collins, viewed the Mule Train as her "once in a lifetime chance to make a contribution, perils and all."[48] Jean Smith also fondly remembered meeting other extraordinary and humble people, for example, the white woman at the grocery store who took bread to the Mule Train and the blind ninety-year-old in a windowless shack wallpapered with newsprint of Dr. King and President Kennedy.[49]

The poor people from Mississippi and across the nation who participated in the PPC completed registration forms. At the top of each form was the ambitious statement "Let's eliminate poverty, let's go to Washington. If you let King lead, Jesus will feed." At the bottom of the form was the King statement that defined the movement: "Let's redeem the soul of America."[50] The form also included a detailed questionnaire, which depicted each person's social status in Mississippi. Participants were required to answer questions on whether they received Social Security benefits, welfare checks, or food stamps. When did they last see a doctor? Were they prepared to go to jail? They had to indicate their availability for training in nonviolence and provide details of previous involvement, if any, in civil rights campaigns, including any arrests for demonstrating.

The Quitman County registration forms, completed by real people at the margins of society, reach out to the reader to this day. They demonstrate that King's aspiration to recruit the poorest in society for the PPC was fulfilled. The data contained in the forms tell us who joined the campaign and why. They reveal structural inequalities and provide compelling insights into the depth and scope of poverty in the area. Jobs, income, welfare, housing, and education were all featured. Helen Jean Holt, age nineteen, from Mount Bayou described high levels of unemployment and child poverty. She was unemployed and had one child. She lived with her parents and wanted more money so that her parents could "buy the home they dreamed of for so long."[51] The written statements confirm that many in the county were without running water in their houses; some had no income yet were not on welfare, including forty-six-year-old Elsie Mitchell and eighteen-year-old Rosa May.[52] The majority in Marks were either unemployed or underemployed and lived in substandard housing with some houses even standing in water. Local resident Willie Brown, a father of ten children, reported that his house was in a "low swamp."[53] Kenneth Lee, age seventeen, had come from Memphis, Mississippi; he was unemployed and had no income. He wrote that he could remain in Washington indefinitely, possibly because he had nothing to return home to in Mississippi. Seventy-six-year-old George Nixon said he wanted "better sewers and better homes," and in order to achieve those basic rights he was determined to stay in D.C. "as long as they let me."[54] Randy King from Marks, only nine years old, wrote that he was "going to Washington for better everything."[55]

Young and old rallied to the cause. Mennie May Simpson, age fourteen, was a member of the Quitman County Youth Movement; some of her fellow members were only eight years old. There was a consent form for parents whose children wanted to go to Washington. At the other end of the age spectrum, eighty-six-year-old Mallie Killingworth from Hattiesburg, a retired sharecropper and mother of eleven children, reported that she always had the "worst of everything," including the "poorest food, worst house, poorest bed to sleep in, poorest heating system." She declared she wanted to "get some of the things I have never had before I die."[56] Rose Kendrick from Marks wrote that poor people do not ever get respect as human beings: "I don't have any money, I am hungry, I need clothes, my house is falling in. Congressmen, you have the job and you have the money. I want some of it, so I can live too. Washington is the center of government power and the national government has the money, we want it right now."[57] The desires for jobs, better education, and better housing were the most common themes highlighted by local people on the registration forms.

All participants signed a pledge to adhere to nonviolence in Washington and on the trip there and back. They agreed not to "hit back" if attacked, not to use abusive or hostile language, and not to resist arrest. If arrested, they agreed to go to jail quietly. Finally, everyone was always required to obey the instructions of official campaign marshals.[58] Holding the line on nonviolence was crucial for the success of the campaign. As the chaotic march in Memphis, Tennessee, had demonstrated, the eyes of the media, Congress, the FBI, and other law enforcement agencies were on the campaign. Violence or other unruly behavior would give Congress an excuse to deny the PPC's demands. The FBI was also ready to use any transgressions from the strict code of behavior imposed by organizers as further evidence of the threat to law and order that the campaign represented.

The involvement of Quitman County residents also demonstrated their courage in being prepared to put the safety of themselves and their families on the line. Activists were aware of the potential threats facing those who put their heads above the parapet. Mississippi remained a dangerous environment for civil rights activists. The SCLC knew from recent experiences that the campaign against poverty in Mississippi in 1968 would be undertaken in a potentially hostile environment. In 1964, for example, extreme violence and intimidation had characterized the white response to Freedom Summer. An organizer described Mississippi in 1964 as "the only place I have ever been where a black person can be fired from his job, evicted from his house, jailed and put in the state penitentiary, shot at, and starved, for attempting to register to vote."[59] A small number of whites were prepared to support the Marks effort. Myrna Copeland, a white resident from Alabama, was able to get involved, apparently because her livelihood did not depend on the city or state government.[60] She viewed the Mule Train "as a symbol of the really poor people of the South, the old mule and the wagon that the very poor dirt farmers of the Old South, both black and white, have been tied to for generations."[61]

The SCLC reported in March 1968 that two hundred to three hundred activists had moved into the Marks Tent City from shacks all around Mississippi.[62] The camp provided a base where poor people could prepare themselves to move on Washington, D.C. The modest temporary tent dwellings occupied by the activists were seen to represent those poor people who "were not allowed to participate in society and who therefore had no voice."[63] Apparently horrified at being held up as a terrible example to the nation, the local well-off whites offered electricity, water, and chemical toilets for the camp and an office with free sodas for the press. Their motives included a desire to speed the activists on their way.[64]

On the other hand, reprisals from whites against those who supported civil and human rights campaigns included economic sanctions. The concept of a tent city had been inspired by the creation of tent communities on southern black-owned land, which had housed those who had lost their jobs and homes because of their participation in voter registration campaigns and other civil rights activities earlier in the 1960s.[65] At least four families in Quitman County were thrown off the land and now lived with extended family. Another forty families were anticipating the same fate.[66] In a personal testimony, a mother of ten children, Lena Evans, reported that her family had no place to live because "the boss man has rented his land out."[67] Seventy-four-year-old Virginia Robinson from Quitman County reported that white people had stolen her land, killed her livestock, and informed her that if "she didn't move away she would be next."[68] The Marks Tent City served as the model for the much larger Resurrection City in Washington.[69] Wooden tent-shaped structures were built in May 1968 to house the demonstrators in Resurrection City in D.C.

Scholars have suggested that while many black people in rural communities in the 1950s and 1960s were aware of racial inequality, they did not always have "the basic information necessary to transform their politics, based on personal experience."[70] However, one event in Marks addressed this issue and had a significant impact on the course of the campaign. Willie Bolden had spent two weeks networking and building contacts and support in Quitman County. He called for a mass meeting to be held on May 1. The projected venue, the local black Quitman County Industrial High School, proved to be controversial. The superintendent of schools, Cecil Sharp, and the school principal, Madison Shannon Palmer, were opposed to the use of school premises for such a purpose. The meeting went ahead anyway and was attended by hundreds of defiant students. It was reported that young black people in Marks were already beginning to shake off the degrading mantle placed on them by oppressors and had received the "baptism of pride in being black."[71]

Seventeen out of thirty teachers decided they were for the campaign.[72] The subsequent arrest of Willie Bolden resulted in students and teachers marching to the local jail in protest of the heavy-handed approach. It was apparent that the "civil rights movement had come to Quitman County."[73] In the blazing sun, Andrew Marrisett informed authorities that he was there to collect Bolden. Refusing to leave until Bolden's release, Marrisett and others were arrested for unlawful picketing and demonstrating near the jail and courthouse. Police beat up protesters, including children as young as twelve years old, and three were hospitalized. *Newsweek* reported that the lead trooper had used the butt of a carbine to club a girl who was sitting peacefully on the lawn. The event ended in chaos as protesters scattered under the onslaught. A highway patrol inspector reportedly growled, "This is the only thing these sons of bitches understand."[74] Throughout the whole incident, protesters adhered to the values and example of Dr. King and were nonviolent. His influence was undoubtedly with them.

The jail protest proved to be the catalyst that brought the community together in Marks. That evening, May 1, 1968, hundreds gathered at Eudora AME Zion Church before heading again to the jailhouse. They sang as they marched, showing that they would not be intimidated or provoked. In previous King campaigns, activists were aware that the disproportionate responses of adversaries often provided the breakthrough. Violence, intimidation, and arrests, when highlighted by television and the press, brought sympathy for the victims and turned public opinion against the perpetrators of such actions. The SCLC got the word out about the disturbance in Marks, and several busloads of supporters, including Ralph Abernathy, headed to Marks. One bus was pulled over by police because they said it did not have a city sticker or Mississippi license plates.[75] Sensing good copy, dozens of reporters also arrived in Marks. Dr. King was gone, but his brother, the Reverend A. D. King, attended a crisis meeting in Marks chaired by Abernathy. Another march followed, supported by representatives of the sanitation workers from Memphis, Tennessee, whose presence added extra poignancy to the occasion. The atmosphere was buoyant and defiant.

A boycott of local schools had just ended when the Mule Train prepared to leave for Washington, D.C. In taking their protest to the streets and in organizing a school boycott, local people had demonstrated their readiness to undertake collective action in response to unjust treatment. In social movements, direct experiences can provide people with information leading them to an understanding of the strategic politics of a campaign.[76] The high school protest and its aftermath were examples of experiential learning: a political demonstration had resulted in the integration of a movement's cultural and political ideals.[77] The school meeting helped to forge a political consciousness among the Marks community that things needed to change. Locals were prepared to challenge the hegemonic practices, values, and expectations that governed life in Marks; they were "not for turning back." The symbolism of the street demonstration and the school boycott set the tone for the campaign in Marks. The SCLC principle that the "community level is where things really count and where people really grow" was vindicated in practice.[78]

Before they departed for Washington and while en route, the Marks contingent learned together in workshops, mass meetings, and demonstrations. Their individual and collective experiences provide unique perspectives on the impact and enduring legacy of the PPC. The experience of earlier campaigns had taught organizers that "understanding the causes of political disfranchisement, social and economic inequities . . . proved to be the basic motivation for involvement."[79] The SCLC used grassroots educational efforts to reach "southern disadvantaged blacks" in Marks.[80] Typically, there were two mass meetings each week in the small town from early March 1968, as well as two workshops as part of an adult education program.[81] Those with no previous experience of campaign participation, who would form the main body of people traveling to Washington, were encouraged to attend. With the planned occupation in D.C. in mind, the primary focus was on providing opportunities for participants to reflect on the causes and manifestations of poverty and to explore how to take nonviolent action to force the government to address those issues.[82] The emphasis on nonviolent tactics reflected the importance of putting into practice the politics and values for which King and poor people were struggling. Andrew Young led the first nonviolence workshop in Marks.[83] The wagon master of the

Mule Train, Willie Bolden, declared, "It was necessary to teach all these new folks the freedom songs, along with nonviolent tactics. . . . It seemed like everybody turned out for these meetings. People were fired up, and we were trying to give them proper direction."[84]

The workshop's pedagogical approaches drew from the SCLC Citizenship Education Program (CEP) principles. The facilitators began with the issues of concern to local people. In his important research, author Charles Payne described the importance of the "organizing tradition" in southern civil rights campaigns, which helped to develop leadership potential in those marginalized by society.[85] This tradition played out in Marks also as workshop leaders drew from rural black culture. Bernice Robinson, the first CEP teacher at the Highlander Folk School in Tennessee, observed that the most important thing she said to students at a new class was "I am here to learn with you."[86] The writings and practices of famed Brazilian educator Paolo Freire offer insights into the approaches to learning adopted in Marks. Freire stressed the importance in learning situations for everyone involved to "help each other grow . . . mutually in the common effort to understand the reality which they seek to transform."[87] Participants were encouraged by the SCLC to "look and then go back for more discussions, then another look and more talk with each other about what you saw and learned about the political process."[88] The workshops in Marks arguably gave local people effective access to knowledge and information, which assisted them to begin to challenge the status quo of poverty and discrimination through the medium of the PPC.

The various activities prepared the people who planned to head to Washington. The marches, demonstrations, and workshops in Marks helped to encourage a common desire for change among the participants and a confidence that they could bring it about. Personal testimonies highlighted the connection between learning and both individual and collective action. A mother of five children living on minimal welfare payments declared that her family was "starving to death. Something needs to be done now—not after a while, now."[89] Bertha Burres Johnson captured the new levels of understanding and the fresh attitudes of determination and defiance in stating that "they are tired of being on these plantations—being poor and not being given their equal rights. So we're going to Washington to let them folks up there know that it is time they treated us right and we ain't gonna take it no more."[90] CEP organizer Dorothy Cotton of the SCLC stressed the importance of the counterhegemonic role of citizenship classes. She observed that they were designed to help "empower" demonstrators and to remove the mental programming that put forth the notion that the government was all-powerful and alien. In her view, the citizenship classes brought participants to "a new place, a new consciousness."[91]

Cotton also noted that people had to "unbrainwash" themselves from the idea they were inferior to others. This idea was particularly relevant to the situation of the black community in Marks, which had experienced generation after generation of racism and discrimination. Freire again offered useful insights on this issue: culture, including history and geography, usually only belongs to the colonizers. He observed that "the history of those colonized was thought to have begun with the civilizing presence of the colonizers."[92] In order to challenge this dominance, Freire argued that "a decolonizing of mentality" was required.[93] Amid extremely challenging circumstances, the PPC helped to bring about a gradual change in the mind-set of people in Marks and to instil a confidence that they could challenge oppression, poverty, and their manifestations in Quitman County and beyond.

Social movement research suggests that those who get involved in civil rights campaigns often ascribe greater meaning to what they had previously thought were possibly only personal or individual problems.[94] Many in Mississippi now understood that they shared the burden of poverty with others. Margaret Wiley, age twenty, from Lambert, Mississippi, wrote that "because the march is for poor people and is for a cause, everyone will have a yearly income and a decent place to live."[95] Ezra Hampton wrote that he wanted to go to Washington "to help to do all I can. We have poor white people here; we are fighting for poor people."[96] The New York Times quoted Marks resident Harry Smiley: "one reason I want to go, is if all towns are like this one, we need to go."[97] Helen Jean Holt wrote, "There are so many people without jobs, and so many of their children don't have clothes to wear to school or any other place. I came out of school with nothing to do."[98] Like so many others, Helen and her family suffered from multiple forms of deprivation. Locals rejected the idea that the poor were responsible for their own poverty. A young person in Marks observed, "Some of the things we learned have taught us that poor folk ain't the stupid ones and besides what could be more stupid than to say somebody deserves to be poor?"[99]

The organizing of the Mule Train provides another example of how the campaign was not inefficient and chaotic, as is often alleged. Organizers addressed the catering of meals and supplying other basic needs of the people undertaking the long trip, as well as those of the animals. A PPC meeting in March 1968 highlighted the resources required for the Mule Train journey to Washington. They included toilet facilities, blacksmith support, mechanics, food and water for travelers and the mules, medical support, laundry, and places to stay en route.[100] Academic staff from institutions in Alabama and other professionals helped to make the covers for the wagons.[101] Ralph Abernathy wrote that the biggest "headache" was the mules. Finding enough mules to make the journey was the first problem. Very few farmers still used mules by 1968, and it took an extensive effort to locate and buy thirty of them.[102] The next problem was getting them shod; several of the mules took exception to wearing shoes. Blacksmiths were hard to find. Even after one was hired, some of the stubborn mules refused to cooperate.[103]

In addition to the Mule Train, some were planning to travel by bus and car from Marks to Washington. The Mule Train was scheduled to head for D.C. in early May. The SCLC reported that Ralph Abernathy planned to march out of Memphis, Tennessee, on May 2 to Marks, where he would hold a mass meeting two days later. The initial plan to head out of Marks for the first destination of Greene County, Alabama, on May 7 was delayed.[104] Due to a combination of bad weather, the aftermath of the King assassination, vandalism when someone cut the fence, allowing the mules to scatter everywhere, and other logistical challenges, the Mule Train did not depart for Washington, D.C., until May 13, 1968. It eventually set off for Batesville and stopped for the night at Mr. Thompson's farm.

As the Mule Train hit the road, it represented the hopes and desires of poor people. Everyone was "on message" and ready to face the uncertainties that lay ahead on the trip. The Mule Train's wagon master, Willie Bolden, noted that "we got folks to understand that this was not going to be an easy journey. It had never been done before. We didn't know of anyone in our time that had undertaken such a task. We were going to have to stick together."[105] Fifteen wagons started the journey. The wagons contained "as many poor people as they'll carry now they are sure nobody's going to turn them around,"[106] including Lee Dora Collins, a mother of thirteen. One hundred of the travelers were poor people, and there were fifteen staffers. They spanned the generations: the youngest was eight months and the oldest was seventy years; twenty children were under the age of thirteen, and more than forty of the travelers were female.[107]

The presence of so many women and children helped to place the PPC's demands for legislation in a gendered context. Those on board, by their very presence, drew national attention to the needs of the family. Women and children provided a powerful antipoverty message, which resonated all the way to Washington. Even before the Mule Train had departed, low-income women from the Mississippi Delta had presented evidence to U.S. Senate hearings in Memphis, which highlighted hunger and health issues.[108] Of the three hundred people who completed PPC registration forms for the state of Mississippi, the majority were female.[109] Their presence was also indicative of how the PPC brought disparate groups together in a common cause. Many of the women were affiliated with either the Mississippi Freedom Democratic Party or the Child Development Group of Mississippi. Women were also involved in different administrative aspects of the Mule Train. Marjorie Hyatt maintained records of supplies, Faye Porche looked after expenses, and Bertha Burres Johnson recorded details about the participants.[110]

The SCLC reported a "carnival atmosphere" as children gathered to view the mules at the start of the journey to Washington.[111] The wagon drivers even "practiced mule-talk" together.[112] With a sense of mischief and to the delight of onlookers, the Mule Train organizers tweaked the noses of the segregationist Mississippi senators by naming the lead mules after them: Stennis and Eastland. According to Ralph Abernathy, the Eastland mule was named because it was old and forgetful; the Stennis mule was stubborn.[113] Abernathy himself sat in the lead wagon as it left Marks. The people on board, through their own life experiences, represented the issues that had emerged in discussion and reflection in Mississippi, which consequently shaped and informed the demands presented to the legislators in Washington. As recorded by the SCLC, the demands embraced a range of civil and human rights, including unemployment and underemployment, a lack of decent housing, and a discriminatory welfare system. Added to this list were the high cost of food stamps, a lack of access to decent education, and inadequate federal programs with local people denied real participation in their management at the grassroots level.[114] Marks resident Joy Miller said that she was going to Washington for "freedom, better houses and better clothes and food."[115] A mother of six, Rosetta Hart, recorded that she was "not able to eat a balanced diet; get jobs and pay, nor medical care. I am not able to pay my bills, my house needs fixing, I cannot keep warm in the winter. These are just some of the reasons I want to go to Washington."[116]

Political slogans emblazoned on the sides of the wagons allowed the Mule Train to reach out to the communities it passed through. The slogans powerfully encapsulated the core campaign messages. They included a celebration of King and the enduring hopes of activists with messages such as "I Have a Dream." The inherent dignity of the travelers and the religious commitment of many of them were celebrated with "Don't Laugh Folks, Jesus Was a Poor Man" and "Jesus Was a Marcher." One message reflected the determination to reach the goal of the nation's capital. It stated simply, "The Mule Train—Washington DC Bound." Other slogans commented on the government's policy priorities: "Which Is Better? Send Man to the Moon or Feed Him on Earth?" Another message articulated the fundamental human rights demands of the campaign as devised by Dr. King: "Everybody's Got a Right to Work, Eat, Live." As it journeyed on, the Mule Train implicitly and explicitly had a pedagogical function to inform onlookers and the press about the focus and significance of the campaign and, at the same time, question the inequities of capitalism.

Spirits were high as the Mule Train set off. Ralph Abernathy claimed that it was a joyous occasion. Television reporter Jean Smith was impressed but later recalled that some of the passengers sat stone-faced or appeared fearful at the prospect of what lay ahead. Freedom songs rang out, and everyone took solace from the fact that trustworthy people would be waiting at every stop en route to look after them.[117] On the first day on the road, the people on the Mule Train ignored the hostility of a few whites. The travelers were feeling good as they arrived for their first overnight stay,[118] but constant rain during the first few days of travel threatened to weaken resolve. The distance of only sixty-five miles to Grenada took three days.[119] The caravan experienced few problems from local officials as they traveled through Mississippi, Alabama, and Georgia. A strong bond of camaraderie built up among those on board. People gifted radios, televisions, food, and toys as the Mule Train passed by.[120] Aside from some harassment from passing cars and spectators, onlookers were generally welcoming as the Mule Train continued to Atlanta. In one frightening episode, however, shots were fired from a passing automobile; fortunately, nobody was injured.[121]

Mississippi State University students waved good luck banners demanding an "end to the war against the poor."[122] Other spectators bore no malice but were amused as the Mule Train passed by. The *Clarksdale Press Register*, for example, reported on May 18 that the people of Grenada reacted "as though it were a circus parade passing through and so far no incidents of consequence have been reported."[123] The forces of the state, especially the FBI, took a much more serious view of what they perceived to be the threat posed by the Mule Train to national stability. All of the different caravans were monitored on their journeys, but the Mule Train attracted a lot of attention, presumably because it was rarely out of the headlines. Author Gerald McKnight pulled no punches in arguing that the intrusive surveillance techniques of the FBI were "unworthy of a democracy and reminiscent of abuses by unchecked secret police of authoritarian regimes."[124] Remarkably, the FBI assigned fourteen agents and one supervisor plus used a network of informants to keep an eye on the Mule Train twenty-four hours a day.[125]

The mules struggled in the hilly terrain between Montgomery and Birmingham, Alabama. This stretch of highway had billboard images of King at the Highlander Folk School in Tennessee proclaiming him to be a communist. Fourteen of the wagons remained to plow on to their destination in Atlanta, where everyone would catch the train to Washington, D.C. Some participants left the Mule Train, and others joined at the rest stops. This changeover replenished the caravan with fresh energies and allowed some to head for home having played their part in the historic initiative. Local media captured the stops in each community. Associated activities at each staging post included regular demonstrations, which both educated the public about the campaign and provided the oxygen of publicity.

At each of the Mule Train stops, local organizers provided resources and support for the poor people and the mules. Local organizers for all the caravans traveling to Washington played crucial roles by setting up contacts on the way and providing clothes, blankets, food, medical attention, and places to sleep.[126] Everyone on the Mule Train had three meals per day, more than they could have afforded at home. Their arrival in each community bolstered existing groups and even helped create new groups.[127] The NAACP in Alabama requested that local branches assist the Mule Train throughout the state.[128] On June 6 in Birmingham, the Mule Train stopped at the historic Sixteenth Street Baptist Church, where the local NAACP officials looked after their needs. Later, the stop in Birmingham would remain in the memories of those on the Mule Train for the worst of reasons. Senator Robert F. Kennedy had been shot in Los Angeles the day before, and he succumbed to his wounds in the early morning of June 6. Now, both King and Kennedy were gone. The Reverend Jesse L. Douglas led a memorial service in Birmingham. Everyone was bereft at the death of Senator Kennedy so soon after Dr. King's assassination. However, the marchers were emboldened and even more determined to finish their journey in memory of those who had been lost. The recent killings became a "source of inspiration."[129]

The only serious opposition experienced by the Mule Train was in Georgia. The Georgia State Patrol met the caravan at the Georgia state line. Captain J. H. Cofer reassured the campaigners that he was there to provide "safety and escort." The Mule Train camped for the night at a local school in Douglasville. Curious residents drove past the location while others watched from vantage points surrounding the school.[130] The Humane Society, concerned about the condition of some of the mules, unsuccessfully offered to buy five of them. Police advised the campaigners that they would escort them, and they could use any route to Atlanta with the exception of Interstate 20. The police stated that for safety reasons, Georgia law prohibited the operation of nonmotorized vehicles on interstate highways. Having been able to travel on interstate highways in Mississippi and Alabama, the marchers were in no mood for compromise. The Mule Train carried on to Interstate 20, where they met a wall of police officers stretched across the road. Arrests followed of sixty-seven demonstrators. Ralph Abernathy, traveling with another caravan at this point, was contacted and informed that members of his family were among those arrested in Georgia. The marchers fell to their knees to pray before being taken away by police in small groups. Wagon master Willie Bolden was not among those arrested because "someone had to stay out of jail."[131]

Georgia governor Lester Maddox announced that the marchers had been arrested for their own safety. They were well treated while in custody in the National Guard Armory in Douglasville. A local restaurant provided them with food. SCLC staffer Andrew Marrisett held a press conference attended by several newspaper correspondents and television crews. In explaining the actions of those on board the Mule Train, Marrisett stressed the Kingian messages of nonviolence and the moral obligation to disobey unjust laws.[132] Maddox was one of the last remaining segregationist governors in the South and had little sympathy for the civil rights movement. In a rabble-rousing quote printed in the Memphis *Commercial Appeal* on May 3, Maddox had staked out his position on the demonstrators. He had accused them of "courting revolution," alleging that they were encouraged by the communists to bring America to its knees.[133] With the Mule Train now in his own backyard, Maddox was determined to pass along the problem as quickly as possible to someone else's jurisdiction. He offered to provide flatbed trucks to pick up the mules and wagons and transport them to Atlanta. To accept such an offer would have defeated the point of the Mule Train in the first place, however. The visibility of the Mule Train traveling sedately on the highways had already captured the attention of the public and media in ways that even the most optimistic demonstrator could not have imagined.

According to activist Tyrone Brooks, the SCLC threatened to build Resurrection City in Georgia unless Governor Maddox was more cooperative with the Mule Train.[134] A federal court order found in favor of the demonstrators, and all charges were dropped. The Mule Train continued its journey in the emergency lane of the highway. The contrast between the Mule Train and the behavior of white political structures, as represented by the police and the governor in Georgia, helped to further transform and empower the poor people traveling in the caravan. Social movement theory has shown that for marginalized groups, the experience of conflict can lead to learning, and it has the potential for growth and development.[135] The very act of participation in the historic effort also brought the group together. Bolden observed that it was fitting that the Mule Train had been temporarily halted in a county where there was little economic opportunity for most people.[136] He also stressed that the unity of the participants was evident in the manner they faced down the challenges and obstacles placed in their path. He observed, "If these people never accomplished anything else in their lives, they accomplished this."[137]

The inevitably slow pace of the Mule Train brought the advantage that unlike those traveling to Washington in buses, cars, and trains, the Marks contingent was constantly visible and could not be ignored by the public or the press. The mules managed to travel an average of twenty-five miles each day.[138] Inevitably, the imperative to get to Resurrection City in time to participate in the planned demonstrations became acute. The decision to complete the journey from Atlanta by train brought some criticism that somehow the poor had failed to meet their objective. In contrast, for the participants, the Mule Train represented a willingness of everyone concerned to undergo hardship and disruption to their lives and those of their families in pursuit of a common goal. Mule Train activist Joan Cashin later reflected that it was easy for outsiders to criticize the campaign. She chose instead to focus on how the whole experience had enlightened and empowered her. She observed that "the effort it took just to get the wagon train together, the people who [were] willing to take this very hard ride, and the symbolism of what it really mean[t] to take mules instead of Cadillacs, these are the most important things to me. Rather than being able to say the mules walked every mile of the way between Marks and Washington."[139] The train journey on the Southern Railway cost the campaign $1,500, a large sum with so many other bills to pay.[140]

The Mule Train was the last of the caravans to make it to Washington, and it arrived by train from Atlanta on June 17, 1968. Thirteen wagons, twenty-eight mules, and four horses remained of those that had set out from Marks, and they were unloaded at the old roundhouse at Duke and Henry Streets in downtown Alexandria, Virginia, along with 150 campaigners from the Mule Train, 80 percent of whom were children or young adults. They disembarked singing "Ain't Gonna Let Nobody Turn Me Around" and immediately boarded buses for the trip to the Northern Virginia Baptist Center in Gainesville, Prince William County, where they stayed for the night.[141] Several local people helped the campaigners who had stayed behind to unload the disassembled wagon parts from the boxcars; they completed the job in about two hours with the aid of floodlights on an Alexandria rescue truck. Veterinarians examined the mules and horses at an improvised corral at the Southern Railway freight depot. Five mules were lame or harness-burned and were taken to a Humane Society farm in Waterford, Virginia. Despite the lameness and burns, the animals were in generally good shape.[142]

Everyone joined together again with the mules on June 18 to make a conspicuous entry into Washington, D.C. Thousands of other demonstrators were already there; indeed, many who had been living in Resurrection City had already departed for home. The short journey of the Mule Train into Washington from Alexandria represented the true fulfillment of King's dream to bring the poor to the nation's capital to dramatize the issue of poverty. The *Washington Post* heralded the caravan's arrival with the ungenerous headline "Rickety Mule Train Plods in to Wait for March."[143] The symbolism of the Mule Train and those on board contrasted sharply with the visible signs of wealth along the highway: advertising signs, expensive cars, and anxious and frustrated commuters in line behind the wagons. The Mule Train traveled north from Alexandria on the George Washington Memorial Parkway to a National Park Service maintenance area near the west end of Memorial Bridge in Virginia. Traffic lined up behind the Mule Train as police shepherded the group in the curb lane on the northbound side of the parkway. The procession moved along steadily with only two disruptions. A wheel rim broke off one wagon, and later a frustrated driver in line behind the last wagon shouted angrily at the activists. A police officer stepped in as youths from the Mule Train challenged the driver to get out of his car. The six-mile trip took three hours.[144]

The Mule Train should have arrived in Washington just in time to take part in Solidarity Day on June 19, the main high-profile day of protest and celebration during the occupation of Washington. However, this last leg of the Mule Train was called off because it would have caused too much "confusion" in the march.[145] The campaigners from the Mule Train instead took part in Solidarity Day without the mules. Anxious to get more involved before the D.C. phase of the campaign was over, some of the Mule Train participants moved into Resurrection City and others into a local church center. By the time of their arrival, much had already occurred during the occupation of Washington. Poor people from different racial backgrounds had been demonstrating for several weeks. But Resurrection City had only a few more days to go before Washington authorities would tear it down.

CHAPTER 7

THE COMMITTEE OF 100

B y late April 1968, the stage was set for Dr. Martin Luther King Jr.'s last wish: to make poverty visible through the presence of the poor in the nation's capital. Before the first caravans began to arrive in town on May 12, their elected representatives to the Poor People's Campaign had already been busy in the nation's capital. The Washington, D.C., phase of the PPC began with the lobbying of Congress over a three-day period from April 29 through May 1, 1968, and the presentation of campaign demands to the different agencies of the U.S. government.[1] A series of press conferences helped the campaigners get their message across to the wider public. This first phase of the campaign in Washington was led by an advance guard known as the Committee of 100.

Two-thirds of the Committee of 100 consisted of representatives of the poor from all over the United States (four from each project), and one-third were national civil rights leaders.[2] Operating under the leadership of the new SCLC president, Ralph Abernathy, the Committee of 100 included Mexican Americans, Puerto Ricans, Native Americans, black and white poor spokespeople, and representatives of religious organizations, labor unions, and peace and interracial support groups. Their diversity demonstrated King's success in pulling together a multiracial coalition prepared to stand together in solidarity. The majority of those involved had attended his Minority Group Conference in March 1968. Their ranks in Washington included well-known and lesser-known names, such as Mario Abreo of the Retail, Wholesale and Department Store Workers of the AFL-CIO; Barbara Brown from Welfare Rights for Cleveland; William Marks Franklin from the Mississippi Freedom Democratic Party; Rose Crow Flies High from the North Dakota Tribal Council; Charles "Buck" Maggard from the Appalachian Volunteers; and Corky Gonzales from the Crusade for Justice in Denver, Colorado.[3] Their cause was given added weight by a Citizens Board of Inquiry report issued earlier in April, which found concrete evidence of "chronic hunger and malnutrition" in every part of America where the group had held hearings and organized field trips.[4]

Unlike previous civil rights campaigns, which sought a single piece of legislation, the PPC's demands were for the development by the federal government of new, costly economic and social policies.[5] The precise nature of the demands was the subject of much discussion from the time of the PPC launch in December 1967 to the arrival of the Committee of 100 in Washington, D.C. The debate then continued through the end of the occupation of Washington by the poor in late June 1968. Bayard Rustin, for example, advised that the demands should be broad enough to ensure some could be won in the short term. In June, he came forward with what he thought was a more achievable set of demands than those advanced by King's successor as president of the SCLC, Abernathy. Press reports sided with Rustin in describing his specific demands as a "concession to reality" by comparison with Abernathy's "nameless demands for an instant millennium."[6]

Opinions varied on the specific demands as individuals and organizations representing the many different faces of the poor had their say on what they wanted to achieve from the campaign. Appalachian regional coordinator Ernest Austin suggested that everyone was looking for something different. While there was consensus on broad areas, such as jobs and income, the political and philosophical differences between the groups were never completely resolved. Austin said this caused him to think about what constituted the "movement." On the one hand, he asserted, there were those talking about changing the whole system because it was corrupt, and on the other hand, there were poor black people from Mississippi who did not see the system as that bad but were angry because they were locked out of it.[7] Many of the poor people who joined the campaign simply wanted what everyone else in America already had. The SCLC observed that it was after "nothing special. All we want is an opportunity with all other Americans to live and work and play, to vote and get an education and be promoted, to fight for our country and hope to be President like everyone else."[8]

The PPC coalition eventually agreed on demands for legislation to address a range of human rights and civil rights issues, including food, housing, welfare, education, and jobs. The main demand was for an Economic Bill of Rights to apply to every citizen, an idea first floated by King in 1964. This included a meaningful guaranteed job with a livable wage, a secure and adequate income, the ability to access land for economic reasons, access to capital for the less well-off, and citizens to have a large role in the government. The campaign also highlighted specific "attainable" goals, including the creation of one million public service jobs; the adoption of the latest Housing and Urban Development Act; the repeal of punitive welfare restrictions; additional funds for antipoverty programs; expanded food distribution; and collective bargaining rights for farm workers. Other important demands—for example, for land and fishing rights—reflected the particular needs of the various racial and cultural groups of poor people involved in the campaign. The campaigners dismissed the potential cost of the demands as missing the point on the basis that their cause was just. They called on the federal government to "qualitatively increase its planned social investments" although the "basic issue was not budgetary but political and moral."[9]

On Saturday, April 27, 1968, the PPC steering committee met in Washington to discuss the strategies, actions, and campaign demands. This committee consisted of SCLC staff, representatives of each geographical area involved in the campaign, and representatives of minority and ethnic groups. The Committee of 100 met the next day to plan its presentation of demands to government officials and congressional leaders. On the morning of Monday, April 29, the Committee of 100 sang freedom songs as the members left the Church of the Reformation on Capitol Street to begin their work. They fanned out across government departments to press their demands for legislation in a range of domestic policy areas. The group was putting the government on notice, giving legislators ten days to prepare their responses before the main nonviolent army of the poor arrived in town. The late Dr. King's influence loomed large. Ralph Abernathy proudly declared that the poor people's presence in Washington was the "last great dream of the Reverend Dr. Martin Luther King Jr., martyred President of the SCLC." He added that they were there to give "conspicuous and detailed witness to the poverty and degradation that rob millions of Americans of their human dignity."[10]

In each presentation to the different government departments, a statement of demands was read, which was followed by testimony of the poor on "how it was" to be destitute in a land of abundance. Thomas Offenburger of the SCLC rejected criticism that the demands as presented were unclear. They were plainly written out and presented to the various government departments.[11] Over a frantic three days, the representatives of the poor had the opportunity to meet with some of the most powerful legislators in the country. At times, cabinet officials were reported to have been kept waiting, while some were referred to as "Brother." Delegates often stayed beyond their allotted times.[12] The specific PPC demands were targeted at the appropriate government departments and agencies. Hunger, housing, education, justice, and welfare were all considered in their turn. The nature of the demands, the composition of the group, and the use of language represented the multiracial coalition that had first come together at the Minority Group Conference in Atlanta in March 1968.

Primed by the National Welfare Rights Organization (NWRO), the Committee of 100 focused its fire on the welfare system. Jesse Jackson read a statement on welfare, describing it as "immoral and disgraceful." He called for an end to unjust welfare laws that led to the humiliation and harassment of mothers and their children by denying them even minimal support. Various regulations often prevented them from getting even a pittance from the system. Jackson called on the government to "simplify, humanize and remedy" the worst aspects of the welfare program. He demanded that the states assist families with unemployed fathers, and he made it clear that no woman should be compelled to work in the absence of adequate daycare for her children.[13] W. Willard Wirtz, the secretary of labor, listened patiently as campaigners rejected the stereotype of the "undeserving poor" who preferred to live off welfare. They wanted him to do more than just "talk about the plight of the poor."[14]

The campaign's focus on hunger brought attention to the Department of Agriculture. Democrat Orville Freeman, the secretary of agriculture, listened intently as Ralph Abernathy cited the government's own reports, which showed clear evidence of acute malnutrition and hunger among families in the Mississippi Delta. Describing the situation as a "national disgrace," Abernathy demanded an end to the farm subsidy program, which paid farmers not to cultivate crops while children starved across the country.[15] On related health issues, Andrew Young and Bernard Lafayette reminded Democrat Wilbur Cohen, the secretary of health, education and welfare, that they were spokespeople for the many Americans "whose poverty does not stop at their pockets but shows up in the state of their health."[16] Damning statistics were produced to show that the infant mortality rate was twice as high among black babies as among whites. Lafayette shamed America, "a rich nation with the most advanced medical knowledge in the world," where some children had never been examined by a doctor or a dentist. Drawing from his experience in the Chicago slums, Lafayette reminded his audience that poor people lived in open contact with serious health hazards, including rats and other vermin, accumulations of garbage, and sewage lines and water lines so close together that their contents sometimes mingled. He demanded "adequate medical care for every citizen," an issue that resonates to this day in U.S. political discourse. Lafayette provided a list of demands, including the expansion of Medicare, effective access to existing health services, comprehensive neighborhood health centers, and improved health care for mothers and children.

The meeting with members of the Senate Subcommittee on Employment, Manpower and Poverty on April 30 typified the high drama of the proceedings. Housing and the living conditions of the poor were on the agenda. Present were Senators Ralph Yarborough, Jennings Randolph, and Claiborne Pell from the Democrats and Senators Winston Prouty and Jacob Javits from the Republicans. Democratic senator Joseph Clark chaired the meeting. Ralph Abernathy, Andrew Young, and Bernard Lee led the SCLC contingent. Corky Gonzales represented the interests of the Chicanos. Several poor people provided testimony at the hearing; they shared the common bond of poverty, but each had personal experiences to impart. They included Robert Fulcher, a poor white man from Appalachia; Lores Tresjan, a migrant farm worker from upstate New York; and Victor Charlo, a Native American from Montana. Lola Mae Brooks, a black woman, was from the Mississippi Delta. Another black woman, Phyllis Robinson from Providence, Rhode Island, represented the NWRO.[17]

In his opening comments, Ralph Abernathy informed the senators that his group represented the poor of all races whom Dr. King had described as "too often forgotten, hungry and jobless outcasts in this land of plenty."[18] He challenged the notion that the representatives of the poor were being unreasonable and unfair in their demands, asking why poor people should continue to care for a country that had so little regard for them that it did not provide for their basic needs for survival.[19] He also detailed the typical squalid living conditions of different races and ethnic groups in every part of the United States. Abernathy argued that few of his fellow Americans "knew or cared" about the inadequacies of housing programs in the "reservations, [the] migrant camps, the shacks and lean-tos in rural Mississippi and Alabama, the teeming ghettos and barrios of the North and West where we and our children are literally perishing."[20] He called on Congress to pass legislation providing for thousands of new units of low-income housing, to support the rent supplement program, and to help poor people to be homeowners rather than "slum renters."[21]

Each poor person had five minutes to deliver their individual testimony. Some went over their time limit. Their presence and their evidence helped to humanize poverty to the lawmakers. Housing and employment dominated this part of the proceedings. The legislators heard of how "children were bitten by rats" and were packed into "barren cubbyholes" with their health threatened by roaches and garbage.[22] The housing issue was also pursued, for example, with Robert Weaver (Democrat), the secretary of the Department of Housing and Urban Development. Urging the Department of Justice to ensure vigorous enforcement of existing fair employment regulations, the campaigners alleged that different racial groups, including black people, Mexican Americans, Native Americans, and Puerto Ricans, experienced illegal discrimination in the areas of employment, housing, and education. They called for action against labor unions and employers that failed to comply with the laws on hiring, training, and promotion.

The Indo-Hispano representatives drew deeply from their historical and cultural roots in shaping their case to elected representatives. Rafael Duran presented his community's demands to Dean Rusk (Democrat), the secretary of state. Duran urged enforcement of the provisions of the Treaty of Guadalupe Hidalgo of February 1848, which guaranteed the cultural and land rights of the Spanish-speaking peoples of New Mexico, Colorado, Arizona, and elsewhere.

Sparing few sensibilities in his choice of language, Duran informed Rusk that his people were victims of a "criminal conspiracy" by "Gringos" to take their land.[23] The theft of their land had left the Indo-Hispanos "powerless" to change their situation and had driven them to the migrant labor fields and cities. Taking full advantage of the opportunity to speak for those he represented, Duran charged that "poverty and city living under the Anglos' colonial system has castrated our people's culture, consciousness of heritage, and language." Consequently, he alleged, they were in an "under-developed condition creating thereby a psychological retardation."[24] Duran echoed King in demanding that action be taken on a range of human rights issues. These included decent living accommodations in a communal style, quality education delivered in schools with "inviting" facilities, Spanish to be the first language in those schools, and a curriculum reflecting the cultural heritage of the Indo-Hispanos, including their contribution to the building of America. In addition, on behalf of his people, Duran called for the return of all "property," including minerals, water, timber, and grazing rights. Jose Ortiz, a Puerto Rican from New York, and Maria Varela from New Mexico added weight to Duran's presentation by condemning the inadequacies of War on Poverty programs.[25]

Both Reies Tijerina and Rodolfo "Corky" Gonzales later complained that their demands on behalf of their peoples were ignored, especially after the death of Dr. King. However, reflecting the multiracial approach of the PPC, it seems that their demands were center stage as the Committee of 100 went about its work. Gonzales informed the Department of Health, Education, and Welfare that the "faulty and regressive educational system of our country has long discriminated against the Mexican American people of our nation." He claimed that Mexican American students and other Mexican American people suffered psychological ethnic destruction through the "overwhelming brainwashing machine called education."[26] Gonzales made a series of related demands on cultural issues in education. He said that the curriculum in all schools should include the history of Mexican American peoples, demanded free education as compensation for the treatment of his people, and said that bilingual instruction should be provided in all areas of education. Other groups also raised the issue of education.

Black representatives, for example, urged affirmative and systematic litigation against northern and southern school segregation.

The Committee of 100 included a contingent of Native Americans. Among their ranks were Rose Crow Flies High, James Bluestone, Melvin D. Thom, Andrew Dreadfulwater, and Hazel Harold.[27] On April 29, 1968, Mel Thom met Bertrand Harding, interim director of the Office of Economic Opportunity, in the Brown Building. Thom was twenty-nine and was director of the National Indian Youth Council. He advised Harding that young people were tired of white interest groups telling them "what to think, to be, and how to act."[28] Native American representatives also met with Department of the Interior staff on May 1, 1968.[29] Ralph Abernathy introduced activist Victor Charlo as "my red brother" at the meeting.[30] The attendees included Secretary of the Interior Stewart L. Udall (Democrat); Ralph Abernathy; Robert L. Bennett, commissioner of Indian affairs; and again Mel Thom. Thom read the opening statement and included King's analysis of "internal colonialism" in his comments. In his position as a representative of the Indigenous peoples of America, Thom asserted that they "were not begging" but had come to Washington to demand what was rightfully theirs. He pulled no punches in describing the Interior Department as "racist, immoral, paternalistic and colonialist."[31] In common with the representatives of other groups, Thom took his lead from the late Dr. King in making the argument that the time had come for radical change. He declared that Native Americans needed to be "heard, not just listened to, or tolerated, the oppressed can be oppressed only so long."[32]

King's influence was also evident in the meeting with Dean Rusk. In the luxurious splendor of a State Department auditorium, poor people asked Rusk why their sons should die in Vietnam when their families lacked freedom at home.[33] Native American activist Martha Grass attacked the shortcomings of the War on Poverty, which led to hunger and unemployment in Indigenous communities, and also slammed the immorality of U.S. foreign policy.[34] The Native Americans' demands had their roots in dealings with the federal government stretching back to the nineteenth century and even earlier. They called for compliance with the legal treaties between tribes and the federal government. One speaker observed that "citizenship is not something you sell for trinkets, blankets and beads."[35] Another key demand was for fishing rights: Washington state was accused of "extinguishing" the legitimate rights of Native Americans to fish for salmon.[36] The Committee of 100 representatives argued that the canning industry accounted for 80 percent of the salmon catch, but "conservation" was used as a pretext to deny Native Americans their legitimate fishing rights.[37] Fish-ins were organized in Washington state while Native Americans demonstrated in Washington, D.C., during the PPC.[38]

Finally, the demand for citizen participation in government programs was a key element in many of the presentations to government agencies. The issue mirrored King's analysis of the "powerless poor": those who had no voice and no influence on the various factors shaping their life circumstances. Reflecting his insights into the powerlessness experienced by residents in the Chicago slums, Bernard Lafayette demanded genuine citizen participation in the planning of housing programs designed to help the poor.[39] The Office of Economic Opportunity (OEO) came in for particular scrutiny on this issue. President Lyndon Johnson had established the OEO to act as the engine of the War on Poverty; however, as Dr. King often alleged, it became a political football and was increasingly starved of funds. The backlash against the poor from 1964 on had undermined Johnson's original commitment to the principle of maximum feasible participation in War on Poverty programs. Community action agencies were supposed to be developed and administered by local people. But politicians alleged that Black Power advocates and other subversives had taken control of projects at the local level to forward their own agendas. Republican representative Paul Fino was on record saying that the federal government had taken complete leave of its senses in bankrolling black segregationists.[40]

King's long-voiced criticisms of the War on Poverty were evident in Andrew Young's presentation. When Young spoke to acting director Bertrand Harding (Democrat), he declared that the OEO, supposedly created to serve poor people and give them the power and money to speak and act for themselves, had failed on all fronts. Young made no secret of his disappointment with that organization, which had been conceived to provide a "doorway into American society." He called for citizen participation in the daily operations of the OEO, including appeals procedures and support for jobs, and representation of the poor on the OEO Citizens Advisory Council. In the view of the PPC leadership, citizen participation was the key to success in government programs. Young cited the positive example of the Child Development Group of Mississippi, where local people were involved in the planning and action of the initiative. Significantly, the Native American representatives wanted to go way beyond mere citizen participation; as proud "Nations" they demanded respect for "sovereignty and self-determination."[41]

PPC campaigners made the most of their time in the spotlight in late April and early May 1968. They secured valuable and quality meetings with the leading politicians in the land and put forward their demands. The voices of the poor were heard at the heart of political power. They exercised their rights in a participatory democracy. The different racial and ethnic groups came together under the common badge of poverty, as King had hoped. One disappointment was the relative lack of interest shown by the press in the proceedings. Very few of the campaign's soundbites found their way into the articles. In fairness to the journalists, they were sometimes shut out of the meetings.[42] Only *Jet* and the *Washington Post* paid much attention.[43] *U.S. News and World Report* was less than balanced in its coverage, commenting on the temerity of the Committee of 100 in keeping elected representatives waiting for them. One article noted that the delegates' "demands were high, their words blunt, and their attitudes often angry," and the author interpreted their demands as "threats."[44] *Newsweek* accused "Abernathy and Co." of making a "shambles" of Washington protocol by keeping Attorney General Ramsey Clark waiting for four hours and Secretary of Labor Willard Wirtz for two. Abernathy refused to apologize for being late for meetings, declaring, "We've been waiting on the white man for 300 years and today we just decided to let them wait on us." *Newsweek* also reported that the meetings turned into "free-form finger waggling oratorical jam sessions."[45] The same article did, however, restore a sense of proportion in its content by acknowledging that the plight of poor people represented a "pressing item of unfinished business."[46] Whereas militants often grabbed the headlines, even they could not drown out the testimony from witness Mrs. Alberta Scott, a "tiny Baltimore black lady in a cotton frock and a shapeless straw hat pulled down to her ears." Scott told the Senate subcommittee that she was sick, and her disabled husband was unable to work. She lived in a slum house filled with rats, roaches, and water leaks.[47]

The efforts of the Committee of 100 represented only the opening salvo in what would become a nonviolent war of attrition. After an exhausting and comprehensive three days of hearings and meetings, Ralph Abernathy reported that congressional leaders were sympathetic but made no guarantees or promises.[48] Abernathy made the best of it, arguing that Washington had "learned from this first great outpouring, unpolished but profound, of the cries and groans of poor people."[49] But he wanted action, not platitudes. He left D.C. on May 1 announcing his intention to return with thousands of demonstrators. In a parting comment, he promised to deliver the most militant, nonviolent, direct action campaign in the nation's history.[50] As events would unfold in Resurrection City later in May and into June, some activists would become frustrated with the SCLC leadership for holding back on King's commitment to civil disobedience. For the moment, however, as the Committee of 100 left Washington, the potential threat of direct action was enough to put the city on high alert, and citizens and politicians alike steeled themselves for the arrival of thousands of demonstrators beginning on May 12. Only weeks after the Washington, D.C., riots following King's assassination, the prospect of thousands of poor people coming to town added to anxiety levels. More broadly, student unrest at Columbia University, anti–Vietnam War protests, and demands for social and political change heightened the tension in Washington and added to a siege mentality.

The various apparent threats to law and order in 1968 also opened the door for those keen to raise the political temperature to advance their own standing. Republican presidential candidate Richard Nixon argued that university disruption, for example, heralded a revolutionary struggle.[51] Nixon could look across the globe beyond the United States for evidence to support his theory. In Paris, left-wing students called for a new social order. Weeks of demonstrations, including worker strikes against alleged political and social oppression, eventually brought the French economy and the country as a whole to a halt. The Prague Spring in Czechoslovakia demanded freedom in Eastern Europe.[52] The planned occupation of Washington by the PPC threatened a perfect storm for residents of the city. In a national context hostile to the idea of the lower classes converging on the capital, conservative distaste for the PPC was obvious. Senator John Stennis of Mississippi called for a blockade of the poor.[53] Conservative Republican senator Strom Thurmond warned that the demonstrators were not coming to petition, but to "intimidate and hold out the threat of violence."[54] Democratic senator Jennings Randolph alleged that communists were behind the PPC.[55] The press contributed to the tense atmosphere in advance of the arrival of poor people in the nation's capital. The *Washington Daily News* editorial on Monday, May 13, claimed that the city had a "sense of foreboding" about the campaign. The editorial writers hoped that poor people would understand their campaign was "political," and this meant they did not have a license to do anything that came to mind, especially considering the riots in Washington one month previously.[56] This article was part of a general narrative that viewed the PPC as a potential threat to peace and stability.

As the authorities prepared for any eventuality, lurid headlines grabbed everyone's attention in the nation's capital. In early May, a series of Washington bus robberies and the murder of a driver led to a wildcat transit strike and added to the sense of crisis across town.[57] The police department placed its Civil Disturbance Team on standby, and troops at nearby Maryland and Virginia bases were set to move, if needed, against the arriving poor people. The Defense Department also was prepared to bring in troops from other states. Army undersecretary David E. McGiffert promised a subcommittee chaired by Senator John L. McClellan (Democrat) that federal troops were ready to carry out a "detailed disturbance" plan, and the Pentagon was prepared to bring a very large force, if necessary, to deal with unruliness. Attorney General Ramsey Clark, who had supported the SCLC license application to set up camp in Washington and was sympathetic to the marchers, confided to the same subcommittee that no disruption of government business or of individuals would be permitted.[58] Speaking on the ABC television network, Clark said that he did not expect any violence but warned that civil disobedience would be met with "adequate law enforcement."[59] Yet the attorney general had long thought that crime and civil rights were closely linked, and he was sympathetic to the King agenda. In April 1967, Clark had urged America to move forward to tackle the problems of education, employment, housing, health, and poverty.[60] One year later, as caravans of poor people approached Washington, D.C., Clark helped to allay fears among the public by talking up Ralph Abernathy as an apostle for nonviolence. He also offered support for the campaign by acknowledging that the demonstrators had an important message to convey, and he hoped they had an opportunity to communicate it. Clark was keen to avoid events like the eviction of the Bonus Army marchers from Washington in 1932. The Justice Department under Clark's direction coordinated all dealings between the executive departments and the PPC representatives.[61]

There was some positive news for the campaigners as thousands were heading for Washington, D.C. On May 7, Hollywood rallied behind the cause of poor people, and a group of prominent entertainers pledged support for the PPC. Their voices helped to get the campaign messages across to the public and added to the pressure on politicians to play their part by passing legislation. Actor Jack Lemmon promised to donate half of his $1 million pay for his next film to the campaign. Coretta Scott King addressed the gathering and rejected media suggestions concerning potential violence in Washington by describing her late husband as an "extremist for good" only. The rally was chaired by Harry Belafonte, one of many still grieving over King, whose death, he claimed, placed his own life "up for reinterpretation."[62] In Washington, government employees formed committees in their places of work and raised money for the campaign. They also donated tools to aid the construction of Resurrection City and later provided sandwiches each evening for the residents.[63]

An overview of public opinion also reported some support for government intervention to address poverty—if protesters behaved themselves.[64] However, there was apparently only limited support for the necessary spending to combat poverty among a public already frustrated by the state of the national economy, high taxes, the rising cost of living, and crime, including urban unrest. A successful outcome to the demands of the PPC did not look promising as the poor people began to arrive in Washington, D.C.

CHAPTER 8

THE POOR ARRIVE IN WASHINGTON

Activity at the local and regional levels across the United States eventually led to caravans, dubbed "Freedom Roads," making the journey in May 1968 to Washington, D.C. All modes of transportation were utilized, including buses, trains, cars, and the iconic Mule Train. The nine major caravans were the chief mobilization channels for people in regions across America: the Eastern Caravan, the Appalachia Trail, the Southern Caravan, the Midwestern Caravan, the Indian Trail, the San Francisco Caravan, the Western Trail, the Mule Train, and the Memphis Freedom Trail.[1] The Eastern Caravan started in New England and went down the eastern seaboard; the Midwestern Caravan began in Milwaukee, Wisconsin; and the Indian Trail in Seattle, Washington. The Appalachia Trail started in West Virginia, while the Western Trail had groups that started from San Francisco and Los Angeles, California, as well as New Mexico, Texas, and Oklahoma, which eventually met up for the final leg to Washington, D.C.[2]

On May 2, Ralph Abernathy led a rally in Memphis, Tennessee, to officially inaugurate the Poor People's Campaign.[3] Following an emotional ceremony at the Lorraine Motel, the Freedom Trail started its journey to D.C. From early May 1968, much activity continued across the United States as poor people made the journey to the nation's capital. Each person on the caravans contributed to the historic effort through their willingness to make America a better place, as visualized by Dr. Martin Luther King Jr. and the leaders of the other racial groups. The idea was for each caravan to attract publicity and attention for the PPC as they made the journey to Washington. Whites from Kentucky, West Virginia, Virginia, and Tennessee were especially prominent on the Appalachia Trail caravan, for example.[4] Doug Blakey of the National Community Union was one of the organizers in Appalachia. Coordinator Ernest Austin suggested later that bringing people together helped participants to understand that they shared the common bond of poverty. Before then, he said, the PPC people in Kentucky did not know what was going on in West Virginia, and people in West Virginia had little idea of what was going on in Tennessee.[5]

The caravans proudly proclaimed the multiracial nature of the PPC coalition. The Mule Train from Marks, Mississippi, attracted most of the media attention and provided the dramatic images much coveted by the press. However, those on board the Mule Train came almost exclusively from southern black communities so that press attention "risked reinforcing a radicalized and regionalized study of poverty."[6] In addition to the relative neglect by journalists of the Minority Group Conference at Paschal's, King's success in building a multiracial coalition went largely unrecognized.[7] In particular, the three western caravans, the Western Trail, the San Francisco Caravan, and the Indian Trail, received only modest press attention.[8] This meant that the sacrifices and endurance of many blacks, whites, Mexican Americans, and Native Americans who made the three-thousand-mile journey to Washington were not adequately acknowledged then or, arguably, since. The Western Trail, for example, drew from mobilization efforts in California, New Mexico, and Oklahoma and brought Mexican Americans and Native Americans to Washington under the PPC banner.

Ralph Abernathy was present at the departure of the Western Trail from Albuquerque, New Mexico, on May 18, and he declared that white people wanted the protesters to turn to violence although those on board had no intention of doing so. The Southwest PPC chair, Reies Tijerina, blamed "enemies" in the news media for a relatively poor turnout at the march that preceded the departure of the buses. Mad Bear Anderson of the Tuscarora nation also addressed the audience.[9] The activists departed from New Mexico in three buses. Three more buses joined them in Denver, Colorado, in addition to three from Los Angeles, and others joined from Texas and Missouri. Tijerina later recalled that twenty buses of Chicanos arrived in Washington.[10] Photographer Karl Kernberger commented on the strong sense of purpose among the participants on the Western Trail.[11] At every overnight stop, the Western Trail organizers maximized publicity for the campaign and made the poor visible by holding a rally, a demonstration, or a symbolic march.[12] On their arrival in Kansas City on May 20, the demonstrators marched through the slum districts alongside Chicano militants, Black Panthers, and Brown Berets. Their contrasting feelings of both "elation and unease" intensified as they drew close to the nation's capital.[13]

The Eastern Caravan mobilized in seven cities across the Northeast and included a large contingent of Puerto Ricans from New York. A conference in New York preceded their departure for Washington. Eighty organizations attended, including the National Council of Churches, the United Federation of

Teachers, the American Jewish Conference, CORE, NAACP, and the National Urban League.[14] The Eastern Caravan joined two thousand supporters for a march in Trenton, New Jersey, to show support for proposals by Governor Richard Hughes to aid welfare mothers. Trenton was the fifth stop on their road to Washington. Many of the demonstrators at the Trenton march were students who were offered the option not to attend classes if they wished to join the rally at the state house.[15] Four youths were arrested following a minor scuffle that was quickly brought under control.[16] A march through Philadelphia, Pennsylvania, attracted huge crowds.[17] The Reverend James Orange hailed Philadelphia on May 15 as the best turnout they had experienced: five thousand marched from a North Philadelphia parking lot to join another five thousand assembled near historic Independence Hall.[18] The crowd marched six abreast and included many children and mothers pushing baby carriages. Ralph Abernathy assured the participants that the PPC intended to stay in Washington until Congress provided jobs and a guaranteed income for everybody. The activists stayed overnight in specially erected large tents in a North Philadelphia area where rioting and looting had taken place in 1964. The situation in 1968 was much more serene. Sandwiches and box meals were handed out.[19]

During the caravan journeys, protesters took time out to have some fun and to bond with their fellow travelers. The twenty buses on the Eastern Caravan left Baltimore, Maryland, for Resurrection City on May 16 after a reported "rollicking night of rock-soul music and Go-Go girls" at the Black Masonic Temple.[20] Several dozen police officers and the police commissioner waited outside the hall, ready to deal with any trouble. The Reverend James Orange, dressed in symbolic baggy blue farm clothes, expressed confidence that the militant young people in his group were under control, would adhere to nonviolence, and were committed to the campaign. He claimed that the militants even referred to white people as "brothers." According to a newspaper report, James Bevel delivered an "antiwhite" speech at the temple, telling his audience not "to help white America to kill off the colored race in Vietnam." The columnist added, however, that Bevel declared his support for nonviolence because "he loved too much to kill anyone."[21]

The Southern Caravan started out from Selma, Alabama, in early May and consisted of 392 people traveling in seven buses and ten cars.[22] Before leaving the city, it stopped in symbolic homage at the Edmund Pettus Bridge, the site of the brutal treatment of protesters by Alabama state troopers in 1965. *Time* magazine reported that Abernathy broke down and wept when delivering a speech in memory of Dr. King. A woman began singing "Jesus Got All the Power" in response.[23] In a gesture of reconciliation, the demonstrators sent a telegram expressing their condolences to Governor George Wallace of Alabama on the death of his wife, Governor Lurleen Wallace.[24] The Southern Caravan later experienced difficulties and holdups en route. An estimated 425 participants arrived three hours behind schedule in Greenville, South Carolina. Undaunted, everyone then took part in a rain-drenched four-mile march to the county hall.

Delays also plagued the Midwestern Caravan. Five hundred poor people departed from Chicago and Milwaukee on May 8.[25] They rallied at the Stone Temple and the Liberty Baptist Church, and then left for a planned four-day stay in Washington.[26] Heavy rain and news of a short-term shortage of housing at Resurrection City hampered their efforts to make progress. Father James Groppi, a "militant open housing priest" from Milwaukee, commended the local people in Pittsburgh, Pennsylvania, for providing accommodations.[27] Detroit mayor Jerome Cavanagh welcomed the Midwestern Caravan when it arrived in town and offered everyone his "physical and moral support."[28] Detroit saw the largest PPC march yet, which was led by a youth from the ghetto carrying a sign announcing "I Have a Dream" with a rat attached to it. Cavanagh apologized to the demonstrators for police violence on May 13, when officers rode horses into the crowd. Five people received treatment for their injuries at a local hospital.[29] But neither weather, resistance, nor the rigors of travel dampened spirits among most of those heading for Washington. As time went on, the numbers at the marches and demonstrations at stops en route grew larger as word spread of the imminent arrival of a caravan in town.

The caravan tactic created an "underground railway," a channel linking the protesters' home communities with the destination of Resurrection City and the return journey.[30] As with the Mule Train, each caravan relied on the preparations made for their arrival at stops en route: arrangements for accommodations, food, medical care if required, publicity, demonstrations, and marches. All of the caravans benefited from the commitment and dedication of innumerable groups and individuals. The Western Trail, for example, drew on the support of key organizers in several cities, including Seattle (Ann Stever), San Francisco (Cassandra Davis), and St. Louis (Mark Harrington). The Eastern Caravan was headed up by, among others, the Reverend Gil Caldwell in Boston, Massachusetts; the Reverend Albert Perry in Providence, Rhode Island; and Edith Savage in Trenton, New Jersey.[31] In New York, the contacts for participants included Jessie Gray of the Tenants Rights Party; the Reverend M. L. Wilson of the Convent Avenue Baptist Church; and M. Rollins, Jimmy Collier, and F. Fitzpatrick of the National Committee of Black Churchmen.[32] Jimmy Webb directed the Baltimore project under the supervision of James Orange. Joseph Hammonds assisted Ben Mack and others in pulling South Carolina together. The Reverend Thomas E. Gilmore supported the campaign in Alabama.[33]

As the first caravans approached the nation's capital on May 12, construction of the camp, Resurrection City, originally known as City of Hope and then Dream City, had not yet commenced. Ralph Abernathy claimed that the name Resurrection City seemed appropriate after King's death; he viewed it as a living memorial to the late leader.[34] Abernathy hoped it would be a model for the rest of the nation to emulate. Comprehensive and impressive arrangements were in place to look after the needs of thousands of protesters. Later criticism that Resurrection City was a fiasco and a shambles presented a harsh and limited view of the camp. While organizational problems arose, especially as time went on, press reports failed to take account of the extensive arrangements put in place to support those planning to live in the temporary community. The design of Resurrection City came under the auspices of the Structures Committee, which consisted of architects and planners, including John Wiebenson from the University of Maryland and Kenneth Jadin from Howard University in Washington, D.C. This group worked with other committees with responsibility for food, medicine, procurement and storage, services, transportation, legal aid, and nonpoor involvement.

The committees operated under the direction of Tony Henry.[35] Henry wanted to ensure that whites did not dominate the chairing of the various committees. To avoid this, he established a superstructure: a group of coordinators who each had three to eight committees working under them.[36] Their overall brief was to build a camp at low cost and in a short time. The biggest challenge, of course, was the requirement to create a sustainable and working small city within Washington to meet the needs of thousands of poor people. The Southern Christian Leadership Conference hoped to create something on a scale never seen before in the history of social movements. To a significant extent, it managed to do just that. Resurrection City provided a pedagogical living space where people came together and learned about each other and their shared issues. It also served as a base where the residents planned and launched daily demonstrations at government buildings and elsewhere.

During its brief existence of only six weeks, Resurrection City had a basic infrastructure, and attempts were made to offer many of the facilities found in larger permanent urban centers. The normal city functions of maintenance, sanitation, supplies, information (scheduling, communications, mail), security (police, fire protection), transportation, health services, food services, childcare, and recreation were all addressed.[37] Resurrection City also had a city hall, a healthcare center, a childcare center, a bakery, a barbershop, its own zip code (20013) and mailbox, its own red-and-white flag, and in recognition of the importance given to learning, a Poor People's University (PPU), Freedom Schools, and a library.

The SCLC worked intensively to prepare for the grand opening of the temporary city in Washington, D.C. The General Services and Administration Committee had oversight of many of the logistical aspects of daily life in Resurrection City. The chair was Al Gollin, and the committee members included Don Mercer, Mike Finkelstein, Faye Zigmond, and Krista Thie. It coordinated the work of subcommittees looking after different Resurrection City functions. These New City subcommittees focused on housing and transportation, building structures and layout, childcare, entertainment and recreation, food, Freedom Schools, nurseries, medical services, sanitation, administration, site selection, workshops, and mass meetings. Working groups with specific responsibilities led on issues such as legal aid to provide legal defense for those arrested during the campaign, legislative research to provide information on proposed and current laws, and public relations.[38] The College Committee developed ways to involve students in the campaign.

The Fund-Raising Committee was tasked to secure enough money to pay for what was the most expensive campaign in the history of the SCLC. King had employed William Rutherford, a former businessman and journalist, to head up SCLC finances.[39] SCLC staff member Stoney Cooks took over the role as part of a general reshuffling of staff later in the campaign. PPC national director Bernard Lafayette was put on the spot about campaign finances at press conferences.[40] During the opening days of Resurrection City, Lafayette announced that $3 million was required to see the campaign through the end of June. When Abernathy retracted this statement, the press seized the opportunity to criticize the apparent lack of communication between campaign officials.[41] Lafayette, however, was correct in his assessment of the pressing need for funds. Efforts continued to find money for the bills even weeks after Resurrection City was torn down. In one notable example, Barbra Streisand, Harry Belafonte, Bill Cosby, and Herb Alpert headlined a PPC benefit concert on July 17, 1968, at the Hollywood Bowl.[42]

The creation of Resurrection City was a remarkable achievement by any standard. Various sites for the camp were initially considered, including Rock Creek Park. One of the early favorites was the airport because it had asphalt, toilets, restaurants, and good access. The details of private discussions about the arrangements appeared in press reports. Tunney Lee, one of the designers of Resurrection City, later revealed that they were continuously monitored by the FBI, which leaked their plans to the press.[43] On March 10, the site for the camp on the Mall was selected on the basis it would be "easiest to handle."[44] Tunney Lee said that nothing happened regarding specific construction planning until after King's assassination.[45] Following five days of negotiations with the Interior and Justice Departments, the General Services Administration, and the District of Columbia government, Walter Fauntroy secured a license for the camp for a temporary period—until June 16. The SCLC was required to post a $5,000 bond to ensure that the grounds would be restored after the campaign ended.[46] An extension to June 23 was eventually granted although no further time was allowed beyond that. The license conditions included a limit of three thousand for the camp population.[47] The historic location for Resurrection City, in the symbolic shadow of the Lincoln Memorial, brought added resonance to the campaign. However, because the campsite was in the heart of tourist areas, it drew criticism that the presence of poor people blighted the landscape.

Resurrection City was described by Lee as an example of "classic modernist" city planning. Designers organized the residential areas into clusters, like neighborhoods, with communal services along a spine. The main axis down the middle of Resurrection City was intended to be more public, like a Main Street.[48] The city hall was situated in the middle of Main Street so that it would be accessible to as many residents as possible since it had telephones, welfare services, and security. The city was divided into administrative units to carry out the many functions. They consisted of three communities of 1,000 people each, broken down into neighborhoods of 250 people each, and further subdivided into blocks of approximately 60 people.[49] Underpinning this model was a desire to build a living and breathing community in which people would communicate and relate with each other in solidarity. Given that the camp residents were poor people who were often alienated from the broader society, the SCLC hoped to promote a sense of connection between them to achieve "a resurrection of the living concept of community."[50] Everyone was encouraged to think of the importance of service, to be responsible to and for others in the camp. Marshals, for example, were instructed not to take on the characteristics of the police by imposing power indiscriminately on people, but to recognize that their authority derived from the residents.

King's analysis of the powerless poor also shaped a determination to facilitate the participation and involvement of the residents in Resurrection City's community affairs. Each tent or hut, with a maximum of five tenants, had one designated representative who reported problems and followed through until the problem was resolved.[51] Decisions on the running of Resurrection City were eventually made by a city council consisting of representatives of each minority group and each geographical area in the camp. Ben Clarke, a veteran SCLC staff member, held the position of city administrator and was responsible for acting on the city council's decisions. He said that his job was to "phase himself out" and train community representatives to take over the running of the city council.[52] Meetings in the city hall in Resurrection City allowed space for all voices to be heard. The SCLC recognized that the "experiment in city government" did not always work, since residents had no experience of participation in decision-making, but it was felt that everyone learned from trial and error.[53] The SCLC leadership was reportedly divided on the extent to which camp residents should have a say in running Resurrection City. Tony Henry alleged that James Bevel and Al Sampson were resistant to the idea of democratic decision-making in the camp on the basis that the "slaved don't make decisions."[54] As it turned out, time was limited given that the camp was forcibly closed down after six weeks.

In anticipation that up to three thousand poor people would live in Resurrection City at any given point, the SCLC issued guidelines to ensure everything ran as smoothly as possible. The registration procedures met a variety of medical, legal, and administrative needs.[55] All prospective residents of Resurrection City were required to go through orientation, registration, and, where necessary, a medical screening before settling in to the New City. Hospitality centers, mainly churches, served as registration facilities, although a special booth was set up near the entrance of Resurrection City for late arrivals and those who came to Washington on their own.[56] Hospitality centers also offered new arrivals in D.C. a place to clean up, rest, and have snacks. The SCLC attempted to provide everyone who came on the various caravans with a supply kit, including soap, toothpaste, a toothbrush, a hand towel, and a washcloth. To cite just one example of what happened with new arrivals, a caravan group of 113 men, women, and children from Marks, Mississippi, were received at Our Lady Queen of Peace Catholic Church in Arlington, Virginia. They were well looked after. The children rode around on tricycles donated by parish members while the adults smoked and watched television. The youngsters washed in tubs at the church while adults went to the YMCA and YWCA to clean up.[57] This particular group won the right to be among the first in Washington because of the large number of elderly people and children in the group. The majority expressed confidence that they could persuade Congress to do something "big" for them after politicians had heard their pleas.[58]

Streams of volunteers, mainly white women, helped in the churches and other reception venues. Louise Winfield, in charge of the reception center at Central Presbyterian Church at Sixteenth and Irving Streets NW, typified the attitude of volunteers in acknowledging that although she was middle class, she wanted to do everything she could to help poor people achieve their goals.[59] All arrivals at the hospitality centers were issued a wristband bearing their name and home state and an SCLC identification card, and they were required to complete a registration form. Volunteer typists and registrars took every arrival through the paperwork. The forms contained basic personal data, including name, address, age, gender, marital status, details of other family members in Resurrection City, religion, home contact, D.C. contact, special issues (for example, diabetes or medication needs), date of arrival, and planned date of departure. Groups were assigned to specific locations in Resurrection City.

Busloads of new arrivals were transferred from the hospitality centers to Resurrection City on an organized basis, in order to prevent "bunching up."[60] Arrangements were in place to ensure that anyone who was not medically fit was supported by social services.[61] Alternative housing to the wooden huts in Resurrection City was available in cases of emergency and for out-of-town students who assisted in various tasks, including recruitment for the campaign, construction of Resurrection City, research, and publicity.[62] Students also joined the demonstrations and assisted at the campsite in a number of other ways, for example, babysitting, fund-raising, and letter writing.[63] The main vehicle for student volunteers was the Summer Task Force project, which prepared them to undertake educational work in Resurrection City.[64] Both black and white students had made significant contributions to previous SCLC campaigns and were a valuable resource for the PPC.[65]

The available data on what became a fluctuating population of Resurrection City provide a useful snapshot of who actually came to Washington to join the campaign. Authentic impoverished people came in the thousands. Bernard Lafayette asked, "Who are these people? They are those who walked from the muddy roads of Mississippi to the muddy roads of Resurrection City. They are those who have journeyed far. They have planted themselves by the Reflecting Pool, until the nation [begins] to respond to poverty."[66] The overall figures of those registered to live in Resurrection City varied from day to day. They were not all there at the same time, of course; otherwise, the camp infrastructure would have collapsed. No daily census was taken, making it difficult to keep track of the comings and goings.[67] Some stayed for a few days and then decided to head for home; arrivals and departures were a feature during the life of Resurrection City. In the first days of the occupation, for example, the *Washington Post* reported that eighty-year-old Lee Buck from Lambert, Mississippi, had packed up to go home almost as soon as he reached Resurrection City.[68] Campaign leaders viewed early press reports of discontent in the first few days as an attempt to undermine the PPC. Reports of people leaving did not consider the arrival of others to replace them.[69] Lafayette asked at a meeting on May 15 if anyone wanted to go home; no hands went up.[70] One report said that the same meeting, called to formulate a new system of government for the camp, turned into a "spirited rally with freedom songs and several emotional speeches."[71] James Bevel conceded that three people had decided to leave by May 16, but only because of illness. On further questioning, Bevel acknowledged that a few people who were homesick and missing their families wished to go home soon after arrival. He was confident that within a short period of time this was less likely to happen. The SCLC, he said, intended to build "group dynamics" and "interpersonal dynamism" in Resurrection City to create a spirit of community.[72]

The official SCLC count of 6,312 protesters included caravan members and those who were resident in the camp for more than a weekend or a night. Al Gollin noted that the gathering of data on those who came to Washington was "unique in the history of social protest movements. It will help to document accurately the character of those whose presence in Washington sharply posed the problem of poverty to the entire nation in the spring of 1968."[73] The data drawn from the PPC registration documents completed by participants in Marks and elsewhere support the proposition that Dr. King's aspiration to mobilize the "hardcore" poor to come to Washington was realized. Many were from the poorest communities in the nation. Registrants came from forty-seven states and a scattering of foreign nations. The South contributed more than one-third of the total, reflecting the strength the SCLC had built there in earlier campaigns. The influence of the churches in particular areas provided not only a spiritual and philosophical basis for the struggle but also access to members and networks. Urbanization and migration in the United States in the post–World War II period had significantly increased the resources available. For example, the concentration of black people in urban centers made it easier to spread word of the campaign and to organize in large cities. Efforts to forge alliances with other organized groups representing the many faces of poverty paid off with 41 percent of those registered coming from groups other than black people.[74]

The 6,312 people who registered included Mexican Americans, Puerto Ricans, blacks, whites, and Native Americans. Just over half were between thirteen and twenty-four years old; the median age was twenty-two. This high percentage of young people reflected well on Dr. King's aspiration to involve them in the campaign.[75] There was a greater concentration of whites in the younger age range; they were thought to be college students or dropouts from society. Three-fifths of the participants were men, and 63 percent were unmarried. Baptists were the largest religious grouping, followed by Catholics and Protestants. At the same time, thousands of PPC participants who did not live in Resurrection City were not registered on the official rolls. They included some who stayed in alternative accommodations. The majority of Mexican Americans and Native Americans, as well as some whites and blacks, moved into the privately owned Hawthorne School in Washington, rather than Resurrection City. In general, Native Americans were said to be "sparsely represented by comparison with other groups, with fewer than 500 in total who, in addition, kept themselves physically apart."[76] But they were an active, vocal, and highly visible group whose presence was magnified by the press. Reporters dashed forward to interview and take photographs of anyone in Indigenous garb, hunted down anyone with a "funny" name, and even made jokes about "Indians on the warpath again."[77]

Also not included in the official count were fifty thousand activists, including several thousand Puerto Ricans, who came from across the nation to take part in the high-profile PPC mass multiracial demonstration: Solidarity Day on June 19, 1968. Many volunteers were not registered, including healthcare professionals, some students, members of religious groups, people who disappeared from caravans, some participants who came for a weekend or a day, and prominent people who did not go through formal registration.[78] Religious community members, including priests, nuns, and laypeople from Catholic Worker Movement houses, offered their support on-site.

The first large caravan, the Freedom Train, pulled into Washington, D.C., on May 12 from its final stop in Danville, Virginia, carrying around five hundred people from the Deep South, including the first people from Marks, Mississippi, who were not traveling on the Mule Train. They had the assignment to start building Resurrection City.[79] They were directed to the reception center at All Souls Unitarian Church at Sixteenth and Harvard Streets.[80] Their arrival at the church at 2 p.m. was greeted by an assortment of anxious officials, curious passersby, and impatient reporters.[81] The mainly youthful group from Marks shouted "Freedom" and "Sock Soul" from the bus windows. SCLC staff member J. T. Johnson suggested that they rest after the long journey. However, many refused to take a break, prompting Johnson to say, "Freedom fighters do not get tired."[82] After a quick snack, some of them joined a march led by Coretta Scott King and then prepared to begin the construction of Resurrection City.

More poor people arrived in the following days. The Midwestern Caravan from Chicago carried a large number of young members of street gangs, including the Blackstone Rangers, many of whom had worked closely with King during the Chicago campaign and who now enlisted as marshals alongside other gang members, including the Commandos from Milwaukee. The thousand-strong Midwest campaigners were among those who had been told to delay their departure from Pittsburgh until accommodations were found for them, since housing construction was still under way in Resurrection City.[83] The instruction to hold off had caused resentment and even some defections among the mainly black people from Chicago, Detroit, and cities in Ohio. However, their delayed arrival was a relief to Resurrection City authorities, who wanted to be certain they were ready to accommodate all arrivals.[84] They finally arrived in Washington on May 15 and were taken to the reception center at Saints Paul and Augustine Church, 1715 Fifteenth Street NW. But some became angry at the further delay at the reception center given their desire to head straight for Resurrection City.[85]

A minority of members of the Saints Paul and Augustine Church were unhappy about hosting street gangs.[86] The church auditorium had to be cleaned after they left, and there were reports of drinking.[87] A group of church leaders met with the Reverend Walter Fauntroy, one of the top PPC officials in D.C., to discuss their anxieties about the large numbers seeking temporary accommodations in churches.[88] However, the churches overall in Washington were welcoming and supportive, and few other problems were reported. The Interreligious Council in D.C. backed the PPC and delegated three clergymen to assist the campaign.[89]

With all the arrangements in place, the stage was set for the campaign to begin in earnest. It was now time to test King's conviction that it was possible for thousands of poor people from different racial backgrounds to share the same space and work together for the common good. Much would depend on the organization of daily life in Resurrection City.

CHAPTER 9

BUILDING RESURRECTION CITY

Beginning on May 12–May 13, 1968, Martin Luther King Jr.'s dream to bring the poor to Washington, D.C., was realized. Although robbed of the chance to greet the impoverished people who traveled from every region in the United States, he remained in the hearts and minds of those who made the long journey to dramatize the issue of poverty. Poor people came to the nation's capital because King and the leaders of the different racial groups had inspired them with a vision of a more just and equitable America and because together they now really believed they could make a difference. Against formidable odds, including opposition from politicians and members of the public, attempts to sabotage the campaign by forces of the state, and tremendous logistical and physical challenges, a multiracial coalition of thousands of poor people from the most deprived communities in America arrived to fight a nonviolent war against economic injustice. Their presence in Washington had extra poignancy because some in the movement believed that Dr. King had been assassinated precisely because he was moving against a racist economic system. Charles Cheng, for example, who organized some of the educational activities in Resurrection City, maintained that King was killed because his plans to mobilize the masses of all racial backgrounds, including whites, represented a threat to the status quo.[1]

The arrival of the first wave of poor people on May 12 coincided with a Mother's Day march in Washington led by the recently widowed Coretta Scott King. Hundreds of participants received an early taste of what was to come in Washington by joining Mrs. King on the march, which was sponsored by the National Welfare Rights Organization (NWRO), a partner of the Poor People's Campaign. The twenty-block march made its way through the riot-scarred Cardozo area where only weeks previously protesters had threatened to lay waste to the district in the wake of the King assassination. Described as a display of "woman power," the event highlighted the plight of "welfare mothers" and typified the crucial role played by women at all stages and levels of the PPC.[2] It helped to frame racism and discrimination to include poverty and the associated areas of home, family, and community. The NWRO later estimated that 73 percent of the women in Resurrection City were poor and working-class welfare recipients.[3] The demonstrators protested pending amendments to the Social Security Act, legislation that threatened to delay federal aid for children with no father in the home and required mothers on welfare to seek work or job training.[4]

Having set off at 3:30 p.m. from the John F. Kennedy Playground at Seventh and O Streets, the march concluded with a rally at the Cardozo High School football field. An estimated crowd of 3,000–3,500 protesters came prepared with posters and buttons bearing a variety of slogans: "New York PPC," "Organize for Poor Power," "Our Children Go to Bed Hungry and Get Up Hungry." In another example of how successful the campaign was in building a multiracial coalition, the demonstrators included representatives of the Puerto Rican, Native American, white, and black communities. Some of the marchers grabbed the attention of onlookers. Native American Cliff Hill sported a full headdress, which he took off when it rained. The hard-core poor people whom King had so desperately wanted to recruit were present in significant numbers. According to reports, the procession included middle-aged black women wearing white dresses and red carnations, elderly men in work clothes, and small children trailing behind their mothers.[5] The march also included women who received Aid to Families with Dependent Children.

Among the marchers was Josie Williams, who came from Marks with her seven children, who ranged in age from two years to thirteen years old. She was looking for a better home, a better job, and more money. She described Marks as "so broke" yet she paid a high rent "for a house not fit to live in."[6] Maxine Mack and Lillian Purdie saw the march as a means of getting better welfare legislation.[7] Brenda Walters, seven years old, had come by bus from Marks, Mississippi, with her mother and three brothers. Children were a visible and prominent presence throughout the occupation of Washington and as residents of Resurrection City; King would have been delighted with their commitment and resilience. As far as the Southern Christian Leadership Conference was concerned, the futures of those children and millions of others—indeed, the very future of the nation—depended on the reaction of the Johnson administration and Congress to their demands.[8]

At the end of the procession, Coretta Scott King entered the Cardozo High School football field flanked by Julie Belafonte (wife of Harry Belafonte) and SCLC aide Bernard Lee. The four King children were also there. Mrs. King shared the platform with Mrs. Belafonte; Ethel Kennedy, wife of Senator Robert F. Kennedy; Iris Cole Clark, wife of Senator Joseph S. Clark; and Jane Hart, wife of Senator Philip A. Hart. The microphones did not work at first, a minor incident that was reported by elements in the press possibly eager to undermine the campaign. With the problem resolved, Coretta Scott King, dressed in black and with her emotions still raw from the loss of her husband, set the tone for the campaign by asking the crowd to honor Dr. King's memory through adherence to the principles of love and nonviolence.[9] She spoke with great conviction. It is worth noting that Mrs. King had a long and distinguished record in her own right of fighting for social justice and against war. She understood poverty, having picked cotton in Alabama as a young child. At college, she was active in the NAACP, joined a race relations committee, and became a lifelong pacifist. Before she had even met her husband for the first time, King was active in Henry Wallace's Progressive Party, attending its convention in 1948. Its platform was a precursor of the issues Dr. King would address in later years. The convention supported an end to segregation, advocated for voting rights, and demanded national health insurance.[10]

Coretta Scott King was therefore a committed activist with a strong sense of social justice. At this crucial first event of the PPC in Washington, D.C., she denounced the forces of racism, poverty, and war. Quaker thinking, especially its advocacy of equal rights for women and of peace, influenced her for much of her life.[11] She had condemned war and nuclear weapons as early as 1961 and supported Women Strike for Peace and the Women's International League for Peace and Freedom.[12] Mrs. King was an early critic of the conflict in Vietnam and helped persuade her husband to call for a halt in the bombing.[13] Her speech to the crowd on May 12 drew from her own experiences and Dr. King's analysis of poverty. She denounced both war and the welfare laws in stating that "starving a child is violence, ghetto housing is violence, punishing a mother and her child is violence."[14] Mrs. King reminded everyone of the significance of Mother's Day and the importance of welfare rights for families. She argued that a discriminatory welfare system, which penalized families that had a man in the house, had accelerated family disintegration and therefore placed America's future well-being in peril. Reflecting Dr. King's inclusive vision for the PPC, she called on women of all backgrounds and races to "remake society based on the principles of love, justice and peace."[15] Finally, she highlighted the key demands of the PPC by calling for a job and/or a guaranteed income for everyone. When it was Julie Belafonte's turn to address the crowd, she received one of the biggest cheers for informing the government that if it did not change its ways, the protesters would "change [the] government."[16]

With the PPC now up and running, a second rally took place at Ebenezer Methodist Church in Washington on the evening of the same day, Sunday, May 12. Cliff Hill, again wearing traditional Native American dress, received a standing ovation as he welcomed everyone with the greeting "This is my country! I welcome you here." He referred to the genocide that had forced his people in the nineteenth century to journey from Georgia to Oklahoma.[17] The audience wore armbands emblazoned with the capital letter *A* to signify their status as the first proud PPC arrivals in D.C.[18] By the time the star, Juanita Abernathy, arrived, the church was rocking with freedom songs. Just like Coretta Scott King, Mrs. Abernathy was a lifelong activist in her own right and a member of the Women's International League for Peace and Freedom. She believed that this background in the peace movement had taught her the possibility of uniting women of all races "into an immoveable force whose strength could erase all semblance of poverty." Highlighting the gendered dimension of much of the campaign, Mrs. Abernathy described the PPC as a "marshalling of interracial womanpower."[19] Juanita Abernathy emphasized the importance of the PPC's multiracial coalition by informing everyone that the government in Washington was "frightened" because "never before have we been able to unite as a non-color body." The success of the campaign, she suggested, depended on the eradication of "the brainwashing" that had resulted in the "division of the races."[20] Aware of the risks many had taken in coming to Washington, Mrs. Abernathy encouraged the audience to stay strong and prepare for reprisals when they returned to the South. Pearlie Mae Byndum from Lambert, Mississippi, made a similar point. Her speech represented the experiences of many poor people who had made the arduous trip to D.C. Having worked in the fields since she was eight years old, she reminded everyone of the threats ordinary people faced in putting their heads above the parapet in support of campaigns for social justice. She said that she risked having her family thrown off the Mississippi plantation where they lived but added defiantly, "I will stay here as long as it takes to get results."[21]

Everything was peaceful on May 12 as the poor began to stream into Washington. Despite warm temperatures, the falling drizzle seemed to reflect the relatively low-key start to the historic campaign. One report noted the absence in the first march led by Coretta Scott King of the exuberant singing so often characteristic of previous campaigns.[22] In a taste of things to come, traffic was jammed bumper to bumper around the Lincoln Memorial and the Reflecting Pool campsite as tourists and Washington residents looked on. The scene was now set for the construction of Resurrection City to begin and for King's final wish to make the poor visible to take practical form.

The next day, May 13, was overcast and humid. The Reverend Ralph Abernathy, wearing blue denim workers clothes, presided over the historic opening ceremony for Resurrection City in West Potomac Park. The proceedings began with a prayer and an address to the assembled crowd by Bernard Lafayette, national director of the PPC. The roar of passenger jets could be heard overhead as he called on God to sanctify the sacred spot on which everyone now stood. Lafayette announced that people of every color had come to "arouse the conscience of the nation." The aim, he declared, was to move the heart of America and a "recalcitrant" Congress to do something about poor and disenfranchised people. In a moving reference to Dr. King, Lafayette declared his confidence that the lost leader was at that moment smiling down on them from heaven.[23]

His wife, Juanita, by his side, Ralph Abernathy then led the singing of "We Shall Overcome" followed by separate choruses of "White and Black Together" and "Red and Black Together," recognizing the different groups represented in the campaign. Native Americans, including Linda Aranayko (Creek), were formally asked for permission to use the land in acknowledgment of their status as the Indigenous peoples. With permission granted, the historic moment had arrived. Abernathy drove a symbolic golden stake into the ground to dedicate the site, and he declared that Resurrection City was now open. With each stroke of the hammer, the group around him chanted "Freedom, freedom!" Abernathy declared that people would come from all parts of the nation to this "hallowed sacred spot for the purpose of building a city, Resurrection City, U.S.A."[24]

Ralph Abernathy announced that they intended to stay a long time—until Congress acted on employment, underemployment, and other aspects of poverty. He reminded the audience that they were there to live together as one family and to build a "community of love and brotherhood." Abernathy's message was both militant and nonviolent, echoing the balance often struck by his lost colleague and friend Dr. King. He declared, "This is a nonviolent movement. We shall not destroy person or property. But we cannot guarantee anything more because we are going to plague the pharaohs of this country until we get meaningful jobs and a guaranteed annual wage."[25] While they had "killed the dreamer," they had not "killed the dream." To great cheers, Abernathy announced "no new business" by Congress until "old business was taken care of."[26] There were nearly as many reporters, photographers, television staff, and curious onlookers as there were participants at the ceremony.[27] Early images in some segments of the press were positive and spoke a thousand words. The *Washington Afro-American* carried a photograph of a Native American woman cradling a young six-year-old black boy with the caption "Tender loving care for six-year-old Carl Hill comes from one of America's original citizens."[28] Some members of the press were already critical of Abernathy, however. According to one report, he looked "exhausted and bewildered" as he was escorted by "officious marshals" to the site of the first wooden hut.[29] Abernathy was scolded, apparently, for not being Dr. King. He was described as not having King's "redeeming sense of an occasion" and for being "neither enlightening nor reassuring" about why the protesters were in Washington.[30]

The police kept their distance from the opening event. On the first day, many of the young marshals in charge of crowd control were not yet equipped with the light blue cotton windbreakers that would be their badge of office. The jackets had the word "Marshal" on them and two red bands on the right sleeve. A press report observed that the marshals wore boots and a "kind of hat identified with Stewart Granger in African movies."[31] They eventually worked thirty hours per week in three-hour shifts. The marshals were criticized for pushing people around in the early days of Resurrection City. Their actions undoubtedly soured members of the press. In one incident on May 14, a journalist claimed that a defiant seventeen-year-old marshal, Melvin Tate, had warned him that the marchers might choose not to adhere to nonviolence.[32] Aware that the eyes of the press, law enforcement officials, and Congress were on them, the SCLC recognized the need to maintain law and order in the camp. The plan was for anyone caught violating camp regulations to be dealt with on-site or handed over to the police.[33] The chief of security, Alvin Jackson, later complained that he received little support from superiors if he wanted to deal with someone accused of a crime.[34]

A small number of the marshals themselves posed disciplinary problems at different points in the life of Resurrection City. Some were sent home for unruly conduct.[35] In general, though, the SCLC leadership was pleased with the behavior and performance of most of the gang members who worked as marshals in the camp. SCLC staff member Al Sampson explained that the PPC had opened up a "creative nonviolent framework of reference for them to express their frustrations."[36] The so-called Tent City Rangers also provided security in the camp. Formed independently of the SCLC and the marshals, the idea for the Tent City Rangers came from twenty-eight-year-old bricklayer Johnny Patterson, who was allegedly later arrested for holding up a restaurant.[37] They wore white outfits and were mostly older black businesspeople. Patterson said they were there to help in emergencies. The marshals resented their presence and referred to them as the "Ranger big shots."[38]

Tensions with the press quickly came to the fore. Eager journalists claimed they were stonewalled in attempts to get quotes from some of the poor people. The SCLC was anxious to control and shape the coverage of the campaign because it was wary of potential negative headlines. Abernathy, for example, pulled back from launching the campaign with arrest-provoking tactics, prefer-ring to keep that option in reserve.[39] Inadvertently, Andrew Young, Abernathy, and James Bevel provided the early soundbites, the tone of which came to char-acterize press coverage. Appearing at an Education Press Association lunch at the Pitts Motor Hotel on May 13, Young and Abernathy confirmed that civil dis-obedience could include demonstrations inside the Department of Agriculture and/or the blocking of Potomac River bridges. Abernathy alleged that Dr. King was killed by a "mean and sick country," and he intended to carry on King's leg-acy by turning the country "upside down."[40] The threats of civil disobedience played into the hands of the opposition, providing a narrative of potential dis-order that the campaign found hard to shake off. Bevel added to the anxieties of politicians by reminding everyone attending the lunch of why they were in Washington. Quoting directly from King's radical rhetoric, Bevel stated, "It's a question of restructuring society so that everyone can share in what this country produces," adding that it did not matter how much the PPC's demands would cost the country.[41]

As the camp began to take shape, leading politicians came to see for them-selves what was going on. Vice President Hubert Humphrey, Mayor Ivan Allen of Atlanta, Mayor John Lindsay of New York, and Mayor Walter E. Washington of D.C. all visited Resurrection City hoping, through personal contact, to reduce the potential for unrest. Years later, Ralph Abernathy recalled that a young con-gressman, George H. W. Bush, who would become the forty-first president of the United States, also dropped in at one point.[42] Humphrey flattered demon-strators that their presence in Washington amounted to the "American way." Hemmed in by marshals, reporters, and onlookers, he informed James Bevel that the government would do everything it could to help. Bevel described Humphrey's visit to the camp as an "expression of concern." Mayor Washington described it as a "big step" toward reducing tensions, and he assured campaign-ers that not everyone was against them.[43] He rejected the idea that the nation's capital was gripped by fear and criticized the businesspeople in particular; he alleged that they had spread rumors about the poor.[44] Polly Shackleton, a city council member, wore a Poor People's Campaign button as she toured the site. Republican senator Charles Percy made a brief visit, chatted with workers, and drove a ceremonial nail into one of the huts. He expressed confidence that the city of Washington, D.C., was responding in an "imaginative way in making ad-equate provision" for the demonstrators.[45] He called on the country to be recep-tive, to listen, and to learn.[46]

Despite the well-intentioned interventions by Hubert Humphrey and others, the threat of violence remained a factor in the thinking of politicians. The arrival of poor people evoked trepidation and even fear among lawmakers. Democratic representative George H. Mahon of Texas doubted that the Appropriations Committee would be influenced one way or the other by the campaign's demands and warned, "We cannot legislate under threats of violence."[47] Democratic senator Herman Talmadge reassured his Georgia constituents in a newsletter that Congress would not legislate with a "racial gun in its back."[48] Staunch right-wing Republicans had little objection to listening politely to the concerns and complaints of their constituents, who may have traveled great distances to come to Washington. What worried them was the prospect of events spinning out of control when thousands demonstrated on the city streets. Some members of the political class were unconvinced by Abernathy's protestations that he was committed to nonviolence. Threats of civil disobedience were partly responsible for the absence of trust between the SCLC and some politicians. The Commerce Department had already stepped up security and closed several entrances to its premises.[49]

A few days after Resurrection City opened, an article in the *Star* newspaper did little to alleviate the sense of impending doom in some quarters. It described a Washington, D.C., and its various communities in conflict. White liberals and middle-class black people were said to be particularly torn in their thoughts on the campaign. The white liberals no longer had the reassuring presence of the nonviolent King, and middle-class black people were either apathetic about the poor or had become more militant under the influence of Black Power. Noting that D.C. had not yet recovered from the recent uprisings following the King assassination, the *Star* journalist wrote that the city was faced with the Poor People's Campaign growing in "size, intensity and rhetoric." The article described a range of conflicting emotions in the broader Washington community, which was "in ferment" through fear and apprehension, anger and alienation, hope and dedication, concern and commitment. It was alleged that people across the city were buying guns for the first time in their lives; others, by contrast, asked how they could help the campaign. One Washington citizen, Warren Diehl, had bought a gun because of the possibility that "a carload of black men who hated whites might come zooming up his street."[50] Another citizen, Bill Price, took the opposite view; he planned to help the campaign achieve its objectives. He had confidence in the nonviolent and multiracial nature of the PPC. Price had spent some time the previous week in New York observing programs in which mixed teams of blacks, Puerto Ricans, and whites went into congregations to get discussions going.[51]

The construction of King's shantytown in Washington began in earnest on May 13. Tony Henry thought it was a mistake for Ralph Abernathy to have delayed the beginning of construction work on Resurrection City until after he had ceremonially driven in the first stake.[52] The delay meant that those involved in the construction of the camp had to work long hours as a logjam of new arrivals of poor people built up. The intention to house the campaigners in tents at Resurrection City, as in Marks earlier in the campaign, did not materialize.[53] However, the important symbolism was retained in that the A-frame wooden huts constructed for the residents of Resurrection City were shaped like tents. The enduring reach of the PPC in this regard is evident in some twenty-first-century campaigns, such as Occupy Wall Street, where protesters carried on the tradition of living in tents, which symbolically for them were "more anarchistic" than conventional dwellings.[54]

On the first day, piles of the materials for prefabricated huts lay on the ground at the campsite, ready for work to begin by the "construction battalion."[55] Materials had begun to arrive on-site on May 11; volunteers began building Resurrection City on the night of May 12–13. Except for three hundred gallons of paint, virtually no building materials were donated.[56] Nash Castro, regional director of the National Park Service, and John Wiebenson, architect for the SCLC shelter program, worked on last-minute revisions of the site. Wiebenson reported that one rather odd problem came up. The locations for huts still to be erected had been marked by small swipes of paint on the grass, which architects felt would be more durable than stakes, which could easily be knocked over. The only thing was that Wiebenson had not counted on workers mowing the grass.[57] There was also a horrible stench because the National Park Service had fertilized the area with manure just before everyone began to arrive.[58]

Wiebenson noted that the hut structures were so light "people can pick them up." He encouraged the occupants to paint their individual huts.[59] Many of the residents personalized what were now their own homes; for example, members of the Blackstone Rangers, a Chicago gang, occupied the Blackstone hut. As the *New York Times* observed on May 24, Resurrection City had its own style, most evident in the graffiti on almost every hut. It was described as "funny, and inspirational by turn, that illustrates the human need to put a personal stamp on even the most primitive and temporary of shelters."[60] Some huts advertised the residents' home states or their hometowns; others announced the dwellers within: "Big House of John Hickman," "Willie the Shoemaker," "Wee Babies Sweet Slums."[61] Big Snake (Ponca) named his hut "Indian Aborigine Lodge" in solidarity with oppressed peoples across the globe.[62] The street names included King Boulevard, Abernathy Street, and Fannie Lou Hamer Drive.[63] James Peterson, an SCLC administrative assistant for the PPC, reflected that he only needed to look at the huts to see how people would live if they had an opportunity; many of them were "really beautiful shantys," they were "homes."[64] As in any other community in America, some residents put locks on their huts.

The first structure to go up was the Information Center tent, erected by Boy Scouts under the direction of the Washington Urban League.[65] Three different ethnic groups erected the first tent, and two hundred volunteers reportedly worked day and night to build the temporary city. Swarms of gnats filled the damp, warm air as work got under way. Progress was not as fast as the SCLC anticipated, however. Problems with lighting halted construction at 8 p.m. on the evening of May 13. At that point, workers had constructed around ninety of the projected five hundred huts. Tom Offenburger, SCLC press spokesperson, announced on May 18 that there was no target date for completion of the city.[66] There was much talk of building a second campsite as more and more demonstrators neared Washington in caravans from across the nation. To alleviate the pressure on space in Resurrection City, the SCLC eventually moved four hundred demonstrators, who had been temporarily living in churches, into the privately owned Washington Coliseum at Third and M Streets NE.[67]

City engineers and utilities officials had visited the site on May 12 to determine how to set up electric, water, sewer, and telephone lines. On the first day in Washington, SCLC officials had to write checks totaling $10,000 to get the power service to Resurrection City started.[68] Much thought went into arrangements to safeguard the health, safety, and security of the temporary city's residents. Builders brought in a ditch-digging machine to excavate for temporary sewage lines and to find old sewer pipes.[69] The sewage lines were for disposing of bathwater only, not toilets. Portable chemical toilets were delivered. The SCLC planned to clean them every day. It was never possible, however, to adequately install drainage systems for showers and sinks, so people were bused to baths.[70] Each dwelling unit had a plastic garbage bag or a large paper bag. Huts were kept clean by the inhabitants.

Fire lanes ran through the center of Resurrection City. On May 13, the D.C. Fire Department stationed a thousand-gallon-per-minute pumper truck onsite. A spokesperson said that the fire department would keep one piece of equipment there every day. There were also six hydrants. Supplies of bedding and linen were provided for all huts, and clothing for those who needed it was available at an off-site warehouse. The childcare center prepared to look after children while their parents were away on protests and testifying before congressional committees. Pay phones were in place by May 13. Phones were also available at the dining hall, the childcare center, and the recreation center. Blueprints were drawn up for an art gallery to display the work of poor people. Information on-site was provided through a public address system, bulletin boards, and runners.[71]

A community like any other began to take shape at the camp over the next few days as construction continued. Resurrection City eventually stretched for six blocks. Members of the Structures Committee were impressed with the way people built the city for themselves and others. They looked on such selfless commitment as part of the community development in the camp.[72] There were doctors, dentists, and a dining hall. Two members of the Diggers, a San Francisco group organized to provide free goods, set up a bakery on Main Street, which became a popular meeting place.[73] The first PPC arrivals enjoyed a lunch near the Reflecting Pool on the Mall on May 13. They ate sandwiches, cupcakes, and fruit supplied by Billy Simpson's restaurant. Some of the new arrivals seemed in awe at their first experience of the nation's capital. One older woman marveled that she had been put up in a house with three bedrooms the previous evening. A young boy pointed excitedly to the sky at the sight of jet planes coming in to land at Washington National Airport.[74]

After their long journeys, some of the poor people expressed relief and gratitude to have a living space in the camp. One woman said that the "Lord has mercy, thank God for giving us a place to live."[75] Poor people settled into their huts with their own sleeping bags, suitcases, and other personal belongings. The first wooden hut was earmarked for Minnie Lee, a mother of twelve children from Marks, Mississippi. She had brought eight of the children with her.[76] Camp children included twelve-year-old twins, Jean and Queen Esther.[77] Two black ninth-grade students, Lorine Doggan and Clara Deal, had never been more than twenty miles away from their home in Crenshaw, Mississippi, population 1,382. They expressed surprise at the sight of slums in Washington, something they thought only existed in Mississippi. Both declared that they were glad they had come to the nation's capital and were determined to stay for as long as possible.[78]

Most of the protesters seemed satisfied with the arrangements made for them. A Mississippi woman ran her hand over the plywood wall of her hut and said, "This is ok, it's better than what we have at home."[79] She was not exaggerating; Resurrection City offered a more pleasant place to live than the dilapidated shacks King had witnessed in Mississippi during his people-to-people tours. The *New York Times* acknowledged that the camp represented the only home some people had ever had.[80] A mother of five children claimed she had no home in Mississippi fit to live in. Her Marks home was infested with roaches, and she had to stay up at night holding a lamp over her children to help them sleep. She had come to Washington, D.C., to do something about it "not after a while, but now."[81] Ellie Stanton, a mother of ten from Mississippi, settled in with the intention of staying for as long as it took to get what she came for. She typified those who came to Washington. Stanton lived on welfare payments of $49 per week; her husband was unable to get a job even after completing a training program. Peeping through the plastic curtains that served as a doorway to her hut, Stanton revealed that her husband had said, "Honey, you go to Washington and shake them up. I'll look after the kids." She shared the tiny hut with four other women and said all she needed was a broom to sweep up. Juanita Perley from Montgomery, Alabama, said her crowded conditions in Resurrection City were no worse than back home. Myrtle Brown from Mississippi, who was in D.C. with four of her five children, said the crowded conditions in her hut, with cots jammed in, were worth it, and she would stay forever if necessary.[82]

Pearlie Bishop from Akron, Alabama, was in high spirits as she chatted outside her hut with fellow campaigners Savannah Stokes from Montgomery, Alabama, and Gertrude Jackson, also from Akron. She expressed confidence that the "Lord would deliver" on their demands. A twelve-year-old boy from Alabama wondered if there were any snakes in the Reflecting Pool.[83] Before long, children were darting everywhere, as in any other community, and scampering across piles of lumber. One woman started to cuff her unruly son but was restrained by another mother, who reminded her no violence was allowed in the camp.[84] Some people spotted an opportunity to make some money, as in any situation where people gather together. San Francisco artist Eugene E. White was busy near the Reflecting Pool on May 13 selling half-tone lithographs of Dr. King. He said that he would keep some of the proceeds and give some to the SCLC. Another trader sold records and King buttons, photos, and ashtrays.[85]

Resurrection City provided many of the resources and facilities found in any small self-contained city. It included a city hall, a library, and a daycare center named after Coretta Scott King. At 8:30 each morning, doctors normally made the rounds of the huts. Two large medical vans, one owned by the Seventh-day Adventists, became focal points for poor people unaccustomed to readily accessible healthcare. Two dental vans were available to the residents also. By May 18, doctors had examined 387 people, and ten dental extraction cases were sent to the Freedman's and D.C. General Hospitals.[86] Health facilities continued to develop in a piecemeal fashion in Resurrection City. In mid-June, these facilities were enhanced with the arrival of a seventy-five-foot trailer that contained a pharmacy, two examination rooms, a mental health room, and a waiting room.[87] Assistance was provided for people with mental health issues on-site, and arrangements were made to look after them when they returned to their home communities.[88]

The residents of Resurrection City enjoyed far better services than many of them had experienced in their home states. Highlighting one of the core demands of the PPC—the need to address the absence of healthcare in communities across America—volunteer doctors and dentists said that many in Resurrection City had never seen a doctor or dentist before.[89] As needed, residents were given injections against measles, diphtheria, whooping cough, and tetanus; they received chest X-rays and blood tests. Healthcare professionals who came to Resurrection City were personally changed by their experiences in the camp. One reflected that although she had previously understood poverty in an intellectual sense, Resurrection City was where she really began to learn the true nature of the issue, and she "intended to communicate this to people outside."[90]

Twenty-seven-year-old volunteer Wendy Pritzker was one of 280 registered nurses who worked in Resurrection City to help the poor. These volunteers worked 5,040 nursing hours over five weeks. Over the same period, doctors contributed 1,680 hours.[91] Pritzker had taken leave from her job to accompany the Eastern Caravan, which left New York for Washington on May 12. She traveled with another nurse and a doctor in a green station wagon equipped with three shoulder-bag first aid kits. One woman on the caravan gave birth in Baltimore and named her child Uhuru, a Swahili word meaning "freedom." According to Pritzker, the woman had wanted to give birth to her baby on the steps of the Capitol building in D.C.[92] Pritzker lived at Number 802, Resurrection City, and served as a medical liaison for the Health Services Coordinating Committee, formed to serve the needs of PPC participants. The committee's partners included the National Medical Association, the Medico-Chirurgical Society of D.C., and the Medical Committee for Human Rights. Wendy Pritzker acted as a link between Resurrection City residents and those who could provide them with medical services. She also liaised with Mexican Americans and others who were living at the private Hawthorne School to make sure they did not miss out on needed healthcare.

The National Capital Area Child Day Care Association took over preschool daycare in the camp and, while there, conducted a study of the children.[93] The subsequent report helped to capture details of the lives of children in the camp who had traveled with their parents to Washington from the poorest communities in America. One woman had started her own daycare program on the road before becoming an "on-site mother" in Resurrection City. For the first few days, the daycare programs were in the basements of churches. When the day-care center finally opened in the camp on May 24, it consisted of three rooms and was staffed by five volunteers. The numbers of children who flocked in surprised the daycare workers. Volunteers from D.C. and Georgetown University took the children out for tours of the city. Among other important insights into the depths of inequality in 1968, the daycare center study reported that many mothers had come from the South where they had no or limited opportunities for education. Many could not write their own name on the registration form. Most of the children came from rural areas where they worked in the fields. Life was tough in Resurrection City but no worse than many of the children were used to back home. The study claimed that it was common to see a seventeen-month-old child arrive in the morning without parents.[94] A handful of children were allegedly stolen, and the victims were said to welcome this. Reports of children abandoned in the daycare center were not unknown.[95] But the study also revealed some uplifting tales. A "freedom baby," born in a jail eight years previously, after his mother had been arrested at a demonstration, acted as an organizer in the daycare center and tried to put the other children into "freedom groups." Another child announced that he was going back to Georgia to build a new poor people's city on someone's land.[96]

In what became a busy and active community, organizational imperatives demanded there be an element of routine in aspects of daily life. Each day in Resurrection City usually began at 7 a.m. with the announcement "Time to get up, breakfast is served." In the outermost neighborhoods of the town, away from the loudspeakers, marshals moved along the dirt paths and tapped the plywood walls to awaken those inside. Long lines then formed at the blue circus tent near the camp's main entrance, where cold cereals, fruit, and coffee were served. The SCLC had hoped to provide three meals a day for everyone living in Resurrection City, including a hot meal in the evening. This was one area, however, where things sometimes fell short of expectations, although contingency plans meant that no one starved. Administrative coordinator John Rutherford was less than impressed with the food on offer, complaining that the same things were provided every day: "baloney, cheese, ham and cheese, salami and cheese." Some people refused to eat it.[97]

The success of the food operation depended on the work of volunteers. Most of the catering was organized by the Food Committee headed by Joseph Danzansky, president of Giant Foods. The supplies came from food chains like Giant and Food Fair and from local dairies. Donations of food also came from sympathetic supporters all over the country. The first flight of Operation Airlift arrived at Washington National Airport on May 14 with a ton of food collected in the Los

Angeles area for the campaign.[98] The *New York Times* reported that a seemingly endless stream of donated food flowed into the camp, as much as twenty-five tons a day and some of it much better fare than the residents had ever known.[99] Food in Resurrection City was stored in a cold truck and two dry vans and prepared on-site.[100] Whenever hot meals were available, they were prepared in kitchens at Howard University, a high school, and churches across the city. According to the camp dietician, Linden Griffith, the day-to-day operation of catering was disrupted by the weather, a lack of volunteers, and the vandalism of food trucks.[101]

Like any other community, Resurrection City was soon noisy with the sounds of transistor radios, babies crying, and guitars being strummed. A voice would typically blare over the loudspeakers from the plywood hut called city hall: "Will a plumber please report to the dental trailer at once?" or "All persons desiring to take showers go to the bus at the front gate."[102] Teenagers were restless, whereas adults expressed "patience and tolerance" with their living conditions. One older man said that he did not come expecting the "Waldorf-Astoria."[103] Conditions in Resurrection City were better than many had at home, but they were not perfect. Residents experienced personal hygiene problems into the month of June due to showers not being hooked up to the water system. Ditches were dug to get around the problem. Residents took buckets of water to their shelters, used rubbing alcohol to keep clean, or were taken to the YMCA or local churches for a shower. Piles of donated clothing were stacked on tables outside a huge truck staffed by Seventh-day Adventists. Riley Lewis, a college graduate, was responsible for camp communications. Ronald Roberts took on social work duties. Tut Tate headed up community activities, coordinated meetings, and took care of the bulletin board outside city hall.[104]

With only a few exceptions, Resurrection City was reserved for the community living there only. Sightseers were not allowed inside the guarded fence that surrounded the site. SCLC field officer Al Sampson justified the exclusion of outsiders by saying, "We are not animals in a zoo, but people trying to establish a nonviolent community." Other explanations were provided to the press. James Bevel said it was to prevent work crews being distracted, and Bernard Lafayette said it was to prevent injuries to outsiders.[105] But some of the curious were determined to find out what was going on behind the perimeter fence. Cars cruised along Independence Avenue as drivers tried to stare inside the camp. Elizabeth Jones of Detroit, whose tiny two-woman hut sat alongside the fence, dismissed such people as "gawkers."[106] Journalists, with special passes, were allowed in for around two hours per day.

The exclusion did not extend to a star visitor, Stokely Carmichael; he made a smiling, hand-shaking visit during the afternoon of May 14. One report said that he moved through Resurrection City like a "ballet dancer," weaving his way through admirers. One young man who shook hands with his idol was so overwhelmed that he announced he would now cut his own "arm off and freeze it."[107] Bevel welcomed Carmichael to the camp by describing him as a "friend and brother, one of the very important and outstanding black leaders in the country."[108] Looking for any opportunity to destabilize the campaign, the director of the FBI, J. Edgar Hoover, undoubtedly paid very close attention to a statement of this nature. For those in the camp, however, it was time to get down to the serious business of protests and demonstrations.

PART III
LEARNING

CHAPTER 10
POOR PEOPLE GET DOWN TO WORK

The mood of the poor people who would arrive in Washington, D.C., was captured in the "Declaration of the Movement" that the Southern Christian Leadership Conference circulated after the period of mourning for Martin Luther King Jr., that is, "the days of weeping are ended; the day of the march has come! We shall overcome."[1] Ordinary citizens came to Resurrection City from all over the United States with purpose and serious intent. Together with the leaders of the different racial groups, many shared the deep desire to fulfill Dr. King's legacy by making poverty visible and to force Congress to pass legislation to address economic injustice. The SCLC's Hosea Williams encapsulated the tone in the first days of Resurrection City by speaking about the most painful subject of all, the recent loss of the "martyred leader." He expressed his determination to see things through in King's name. Williams announced, "By the time we are through in D.C., white people will say, wake up Dr. King! These white people killed the dreamer, but we are going to show these white people what became of the dream."[2]

With the occupation of Washington about to get under way, the SCLC reiterated that protest was necessary because the federal government had acted in the past on behalf of only one segment of the population. In the belief that the government did not wish to change direction because this would imply a "redistribution of power and wealth," leaders of the Poor People's Campaign called on the people who had arrived in the nation's capital to set aside their fears and to unite under one cause.[3] The SCLC stressed its determination to bring about a change in the "structure" of society, not merely "reform." A commitment to nonviolence to achieve such radical change underpinned the demonstrations and protests,[4] despite warnings in Congress and in the press that the poor were there to bring violence and disorder to the streets of the nation's capital. Soon after Resurrection City was declared open, the national director of the PPC, Bernard Lafayette, restated the SCLC's intention to maintain good order among the ranks of the protesters.[5] He promised that the camp would be the first nonviolent city in the United States.[6]

The PPC strategy was to organize events on a mass scale, including demonstrations, lobbying Congress, and civil disobedience, if required.[7] King had envisaged that Resurrection City would be the launch pad for such activism across Washington, D.C. In his estimation people had to get out of the camp and into the city to press their case. The Reverend James Bevel set out the same vision in stating that Resurrection City "cannot remain an island; it must be a church that goes out to Washington and moves Washington to fight for the poor. We must demonstrate every day, but in the afternoon we must get out into Washington, we must come back and canvass, knock on doors, talk to people about the reality of poverty in this country."[8]

The demonstrators needed to win politicians over to their cause. Bevel claimed that the protesters would practice "political psychiatry" on the elected representatives and educate them on the need to eliminate poverty now.[9] The task of educating politicians posed significant challenges. In the political climate of May 1968, an unreceptive Congress was hostile to both the presence of the poor and the costly demands they brought with them. Politicians simply cited a shortage of money to justify their inaction. Tax hikes to pay for fighting both the Vietnam War and poverty were unlikely to receive congressional approval. As previously mentioned, under increasing pressure to fund the war, President Lyndon B. Johnson had enacted a 10 percent surcharge but had agreed to cut expenditures by $6 billion.[10] In this context Congress balked at the huge estimated bill of $25 billion per year to meet the PPC's demands. Even supporters of the PPC in Congress were skeptical. Democratic representative Emanuel Celler of New York, chair of the House Judiciary Committee, doubted that a "stingy" Congress would do anything to meet the PPC's demands.[11] Democratic senator George McGovern observed that Congress could only do what was "politically possible."[12] Liberal Democrats were trying to stand up against budget cuts, and greatly increased spending was not on the agenda.

Support for the PPC's demand for increased spending was forthcoming from a dozen members of Congress in the form of the Full Opportunity Act. Democratic representative John Conyers had raised this idea at the 1967 SCLC convention. It would have added an estimated $30 billion to the annual federal budget, including money for three million public service jobs, child allowances, one million new homes a year, special aid for ghetto schools, the construction of colleges, vocational and technical schools, and student loans. However, skepticism remained about the chances of winning such huge sums to wage war against poverty. Democratic representative Joseph Y. Resnick, a cosponsor of the Full Opportunity Act, said the campaigners were engaged in a "pretty useless" exercise in that all they would get was media coverage.[13]

The request for an annual guaranteed income was particularly problematic for politicians and the public alike. Republican senator Milton R. Young of North Dakota, who regarded the PPC's demands as "unreasonable and unrealistic," vowed to oppose the call for a guaranteed annual income, adding that the "most socialistic countries in the world never attempted this or believed it feasible."[14] Democratic senator Russell Long of Louisiana was already on record in stating his opposition. Showing a lack of any sympathy for the poor, he declared, "If they think they are going to push into bankrupting this country to pay worthless people to be more worthless, they are making a mistake."[15] The SCLC, however, showed little inclination to back away from this demand, which was closely associated with Dr. King. Support for the idea came from a leading economist, Leonard Fein of the Massachusetts Institute of Technology, just as the occupation of Washington got under way. Sitting at a conference table alongside SCLC executive vice president Andrew Young, he criticized government policies that were aimed at "racial brotherhood" but did not help black babies live longer. He called for the adoption of the A. Philip Randolph Institute's Freedom Budget.[16] One thousand academics endorsed the idea of a guaranteed income later that month, although one of them perhaps got to the heart of the issue by stating, "The only ones against it are the people."[17] The PPC leaders knew they had a hard sell to persuade the public that a guaranteed income did not amount to a handout. With House, Senate, and presidential races all taking place later in the year, many politicians were reluctant to go out on a limb by endorsing massively increased public spending. The *Daily News* regarded the guaranteed proposal as "startling" and stated that once embarked upon it would be a "road with no ending."[18]

The highly polarized presidential election in 1968 added to the complexities of the situation facing PPC leaders. Republican presidential frontrunner Richard Nixon warned Congress that it was a "mistake to legislate from behind a barricade or bow to the demands of the PPC." He dismissed the campaign demands as "not a freedom budget at all but a blueprint for continued dependency."[19] He called for more private investment in ghetto areas, arguing that the country could not afford to meet the PPC's demands. Later in the summer, Andrew Young would charge the former vice president with toying with the "white backlash" and not facing up to poverty. Nixon's staff responded to the accusation by pointing to their candidate's recent speech on black capitalism with its emphasis on individual initiative, which they claimed was highly praised by the leaders of other groups, including the Congress of Racial Equality.[20] The Nixon plan suggested that the federal government give tax write-offs and encourage locally owned businesses in the ghetto areas.

When planning the Washington demonstrations, the PPC leaders felt they had learned in previous campaigns how to effect change, which provided them with the confidence and knowledge associated in social movements with "activist wisdom."[21] The Selma and Birmingham campaigns, in particular, represented the kind of positive experience, a "historical consciousness," which social movement theory suggests can contribute to the building of solidarity among activists.[22] King had regularly cited the success of previous campaigns in placing pressure on the government to change direction. An estimated forty marches took place over six weeks in Washington, D.C., during the life of Resurrection City. The targets included the Departments of Agriculture and State; the home of Wilbur Mills, chair of the House Ways and Means Committee; the Capitol building; the Bureau of Indian Affairs; and the Supreme Court. Although supportive of the right of demonstrators to be in Washington, Attorney General Ramsey Clark set conditions on the size of the marches, and a few areas remained off-limits to demonstrators.[23]

On May 14, two days after the march of welfare mothers led by Coretta Scott King, Tony Henry represented the PPC at a meeting with staff of the Office of Economic Opportunity (OEO) and received a promise of their cooperation for the duration of the campaign. While pleased to receive such reassurances, he warned the OEO representatives not to expect an easy ride when they met with genuinely poor people in the days and weeks ahead. On May 15, in what would become a regular sight throughout the campaign in Washington over the next few weeks, a group of one hundred demonstrators, mainly black people and Native Americans on this occasion, proudly marched to a Senate hearing to press their case for legislation. The Senate Committee on Indian Affairs heard testimony from the Reverend Al Sampson, who had arrived in D.C. with the southern group from Marks and Memphis. Sampson accused the government of "theft" from poor people, comparing the politicians to robbers who "knocked people over the head on the streets."[24] In an acrimonious meeting, there was a degree of farce when one legislator assumed that the cry from the demonstrators of "Soul Sock" was a Native American language. Sampson had Mohawk ancestors, hence his position as one of the group leaders presenting testimony and other evidence to the senators on behalf of Native Americans.

Al Sampson wore a pinstriped suit and an orange turtleneck sweater. Clint Hill, wearing a purple shirt and a beaded "war belt," followed Sampson into the hearing room. Together, they made a great impression on the proceedings and not only because of their attire. Hill introduced members of the hundred-strong group of demonstrators, including representatives of the Snake Clan of Oklahoma. Sampson had an angry exchange with the senators; one press account used the headline "Senate Ambush by Campaign 'Truth Squad.'"[25] Unperturbed, Sampson provided hard evidence to challenge legislation that allegedly discriminated against Native Americans in the area of welfare. The campaigners were invariably well prepared to present their arguments, thanks to the work behind the scenes of the PPC Legislative Research Committee led by Phillip Buskirk, which provided them with information on current and proposed government legislation.

On the same day as the Senate Committee on Indian Affairs hearing, May 15, 1968, Ralph Abernathy and Andrew Young met with a group of more than seventy House representatives and senators. The closed meeting was described as "calm and rational" with the politicians reported to be sympathetic to both SCLC leaders.[26] Abernathy sought to reassure the politicians that his army of the poor would only disrupt Washington as a last resort. While King had suggested "going for broke" to confront the government through civil disobedience, Abernathy and other SCLC leaders initially adopted persuasion rather than coercion. Attempts to force the government into making concessions were for the most part held back until after the massive Solidarity Day demonstration on June 19. This relatively cautious approach in the early stages of the occupation of Washington did not play well with grassroots activists desperate to place maximum pressure on the authorities. Abernathy also put the onus on the politicians by refusing to make specific demands beyond those of jobs, housing, and income. He declared that the task of writing laws belonged to Congress, and he would not tell them how to do it.[27] His stance regarding the campaign demands was a constant source of frustration for the politicians. Republican senator Charles Percy was, however, upbeat in his support for the campaign, stating that he understood the demonstrators just wanted to feel that "they are a part of the country."[28] Although sympathetic to Andrew Young's plea for an "expression of deep concern" from Congress, Percy warned the SCLC that any disruption of government activity in the coming weeks would irreparably set back and injure its cause.[29]

The meeting with the politicians on May 15 had one concrete outcome. Congress established an ad hoc committee on poverty.[30] Republican senator Edward W. Brooke chaired the committee.[31] Other members included Democratic senator Philip A. Hart and Republican representative Ogden R. Reid. It met weekly with representatives of the PPC to assist them to liaise with Congress and to provide a forum for legislative and administrative solutions to the problems of poverty. The regular discussions ensured that channels of communication were maintained between campaign leaders and elected representatives as the occupation of the Mall continued. After the initial meeting, Ralph Abernathy put the nation on alert by repeating King's dire warnings of chaos in America should the needs of the poor continue to be ignored. He observed, "The bill for generations of irresponsibility is being presented to the nation; it will be collected in human decency and love or the flames of destruction."[32]

Echoes of the final Selma march for voting rights in 1965 could be identified in the enthusiasm and determination of the protesters in a demonstration near the Capitol building on May 23, which was the first major event of the PPC following the official opening of Resurrection City. The demonstration drew hundreds of congressional staff to their windows and balconies, attracted dozens of reporters, and brought unwanted attention from the police. A handful of politicians ventured onto the pavement to discuss the situation with police officers. Representative Clarence D. Long, a Democrat from Maryland, said that the demonstrations revealed the marchers' "attitude of truculence and menace."[33] His criticism seems harsh and unfounded. The march was far from intimidating: the protesters sang and shouted slogans, but there was no violence. Yet several demonstrators were arrested even as the protest's leader, George A. Wiley, executive director of the National Welfare Rights Organization, negotiated with James M. Powell, chief of the Capitol police. All of those taken into custody were later acquitted of disorderly conduct charges, including William R. Riley, twenty-six, of Pittsburgh, and Lonzy West, forty-five, of Selma. No evidence was found to show they had disrupted either congressional business or the free flow of tourists, nor had they damaged property.[34]

The arrival on the scene of Resurrection City mayor Jesse Jackson at the May 23 protest soothed tensions. He reached an agreement with the police chief that there would be no further arrests. Jackson, in a smart public relations gesture, praised the diplomacy of Powell in taking steps to stop further arrests and to deescalate the situation. Jackson announced that the campaigners were not yet ready to up the tempo of the movement to mass arrests nor to engage in massive civil disobedience.[35] Jackson, Wiley, two hundred protesters, and fifty reporters then all jammed into a room in the Rayburn Building, where they confronted Secretary of Agriculture Orville Freeman, demanding he liberalize the federal food stamps program and the distribution of surplus food. Jesse Jackson gave a rousing address, pointing out it was time to back the poor for all they had contributed to America. In a portent of a similar speech he would make many years later when running for the Democratic Party nomination for president, Jackson declared, "We have been the nation's laborers, its waiters. Our women have raised its presidents on their knees. We have built the highways. We have died in wartime fighting people we were not even mad at. America worked us for three hundred and fifty years without paying us, now we deserve a job or an income."[36]

Despite Jackson's passion and eloquence, "Brother" Orville Freeman was unmoved. He made no fresh concessions and referred instead to an announcement a year earlier that the Department of Agriculture would begin the distribution of surplus food in the 331 counties across the country not covered by food stamp plans. Freeman refused to authorize the "emergency" use of both food stamp and surplus programs simultaneously in any county.[37] He felt aggrieved that he had been made the "fall guy" by the PPC. In his view, the campaigners had come to his department because food was an "emotional thing," and they were organizing a "publicity stunt." Defending his corner, Freeman said he was unable to give them free food stamps because that was against the law.[38]

In a dramatic gesture that entered the folklore of the PPC, Jackson led demonstrators into the Department of Agriculture cafeteria, where they helped themselves to a meal and declared that this "eat-in" was only a down payment on what the government owed poor people. The protest was effective in capturing the attention of the press, and everyone enjoyed a good meal, although the SCLC eventually paid the bill. Ralph Abernathy justified the exercise: "We came here because we were hungry, this is our Department of Agriculture, it is owned by us."[39] Secretary Freeman, by contrast, felt that the tactics of banging drums outside the agriculture building and helping themselves to food in the cafeteria did the cause of the PPC no good.[40] He added dismissively that you can be militant "without being screwball."[41]

The demonstrations did not occur in isolation and regularly offered the participants opportunities for dialogue and reflection. Staff from the independent national organization the Scholarship, Education, and Defense Fund for Racial Equality (SEDFRE) were on hand to provide support and advice after the cafeteria protest. SEDFRE trainers encouraged Ralph Abernathy to allow the protesters space and time to sit down and discuss what talking to Department of Agriculture staff meant and what the eat-in was about; this was described as an "evaluation-type" session.[42] The conversations took place at Resurrection City when everyone returned from the protest. In discussing her feelings about what had gone on, an elderly woman from New York advised that they all stick together because the problems of poverty in her supposedly progressive home state were the same as everywhere else. She told everyone not to be put off by the delaying tactics they had experienced from the Department of Agriculture staff but to stay the course.[43] A man commented that the food was good in the cafeteria, much better than he had in Alabama, and stated that his children, who were not with him in Washington, probably had nothing to eat that day back home. The SEDFRE trainer expressed his satisfaction with how things had gone; the protesters had managed to encourage dialogue that made the demonstrations and activities meaningful for people. His only regret was that he felt the SCLC had not made enough use of the SEDFRE expertise in the camp to train and educate people to a higher degree.[44]

Hosea Williams took over from Jesse Jackson as chair of direct action in Resurrection City in early June. Campaign leaders were at pains to stress that Jackson had not been demoted in being reassigned to organize "action cadres" in other cities, including Baltimore, Maryland; Richmond, Virginia; Wilmington, North Carolina; Philadelphia, Pennsylvania; and New York. Williams maintained that Jackson had to go because "Dr. King and others had given their lives and that if he had to, he [Jackson] was willing to give his also."[45] Jesse Jackson had made his mark in Resurrection City, and there was a perception that some of the SCLC leaders were envious of his oratory skill and popularity with the camp residents. The internal politics of the SCLC also may have played a part in the decision to exile him.[46] Williams later made his own presence felt at a civil disobedience protest at the Department of Agriculture. He had traveled to Resurrection City as part of the Mule Train.[47] Wearing a one-piece khaki garment, in contrast to the blue denims worn by other campaign leaders, he announced to the crowd standing around that the "picnic was over." He berated the police on duty, declaring that the government would make them "beat" the demonstrators, adding that he understood that was their job.[48] The focus on the Department of Agriculture intensified from mid-June following the decision at an SCLC strategy meeting to give even greater emphasis to the issue of hunger.[49] Later that month, a direct action group initiated by James Bevel engaged in civil disobedience with the intention to close down the Department of Agriculture and to fill the jails in Washington. Dozens were arrested.[50]

Other locations also attracted the attention of PPC demonstrators. Women activists decided to protest at the Capitol building, the seat of U.S. political power. In a standoff with police, the women, who did not have a permit to march that day, declared they were there as "tourists" and wanted to meet their senators.[51] It was reported that the "side[s] knew each other too well," and a compromise was reached that allowed the women to enter the Capitol to use the rest rooms and then claim they had "liberated" the building as part of the first Washington "pee-in."[52] On June 3, four hundred poor people demonstrated at the Justice Department. They had an agreement with Attorney General Ramsey Clark to meet them. Hosea Williams asked the demonstrators to block the entrance to the Justice Department, although Clark eventually left from the rear of the building to avoid them.[53]

One of the most iconic Native American demonstrations during the occupation of Washington took place at the Supreme Court on May 29. It began at the private Hawthorne School, where most of the planning for the event took place.[54] To the PPC activists in D.C., the Supreme Court represented the injustices of the entire legal system. Native Americans led the protest, and their mood typified the militancy and solidarity often evidenced in the various demonstrations during the campaign. Although initially opposed to the action on the grounds that the location was too controversial, Ralph Abernathy joined in and marched arm in arm with Native American and Mexican American leaders. They were all there to protest a Supreme Court ruling, the *Puyallup* decision, which had upheld Washington state's conviction of twenty-four Native Americans who had staged a fish-in off the reservation to demand their fishing rights.[55] Washington state had cited conservation reasons for its action against the twenty-four Nisquallys and Puyallups.[56] Abernathy described the decision of the Supreme Court as another attempt to deny citizens their right to survival. He condemned America as a country "controlled by racists who now deny the right to fish in God's waters."[57] Reies Tijerina was equally scathing, accusing the Supreme Court of being in contempt of the Constitution of the United States.

The Supreme Court protest attracted the attention of press and television. The demonstrators included five hundred Chicanos, one hundred Native Americans, "some Anglos pretending to be poor," according to Reies Tijerina, and fifteen black people accompanied by Ralph Abernathy.[58] Tijerina repeatedly declared his support for Native Americans throughout the PPC on the basis that our fight is "one and the same."[59] Hidatsa elder George Crow Flies High wore an eagle feather headdress, a clamshell necklace, dark sunglasses, and a pin saying "Indian Power." Some protesters smoked "peace pipes," satisfying press demands for photographs. Al Bridges held up a banner saying "Supreme Court Starves Indians."[60] Several women banged on the doors of the Supreme Court to demand entry and were able to hand over a petition to Court clerk John F. Davis. Small victories meant a great deal to the protesters. The agreement of Davis to meet with a delegation was regarded as a further triumph for the protesters. Things got out of hand, however, and two arrests were made after a few windows were smashed and an American flag was flown at half-staff.[61]

Some newspapers reported on the disturbances with great glee, for example, the *Washington Post* demanded that ordinary Americans react to the "disgraceful behavior of those who besieged the Supreme Court with outrage and indignation." The article included patronizing comments that "those deprived of the advantages of affluence and a polite education cannot be expected to have the manners of finishing school graduates or the vocabulary of parliamentarians."[62] The *Post* called on friends of the campaign to "reflect on the episode with sorrow," adding that only black militants would benefit from the disorder. It seemed to elements in the press that the sacred Supreme Court had been tarnished by the presence of a rabble. The substance of the protest—the Supreme Court ruling on fishing rights, which the demonstrators contended was flawed and biased against them—was ignored by the *Post* and in some other accounts of the event. Reies Tijerina, however, celebrated as protesters climbed on the statue of Athens outside the Supreme Court, "an act of symbolic conquest over Anglo justice."[63] He was proud that his people had rejected "passivity" in the face of injustice. Social movement theory supports his analysis. Although it was reported that other activities, including Freedom School workshops and other forms of learning in Resurrection City, were "very good" with a lot of debate and discussion, just as important was the experience of marching to "and challenging the Supreme Court as the Native Americans did one afternoon."[64] Social movement theory suggests that such unacknowledged learning is common within movements and is "embedded in action and is often not recognized as learning."[65]

The Supreme Court demonstration ended on a low note, however. On the way back to Hawthorne School, police and marchers clashed, and twelve arrests were made. The conflict merely galvanized the Chicanos, who continued to make their presence felt in demonstrations until the end of the occupation of Washington. Tijerina led a small group to the State Department on June 13 to demand an investigation into the Treaty of Guadalupe Hidalgo. In a sign of tensions within the PPC leadership, he asserted his right to lead the Indo-Hispanos on their demonstrations and regularly complained that black people's interests often took precedence, to the detriment of other minority groups.

On June 10, Abernathy repeated his intention to stay in D.C. until the campaign goals were met and warned that any attempt to move them might spark violence. He added that the demonstrations so far had been successful in dramatizing the "old issue of poverty," but further progress needed to be made. He expressed satisfaction with specific outcomes already achieved, including the agreement of Secretary Orville Freeman to finally provide food in the neediest counties, Senate approval of an amendment removing restrictions on the Agriculture Department's use of millions of dollars in the contingency fund, Senate passage of a bill to increase housing for low-income families, and the Office of Economic Opportunity decision to free $25 million for expanded antipoverty programs, such as Head Start.[66] There was, however, a note of caution in relation to the public mood over the presence of the poor in the nation's capital. A Lomax Poll showed that among whites there were lingering fears that the encampment would erupt in violence, despite pledges that the demonstrations would remain peaceful.[67]

In addition to the marches and demonstrations, King's aspiration to make poor people visible was achieved through lobbying Congress. The PPC Legislative Committee, including Phil Buskirk and Sarah Alter, prepared individuals for this crucial work.[68] Many poor people provided testimony at Senate hearings. In one powerful example, the Senate Subcommittee on Employment, Manpower and Poverty meeting on May 23 in room G-308 of the new Senate Office Building heard heartbreaking and compelling testimony on hunger from several poor people, mainly women. Their presence reflected their courage and heroism in traveling often immensely long distances and then having the confidence to speak before the most influential people in the land. In his opening comments, the committee chair, Democratic senator Gaylord Nelson of Wisconsin, a strong supporter of the movement and an early critic of the Vietnam War, acknowledged the increasing public awareness of the issue of poverty. Only two days previously, CBS had broadcast a landmark exposé called *Hunger in America*. The documentary was extremely timely for the campaigners. Its content shocked the nation and put hunger firmly in the spotlight. Dr. King would have been happy to hear Senator Nelson praise the PPC for attracting the attention of media outlets, including CBS and *Time* magazine, to the issue of poverty. In Nelson's view, they had achieved something no one else had done. He observed that they had managed "to dramatize and sharply call to public attention" the issue of poverty, which had been ignored for too long.[69] Senator Nelson shared correspondence he had received from ordinary citizens from across the country in the wake of the *Hunger in America* broadcast. A hundred to one were apparently in favor of the government doing whatever it could to assist. Moderate Republican senator Jacob Javits added his praise in commending Abernathy for staying true to Dr. King's nonviolent vision of the campaign.

Marian Wright Edelman, who had been appointed as congressional liaison for the PPC, introduced the witnesses. Edelman saw her role during the Washington campaign as "supportive": "the poor can speak for themselves more eloquently than anyone can speak for them."[70] Among the witnesses was Willie J. Hardy of the Metropolitan Community Aid Council; she alleged that some poor people were reluctant to appear before the committee for fear of being "sanctioned" by the government departments in a position to help them out.[71] Others were willing to take the risk. Several people provided firsthand accounts of what it was like to be impoverished in America. Lupe Martinez of Denver, Colorado, like so many others who joined the campaign, confirmed this was the first time she had left her state because she never had the money to do so previously. She revealed that her son was in Vietnam with the navy because there were no opportunities for him at home. She attributed his plight to "racism and discrimination" because he was a Spanish speaker. A mother of eleven children, she barely subsisted on $200 a month. Her children often went hungry because she could not afford to pay the thirty cents for each of them to have a school dinner. Martinez said, "This is not justice. This is why I am in Washington. Nobody listens to you in Denver." She had come to Washington to let Congress know what she was "going through."[72]

Andres De Pineda from Denver, a father of two who claimed he had no money to buy food stamps, read a statement on behalf of the Mexican Americans of the Southwest. His statement was dramatic, compelling, and to the point. It expressed the solidarity the PPC had achieved among the poor of different racial and ethnic backgrounds. Showing an impressive degree of confidence, De Pineda requested that the senators not interrupt him until he had concluded his statement. He declared, "The Mexican American people of the Southwest are not here to entertain you or be part of a sideshow in a carnival. We are not a group of gypsies trying to scheme or connive you out of your dollar bill Bible. We are not here to let you do our thinking for us anymore. We are not here to make you feel comfortable. We are here with brothers of other races, here in unity, in love for each other. We are all poor; we speak for the oppressed, for the hungry thousands that exist in this country."[73] De Pineda went on to describe how a previous conviction for assault—he claimed to be the victim and not the perpetrator—made it very difficult for him to get a job. His authentic voice made an impression on the panel. Senator Jennings Randolph thanked him for the statement, which was delivered in De Pineda's "own rather blunt but clear and understandable language."[74]

Other testimony followed on May 29; taken together, the statements revealed a disturbing picture of poverty in America. Lupi Trujillo from Denver was accompanied by her son John. She had no education, and her son had already dropped out of school at age fifteen. He explained he was embarrassed at being unable to pay for school sports equipment and had been forced to use a different color card when ordering his free school lunch. John said that the whole experience of school had knocked the enthusiasm out of him.[75] The campaign highlighted such indignities, which represented just some of the ways in which poor people were regularly humiliated when claiming what should have been theirs by right. Tina Kruger from Texas delivered a graphic account of life in poor communities and in so doing provided compelling evidence as to why Dr.

King wanted to bring the poor to Washington. She worked with poor families and was shocked at the poverty and hunger in the "great state of Texas." Kruger informed the senators that she had spent three years in Honduras but saw few starving people there.[76] She alleged that 51 percent of Mexican Americans in Texas were poor. Kruger claimed she knew a mother of eight children who refused to go to the welfare office because it "intimidated her." Kruger highlighted some horrific cases she had encountered of mothers who gave up their children because they could not feed them. She claimed to know of dozens of cases where current welfare laws forced parents to separate to make sure their family had an income.[77] Kruger spoke for so many others often looked upon as the "unworthy poor" who needed to pull themselves up by their bootstraps. She asked that people not be treated like "scum" when they turned up to request help from the authorities: "We want jobs, we like to work, we want education, we want justice."[78]

Native Americans also provided powerful evidence of hunger in America. Perhaps the most remarkable witness was 101-year-old Mattie Grinnell from the Fort Berthold reservation. Her presence confirmed that even some of the oldest people in the country were motivated by the PPC to come to Washington. She was there to help the generations coming after her but personified an attitude among older participants that they wanted "some of that" for themselves also. She was old and could have stayed where she was in North Dakota, but she had wanted to come to explain to President Johnson that she received no help back home. She said, "I didn't go much to school. So, I can't talk very good, and I don't understand very much too. Anyway, I am talking." Grinnell reflected on a past when things had been better, when her people could live off the land. She said that people were starving on the reservation. They received "commodities" from white people, typically cornmeal, oats, and rice, but the grains were often infested with worms. Educated in the issues underpinning the campaign demands, she added that she could not understand why Johnson continued to send troops to fight in Vietnam.[79] Another Native American woman, Ellis Blackhorse, revealed she had had no income at all for several months following the death of her husband, an armed forces veteran, the previous year. She told the Senate subcommittee, "I am starved, that's all I can say."[80]

Leona Hale of the Fort Berthold reservation expressed the kind of powerlessness experienced by the poor in several areas of life. She alleged that an oil company had taken away the rights to the land from the people on the reservation and claimed that whites with "forked tongue take . . . everything away from us Indians." She thanked "Brother Abernathy" for his support and concluded with a warning about the possible consequences of atomic weapons by declaring that the Great Spirit said, "If men hardened their hearts to the Maker, there shall be war, atomic war."[81] Lucille Knight alluded to the multiracial nature of the campaign in asserting she was there to speak for all of the people, "red, white and blue." She was a widow with two children she could barely feed. She suffered from a number of ailments, including failing eyesight due to complications from diabetes, cirrhosis of the liver, and a heart condition. Participation in the PPC apparently had provided Knight with the necessary knowledge and information to help her understand why she was poor, and the confidence and means to do something about it. In thanking black people for "waking Indians up to how whites are treating us, how they are feeding us [with low-quality commodity food], and depriving us of things of our heritage, our agriculture," she showed the inherent value of King's idea to build a multiracial coalition.[82]

The testimony of black people from the South provided additional evidence about several of the issues that had been revealed during the Senate field hearings in Mississippi in 1967. Myrtle Brown, an unemployed mother of five from Marks, Mississippi, paid tribute to Dr. King for getting her involved in the campaign. She had completed the PPC registration form to join the campaign on the same day he had visited her community to hand out circulars promoting the initiative. She told the Senate hearing that she had come to Washington to "get some rights," and she was there on behalf of the "whole nation of poor people."[83] Josie Williams also had come all the way from Marks, Mississippi. A mother of seven, she had brought all of the children to live with her in Resurrection City. Her testimony demonstrated how life back in Marks had, in some respects, barely changed since the days of slavery. She alleged, substantiated by the testimonies of others at the hearing, including Marian Wright Edelman herself, that a local plantation owner exploited the food stamp system for his own financial gain while the poor missed out. A shocked Senator Randolph promised to investigate the situation. On a related issue, Margaret Goodman testified on the unfairness of the welfare system as it affected numerous families in her community in Atlanta. Although she had a heart condition, she was on the "commodities" diet of grits and beans, which was bad for her health. Her welfare payments had been cut after she received an increase in Social Security payments.[84]

Speaker after speaker revealed the depth and injustice of poverty in America. Shirley Ann Simmons from Atlanta told a horrific tale of how she had to wait in the snow and rain to get food for her blind child. But the food she was given had bugs in it, a claim made by several of the witnesses. She had less than $30 per month to pay for food, clothes, and other essentials; this was not enough to feed her two children.[85] Shirley Robinson was one of the students who had been inspired by events at Quitman High School in Marks. She described the poor quality of the food offered for school lunch—usually "pieces of cornbread with bugs in it." She lived with her mother and six siblings in a house with "cardboard walls," yet they had to pay $75/month rent for the property. Her father had died the previous year.[86]

Nineteen-year-old student Benjamin Ortiz from Camden, New Jersey, was introduced by Marian Wright Edelman as a spokesperson for young people. He confidently announced that he was not there to "beg and submit, I am here to tell you what to do and see that you do it, and if you don't do it, then it is my turn." Ortiz alluded to the rhetoric of Malcolm X in saying that his own attitude was "by any means possible." He was committed to nonviolence but typically for many of his generation could not promise that things would stay that way if action were not taken to meet campaign demands. He told of how his family had been on welfare for sixteen years; since his father's death, he was effectively head of the household. Ortiz had been given a leave of absence from school to join the PPC, and he declared that in common with the other young people who had come to Washington, he was there to build a better future. By the close of his testimony, he was in a defiant mode, informing the senators that if they really wanted to understand poverty, they should come down to Resurrection City, not for a day, but "to live with me man."[87]

The SCLC reported later that many politicians were personally touched by meeting people from their districts or states who were in crisis. The eyes of politicians were opened to the poverty in their midst. The human contact between poor people and their elected political representatives was a key element of the campaign strategy.[88] The poor people who participated in the protests, demonstrations, and lobbying of Congress also grasped the essence and significance of the campaign. They made their voices heard and their presence felt during the occupation of D.C. They understood that the poor were not to blame for their own poverty, and they had the confidence and belief they could make a difference. Some of this knowledge was gained through learning activities in Resurrection City itself, and some before participants arrived in Washington. The camp brought many people together and helped prepare them to join the protests as nonviolent, well-informed, and knowledgeable activists.

CHAPTER 11

LEARNING IN RESURRECTION CITY

The assumptions that the Poor People's Campaign was badly organized and that it achieved very little has prevailed.[1] This narrow view fails to take account of the role of educational activities in Resurrection City and in the PPC more generally. The camp in Washington, D.C., provided a pedagogical space for people to come together to share their experiences and reflect on what they had in common. Scholars have recognized the important place of learning in social movements.[2] The contribution of adult education to the civil rights movement, for example, has been documented.[3] However, little consideration has been given to the learning opportunities involving poor people during the PPC. A close examination of how and what many people learned during their occupation of Washington in 1968 provides fresh insights into the impact of the campaign on the ordinary citizens who hoped to end poverty in America. Education was an important component of the campaign as the poor headed to D.C.; it also helped to define daily life in the camp and arguably provided a launch pad for future activism after the temporary city closed.

On May 12, 1968, as demonstrations and the lobbying of Congress got under way, the renowned activist Ella Baker reminded PPC participants of why they were in Washington. They were not there just to have a good time, she maintained, but to gain knowledge and use this unique opportunity to reflect on how poor people of all races had been divided until now.[4] She advised poor people to adopt the fundamental King message that "the only way to beat this rap [poverty] is for people [of all races] to work together for themselves."[5] At the official launch of the PPC in December 1967, Dr. Martin Luther King Jr. also had flagged the important role to be played by education and training in the campaign effort. He had promised that the Southern Christian Leadership Conference would train a nonviolent army to prepare them to protest in Washington, and while there would equip them to continue the struggle when they returned to their home communities. This task was in keeping with SCLC approaches to the education of activists in previous campaigns. As an organization, the SCLC was committed to the notion of lifelong learning based on the understanding that "modern society does not live by asking is everybody happy but rather is everybody learning."[6] King believed that education and social action were meaningless in isolation from each other.[7]

Resurrection City drew from a rich legacy. The seeds of activism in the civil rights movement were planted in part by adult education. In 1961, the SCLC took over the Citizenship Education Program (CEP). Black women, in particular, were at the heart of the SCLC attempts to organize and educate at the grassroots under the CEP initiative.[8] The CEP owed much to the efforts of individuals such as Septima Clark and Dorothy Cotton.[9] The program grew out of the work of the renowned, integrated Highlander Folk School in Tennessee and its collaboration with grassroots organizers in Sea Island communities off the coasts of Georgia and South Carolina.[10] Highlander, under the leadership of Myles Horton, became a powerful tool for the development of movement organizing.[11] For example, Rosa Parks entered into the national consciousness through her role in the Montgomery Bus Boycott only months after she attended one of the regular Highlander workshops.[12] Horton used education as one of the instruments for bringing about a new social order.[13] He observed, "The poor who can't read and write have a sense that, without structural changes, nothing is worth really getting excited about."[14]

Elements in the right wing of U.S. politics regarded Highlander as a hotbed of communism. FBI director Hoover's attention was drawn because the institution was so successful in educating and preparing civil rights activists to work for change across the South. He regarded Highlander as a threat to the status quo in race relations. King's connections with Highlander contributed to the right-wing backlash against him, which reached a crescendo when he began to plan the PPC in 1967. A widely circulated photograph of King "consorting" with alleged communists at Highlander in the late 1950s was repeatedly used by right-wing elements to try to discredit the SCLC leader.

Dr. King came to view the Citizenship Education Program as an example of a "constructive program project" as distinct from public protest. He anticipated that the CEP would assist the SCLC to fulfill its mission to educate and politicize black people. Ella Baker urged the SCLC to get involved in the program. Andrew Young was appointed by King to help expand the CEP, and Dorothy Cotton was in charge of field operations.[15] The decision to incorporate the CEP had far-reaching consequences for King's continuing struggle to achieve social and economic justice. From the early 1960s to the Poor People's Campaign in 1968, the CEP trained thousands of poor people and encouraged them to transform their communities, their nation, and their world.[16] It provided the foundation for the SCLC mobilization strategies; those who completed the program played a strategic role in SCLC campaigns, including the PPC.

The CEP focus was initially on teaching literacy and, more fundamentally, linking personal concerns to the overall civil rights movement.[17] By 1965, the program's curriculum had developed from an almost exclusive focus on basic reading and writing to include courses and workshops in political education, consumer education, and the "techniques of group organization designed to facilitate massive social change."[18] The initiative was underpinned by a philosophy that the social, political, and economic problems facing black people could be effectively removed through active citizenship participation.[19] In the early to mid-1960s, the CEP prepared marginalized individuals and communities to work with local government systems to gain access to services and resources. Organizer Dorothy Cotton described it as a "runaway train that could not be stopped."[20] Field workers dealt with issues, including equal access to welfare, housing, and jobs, that would underpin the demands articulated for the national effort of the Poor People's Campaign. The impact on those who participated was potentially profound. Some scholars have argued that in myriad ways, the CEP assisted black southerners to discover for themselves the links between civil and political rights and their aspirations for economic citizenship.[21]

The CEP and other programs of learning were pivotal to the success of civil rights campaigns throughout the 1960s. In the fight for the ballot, citizenship education, including Freedom Schools, advanced the cause of voter registration in the Deep South during Freedom Summer in 1964.[22] Education and citizenship were viewed as parallel institutions in the community. It was thought to be crucial for poor black people to build their own educational institutions instead of relying on those handed down by white power structures. Myles Horton described voter registration classes as more akin to a community organization where "the students were talking about using their citizenship to do something."[23] The experience of Freedom Schools also was believed to have educated and matured those involved in their delivery.[24] Among the most remarkable outcomes of the citizenship class approach was the willingness of ordinary people to wait in line either to register to vote or to cast a ballot. According to the SCLC, this showed "the courage that had been instilled in these people who earlier faced jail, beatings and other reprisals. They also knew why they needed to vote."[25]

From the moment that poor people began their journey to Washington, many felt as if they were part of something historic. Their experience was an example of the kind of learning associated with participation in social movements. PPC education organizer Charles Cheng maintained, "People had the [experience of a] Freedom School through the action of being in the PPC."[26] An activist revealed that traveling on the bus to Washington opened his eyes to the fact that many white people who were financially well-off were unhappy because others were enslaved. This led them to want to do something to make a difference. Dr. King similarly argued that equality for all would free the oppressor as well as the oppressed. For the activist on the bus, the experience of simply spending days sitting alongside others, sharing knowledge and discussing poverty, opened his eyes.[27] Another participant related how en route to Washington, some dogs behind a garden fence unsuccessfully attempted to get at them. Unfazed by the threat posed by the dogs, he announced, "We marched by, knowing we couldn't be touched, we who were tomorrow, sailing past all the fenced-in yesterdays."[28] A thirty-three-year-old man who traveled on the Freedom Trail from Memphis described the trip as "the greatest experience of his life." He said he learned so much on the journey through Alabama, Virginia, and North Carolina that he felt as if he were eighty years old.[29]

The solution to the related challenges of building a sense of community and creating the capacity for activism in the PPC lay in great measure with the learning opportunities provided for participants in Resurrection City. The PPC demonstrations, marches, and lobbying of Congress required active, committed, and informed campaigners who would adhere to nonviolence and work toward a common agenda. The Reverend Al Sampson encapsulated the challenge in noting, "Resurrection City brought people into a 'domestic' relationship with each other, but it was now important to harness this potential to bring everyone forward into a philosophical context, to be used as a vehicle for nonviolent direct action."[30] Some of the groundwork had been laid in Marks and other areas of mobilization before the poor arrived in Washington. A range of formal and informal learning opportunities were then employed in Resurrection City: Freedom Schools, workshops, meetings, and discussions in addition to the demonstrations across town. The curriculum was intended to reflect the economic and social realities faced by community members in their everyday lives and how they could change their root condition. For the most part, the learning opportunities at Resurrection City provided alternatives to conventional teaching practices. Organized outside of the formal public school and college systems, the various activities sought to avoid a form of banking education, which would disempower the poor. The term "banking education" refers to the metaphor of students as containers into which educators pour knowledge, which reinforces a lack of both critical thinking and knowledge ownership. Teachers instead adopted a peer teaching approach; they were often barely better educated than those they were teaching to read and write.[31] All education volunteers were screened to determine as far as possible whether they had any degree of racism.[32]

The centerpiece of the education effort at Resurrection City was the Poor People's University. The PPU was intended to be a special school for the study of poverty, its problems, and tactics for its elimination. It was directed at participants living in Resurrection City and the students who had come to help the campaign. Campaign organizers had lofty ambitions for this initiative, which they believed would educate participants on the many facets of poverty and thereby act as a springboard for activism in Washington and thereafter in countless communities across the nation. The PPU fitted the climate of 1968 when radical sentiments and alternative educational solutions to societal problems were in the air in the United States and elsewhere in the world. The PPU was described as "a true university in that it will serve people of greatly varying educational backgrounds, its purpose is to produce a greater level of awareness and action on the need to confront the American social structure."[33] The SCLC promised that nationally known authorities and poor people would lead the initiative and would with "no holds barred, explore the impact poverty and cultural deprivation has on America today. . . . It will prod the economics of depravity and the influence of disparity."[34]

The PPU sought to provide an opportunity for young adults to get involved in the campaign and to assist them to learn more about why poor people had come to Washington, D.C. The Summer Task Force of students would then fan out across the nation and fight poverty from the beachheads of their respective colleges and universities. Student volunteers did not need formal qualifications or experience to participate. Stoney Cooks, director of Campaign and Student Activities at Resurrection City and later the SCLC finance officer, visited college campuses from November 26, 1967, until around April 23, 1968, recruiting students to join the campaign. He expected students to personally benefit from the experience and described the students' involvement as part of a work-study program for them.[35] With students in revolutionary mode across the United States and Western Europe in the summer of 1968, Cooks was able to evoke significant interest in the PPC among some of the more militant students. During the Columbia University uprising, for example, the citizenship council there organized a benefit for the PPC: it raised money and had a clothing shack in Broadway Hall.[36] Other support came from UCLA and elsewhere. Students from the University of Michigan who were studying nonviolence held workshops at American University in Washington for the residents of Resurrection

City. They also helped to build some of the huts and to set up the camp library.[37] At American University, the Social Action Committee members moved their institution toward support of the PPC. Gary Aires and Ross Connelly from Howard University were especially prominent in mobilizing students to support the campaign. Some of the more militant Howard students, however, regarded the PPC as a farce and did not wish to get involved.[38]

The PPU ran on small donations and had an office ten minutes away from Resurrection City in the basement of the Concordia Church of Christ, located at 1920 G Street NW. Stoney Cooks, Ross Connelly, and Bill Treanor, with the assistance of numerous others, organized the initiative.[39] The SCLC worked with a committee of faculty members in area colleges and universities to get things up and running. The faculty of Howard University's School of Social Work pledged to help "make visible and to dramatize poverty."[40] Active members of the PPU Faculty Committee included Grady Tyson and Bernard Ross of American University, Sister Mary Gerald of Trinity College, Cynthia Thomas of Georgetown University, Clifton Jones and Roy D. Jones of Howard University, Mal Harris of George Washington University, and Sister Mary Frieda of Catholic University.[41] John Lewis, former chair of the Student Nonviolent Coordinating Committee (SNCC) and later a long-serving congressman, was chancellor of the PPU.[42] The great and the good across America offered their support. PPU affiliate faculty members included Kenneth Clark, a noted psychologist; singers Harry Belafonte and Joan Baez; David Dellinger, one of the organizers of the march on the Pentagon in the fall of 1967; Ivanhoe Donaldson of SNCC; and Michael Harrington, writer of *The Other America*.[43]

The PPU operations began on May 29 at the downtown American University campus in D.C., although the initiative was officially inaugurated at a mass rally in Lisner Auditorium on the George Washington University campus.[44] Local universities gave dormitory space and the use of a downtown campus, showed films, and organized teach-ins involving faculty, staff, and poor people.[45] "Confronting" the issue of poverty was to be achieved through meetings, lectures, films, presentations, and discussion groups.[46] Keynote addresses in front of the Reflecting Pool alongside Resurrection City were often delivered by well-known speakers, a who's who of radical thought in America in 1968, including Alex Haley, Howard Zinn, Dave Dellinger, Corky Gonzales, and Chuck Stone.[47] Notable thinkers such as Robert Theobald provided the background for workshops and seminars.[48]

Classes were typically held every day at 1:00 p.m. and 5:30 p.m. Workshop topics on the first day of the PPU included "The Problems of Human Communications," "Man's First Literature," and "Social Welfare Problems."[49] Other topics included "Welfare Regulations and Qualifications," "The Psychology of Racism," and the "Corporate Establishment." The schedule for June 9–15 included "The Politics of Race" and "American Black Literature."[50] One event focused on Puerto Rican and Native American poverty and included contributions from Ossie Davis, James Bevel, and Michael Harrington.[51] The idea of starting where people were—reflecting on the poverty affecting their lives—came straight out of the Highlander Folk School and CEP textbooks. Social movement theory suggests that such an approach brings positive outcomes. The theory holds that education based on the lived realities of subjects "is key to making them aware of the revolutionary nature of their objective situation as a part of the development of a critical revolutionary practice."[52]

The PPU activities were free and open to all. It was a fluid entity. Courses, discussions, and events were organized wherever space could be found and a need had been identified. Lectures and associated events were held at the George Washington University, Howard University, and American University campuses. American University made available twenty-one classrooms.[53] In addition to various university locations, discussions often took place in a tent in Resurrection City or "under the trees."[54] One interviewee recounted how magazine editor I. F. Stone was wandering around looking for the PPU and was taken off by young people for a spontaneous discussion on the grounds of Resurrection City.[55] Camp residents were also provided with reading materials. The PPU library was stocked with books, particularly those "dealing with minorities and their needs such as Dick Gregory's 'Vote for Me.'"[56] A film was presented most nights, including *Walk in My Shoes* and *A Time for Burning*.[57]

Organizers were keen to make the learning experiences in the camp as democratic as possible. Poor people often sat alongside the high-profile speakers during the workshops.[58] Discussion groups that evolved out of the lectures were said to include the other "experts": poor people themselves.[59] The SCLC's intention was to encourage learning activities that were, whenever possible, nonhierarchical, collaborative, and not confined to a formal classroom environment. In one of many examples, a facilitator was assigned to encourage dialogue among women in the Resurrection City beauty parlor.[60] The different cultural and racial groups at times jostled for position to ensure that the voices of the poorest in their midst could be heard in the various forums. For example, Native Americans insisted that mothers from their group be given a platform to help counter discrimination against their race.[61] The overall goal was "to focus and centralize the thought" of everyone involved.[62] The philosophy of the PPU reflected the vision of a campaign that aspired to be shaped and led by the needs of poor people. Stoney Cooks observed that it was not a traditional university but instead provided a platform for the poor and gave everyone an opportunity to think about poverty. With colleges across America in ferment in the revolutionary year of 1968, Cooks rather grandly maintained that the PPC, thanks to the PPU and other learning opportunities in the camp, was the most significant thing going on that summer in the social sciences. He argued that the PPU fostered participation, thinking, and perceiving and was educational.[63]

The PPU organizers inevitably faced some challenges in putting theory into practice. Some camp residents were not willing to join the various workshops and were more concerned with trying to cope with the incessant rainfall and other challenging conditions in Resurrection City. This meant that some classes were canceled due to a lack of interest. Others in Resurrection City felt excluded from some learning sessions. The *Washington Post* reported that a few older and poor-looking people seemed to be remote from the talk of "co-option" and the "rhetoric."[64] Those from different racial and political backgrounds regularly locked horns when discussing contentious issues. The more militant black students from Howard University who chose to participate changed the dynamics of some sessions when putting forward their views of the movement. In one example, some SCLC staff came together to discuss campaign issues with around thirty whites and fifty blacks, and some students who strolled by listened to the talk. One Howard University student made it clear that black people were the "teachers" and whites needed to listen. A white student objected to the suggestion that he should be silent, stating he was ready to go to the "front lines" to fight for equality. Another white man argued for the value of real interracial dialogue, and another reportedly went into a huff, protesting that he was only there because he had been invited.[65]

The challenges to maintaining black and white unity were as evident in Resurrection City as in other parts of the nation in 1968. Highlighting tensions that were never far from the surface, a militant Howard University student rejected white involvement in the campaign and cited Sartre and Malcolm X in his condemnation of what he saw as the "half black, half white" approached adopted by the PPC.[66] Some residents in Resurrection City had tired of King's philosophy of nonviolence and had little interest in peaceful demonstrations. Tony Henry felt that some of the people who had come to Washington had not been properly screened and had not been trained in nonviolence. This was especially true, he felt, of some of the younger participants.[67] Again, this mirrored the attitudes of many young people across the United States in 1968: they were impatient and wanted results. An "Uncle Tom Day" was organized to unpack some of the tensions between those content with a gradual pace of change and those more inclined to push for immediate and dramatic progress against the different manifestations of poverty.[68]

Stoney Cooks argued that the PPU, in terms of its philosophical approach, was planned and conceived as a greatly expanded Freedom School. The Freedom Schools themselves provided another strand of learning in Resurrection City. They aimed to involve children, young people, and adults.[69] The PPU joined with Telford Anderson of Resurrection City's Freedom School to present "freedom" subjects of interest to younger campaigners in the Freedom School tent at the extreme rear of the city. In the final week of the camp's existence, the National Education Association collected older children from the camp in a bus to take them into town for more traditional classes. Organizer Charles Cheng of the Washington Teachers Union reported that the Freedom Schools in Resurrection City adhered to the nonviolent philosophy of the SCLC.[70] A press article heralded the arrival of Freedom Schools in Resurrection City with the headline "Freedom Schools Open: No Philosophy and No Pencils."[71] Cheng said, "We are not going to make decisions for the community"; we "will radically depart from traditional educational methods."[72] The classes drew inspiration from the student-centered example of Freedom Summer in 1964, although they placed less emphasis in Resurrection City on reading and writing.[73] It was anticipated that teachers would learn more than they taught.[74] Cheng insisted that teachers needed to be opposed to racism and the war in Vietnam; otherwise, they were not appointed.

An all-black Freedom School steering committee was formed although whites participated at different levels in the program. Teachers were recruited who included "drop-outs" and professors, and poor people led some classes. Sixty percent of the teachers were black, and 40 percent were white.[75] The training of teachers was held at the local, community-controlled Morgan School, a fact Charles Cheng observed was important since, from his perspective, Freedom Schools were about empowering people to take control of their own lives, including their own institutions.[76] The Freedom School classes were organized each day depending on what was happening in the campaign. Although not all camp residents chose to participate, one hundred to two hundred people regularly attended each session. The basic curriculum focused on issues of racism, poverty, and oppression, including discussion of the participants' personal experiences of poverty.[77] Cheng reflected on the intrapersonal dimension of the learning that occurred in Resurrection City: "I think that someday somebody will see as much in that [bringing groups from different backgrounds together] as . . . in many of Malcolm [X]'s contributions. Now I'm only talking now in terms of the solidifying of those of us who for so many years have been at least if not outright enemies we've certainly been silent ones."[78] He maintained that Freedom Schools in the broadest sense started the day that poor people began to leave their homes. From then on, he insisted, "they probably had one of the most educational experiences that has been completely denied by the white educational system."[79]

The PPC learning activities also benefited from the contributions of educators from the independent national organization the Scholarship, Education, and Defense Fund for Racial Equality (SEDFRE). This organization worked at the grassroots level to effect social change. It provided leadership training for disenfranchised and poor people to meet needs ranging from voting rights and improved schools to street lights and paved streets.[80] SEDFRE delivered workshops on the theory and practice of community development, and its members organized discussions and workshops on the techniques and strategies of citizen participation and nonviolent civil disobedience.[81] Ronnie Moore of SEDFRE described the PPC as "the greatest test of nonviolence of our times." He argued that in Resurrection City nonviolence was undergoing an "experiment of community development, a live-in, and not the traditional mobilization marching." It was his job, as he saw it, to develop leadership in the camp; to help the residents learn about protest, collaboration, and the management of conflict; and to help them seek a deeper understanding of their dilemma.[82] As previously mentioned, SEDFRE provided forums where camp residents discussed the purposes of demonstrations and protests, for example, following the eat-in at the Department of Agriculture.

A SEDFRE tent was open in the city for a minimum of eighteen hours a day; residents attended two- to three-hour sessions in groups of fifty or more on a regular basis. The notion of the activist educator in social movements, who helps people translate their anger and frustration into forms of action, is particularly helpful here in understanding the SEDFRE approach.[83] SEDFRE staff attended the first city council meeting of Resurrection City. Immediately afterward thirty-five people participated in a session in the SEDFRE tent. A lively discussion ensued about how people in the camp viewed Resurrection City. Some concerns were expressed by the participants about the behavior of the marshals, and it was agreed to form small committees of residents to deal with such situations. SEDFRE staff were keen to see the participants themselves take up the issues they had identified rather than rely on the trainers to do so on their behalf. In one discussion, some camp residents from the South came to the defense of Ralph Abernathy and others in the SCLC leadership who were being criticized on several fronts, including the fact they were not living in Resurrection City alongside the poor people. Spiver Gordon from SEDFRE believed that these town hall meetings acted as "a drainage of the frustration" that built up and helped to bolster morale in the camp.[84] One meeting was reportedly constantly interrupted by a Black Power advocate who would not let the other people get a word in. The group asked him to leave.

Although Resurrection City predated the writings of Brazilian educator Paulo Freire, much of the learning activity in Resurrection City was similar to his work with poor people in Brazil. His relevance for understanding the Freedom Schools has already been considered by scholars, in particular the example of Freedom Summer in 1964 in Mississippi. One author observed that "although presumably unknown to planners of Freedom Schools, [Freire also] saw literacy instruction [as] rooted in the social, political and economic realities of the student, leading to critical consciousness or conscientization as an essential weapon in empowerment."[85] Freire's rejection of "banking" education and his emphasis on "conscientization" can be identified in the forms of learning in Resurrection City.[86] In considering the relationship between education and consciousness, he wrote about education that "domesticates" and education that "liberates." He argued that oppression in all societies derives from the distribution of power, which powerless people can understand partly through education.[87] Dr. King's concept of the "powerless poor," shaped through his experiences in Chicago, also seems relevant for an understanding of the approaches to learning in Resurrection City. Like Freire, King appeared to understand that people's ideas, beliefs, and values arise from their position within the capitalist system, and this social experience shapes their view of the world. This analysis holds that through education, people can become more aware and conscious of the economic, historical, and political factors that have influenced their place in society.

The SCLC argued that it was essential for poor people "to be free to articulate their problems."[88] Through the learning opportunities in Resurrection City, participants were encouraged to dig deeply into their own history and the roots of poverty. Jesse Jackson reflected that the informal meetings provided a forum for the poor to come together to understand the history of discrimination from their different perspectives and legacies; for example, as a consequence of their history the Native Americans were "anticolonial" and made this clear to other groups.[89] Analytical sessions assisted participants to discuss their felt needs, to seek a deeper understanding of their dilemma, and to learn about protest, collaboration, and the management of conflict.[90] Some of the poor people in Resurrection City were arguably politicized in the process. As one young resident from Marks, Mississippi, commented, "We've been learning here that we have responsibilities—that we have to think about changing things, because if we don't they're going to get worse. Like the air being polluted, you think you want to breathe that? And the water too. We've been learning a lot, like how this country made the Congress vote a lot of money to end the poverty in this country."[91]

Paulo Freire showed through his educational work that individual development and collective consciousness go together when exploited and oppressed classes or groups take education seriously as a liberating experience worth working hard at.[92] The PPC was an example of a social movement that provided opportunities for such learning to take place. One scholar stated that "consciousness-raising is a process, one through which members transcend the false consciousness of individualism and build a new consciousness of participation grounded in solidarity and cooperation."[93] Antonio Gramsci's notion of cultural hegemony also offers a framework for understanding learning in Resurrection City. It can be seen that hegemony operates persuasively rather than coercively, through the medium of cultural institutions.[94] Gramsci showed how hegemony constitutes a sense of absolute reality, beyond which it is difficult for most members of society to move in most areas of their lives.[95] Ruling ideas are so powerful that they limit the possibilities for thought among the dominated classes.[96] The counterhegemonic project, therefore, is about the formation of alternatives within an existing political system.[97] Some autonomy is possible, which can bring about critical consciousness. Gramsci argued that the development of counterhegemony is an essentially educational enterprise: the key is found in learning.[98] Some scholarship has suggested that with education, the groups in Resurrection City came to an understanding of the economic component of their oppression and "how racism and economic exploitation had contributed to their situation."[99] The organizer of the Appalachian caravan put his finger on the issue in commenting that the purpose of the Poor People's University was to educate poor people. The PPU was conceived, he maintained, "primarily to do that job with the poor people which would give them that degree of sophistication—to go beyond just wanting another pair of shoes or to figure their welfare handouts."[100]

While some residents chose to stand apart from others in the camp, Resurrection City arguably housed a more vibrant and active community than has ever been acknowledged. The evidence from numerous case studies indicates that learning in social movements can occur in concentrated moments of struggle, as people learn it is possible to challenge the unchallengeable and learn the practical processes of making this happen.[101] Social movement theory suggests that engagement by individuals and groups in local communities and in campaigns is an important factor for learning solidarity and coalition-building strategies.[102] A campaign leader observed of Resurrection City, "It was a hard place to live in, but you develop within a movement . . . because you know what you're working for within that structure. They felt good about coming to their [nation's] capital and making a statement about themselves."[103]

In focusing on an inaccurate stereotype of lazy, grasping, and potentially disruptive poor people in Resurrection City, scholars have distorted the purpose of the campaign and denied ordinary citizens their historic contribution to fighting poverty. In the next chapter I consider further evidence of how some of the residents in Resurrection City who were proud of their own identities came to trust others from different racial groups through the medium of cultural activities and shared pedagogical space.

CHAPTER 12
A CITY LIKE ANY OTHER

The learning activities in Resurrection City notwithstanding, the enduring image of the camp is of discontent and disorganization with people living uneasily together in a sea of mud. The core themes of the campaign were largely forgotten in the tide of adverse publicity, which has helped to define the initiative ever since. The shantytown of Resurrection City became the story—to the detriment of the campaign. The press described a camp divided and in chaos. The *New York Times Magazine*, for example, observed that the "anger and problems of the poor of the whole nation were in this one shantytown."[1]

Undoubtedly, different groups strived to make their presence felt in the shared space. The Southern Christian Leadership Conference reported on tensions between experienced activists and "youthful, poorly disciplined poverty warriors."[2] Accounts of daily life referred to the literal dampening of morale caused by incessant rain. Especially severe rainstorms on May 23–24 and 27–28 made life almost impossible for vulnerable residents in the camp. The *Washington Post* carried an image on May 29 of a rain-sodden and collapsed dining tent in Resurrection City.[3] Half of the estimated 2,400 residents were evacuated because of the drenched conditions. The evacuees, mainly women, children, the elderly, and the sick, were accommodated in private homes and churches. A resident described the brown, sticky, smelly mud, sometimes ankle deep: "You mince along, leaping over a treacherously deep section of slimy brownness, only to end up with your feet in mud, less deep, but no less slimy and stinking."[4]

On June 3, following yet another deluge, the *Washington Post* described a bleak scene in Resurrection City. It reported that bread, fruit, opened food tins, and empty cartons were scattered around. At least thirty fires burned in open oil drums. Smoke, black ash, and the odor of rotting food hung in the air. A Washington, D.C., water truck arrived on the scene, allowing residents to brush their teeth.[5] Jesse Jackson tried to be upbeat about the situation, but conceded that some poor people had left the camp: "Some just honestly can't cut it, but for many of us it's a matter of going for broke."[6]

There was disorganization in Resurrection City in part due to the challenges involved in running such a complex enterprise. The assassination of the charismatic Dr. Martin Luther King Jr. on April 4, 1968, had left a void that others, including Ralph Abernathy, struggled to fill. But Abernathy and some SCLC colleagues played into the hands of their critics by sleeping in the Pitts Motor Hotel while their "black brothers and sisters slept in the rain and mud" of Resurrection City.[7] Abernathy tried to claim he needed to be near telephones, but this excuse did not wash with critics.[8] Marian Logan of the SCLC was outraged at the apparent selfishness of Abernathy and others.[9] The bad press over the issue was a public relations disaster for the Poor People's Campaign.

Some scholars have suggested that the remaining leaders of the SCLC were less astute than King had been in handling the news media.[10] The SCLC later described relationships with the media as "experimental, tense and at times volatile."[11] Lurid reports alarmed D.C. residents already worried at the presence of poor people in their midst. Those in Resurrection City rejected such reports as exaggerated and intended to derail the campaign. James Peterson, administrative assistant to the national director of the PPC, described the press attitude as "derogatory," stating that journalists were only interested in what sells newspapers.[12] Jesse Jackson wrote that problems in the city were amplified out of all proportion by the news media.[13] One SCLC official was less generous and criticized what had gone on in Resurrection City in unflattering terms: "In retrospect, I'm not sure that our version of a 'Utopian Auschwitz' would have been a significant improvement over the 'chaotic Auschwitz' that developed. It was quite a shattering experience to learn that the 'noble poor' have as many hustlers as we 'rich folk.'"[14] However, even SCLC outsiders recognized that at least some press reporting was biased against the campaign. A local government employee expressed disappointment with the media: "The press and the American public failed to recognize that the PPC brought together the poor and the militant from all areas—people who had not known each other before. What we had was a simulated ghetto and what can happen there."[15] The Reverend David Eaton of the Washington Opportunities Industrialization Center argued that the press overplayed many of the problems in the camp and underplayed the real reason—poverty—that people were in D.C.[16]

It is naïve to assume that life in the city was unproblematic for those living there. As in any community, "there were people there who'd give you the shirts off their backs, and others who'd kill you for yours, and every type in between, just [like] a city."[17] Resurrection City arguably posed no more challenges for law enforcement agencies than any other community of a similar size. Hosea Williams dismissed suggestions that the camp was some sort of lawless Wild West town. Following reports in the press of rapes, robberies, and general mayhem, he said that nothing took place in Resurrection City that did not happen in New York or Chicago. An activist blamed the SCLC for failing to maintain order but scoffed at the idea that any hoodlum in the camp could threaten him. "We'd break his jaw," he declared; his working-class background meant he could handle himself.[18] In order to establish a sense of proportion about what was going on, the gates of the camp were opened temporarily so that the public could come in and see for themselves the realities of life there, rather than read reports in the newspapers.[19]

With many different groups of poor people sharing the same space, a complete unity of purpose was impossible. It was reported that "cultural, programmatic and ideological differences present[ed] a serious organizational problem for the city."[20] The Reverend Al Sampson conceded that his role was to stay up sometimes to 5:00 a.m. in order to get people to relate although they came from different backgrounds: "maybe the same social economic level but they came from different habitats."[21] Tensions existed between different racial groups and within them. Perhaps no one should be surprised by this. The Resurrection City experiment of bringing together so many different people with conflicting world views was unprecedented. A key activist observed, "You had a city going; and like in any other city, everybody wanted to be the top politician in that city. So there was a normal, healthy struggle of poor people finding out that they had power and wanting to exercise it."[22]

As mentioned above, the decision by some participants to live outside of Resurrection City proved to be controversial and fueled rumors of divisions within the campaign leadership. Ernest Austin, coordinator of the PPC Appalachian group, explained that his first arrivals in Washington, D.C., came on a three-day "inspection tour" and then simply accepted an invitation to live in the Hawthorne School, owned by Alexander and Eleanor Orr. The school provided the best refuge from the incessant rain. Some Appalachians decided to remain there because, in their view, Resurrection City was not run as a model community should be; for example, three good meals a day were available at the private Hawthorne School.[23] Less well reported was the fact that other Appalachians did live in Resurrection City near the Washington Monument, where they had a campfire and held workshops. Austin described that group as one of the "strongest sections of the city as far as community spirit and bearing in an interracial community were concerned."[24]

Approximately five hundred PPC participants lived in Hawthorne School, including Native Americans, Indo-Hispanos, whites from Appalachia, and black people. The D.C. Department of Licenses and Inspectors repeatedly threatened to evict the PPC activists because Hawthorne did not have a license to lodge them.[25] But the Orrs played host to the various PPC contingents until mid-July, when they closed for the summer and left for a tour of Europe. Reies Tijerina had opted to house "his people," the Indo-Hispanos, at Hawthorne School. Their physical separation from Resurrection City was symbolic of a broader rift between him and the SCLC leadership. He felt disrespected because, in his opinion, his group did not get the same support as others did from the campaign leaders; for example, they were not provided with new clothing. Press reports claimed that Tijerina briefly quarreled with Bernard Lafayette over an alleged failure by the SCLC to pay travel and other expenses of Native American leaders, including Mad Bear Anderson from the Tuscarora reservation in New York and Hank Adams from Washington state.[26] Tijerina regularly complained at press conferences about his treatment by black leaders.

In the opinion of Andrew Young, the decision of some groups to live apart from the others was understandable in that friction was a "part of the nature of the poor." He acknowledged that the outspoken and defiant Tijerina was "more Stokely Carmichael than Ralph Abernathy."[27] SCLC staffer Katherine Shannon felt that Tijerina only ever wanted to talk to the "top man" because he assumed that such a person spoke for all.[28] Rodolfo "Corky" Gonzales from Denver, Colorado; the Reverend Leo Nieto from Austin, Texas; two young Puerto Ricans; and a young woman identified only as Escalante from Los Angeles worked with Tijerina in the Hawthorne School. Gonzales was another frequent critic of the black leadership of the PPC. He declared he would not move into Resurrection City until there was "honesty on both sides."[29] In addition to those at the Hawthorne School location, one hundred Native Americans also set up a headquarters in St. Augustine's Episcopal Church, which was close to Resurrection City. The Reverend Alfred R. Shands of St. Augustine's identified with the values and objectives of the PPC and even joined the marches. He provided the Native Americans with a kitchen, sleeping areas, and a rest room.[30] Other Indigenous people did occupy space in Resurrection City. They erected tepees at the edge of the camp, held planning sessions there, sang freedom songs, and had snacks from the God's Eye Bakery.[31]

Critics of the campaign contend that integration within the PPC was an illusion, given that most of the Spanish speakers and Native Americans chose to live outside of the camp. Tom Houk argued that this was one of the biggest splits in the campaign: some in the SCLC were unhappy that the people did not all live together.[32] However, there are two ways to look at this issue. King's aspiration to bring the different races together was achieved in part during the occupation of Washington, D.C., but the action was not confined to Resurrection City. The different groups that gathered at Hawthorne created a multiracial community in microcosm. They met, socialized, and devised protest strategies.[33] The location provided a focal point for those of Indo-Hispano origin to come together, for example, to claim land that had been stolen from them. The different racial groups at Hawthorne also organized a new educational program called AIM (African American, Indian, and Mexican American), celebrating their different cultures, which grew out of a meeting they all attended at the Department of Health, Education and Welfare. Participants in AIM included Lance "Sweet Willie" Watson and other members of the Invaders gang from Memphis, Tennessee, which had been implicated in the disturbances at the sanitation workers protest in March.[34] The different groups found common ground at Hawthorne and worked in solidarity. In one notable incident, the residents resisted an attempt by police to arrest a boy by making a fortress against the doors at the Hawthorne School.[35]

Despite press suggestions to the contrary, the Native American contingent forged close emotional bonds with other racial groups in Washington, D.C.[36] Charlie Cambridge, for example, worked closely with people from Appalachia. Tillie Walker, Mel Thom, and Victor Charlo coordinated efforts with the SCLC steering committee.[37] They organized combined and separate demonstrations for the Indigenous group, including visits to the Indian Claims Commission, the Forest Service, the Department of Health, Education and Welfare, the State and Justice Departments, and the Smithsonian Institution.[38] Ralph Abernathy later implied in his autobiography, published in 1989, that he had been uncomfortable with certain aspects of a multiracial campaign. He wrote that "no longer did the cause seem as clear cut or the motives as pure."[39] Perhaps his unease is understandable; the campaigns in the South in the earlier phases of the movement had focused on clearly understood objectives—to bring an end to segregation and assure the right to vote—because they affected black people only.

In Resurrection City, other groups had their own priorities and were therefore not always "on message." Individuals such as Reies Tijerina were impressive leaders and had their own constituencies. Reporters jumped all over an incident at an Abernathy press conference when Kahn-Tineta Horn (Mohawk) interrupted his flow by delivering a letter accusing the campaign of exploiting Native Americans. Her letter acknowledged that Abernathy acted with good intentions but alleged he had no knowledge of the real needs of Native Americans.[40] Her intervention got to the heart of the matter. The needs of Native Americans coincided with other groups around the broad issue of poverty, but the specifics of each group often differed. Abernathy pleaded innocence by responding that the Indigenous people's demands had been included in the presentations to Congress, and on this issue, he could claim to be on safe ground. Interestingly, Abernathy later disagreed with the shorter list of campaign demands drawn up by Bayard Rustin in the run-up to the Solidarity Day demonstration scheduled for June 19, partly because the demands of nonblack groups were not included.

The real bone of contention for other racial groups was around the issue of leadership and the perception that Abernathy and the SCLC made all of the important decisions. King had set a standard at the Minority Group Conference in March 1968 by bringing minority group leaders together on an equal footing. He had created a coalition of the willing that drew together both the common and disparate aspirations and demands of the various groups that signed up for the PPC. However, Ella Baker, for one, had long thought the leader-centered approach of the SCLC as opposed to group-centered leadership stifled self-sufficiency and was inherently less democratic.[41] If King had lived, the tensions between the groups may or may not have been less acute, but that is all conjecture.

Against the legitimate criticism of the SCLC by Reies Tijerina and others should be weighed the reality that divisions within social movements are not unknown, especially regarding a campaign as diverse as the PPC. Conflicts on the ground in Resurrection City made cooperation difficult but were a learning experience for some. For example, Tillie Walker, executive director of the United Scholarship Service, acknowledged that many in her community thought it was wrong to mix with black people, but she actively went around "educating people" to try to change their minds.[42] Walker claimed that black people in Washington treated the Indigenous people better than the Mexican Americans did.[43] Reflecting that there was also a gender issue, she stood her ground by refusing to let Tijerina and other male leaders speak for Native Americans. When the opportunities arose to press their case in public forums, she insisted that individuals such as Martha Grass, a Native American low-income mother of eight, be given the floor.[44]

For those who chose to live in Resurrection City, there is no doubt that people did not get along all the time. Confrontations between some blacks and whites were reported.[45] Jesse Jackson observed that tension between people was not surprising since throughout U.S. history the poor were taught that other poor groups were their "enemies."[46] Yet the disagreements between and within the different racial and ethnic groups were not terminal to the spirit of solidarity that often characterized life in Resurrection City. On June 22, George Crow Flies

High, in a mark of respect for King's successor, presented Ralph Abernathy with a Proclamation of Temporary Cession inscribed on a tanned hide and signed by Mad Bear Anderson and others.[47] Corky Gonzales, president and director of the Crusade for Justice in Denver, thought Resurrection City was a great success in pulling people together despite his dismay with SCLC leaders who, he argued, had not lived up to Dr. King's dream. He felt let down by the failure, as he saw it, of the SCLC leadership to take a strong enough stand against Vietnam: "It's poor people fighting that war."[48] Even Tijerina later conceded that the PPC was "one of the best opportunities to give our own version of our history, not the Anglo version, to the world."[49] He recalled with pleasure taking more than three hundred southwesterners of all backgrounds to the Mexican embassy on June 3 to request assistance over the Treaty of Guadalupe Hidalgo.[50]

It is possible to see aspects of Resurrection City in a more positive light. Activist John Reynolds brought some perspective by acknowledging that it "was not a place of comfort, it represented the way people lived their lives, they brought their issues with them."[51] Daily life was arguably better organized and more diverse than press coverage suggested. For example, the varied schedule for Friday, June 14, 1968, included a protest on school conditions by Mexican Americans at the Department of Education and a variety of other demonstrations and lobbying across town; activists addressed the Press Club, and the news media were briefed on the responses of three federal agencies to campaign demands.[52] The reality that the majority of people had no option but to live together in the camp also was a factor; they could either work together in solidarity or splinter apart. Through his involvement in the PPC, Buck Maggard from Appalachia recognized for the first time in his life that black and white miners had similar priorities.[53] One campaigner summarized it best. He recalled how "plain citizens" had come together in coalition: "We sat in little sessions around fires and talked about it. It took four or five weeks to get people to the point where folks . . . said, all right, when are we going to form it."[54]

Despite the problems of the multiracial community, an impressive aspect of life in the camp was the cross-cultural interactions made possible by the shared space. These activities fostered friendship, respect, and understanding between some of the poor, although not all of them. Resident Marguerite Lopes observed that outsiders might get the impression that people "idled" about the camp, but there were numerous cultural and educational programs to occupy everyone in a productive fashion.[55] Campaigners from all kinds of backgrounds met and interacted at the focal point of the Many Races Soul Center, which was under the leadership of the Reverend Frederick Douglass Kirkpatrick, director of the PPC cultural program, and Jimmy Collier.[56] Collier composed and produced a record of freedom songs, *Everybody's Got a Right to Live*, in cooperation with Kirkpatrick. Cultural activities generally have pedagogical functions in bringing people together. Singing and storytelling, for example, have traditionally been associated with learning in social movements.[57] The Soul Center played host to a variety of activities, including music projects, where residents could teach others and at the same time explore the roots of their own cultures. Talent shows featured songs and acts by those living in the city. High-profile guest performers included folk musician Pete Seeger and the Georgia Sea Island Singers.

The cultural program validated the backgrounds of the groups represented in the PPC, giving Mexican Americans, Native Americans, Appalachian whites, black people, and others an opportunity to share their distinctive cultures. The expressed aim in the Soul Center tent "was not merely to give release or entertainment, but to educate people about their past."[58] Musicians related and shifted their material as they acknowledged the relationship "between who they were and who somebody else was."[59] Activist photographer Jill Freedman related how "one granny in her 80s" from Mississippi marched through the mud and stood on the platform to sing "Ain't Gonna Let Nobody Turn Me Around."[60] Reverend Kirkpatrick viewed the Soul Center as the "birthplace of a new nation, because, through their folk art, oppressed people can testify to their deepest feelings, purge themselves of fear and passivity and become a history-making movement."[61] Reflecting the ideas of Brazilian educator Paulo Freire, Kirkpatrick argued that poor people need to be freed from "cultural oppression" at the same time as they exert pressure to end economic deprivation.[62] The cultural events provided entertainment but were also educational. The Soul Center activities developed within people an awareness of and a pride in their own heritage and an awareness of the heritage of others sharing the space in the camp.[63] The Many Races Soul Center also hosted city council meetings and held the occasional "press seminar," where residents met the news media. All such events were announced over Resurrection City's loudspeaker system.[64]

Before coming to Resurrection City, Anne Romasco from New York City worked at the Highlander Folk School, using the mediums of art, music, literature, and dance to develop interracial understanding. She believed that the cultural programs at Resurrection City gave visibility to all the groups represented in the PPC.[65] On one memorable evening, May 29, many groups contributed to a varied evening of folk music and poetry. There were harmonicas, trumpets, guitars, and drums of different makes and kinds, including a barrel and a biscuit tin. Native Americans offered songs and spoke of their solidarity with all poor people.[66] A resident identified only as Mr. Perkins, an older Native American from North Dakota, spoke Dr. King's language in declaring his opposition to the Vietnam War. Jimmy Collier compared Perkins to great black leaders who "could talk music."[67] A performance by Bernice Johnson Reagon had the whole tent city "singing and shouting" the old spirituals.[68] Pete Seeger rounded off the evening, expressing the protest and longing of all of America's poor and powerless.[69]

A large sculpture of a hand celebrating the black struggle was created for Resurrection City although the camp was torn down before it was put in place. The sculpture remained in a backyard before being recovered many years later and placed outside the Historical Society of Washington building in D.C. The hand represented yet another example of the celebration of cultural life engendered by the PPC. Commissioned by SCLC staff member Vincent DeForest, the sculpture was envisioned as part of the Hunger Wall plywood mural already in place in Resurrection City. The Hunger Wall helped the residents to declare the space on the Mall as their own. They used the panels to display words and images to convey to the world at large their messages and identities and solidarity. Conceived as part of a PPC narrative to "tell it like it is," the murals' messages were multilingual and multicultural. They included "Chicano Power," "Guerrilla," "Love the Viet Cong," "Black That's It," "Let's Get Human Understanding," "Sisters of Watts for Human Dignity," "Brothers and Sisters' Hunger Is Real and You'd Better Believe It," "Small House and No Work for My Family," and "Ask It Shall Be Given." Some of the Hunger Wall panels are today part of the collection of the Smithsonian's National Museum of African American History and Culture in Washington, D.C.

The campaigners also produced their own internal media, including *Soul Force*, the official organ of the SCLC. The director of information, Thomas Offenburger, together with an editorial board had oversight of the publication.[70] Alongside regular position statements and press releases, the publication was an important tool intended to heighten awareness of the campaign and sway public opinion. The SCLC had learned from previous campaigns, including Student Nonviolent Coordinating Committee activism during Freedom Summer in 1964, the value of providing local communities with a variety of media, including books and newspapers, that offered counterhegemonic messages to those normally received from official channels.[71] Among a wide range of articles written by activists, the *Soul Force* edition dated June 19, 1968, highlighted the exploitation of cheap labor among different racial groups. It stressed that the presence of poor people in Resurrection City was evidence that they "were tired of the rich getting richer and the poor getting poorer." Another article declared, "We are here for revolution—the continuing revolution of America."[72] It also celebrated the great tradition of dissent in American life by recollecting the abolitionist orators and socialist songwriter, poet, and labor activist Joe Hill's *Red Songbook*.[73] *Soul Force* offered a searing critique of capitalism, sought to raise the consciousness of those involved in the campaign as to their place in the system, and stressed the importance of nonviolent collective action in bringing about change. A powerful piece written by Howard McConnell seems to transcend the decades that have passed since the PPC. He called for a "human revolution" in the United States, requiring investment in people and an end to the "cage of the ghetto" and the "squalor of the shack."[74]

Camp residents also wanted a community newspaper and agreed it should not be an SCLC organ but something completely assembled and written by people living in Resurrection City. *True Unity News* was viewed as "a people's newspaper, a grass-roots thing" and included poetry and stories written by poor people themselves.[75] Printed in a rudimentary fashion, which belied the seriousness of the content, its statement of purpose was "to write what has to be said to help advance the goals of the people." It advocated self-help, economic control, and cultural pride, ideas central to Black Power. The newspaper also described its statement of philosophy as one of "unity" regardless of religion or philosophy. "Let's get ourselves together," it proclaimed.[76] It featured regular bulletins called "Abernathy Speaks" and was edited by Gordon White, J. Edward Haycraft, "Akbar," and Bill Mahoney. Haycraft, an accomplished writer known as the "Black Soldier," was reportedly born in an alley in Louisville, Kentucky.[77]

Encouraged by the general creativity brought about by educational and related cultural activities in Resurrection City, the residents wrote songs to document their thoughts and experiences of the PPC. Haycraft distributed numerous songs while living in Resurrection City, including "Mother Take Me Back," "In Resurrection City," and "Crosses on Freedom Fighters' Graves."[78] He sold songbooks for fifty cents.[79] Most important, poems published in *Soul Force* allowed the voices of poor people to be heard. Haycraft stressed the importance of poetry as a medium of expression for camp residents. He noted that "the culture of peasants, poor industrial workers and unemployed people is an oral culture; thus, the most profound statements are verbal and not written." He saw poetry as the best vehicle to express the "great ideas" of poor people.[80] A Native American calling himself "Free Man" eloquently expressed his thoughts on the immorality of the Vietnam War in his poem "A Curse on the Men in Washington." An extract reads: "As you shoot down the Vietnamese girls and men in their fields, burning and shooting, poisoning and fighting, so surely hunt the white man down in my heart."[81]

Despite this activity, frightening tales of crime and anarchy clouded the realities of life in Resurrection City. The *Boston Globe* sought to bring a different slant, however. It published a revealing interview with Marguerite Lopes during the occupation of Washington in which she provided a detailed description of life in Resurrection City from the perspective of a resident. She told a tale of ordinary people going about their business while at the same time doing extraordinary things. Arriving early in the morning in D.C. on a bus from Mississippi, Lopes's first thought was to find coffee to put some life into her "fatigued aching" body. She ducked under a canvas into Resurrection City and from that point became acquainted with some "proud, committed and articulate victims of abject poverty." These included Eddie and Dolores Boynes from Newark, New Jersey, the parents of ten children. Eddie Boynes acted as the chief coffee maker in the camp. Every morning, tenants from all over Resurrection City drifted toward the plywood-roofed extension of his shack for coffee and conversation. He poured Lopes and her two friends cups of coffee from a large pot that sat on a grate placed over a shallow pile of burning charcoal. Boynes informed them that he had built his five-room plywood and plastic domain in thirty-five minutes in the pouring rain while his ten children waited in another hut. He had come to Resurrection City because he knew how difficult it was to eke out a bare existence but wanted to give a little hope to those who "have it harder than I have."[82]

Newspaper reporting on the campaign rarely captured the kind of selfless spirit demonstrated by Eddie Boynes and so many like him living in the camp. He was there to help others as well as his own family, even though he was so poor himself that his wife had no shoes because the mud had chewed up the only ones she had. Lopes described him as a kind and genuine person who hoped that "something good will give hope to the despairingly poor."[83] Lopes was embarrassed to see one of the Boynes children give his mom a pair of shoes that were far too small for her. The apparently innocuous incident led Lopes to walk away feeling a "little sick and very angry, every time I recall the hurt in the eyes of every member of the family, the sickness and anger will return."[84]

Lopes was surprised that there had been no epidemic in the camp because of the mud and the mosquitoes. However, she was impressed with the "neighborhood concept" practiced in Resurrection City; people were happy to socialize with her and everyone else. A mother of five children from Concord, Massachusetts, explained to Lopes that she had come without her children "to help out others who are as poor as I am."[85] The mother expressed optimism that the efforts of the poor in Washington had "shaken them" (members of the government). A twenty-eight-year-old mother of four from Roxbury, Massachusetts, stated that she was there because the welfare system left her unable to clothe her children properly. She explained to Marguerite Lopes that she had cried most nights since arriving in Resurrection City, but she did not want to leave. She had become attached to many people, everyone was good to each other, and her children were treated kindly, therefore she never needed to worry when they ran off. Lopes observed that this testimony filled her with pride, especially when the mother from Roxbury added, "I'm going to stay just as long as I am needed. I used to feel awful all of the time I was in Roxbury, poor and ashamed, but I am a different person now, I am proud, I know I am black and even though I am poor, I am proud."[86] While only part of a complex situation in the camp, the commitment of this young woman spoke volumes about the way some people reached out to each other in Resurrection City in genuine and sincere ways.

Some other press coverage also helped to provide a more complete and balanced view of life in Resurrection City. One article captured some of the contradictory and conflicting aspects of the camp and by implication reminded readers of the sacrifices made by so many poor people in traveling to Washington and putting up with so much. The writer tried to view the world from the perspective of the residents. The article began by observing that "from the outside, there is a certain amount of physical ugliness in the place." The author claimed that marshals harshly chased away any curious people who tried to look in through the main entrance. He also suggested that outsiders might gag at the "stench of burning trash," or flinch at the "ragged clothing" hanging on lines stretched between the wooden and plastic huts, or even be taken aback by an "old overstuffed chair drooping unevenly on three legs on the grass." Readers were encouraged, however, to look beyond the superficial impressions of the camp and those living there. A camp "militant" informed the journalist, "There is no hate in here. When you walk through that gate, we tell you to get yourself together . . . to make peace with yourself."[87]

The article also cited the example of Peggy and Ray, who in another time and place might have mistrusted and perhaps even fought with each other. Peggy was a white grandmother from Alabama, described in the article as a "hillbilly," who was in Resurrection City with her children and grandchildren. Ray was a young black man who had lived with his wife and children in ghettos in the North, ghettos in the South, and ghettos in Washington, D.C. Both represented the people Dr. King had attempted to bring on board in the grand struggle against poverty. Ray had a simple but evocative sign hanging outside his hut: "We have lived in many houses. This is our first home. Welcome."[88] Peggy and Ray sat on the grass between their huts and talked as neighbors would normally do. It was a typical scene one might find anywhere across America, except that one individual was white and one was black. Other neighbors stopped by to say hello or drop off something they had borrowed. Ray explained they were over the "hate stuff": "We have learned it's not race, the enemy is the whole sick American system." Another man added that the problem was not in Resurrection City but outside in the wider society. Later, Ray strolled over to the dinner tent, where a band was playing for several hundred residents of the camp. The newspaper article pointed out that the "crowd was one that people said could never be."[89] A member of the Blackstone Rangers from Chicago sat clapping on the edge of his chair with a young white couple from Baltimore seated beside him. Women from Mississippi and Tennessee sat with small children on their laps. One mother said, "There is no fear in here," and another said, "This is our home, now."[90]

The New York Times, in one report, also tried to look beyond the first impressions of an unkempt camp sitting in the heart of the tourist area. The presence of the poor was acknowledged to be a "shock amid the fountains and magnificent lawns and cool formality of white marble monuments to dead presidents." The article added that as "untidy and impermanent it may be Resurrection City has a life of its own."[91] The community was described as a "restless but spirited union of farmers, preachers, factory workers, community organizers, welfare mothers, maids, children and students."[92] Reports that the Invaders group from Memphis was terrorizing the camp were unfounded, according to the New York Times. Journalist Faith Berry wrote that a leading Invader, Lance Watson, seemed to have begun a new "constructive program." She witnessed the Invaders helping blind and sick people in the dining tent and medical unit. Berry said that if she had believed all of the stories about gangs, she would have run for her life. Wild stories about the Rat Patrol gang and the Commandos from Milwaukee seemed untrue from her firsthand experience. In fact, she wrote, the Commandos were not a gang at all, but part of the youth council of the NAACP.[93] Berry mentioned an important aspect of the matter in describing Resurrection City as a "city of rumor." On the night of June 22, for example, a story spread that Stokely Carmichael had been shot. Fake news was indeed alive and well in 1968. Ralph Abernathy dismissed the story over the camp's loudspeaker system.

Abernathy hoped that the Resurrection City experiment would teach people how to live with each other in their home cities and would act as a model for a just society. He wrote optimistically, "We would all be back on the frontier, where liberty and equality were achievable goals."[94] Despite disagreements between the constituencies represented in the camp, some important progress was made in creating a critical mass of politicized poor people who now considered that their experiences of poverty constituted a common bond. They gained new knowledge and confidence to carry forward the struggle for economic equality. Jesse Jackson argued that Resurrection City allowed poor people from different backgrounds to come together and in the process begin "learning to appreciate the other and to gather information about the other." He added that by "wallowing together in the mud . . . we were allowed to hear, to feel and to see each other for the first time in our American experience."[95]

Administrative coordinator John Rutherford asserted that poor people would take back the message of the camp to their communities. He claimed it was the first time he had witnessed blacks and whites getting up in the morning to greet each other with "Brother" and "Sister" and meaning it. Living together in Resurrection City had proved that people of different races could get along: "We were a living example that it could work."[96] He added that people really tried to reach each other, even though they did not know how to go about it.[97] Camp resident Marguerite Lopes observed that contrary to what the press reported, she never sensed any real tensions between people. Personality clashes were to be expected, she conceded, and the occasional "explosion" was unsurprising given the circumstances in which people were living.[98]

James Peterson, administrative assistant to the deputy national coordinator of the PPC, reflected that some people came to the model city expecting luxury. However, he argued, they were not supposed to think of it in that way; it was in fact a "communion dream of Dr. Martin Luther King Jr." He argued that Resurrection City was set up primarily to show the nation and the world how people from all backgrounds could live in togetherness.[99] Based on the daily interactions between people of different races and backgrounds, the SCLC felt justified in making the optimistic claim that the campaign had succeeded in "uniting the poor in community and breaking down the racial barriers that have long prevented America's poor people from joining together in a common cause."[100] Philosopher Cornel West has observed that it is politically and culturally difficult to build coalitions because of the mistrust between disenfranchised groups.[101] The evidence suggests that in Resurrection City some progress was made in breaking down the barriers between people. An architect responsible for designing Resurrection City noted that people were separated not by race but by geography and that "there was more mixing than you would have seen elsewhere in 1968." He added, "They were there because of King; it was all inspired by him."[102]

One scholar has argued that Resurrection City became a "casualty of its very nature as a metaphor, its problem as a strategy for continuing the movement after King being precisely that it was not movement but emblem, static and so passive."[103] However, the disorganization in Resurrection City and the reluctance of the U.S. government to meet the PPC's demands obscured much of what was achieved. In any social movement, things—often the most significant things—go on behind the scenes.[104] If one drills down to look at the realities of life as experienced by the poor people who were there, it is possible to see that the campaign was arguably life-changing for many of them. The sacrifices made in traveling to Washington, the marches and demonstrations, the formal and informal learning activities, the incidental contact between individuals, and the cultural exchanges among people of different races meant that the participants would never be the same again. Their effort was historic, and at a personal level the impact on them should not be underestimated. Sixty-eight-year-old Mr. Tilly from Marks, Mississippi, told of how he would stay in Washington until "we get straight." Even at his age, he worked ten hours a day in the cotton fields under a broiling sun. He lived in no more than a hut back home.[105] The life story of a disabled merchant marine typified the fresh belief many found in the camp. A formidable fighter for justice, he had been refused Social Security several years previously and wrote to President Lyndon Johnson to complain about the decision. In 1965, he had hitchhiked from Tennessee to picket the White House in protest at his treatment. Returning to Tennessee, he refused to back down and continued his one-person campaign for justice. In yet another trip to Washington in 1965 to press his case for Social Security, he slept on the streets and ate from garbage cans. Three years later, he claimed, the PPC had offered him the hope he thought had been extinguished by the system in the United States.[106]

James Peterson, PPC administrative assistant, pointed to the tragedy of Resurrection City being regarded as the problem. He observed that poor people did not come to Washington to "be scandalized, to be looked at as being hoodlums, gangsters, beasts living in Resurrection City." They had come primarily, he argued, to raise the problem of poverty in America.[107] There were some criminals and others who behaved badly in Resurrection City, but the negative press coverage often failed to acknowledge the heroic efforts made by dignified ordinary people who had made long journeys to Washington, D.C., to end poverty in the nation. Nor had the press fully captured their contribution to community life in Resurrection City, nor the impact on them of their residence in the camp. One of the designers of Resurrection City, Tunney Lee, said of the camp that "it worked," and it was a privilege to work with the kind of people that he encountered.[108] For the first time, people felt that their voices were truly heard, and many had been empowered by the whole experience. The campaign gave them hope. Twenty-two-year-old Dallis E. Carr from Marks managed to find a job at a filling station in Washington. He claimed that his eyes had been opened by participation in the PPC to new possibilities, however modest they may have appeared to others. Looking out of Resurrection City to the world beyond the perimeter fence, he described the "big green park with green trees, birds flying and singing all over. There is freedom in the air. I feel I am in the free world I heard so much about."[109]

Resurrection City was not a five-star hotel, but it was a community where many people came together and where some of them found hope. SCLC leader Andrew Young later wrote optimistically, "Looking back, I can see that it [the PPC] marked the emergence of a broad-based progressive coalition—poor people who were black, white, brown and red; religious leaders, union leaders; peace activists. Jobs, peace, freedom would be linked, sustained through a loose, shifting, but persistent coalition of organizations."[110] The shared space in Resurrection City helped make all of this possible. However, the life of the camp was short, and a number of circumstances led to its demise.

CHAPTER 13

THE FINAL DAYS OF THE POOR PEOPLE'S CAMPAIGN

Over the course of Resurrection City's brief six-week existence, the residents experienced highs and lows. One of the lowest points was the assassination of campaign friend and supporter Senator Robert F. Kennedy. Still reeling from the shock of Dr. Martin Luther King Jr.'s slaying just two months earlier, residents of the camp were devastated by Kennedy's death on June 6 following his shooting a little more than twenty-four hours earlier. His assassination while campaigning for the presidency came as a great blow to the movement. Robert Kennedy, of course, had suggested through his emissary Marian Wright Edelman that Dr. King bring the poor to Washington, D.C.

Kennedy's relationship with King was complex and had evolved over several years. King was regarded in 1961 by the Kennedy brothers as a "troublemaker" and difficult to control.[1] Peter Edelman, an aide to Robert Kennedy and Marian Wright Edelman's husband, observed that when Kennedy was attorney general, he had a "relationship of discomfort" with King.[2] As attorney general, Robert Kennedy had authorized FBI wiretapping of King, helping to fuel rumors about the private life of the civil rights leader. The attempts to ruin King's reputation lived on long after his death. In 2019 King biographer David Garrow discovered summaries of FBI transcripts obtained from bugging and wiretapping. The unsubstantiated summaries presented lurid and disturbing tales that if made public at the time would have ended King's career.[3] During the John Kennedy administration, Robert Kennedy and Dr. King had different priorities and viewed the desired pace of change on civil rights differently.[4] Before the Chicago campaign in 1966, King heard that Kennedy felt the movement had neglected the northern urban centers. In Andrew Young's view, King took the Kennedy remark personally and "was wounded" by it.[5] It was not until 1967 that Senator Kennedy and Dr. King grew to trust and respect each other; opposition to the war in Vietnam and their shared determination to tackle poverty brought them closer. Both believed that the lack of educational and economic opportunities for young people in the slums was at least in part responsible for unrest in urban centers.

In his bid to win the Democratic Party nomination for president in 1968, Robert Kennedy, in common with King's agenda for the Poor People's Campaign, sought to build a multiclass and multiracial coalition. (Barack Obama would succeeded in achieving this forty years later.) Robert Kennedy announced the news of King's murder to a mainly black audience while campaigning in Indiana on April 4, 1968. Rarely a comfortable public speaker, Kennedy's speech that night saw him at his best. He only used a few notes he had scribbled himself. His tribute to King included an appeal for calm in the wake of the assassination in Memphis. He also fused the deaths of his late brother, President John F. Kennedy, and Dr. King in stating that white men killed both of them. Robert Kennedy viewed King's body the night before the SCLC leader's funeral in Atlanta and marched in the procession from Ebenezer Baptist Church to the campuses of Atlanta University and Morehouse College after the funeral service.[6]

Ralph Abernathy, Andrew Young, and others in the Southern Christian Leadership Conference had come to regard Robert Kennedy as a standard-bearer in the fight against poverty.[7] Kennedy had attacked the inadequacies of the War on Poverty, especially as it affected urban ghettos, from at least 1966. Like King, he was looking for solutions to urban problems. Kennedy started his own regeneration initiative in Bedford-Stuyvesant, New York, which had some private investment from large corporations, including Ford and IBM. Since King's assassination, Kennedy in part at least had replaced King in the hearts and minds of the SCLC leaders. He was also loved and respected by many of the poor people living in the camp. Kennedy's advocacy on their behalf seemed genuine and sincere. Earlier in 1968, he had added to his already high stock with poor people by chairing the Senate's committee hearings on hunger in Kentucky, which examined the outcomes of the War on Poverty.[8] Kentucky resident Zona Belle Akemon commented that he "was here with a purpose and it wasn't a vote getting thing. I think he had a real feel for the people here."[9] Even Stokely Carmichael apparently respected Kennedy and voiced concerns that the senator might co-opt Carmichael's own power in black communities.[10] For the poor people in Washington, D.C., and their leaders, Robert Kennedy's assassination became a second important what-if. Marian Wright Edelman believed that Kennedy would have gone all the way and defeated Republican candidate Richard Nixon in the November 1968 presidential election.[11]

Abernathy saw great significance in the circumstances of Robert Kennedy's passing, reflecting that his death was another manifestation of the "daily violence and oppression" in the United States, which was visited on citizens through inadequate housing, a lack of decent education, and hunger. He urged America to honor Senator Kennedy by bringing forward reforms, including a more equal distribution of wealth, better housing, decent jobs, adequate income, and education of the highest quality.[12] In a moving, symbolic, and memorable gesture, the Kennedy funeral cortege stopped briefly in front of Resurrection City on its way to the burial site in Arlington National Cemetery. The residents of Resurrection City came out of the camp to stand with raised fists in homage and joined a choir in singing "Battle Hymn of the Republic," an anthem associated with the Kennedy brothers and the civil rights movement. Abernathy also remarked that the "news media did not see the stop at Resurrection City as a tribute to the poor, but it was."[13] Representatives of the city attended the burial ceremony. In the spirit of the multiracial city itself, the representatives included poor blacks and whites, Mexican Americans, Puerto Ricans, and representatives of three Indigenous nations.[14] They waited patiently for six and a half hours on the grassy slopes surrounding the gravesite, which was near John F. Kennedy's final resting place with its eternal flame.[15] The threat of rain and the sound of thunder added to the somber nature of the scene.

The loss of Robert Kennedy compounded the sense of grief still felt over the death of Dr. King and contributed to a lowering of morale in the camp as the month of June 1968 progressed. A welcome renewal of the camp license until June 23 breathed a little more energy into everyone. The largest PPC crowd thus far, fifty thousand people, was attracted to the Solidarity Day rally against poverty on June 19. Originally scheduled for Memorial Day, the event was postponed until Juneteenth, the annual celebration of emancipation from slavery. It was perhaps the highlight demonstration of the campaign. Participants included around seven thousand Puerto Ricans from New York under the leadership of Annibal Sullivan and Bill Rodriguez. Puerto Ricans had collaborated on civil rights issues with other racial groups beginning in the 1950s, and their presence in Washington represented a determination to stress their own identity and to make their voices heard.[16] Sullivan later worked to establish the Poor People's Embassy, based in the Hawthorne School, to look after the needs of poor people after Resurrection City closed down.[17] The embassy was intended to provide a place where people could go to seek a redress of grievances and to call elected officials to account.[18] It failed to have an impact, however, and the idea was shelved not long after Resurrection City was bulldozed into the ground.

Bayard Rustin came back briefly into the spotlight when Ralph Abernathy asked him to organize Solidarity Day. Rustin suggested a list of what he believed were easily understandable and achievable campaign demands to underpin the event. He viewed Solidarity Day as an opportunity to make one last push to win support from Congress for specific legislation. His list of demands was to be taken forward in coalition with other civil rights organizations under the auspices of the Leadership Council on Civil Rights, whose executive council Rustin chaired.[19] Rustin asked the government to recommit to the Full Employment Act and legislate the creation of one million socially useful career jobs in public service; adopt the pending Housing and Urban Development Act of 1968; repeal punitive welfare restrictions in the 1967 Social Security Act; extend to farm workers the guaranteed right to organize trade unions; and restore funds that had been cut in War on Poverty programs.[20] Politicians warmed to the clarity and apparent reasonableness of his demands.[21] But Hosea Williams and Ralph Abernathy both turned on Rustin because his more modest demands represented a step back for the campaign and did not include the main demands of the other racial groups. Rustin's omission of demands for the return of stolen land, for example, confirmed the view of some of the Mexican American representatives that their needs continued to be marginalized.[22] Under pressure, Rustin resigned from his position as head of planning for Solidarity Day. His effective firing provoked much adverse comment in the press about further splits in the leadership of the campaign.[23]

Solidarity Day continued without Rustin and under the guidance of Sterling Tucker, director of the Washington Urban League, ably assisted by David Rusk. The SCLC leaders lowered their demands because the campaign was due to close in any case.[24] They were reduced to only the priority items of food, welfare, jobs, and housing. Marian Wright Edelman helped formulate a revised list, which mapped onto legislation already in the pipeline.[25] She led a deputation of around 155 clergy and church officials to meet members of Congress on July 10–11, after Resurrection City had closed. The National Council of Churches, the Social Action Department of the U.S. Conference of Catholic Bishops, and the Synagogue Council of America sponsored the group.[26] Over the course of the campaign in Washington, Edelman reportedly negotiated with eight government agencies and attended meetings of five subcommittees of the ad hoc committee set up by Congress to maintain communication with campaign leaders. One Capitol Hill insider observed that "the campaign should have had a dozen of her," such was the impact she made on elected officials.[27]

Washington, D.C., authorities set several provisions for the organization of Solidarity Day. They agreed on a timetable for the event with the PPC leadership. Assembly took place between 5:00 a.m. and 10:00 a.m. at the Washington Monument; entertainment and march formation occurred between 10:00 a.m.

and 12:30 p.m.; the march to the Lincoln Memorial via Independence Avenue and the Mall was scheduled for 12:30–2:00 p.m. The program was held in front of the Lincoln Memorial from 2:00 p.m. to 4:30 p.m., and everyone dispersed thereafter. Traffic and parking restrictions were imposed.[28] The evening before the event, as King had highlighted on many occasions, Abernathy encouraged America to think what the alternatives to nonviolence might be. He described the scheduled speakers at the event as the voices of reason and judgment, the voices of the democratic process and nonviolence. Nevertheless, he added, "there will be anger in our voices; our tramping fear must be heard."[29]

Campaign organizers prepared and distributed twenty-five thousand signs, bumper stickers, and badges.[30] The buttons represented the new confidence of many by declaring "Black Is Beautiful." Some placards identified individual groups, such as "Sisters of Watts" and "Concerned Citizens from Slippery Rock." A "grizzled man in denim overalls" carried a placard proclaiming the aspirations of countless thousands: "Happiness—No Rats, or Roaches: Lots of Good Food, a Warm Dry House."[31] One man proudly carried a handmade sign on which was written a George Bernard Shaw quote often used by the late Robert Kennedy: "Some men see things as they are and ask why. I dream of things that never were and say why not." A gray-haired man sat under a tree holding a small sign with the poignant message "The King Is Dead, Long Live His Thing."[32]

The crowd at Solidarity Day was an eclectic mix, as King would have wanted. It attracted participants from across the country with many different motivations for joining in the event. Some, including trade unionists, had long supported the rights of workers. The event attracted civic action groups and supporters of civil rights and human rights. The crowd presented an image of both diversity and solidarity. The marchers' clothing included "sandals, dungarees, business suits, nuns' habits and miniskirts."[33] Church representatives included Arthur S. Flemming, president of the National Council of Churches. The Protestant Council of the City of New York sent several dozen busloads of church members.[34] The U.S. National Student Association (NSA) mobilized nationwide support. More than seventy-five colleges and universities had already contributed food, money, and clothing to the campaign. Moved by the assassinations of King and Kennedy, the NSA vowed that "for every person who is killed in pursuit of change, there will be thousands to continue the struggle."[35] While the event took place, hundreds of white hippies and young black people splashed around in the Reflecting Pool ignoring announcements for them to "come back to land."[36]

The event also celebrated woman power. The first march of the Washington campaign, led by Coretta Scott King and symbolically held on Mother's Day

(May 12), had highlighted the contributions of women to the campaign while also focusing on the issues of welfare as they affected families. This momentum carried through all the way to the end of the PPC. More than 50 percent of the Solidarity Day crowd was female; the *Washington Afro-American* reported that women were a dominant presence in the program.[37] This contrasted with the all-male speaker platform five years earlier during the March on Washington. Organizations represented on Solidarity Day included the League of Women Voters, the National Council of Negro Women, the Young Women's Christian Association, the Women's International League for Peace and Freedom, Women Strike for Peace, Church Women United, the National Welfare Rights Organization, Women for McCarthy, and the National Association of Social Workers.

White women from the suburbs paid $1.75 each to ride from Bethesda, Maryland, on buses sponsored by Montgomery County church groups. Several of them said this was the first time they had participated in any kind of demonstration but regarded the event as a "just cause."[38] Mrs. John Woolverton, who lived at the Episcopal seminary in Alexandria, Virgina, had helped to find food and supplies for Resurrection City. At first when she phoned others to ask for help, they would get angry and describe the poor as "riffraff." It is to the great credit of the campaign that this negative and hostile attitude changed, and many people started to come forward with donations; Mrs. Woolverton thought this was "very moving."[39] Mrs. Lucy Wilson Benson, president of the League of Women Voters, announced her intention to the press to bring a large contingent on June 19, reflecting the important role that women and the issues they represented played throughout the campaign. She noted that her group's involvement in the PPC was merely an extension of the activities of the League of Women Voters, including their long-standing support of equality in education and employment. She rejected the suggestion that poor people needed to pull themselves up "by their bootstraps" and placed the onus on Congress to take action against poverty.[40]

The march was notable for its excellent organization. Three hundred buses brought protesters from Boston, New York, Detroit, Pittsburgh, Chicago, and dozens of other places. On one bus from Baltimore, SCLC marshal Earle Flemming collected the names of the people on board and made sure everyone had an identification tag. The bus travelers sang "Michael, Row the Boat Ashore" as they sped toward Washington.[41] Seven hundred northern Virginians assembled at a parking lot north of Washington National Airport and walked two miles, two abreast, and across the Fourteenth Street Bridge to the Washington Monument. A North Arlington college student identified himself as coming from a white, middle-class, suburban neighborhood. He said he had come to change the minds of those "who didn't give a damn" about poor people.[42] A *Washington Post* report suggested that the excitement of the day reached the poorest quarters of Washington, D.C. A journalist spoke to a few men standing at a street corner who if they were very lucky might get a day's work cutting underbrush, cleaning out a basement, or handling rubbish. They were Dr. King's people. Dressed in rags, they fed on "tepid" baked beans with two slices of white bread on the side. Although reluctant to join the throngs at Solidarity Day, most were "abuzz" about what was going on downtown and thought it was a significant event. "Slim," one of the group, declared that this time "the white man knows we ain't kidding." He went on to suggest that violence could be the way forward should the campaign fail to make a difference in their lives.[43]

The demonstrators on the Mall picnicked and enjoyed listening to a range of entertainers and speakers.[44] A generally positive mood prevailed although twenty-one-year-old Zanette Lewis of Richmond, Virgina, complained that this type of demonstration was for the older people; it was no longer relevant.[45] Other views reflected the presence of Black Power advocates amid the multiracial nonviolent demonstration. There was certainly an underlying tension that this might just be the final nonviolent event. The *New York Times* described a young black woman in a red T-shirt sitting under a tree wearing a sign around her neck: "This Is Your Last Chance for Nonviolence." The article commended the marchers who had tried to bring change over many years and were nearing the end of their patience.[46] Standing across from the PPC headquarters in Washington, a black youth declared that the march would not change a thing. "Black folks have [to] quit marching," he asserted. Walter Shepherd, age sixteen, said he now felt "good" about white people after seeing so many of them turning up to support the cause. He wanted to help poor whites but predicted there would be a lot of violence if things did not turn out well.[47] Groups of older teenagers, including the Zulu 1200s from St. Louis, Missouri, came to Solidarity Day because they said they wanted to be close to the action. They confirmed they were not supporters of nonviolence but adhered to King's principles on this momentous day.[48]

Protests against the Vietnam War often were couched in terms of the importance of nonviolence.[49] In a powerful address, Jesse Jackson offered America "soul power" as an alternative to war. He declared that "instead of military power to kill, and economic power to enslave, and political power to disenfranchise . . . with steady persistence and determination, we offer soul power, an expression of our internal toughness and capacity to endure and not submit to tyranny and oppression."[50] Despite Jackson's rejection of violence, the D.C.

authorities used local National Guardsmen and police reservists to bolster the Metropolitan Police Department, providing a total security force of 4,300 for the event. The U.S. Army was also on "high alert" to intervene if required.[51] On Solidarity Day, the police and National Guardsmen on duty remained mainly on the fringes.

The event was said to resemble an old-style political rally with music and rousing speeches.[52] It also captured the cultural scene in 1968. Celebrities turned out in force. Well-known musicians helped to educate the public about the PPC through their songs of social protest. While onlookers munched hot dogs, the Roberta Flack Trio performed; Peter, Paul, and Mary were well received; singer and composer Noble Sissle eulogized Dr. King; and Pete Seeger sang "Banks of Marble."[53] Eartha Kitt was introduced as the "First Lady," and she spoke and sang a little in Spanish. Inspired by Dr. King, she hoped to persuade America to change direction and to stop losing face across the world due to its failure to solve the problems of poverty and peace.[54] Marlon Brando turned up wearing cowboy boots, "tight fitting pants," and a navy blue pea jacket. The *Washington Afro-American* described him as "standing alone like the world had forsaken him."[55] Brando took time to speak to the press, describing hunger as "obscene" in the richest nation in the world.[56]

While the marchers sweated together in the sweltering heat, a congressional delegation provided a sharp contrast by arriving in air-conditioned buses. Democratic representative Kenneth J. Gray from Illinois reportedly had an "uneasy" look on his face, perhaps because he was the chief architect of a bill intended to close Resurrection City for good. The politicians looked like fish out of water; the majority seemed relieved to escape after an hour when word arrived of a quorum call on the Hill.[57] Cabinet secretaries Orville Freeman of the Agriculture Department and Robert Weaver of the Department of Housing and Urban Development, the focus of the food and housing protests, made an appearance at the Lincoln Memorial. Presidential candidates Senator Eugene McCarthy and Vice President Hubert Humphrey joined them. Humphrey was booed because of his close association with the policies of LBJ, despite his career-long advocacy for civil rights.

As ever, Dr. King was never far from some people's thoughts. Solidarity Day seemed to provide further evidence of how some people had not come to terms with his loss. The *Washington Examiner* wrote that his physical absence "created a pervasive and all-encompassing spiritual presence, he was the sub-theme of a whole day's program, whose main theme was an appeal to Congress for food, housing and job aid for the poor."[58] Constant reference was made to King, and many of the signs in the crowd paid homage to his memory. The presence of people who had been close to King added extra poignancy to the occasion. His Morehouse College mentor Benjamin E. Mays presided over the early portion of the program, and Rosa Parks was present in the audience. The speakers in the main event and the concluding ceremonies included Dorothy Height of the National Council of Negro Women, Ralph Abernathy, Coretta Scott King, Republican senator Edward W. Brooke, Walter Reuther of the United Auto Workers, Johnnie Tillmon of the National Welfare Rights Organization, Whitney Young of the National Urban League, Roy Wilkins of the NAACP, Reies Tijerina, Corky Gonzales, Peggy Terry, Martha Grass, Gilberto Gerena Valentin, and Jesse Jackson.[59] The majority of them called for a guaranteed income, jobs, healthcare, and other measures.

Abernathy gave the speech King might have delivered himself. He declared that the frustrations of the ghettos and Vietnam "caused the nonviolent idealism of the black community to become a violent cynicism for many." In reference to the March on Washington five years earlier, he noted that on that iconic day the marchers had come for black people, whereas now "we plead for the Indians, Mexican Americans, the white Appalachian, the Puerto Rican, and the black man."[60] Abernathy reflected later that the positive response of the crowd to his speech helped him feel comfortable for the first time in his new role as successor to King.[61] Coretta Scott King was one of the main centers of attention: children in the audience chorused her name, and the crowd gave her standing ovations. Her children accompanied her. Yolanda wore a blue denim dress; Martin, Dexter, and Bernice were all clad in blue denim work clothes. Mrs. King's emotions must have been mixed as she delivered an address from the same spot where her husband had stood five years earlier when he made his "I Have a Dream" speech. She read words she had composed on her fifteenth wedding anniversary.[62] She referred to the violence of poverty and how it affected women more than others. She spoke of the need to get more women into leadership positions and made a plea for united womanpower to fight poverty and war.[63] King's widow then sang the spiritual "Come by Here, My Lord" and read an emotive telegram from Ethel Kennedy, widow of Senator Robert Kennedy. It said, "Today my heart and prayers go with you; the best monument to Martin Luther King would be the programs he and my husband cared about deeply."[64]

The speakers brought their own particular perspectives to bear on the proceedings. Walter Reuther, president of the United Auto Workers, provided welcome support from labor unions. He urged renewed efforts in declaring, "Progress must not be judged by how far we have come but how far we must still go." Like King, he called for an end to the slums and ghettos.[65] Whitney Young of the

National Urban League warned that unless things changed, this would be the last nonviolent march.[66] In a newspaper column a few days later, Young seemed to draw back from this prediction, observing that the poor had limitless power to deepen the scars of hate and violence, but they had chosen a different kind of power, "the power of reason; the power to build; the power to organize together to loosen the bonds of poverty and to turn the nation around."[67]

On behalf of Mexican Americans, Reies Tijerina once again made his presence felt. He struck a militant note by accusing the United States of an "organized criminal conspiracy against his people."[68] Although Solidarity Day was peaceful and respected King's philosophy of nonviolence, Tijerina's rhetoric encouraged the press to compare the event unfavorably with the March on Washington in 1963. The *New York Times* reported that "anger replaces the hopes of 1963."[69] Other media outlets saw it differently; the *Washington Post* described a "day of hope and challenge, not a day of disaster and despair." It noted that the appeals over the loudspeaker were not for violence and revolution but to drive home the message that the nation had problems. The predominant tone, the article said, was a plea for people of all races to come together to fight poverty.[70] The *Washington Afro-American* hoped that the federal government would respond to the "constructive criticism" as opposed to the "violent civil disturbance" by marchers from the seamy side of America.[71]

Many outsiders to the campaign believed that the leadership should have closed down the PPC and gone home after the relative high of Solidarity Day.[72] However, those remaining in Resurrection City were determined to stay the course. While Solidarity Day was taking place, the camp was quiet and depopulated. The *Washington Post* reported that "an air of subdued tension" prevailed in Resurrection City. Park police reported at least six incidents in which people were beaten up, robbed, or both allegedly by young people from the camp.[73] Almost as if preordained by the negative coverage from some press outlets, Solidarity Day on June 19 was followed by heightened tension and a more militant mood in the camp. The next few days brought the "most overtly disruptive action taken by the frustrated Native contingent."[74] A march to the Department of Agriculture on June 21 ended in chaos after protesters nonviolently blocked the building doors. The police responded by wading into the demonstrators with billy clubs in a bid to disperse them. King's promise to dislocate Washington had come to pass.

The date of June 23, when the license for the camp was due to expire, fast approached. Abernathy called for a National Day of Prayer. Only around five hundred people remained in Resurrection City; the others had left for home. Police made their plans, and by the early morning of June 23 were in place around

Resurrection City and ready to move in. A tear gas attack in response to an alleged rock-throwing incident saw residents run in panic toward the Washington Monument before returning to the camp. *True Unity News* later gave its version of events. It reported that Andrew Young's pleas to remember there were women and children in the camp were ignored by the police.[75] An officer apparently threatened to arrest Young and reloaded his tear gas gun in front of him. The tear gas covered more than half of Resurrection City, according to the *True Unity News* account; some of the residents were hospitalized. A man who identified himself to police as a physician was treated with great disrespect, and his medical bag was confiscated. Around 3:00 a.m., a police car was observed approaching, and broken bottle glass was then found scattered around the edge of the camp. In the view of *True Unity News*, police had scattered the glass in a blatant attempt to both smear and incriminate the residents in order to justify the tear gas attack.[76]

The determination of camp residents to see things through to the end was powerful. Their adherence to nonviolence can be contrasted with the actions of some police officers as the life ebbed out of Resurrection City. Activist Jill Freedman asserted that the community was attacked because police and the overall system were afraid of them.[77] On June 23, the day before the camp was bulldozed into historical memory, Jesse Jackson showed one last act of defiance. He spoke from the back of a truck in Resurrection City to a "rainbow" coalition of the remaining residents, mainly women and children. Greatly moved by their plight, Jackson called on each of them to repeat the words "I may be poor, but I am somebody, red, yellow, brown, black, and white, we are all precious in God's sight, I am somebody."[78] Dr. King had used the phrase "I am somebody" from at least 1964. Jackson's actions and words on that morning in front of a dispirited crowd recaptured the essence of the campaign and in a real way offered hope for the future. The federal permit for the camp expired on June 23 at 8:00 p.m. The few remaining residents of Resurrection City were permitted to stay overnight. There was to be no further reprieve, however; authorities intended to put a stop to the occupation and the demonstrations.

The next day, heavy humidity hung over the campsite; it had rained on twenty-two of the forty-three days of existence of Resurrection City. The *New York Times Magazine* described the death throes of the camp. At precisely 9:44 a.m., a police chief using a bullhorn announced, "The permit of this property has expired; you must leave here within the next 56 minutes to avoid arrest and prosecution."[79] Abernathy stood his ground by reiterating his intention "to honor the permit granted to us by the Indians, who hold a more rightful claim to the land than the government of the United States."[80] But by 1:00 p.m. on June

24, King's dream to occupy Washington, D.C., had come to its inevitable conclusion. Two hundred and fifty members of the Civil Disturbance Unit backed up "by a battery of weapons from tear gas to shotguns and one thousand Metropolitan police officers" moved in. Workers destroyed the site. All that remained were piles of rubbish, destroyed huts, and a few defiant placards and signs. A plywood board against a tree pronounced, "Now Occupied by the U.S. Government."[81] Another wooden sign left behind said, "We came in droves with new hope, the young—the old—the gritty; / We dared to build a dream in Resurrection City. / We left behind hopelessness, for we were tired of pity, / We seek only true dignity."[82]

Defiant as ever, dozens of poor people and their supporters were arrested and jailed for some final acts of civil disobedience. Chief Judge Harold H. Greene of the Court of General Sessions sentenced Abernathy, for example, to twenty days on an unlawful assembly charge after the SCLC president joined more than two hundred other campaigners at a demonstration at the Capitol grounds on June 24.[83] Federal law prohibited demonstrations on those grounds. Other campaigners followed Abernathy's example. One hundred and twenty of the stragglers in Resurrection City who refused to budge were arrested. As they were led away, all adhered to nonviolence. King's spirit was with them all.

The closure marked the end of a turbulent and short life for a community that had endured the constant attention of the forces of law and order, including infiltration by the FBI, the tear gas attack by police, and the repeated calls of politicians to close the camp down. A major critic of the PPC, Senator Strom Thurmond, had no sympathy and in July complained that the whole enterprise had cost the taxpayers $1 million, including overtime pay for the police and the resodding of the area where Resurrection City stood.[84] A national campaign, which had begun at the local level, now made ready to return to its origins at the grassroots. The groundbreaking *Eyes on the Prize* documentary on the civil rights movement would later advance the notion that Resurrection City represented a battle between rich and poor—and the poor had lost.[85] Michael Harrington also assumed that Resurrection City was the end of a long journey. He wrote, "One of the most marvelous political movements in America in the form which it took under Dr. Martin Luther King Jr. from 1955 to 1968 had come to an end. And the beloved community was gone forever."[86]

The stragglers were given bus fare home by the Travel Aid Society.[87] The demise of the city and the circumstances surrounding the closure were a huge psychological blow to the camp's residents. Activist John Rutherford recognized that there had been organizational difficulties in the camp, but he believed it was closed because of its growing efficiency and argued that it had been well run and well structured.[88] This was achieved despite the wet weather, which "had a drastic, if immeasurable, effect on continued residency as it created difficult living conditions."[89] However, the residents had remained proud and resilient. For many of the poor, "the mud hole was a paradise," and they had raised their standard of living by moving in.[90] A resident claimed that the authorities "were afraid of the strength that had withstood the endless rain."[91]

Ralph Abernathy justifiably postulated that the very existence of Resurrection City was a triumph because critics said "we couldn't build it but we did," and in his estimation this meant the nation could no longer hide from the poverty in its midst.[92] He later described the camp as "a beautiful and eternal symbol of hope and determination to end poverty and redeem America."[93] He was frustrated because the negative press coverage was a distraction from the campaign demands and complained, "The world knew about the mud in Resurrection City, but not about the progress we made."[94] It was a source of regret to Abernathy that the camp was closed down just as he felt that all of the logistical problems in running a small city had been overcome. Hot meals were being provided for all; pipes and sewers were being put in. He took pride in the other successes of Resurrection City, for example, the daily newspaper appropriately called *True Unity News*, the Poor People's University, the New Breed Art Center, and an arrangement for poor people to sign up to meet directly with elected representatives.[95]

With Resurrection City gone, a few hardy souls remained behind in Washington, D.C., and looked to the SCLC to provide shelter and support for them. One campaigner noted that people had been involved in the process of building the city together and did not want to leave, no matter what happened: "They really felt, this is what we made."[96] A group of around forty calling themselves the Refugees from Resurrection City for Human Rights ended up on July 10 huddled outside Alexandria's Episcopal seminary waiting to be provided with places to go. The closure of Hawthorne School had left the SCLC with the task of finding them temporary accommodations.[97]

The destruction of Resurrection City did not spell an immediate end to the PPC in Washington. The headquarters, originally situated in a plywood building in Resurrection City, relocated to a former National Urban League office in D.C. The SCLC planned further acts of civil disobedience, although Andrew Young feared that not enough people were willing to go to jail.[98] Morale was high, however, among the small band of determined people. Two jailed activists, Andrew Papillon and Phil Harris, demonstrated their spirited refusal to buckle to what they regarded as unjust authority by refusing to undertake the routine duties expected of all inmates in prison. Papillon argued that if he did the work, it would be "just like the slavery that we are trying to escape."[99]

On June 28, five men from Georgia, including Willie Bolden, wagon master of the Mule Train, were arrested for a demonstration at the Capitol. Bolden was undaunted by his subsequent sentence of twenty-five days in jail, saying, "I have never run from jail, I believe in what I am doing." Jim Mock, head of SCLC's direct-action group, promised a change of tactics in late June and canceled a small demonstration.[100] The SCLC thereafter stepped up the pace, and more arrests followed for civil disobedience. Fifteen PPC activists were arrested on July 4 after 150 police officers blocked an attempt by protesters to take three mule-drawn wagons from the iconic Mule Train onto the Capitol grounds for a watermelon picnic. A demonstration led by Herman O'Neil at the Capitol building on July 9 ended in eighteen arrests, including that of Melberta Meadow, age nineteen, for unlawful assembly.[101] All but one were ordered held on $200 bail (the freed individual was not accounted for in some press reports).[102] That person was arrested after cursing policemen and running across a lawn; it is unclear if he was a campaigner or not. It was only the latest in a fresh series of sporadic protests.[103] More than fifty Capitol and Metropolitan police converged on the scene; they processed and photographed the demonstrators and put them in two patrol wagons.[104] The arrests of the five men, six women, and several juveniles took place in front of tourists, who listened as the group sang "We Shall Overcome" and chanted "Oh Johnson, You Know You Can't Jail Us All."[105] Sympathetic supporters held vigils outside the prisons.[106]

The remaining activists continued to make an impact. A group of one hundred Detroit priests accused General Sessions judge Tim Murphy of imposing an "apparently excessive" ninety-day sentence on the Reverend Dennis Maloney of Detroit on a charge of unlawful assembly.[107] On July 12, SCLC staff member Jerry Spriggs from New York received the same harsh sentence: ninety days in jail and a fine of $250. Spriggs had been a marshal at Resurrection City and was convicted of blocking driveways and rush hour traffic at an Agriculture Department sit-in.[108] He was among seventy-five protesters put behind bars. The SCLC provided clear guidance in advance to those planning civil disobedience to support and prepare them for the inevitable period in jail. Individuals were required to register in advance with the PPC Legal Redress Committee (the Jail Committee) and to declare any special medical issue, such as the use of glasses or hearing aids. The SCLC supplied those in jail with cigarettes, candy, and magazines and looked after their medical needs.[109] It also provided housing and other support for at least two days after each protester's release.[110]

Civil rights activists regarded arrest as a badge of honor. While serving his sentence, Ralph Abernathy kept the prison officials busy with a steady stream of visitors and incoming phone calls; however, his conduct was described as causing "no problem."[111] Inspired by Dr. King's "Letter from a Birmingham Jail," he wrote to fellow clergy from "a jail in Washington DC." He reminded them of how they were all charged in the Bible to "defend the poor and fatherless; do justice to the afflicted and needy, deliver the poor and needy, rid them . . . of the hand of the wicked."[112] Writing that he was in jail "with" and "for" poor people, Abernathy called on other clergy to join future planned confrontations with the government, adding that "words are no longer sufficient."[113] He went on a liquid-only fast while incarcerated and lost twelve pounds, which left him feeling "mighty weak."[114]

Ralph Abernathy was released from jail on July 13. Three hundred of his followers cheered and some even wept as he left the Washington, D.C., red brick prison at 9:20 a.m. In a gesture of reconciliation, Abernathy shook hands with prison guards before embracing nurses and orderlies from a Washington, D.C., hospital. The Tent Rangers, reportedly making their first appearance since the closure of Resurrection City, protected him.[115] His wife, Juanita, and close colleagues the Reverend John Adams and the Reverend Fred L. Bennett greeted Abernathy. He then climbed onto the fender of a car to inform the cheering crowd that he would use all the strength at his command to "make the dream of our founding father, the late Dr. Martin Luther King Jr., come true." Alluding to King's main objective for the PPC, Abernathy concluded, "We have made the invisible visible; never again will the poor be invisible in this country."[116]

With the occupation of Washington over and the camp and people now gone, the immediate concern was how to continue a campaign that had united the poor, the alienated, and the disenfranchised from all over the nation.[117] Abernathy sought to dispel any notions people may have had that the campaign was now officially over. At the Mount Carmel Baptist Church on July 13, he declared that he was more determined than ever to complete Dr. King's "unfinished task to subpoena the conscience of the nation." He used the same phrase King had uttered five years earlier during the March on Washington. Abernathy said the country had given the poor a "bad check that was returned marked insufficient funds."[118] Abernathy gave no specifics but suggested that he would target the national political nomination conventions later in the summer. He planned to lead around twenty-five people trained in nonviolence to each political convention.[119] Andrew Young described this new phase as "moving from the realm of symbol to the realm of power."[120]

The few campaigners who remained in Washington, D.C., after Resurrection

City closed were now advised to return to their homes across the nation and join the local leadership of activities for other poor people.[121] In short, they should now put into practice all that they had learned as participants in the great effort to end poverty in America. The proposed fresh phase of the campaign had several other facets, including direct economic action against companies with ties to politicians. During the afternoon of his release from prison on July 13, Abernathy made a sentimental return to the hallowed ground where Resurrection City had stood only three weeks previously. Bulldozers created clouds of dust in the background as they continued their work. Picking up a small sample of soil, Abernathy claimed that the shantytown had been a success; it was a "true city of love and brotherhood."[122] While depressed at what had happened to the camp, he predicted that for generations to come people would visit the site "to see what it symbolized and what it still symbolizes."[123]

CONCLUSION

n common with other leaders of the Southern Christian Leadership Conference, Jesse Jackson refused to be downhearted by the end of the Poor People's Campaign. He wrote, "Resurrection City cannot be seen as a mudhole in Washington, but it is rather an idea unleashed in history. . . . the idea has taken root and is growing across the country."[1] His optimism reflected a determination among those who had traveled to Washington, D.C., to continue to do everything they could to fulfill Martin Luther King Jr.'s dream to end poverty in the United States.

With the occupation of the nation's capital over, some PPC activists followed through on Ralph Abernathy's commitment to lobby the Republicans and the Democrats at their respective nominating conventions in 1968. Both conventions mirrored a nation divided against itself and reflected the social and political contexts in which the PPC had taken place. The less than warm reception received by the protesters at the conventions typified the mood toward the poor and the PPC at this point. The Republican convention in July 1968 in Miami confirmed the nomination of Richard M. Nixon as the party's presidential candidate. Nixon's acceptance address captured the rhetoric of a backlash against the liberal consensus and against what the politics of the PPC largely represented to many delegates. Nixon reached out to "forgotten" Americans who were not engaged in rioting; he emphasized a lean government and supported a crackdown on crime in favor of law and order.[2] In a jab at the counterculture and the antiwar protesters, he promised that no one would use the U.S. flag as a doormat as long as he was in charge.

Nixon's choice of Maryland governor Spiro Agnew as his running mate played well with those who supported the backlash against the perceived excesses of the 1960s. The *Washington Post*, in contrast, described Agnew's selection as the most eccentric political appointment since Emperor Caligula named his horse a consul.[3] Agnew was on record as saying that if "you've seen one slum you've seen them all."[4] Among other eccentric actions, Agnew added the Beatles to his list of cultural outcasts because they sang about "getting high." He ran with the tide of political opinion. Although initially a reasonably progressive governor of Maryland, the urban riots in Baltimore following King's assassination had helped to turn him into a law-and-order man. He had used the National Guard and federal troops to quell the disturbances. A visit by Stokely Carmichael to Baltimore just before trouble broke out had led Agnew to believe in common with others on the right wing that a conspiracy was to blame. He called a meeting of moderate black leaders after the riots and let them know he expected more of them. He also used the meeting to denounce the black leaders as "circuit-riding, Hanoi visiting . . . caterwauling, riot-inciting, burn-America-down type of leaders."[5] Most of the audience walked out.[6] Agnew had denounced the Kerner Commission for its references to "white racism," said looters should be shot, and claimed that the cause of urban unrest was "the misguided compassion of public opinion."[7] He also turned his fire on the media for giving antiwar demonstrators an easy time. His humble origins appealed to Nixon. A son of a Greek immigrant, Agnew resented black people who in his view were rewarded for causing disorder while his father had worked for what he earned. He secured the admiration of right-wing Republicans by denouncing the PPC. On June 20, he had met with Richard Nixon in the aftermath of Solidarity Day. Agnew positioned himself as the right candidate to be Nixon's running mate by using the meeting to declare that the people in Resurrection City were not genuinely poor but were "lobbyists for opportunism."[8]

Support for the poor people who had participated in the PPC was also in short supply at the chaotic Democratic Party convention in Chicago in August 1968. Divisions in the Democratic Party were on show to the world as Senator Abraham Ribicoff took to the platform to denounce the "Gestapo tactics" of Chicago mayor Daley's handling of the anti–Vietnam War protests outside the hall. Representatives of the Mule Train, including Ralph Abernathy, turned up at the convention but were a mere sideshow to the general mayhem. The police allowed the mules and their handlers to pass through their cordon near the convention hall before turning on the protesters coming up behind.[9] Highlighting a polarized nation in 1968, members of Students for a Democratic Society, hippies, and antiwar demonstrators were battered by police determined to stop them from reaching the convention hall. The disarray helped to pave the way for a Republican victory in the presidential election.

Despite a late bid from Senator George McGovern to snatch the prize, Vice President Hubert Humphrey was selected as the Democratic Party nominee for president. Humphrey's campaign message of the "politics of joy" seemed hollow amid the chaos. Democrat Lawrence O'Brien said that the Hilton Hotel became a battle area. Police used tear gas and fought with demonstrators. It was reported that the Chicago Police Department contained many admirers of George Wallace.[10] Even members of the clergy were beaten up. CBS correspondent Dan Rather was roughed up in the convention hall, which led to Walter Cronkite describing his assailants as a "bunch of thugs." Cronkite denounced the situation in Chicago as akin to a "police state" and noted that King's old foe, Mayor Richard Daley, did not want "unpatriotic, dirty unwashed people there."[11] Daley's message of "go home" to the activists was familiar to the poor people who had joined the PPC occupation of Washington just a few months earlier. Daley had little time for radicals and the counterculture. Following the news of King's assassination, he had given the order to "kill arsonists and shoot to maim looters."[12]

As fresh plans were laid for the immediate future in the troubled summer of 1968, the PPC leaders and the poor people who had taken up Dr. King's call to go to Washington reflected on their achievements. At first glance, the campaign had fallen far short of its objective to end poverty in America. The federal government had dashed the hopes of thousands of poor people who had traveled to Washington in pursuit of significant and immediate legislative action against economic injustice. The actual legislative gains were relatively modest. Insisting that the PPC had not been in vain, activist John Reynolds argued that the achievements included additional nutrition programs for the poor, new food stamp programs, and free school lunches.[13] An additional $25 million had been provided for new antipoverty projects. Another measurable outcome of the PPC was that nonprofit organizations took on responsibility for food storage and distribution. PPC national director Bernard Lafayette claimed that campaign leaders were most pleased with their successes in relation to the Department of Agriculture and the issue of hunger in America. He asserted that the visible gains included the initiation of food programs in all thousand neediest counties, a program of supplementary food packages for mothers and children, the inclusion of six new commodities in the food distribution program, and congressional appropriation of almost $10 million for an expanded and revamped school lunch program.[14]

In the three major areas where legislation was demanded—housing, employment, and welfare—the only significant action came through a housing bill.[15] A $5.5 billion, three-year housing bill that included major new programs to help poor families buy homes or rent apartments was approved by the House Banking Committee on June 19, 1968, Solidarity Day. PPC organizers described the bill as going a long way toward meeting their housing goals. The key feature of the bill was government-subsidized monthly mortgage payments for low- and moderate-income families to help them buy homes. The bill passed into law in August 1968.

The relatively weak response of the government to the PPC's demands in 1968 has contributed to the view that the initiative was a failure. However, government inaction has also obscured more substantive outcomes of the campaign. The key PPC coalition partner, the American Friends Service Committee, agreed in its annual report for 1968 that the campaign fell short in many ways. The report also asserted that it had "made the reality and harshness of poverty visible to all Americans, it resulted in improved administration of existing legislation, in the stimulation of other pending legislation, and in the establishment of a viable, if still fragile, coalition of the poor."[16] Marian Wright Edelman also suggested that the ripples from the campaign continued to have an impact long after the demonstrators had packed up and gone home. She said that after the PPC finished, she started planting seeds, which resulted in the expansion of Medicaid and child health insurance, to cite just two examples. She attributed these advances to the efforts of both Dr. King and Senator Robert Kennedy. She claimed they had "started something."[17]

The Poor People's Campaign has often been misunderstood and even forgotten. It was better organized than the SCLC and the other PPC partners were given credit for. Careful plans in fine detail were made, and despite the problems caused by the weather and other factors the achievement in creating a national movement and in taking up to six thousand people to Washington should not be underestimated. While Resurrection City had its problems, the campaigners created a living community in a short space of time. The legitimate claim of the PPC to be the first example in U.S. history of a truly national and inclusive multiracial social movement has not been fully recognized. For example, the poor people's March for Our Lives, which targeted the Republican Party convention in 2008 (and again in 2012), is seen by some scholars to have broken new ground and to have brought a "sense of newness" in that it was led by the poor and was multiracial.[18] Apparently, many on the Left have never even heard of the PPC. Yet we should acknowledge that the PPC in 1968 attracted grassroots poor people of all races who coalesced around the demand for economic justice.

The poor people who contributed to the campaign deserve recognition for making their presence felt and their voices heard. They were willing to stand up for change in the face of the backlash directed against them. They set aside anger and frustration at their lot in life and did the hard work to try to turn things around. The greatest triumph, in SCLC president Abernathy's view, was the historic victory of the poor in exposing the issue of poverty, and he hoped that the nation would never be permitted to ignore it again. The national director of the PPC, Bernard Lafayette, emphasized that the "presence" of poor people in the nation's capital was a powerful form of protest. Until they joined the PPC for the trip to Washington, D.C., the poorest people in communities across the United States were marginalized, and their voices went unheard. They overcame this during their journeys to Washington and in the nation's capital. It can be seen that without visibility, there is no history.[19] The demonstrations and the lobbying of Congress dramatized the plight of those living in poverty. The actions of peaceful nonviolent protesters countered in part the media and political onslaught against the initiative and the dominant view that the "great unwashed" were feckless and represented a threat to law and order. Thanks to the diversity of those involved in the multiracial Poor People's Campaign, the nation understood that the poverty in its midst was not restricted to any group or any region.

Social movements can create "counterpublics" and "counterknowledge," which challenge the hegemony of dominant corporate and state discourses.[20] The PPC was one example of such a movement whose impact was felt in the corridors of power. It forced America to look at and learn about the ugliness of poverty and to consider its treatment of those who suffered through no fault of their own. The presence of poor people in 1968 in Washington can be seen as an example of something that, as Cornel West argued, "puts the focus where it belongs": on any form of discrimination, including economic injustice, that "impedes the opportunities of everyday people to live lives of dignity and decency."[21] As one campaigner observed, the PPC was an extremely valuable educational tool for the whole society.[22] Many PPC participants understood that their occupation of the Mall was in practice a form of public pedagogy, a fundamental rejection of the dominant narrative that the poor needed to change themselves in order to achieve economic justice. The campaigners insisted that it was the nation and the world that were in desperate need of education.[23]

Many of the poor people who traveled to Washington had never before left their home communities. Throughout the campaign, many shared a sense of determination and the realization that they had embarked on a historic mission. The Mule Train participant testimonies, for example, tell of how they returned to their communities vowing that things would never again be the same. Lee Dora Collins observed, "I really enjoyed the whole experience, and I learned what we could do if we stuck together. I had never marched like that before. I saw my government turned us down. But, the experience lifted my spirits and changed the way I think forever. I got back here, and I don't say 'yes, suh, boss,' anymore."[24] She said that her son did not need to work in the cotton fields and added, "That's all I was hoping for when I went to Washington, was to make things better for my family."[25] Although Collins understood that change at the national level had been limited following the PPC, she nevertheless articulated a strong case that her involvement had changed her both as an individual and as a member of a broader community of poor people. During a great period of social and personal upheaval, she stood up for justice in the firm belief that a better quality of life for her family was within reach.

The PPC initiative also encouraged a sense of common purpose among many of the participants. The Appalachian people's group illustrated this point as they prepared to depart for Washington. In May 1968, seven hundred people from several states participated in workshops on issues considered of importance to the people of Appalachia. The experience of coming together brought new understanding of their common bond as poor people and helped set the tone for the remainder of the campaign. A coal miner said, "Poor people are waking up and finding they are all on the same side."[26] Another speaker said, "The press has led everyone to believe that the march to Washington is mostly black, which is not true—it is the American people, Appalachians, Mexicans, Indians, Puerto Ricans, Blacks all together."[27]

The campaign was particularly important in that it afforded space for the poor of different races and cultural backgrounds to come together in solidarity in ways unparalleled in U.S. history until this point. The tales in the press of tension and conflict between and even within some of the racial groups in the camp have validity. Yet they tell only part of the story. While some camp residents remained aloof and chose to stand apart from other participants, others described the importance of "fellowship" in Resurrection City.[28] The various traveling caravans and Resurrection City itself were impressive examples of what can be described in social movement terms as sites of "dialogue and interaction."[29] PPC administrative assistant James Peterson claimed that this was the point of the exercise, arguing that the Resurrection City experiment "was set up primarily to show the world, the nation, how people can live in togetherness from all walks of life."[30] Jesse Jackson, who later built his own Rainbow Coalition when running for the presidency of the United States in 1984 and 1988, claimed that the various victories of Resurrection City included "the poor of all races coming together" and the "new relationships created and the lessons learned."[31] He observed that the shared turf in Resurrection City allowed people to hear each other for the first time and helped some of them begin to understand the discrimination experienced by other groups.[32] Just as King had hoped, some potential adversaries reached out to each other in solidarity to address the common bond of economic injustice.

The emergence of new grassroots leadership in Resurrection City meant that the camp had acted as a launch pad for protest after the poor returned to their home communities. Groups that were already organizing around their own identity gained significantly at Resurrection City in terms of confidence, experience, and knowledge. New leaders were prominent and highly visible in their own communities in subsequent years. Cornelius Givens, one of the founders of the Poor People's Embassy and the Poor People's Development Foundation, which helped poor communities establish cooperatives, claimed that Resurrection City had afforded an opportunity he did not think would occur again for a hundred years. It had brought people together who shared common concerns, and they came from all over the country. He thought the camp had provided "the seed for revolution."[33] Native American Tillie Walker observed that the campaign represented a new beginning for those who previously had never been involved in anything larger than their own groups.[34] The evidence shows that Native Americans were central to the campaign, and their participation served as a defining moment in their lives, yet their stories have remained largely untold. The PPC arguably served as an impetus for many participants to devote their lives to grassroots activism.[35]

The Poor People's Campaign is an important part of the history of education for social change. It relates to racism, class, and basic struggles around poverty. The PPC brought together ordinary people who fought nonviolently for decent housing, jobs, a fairer welfare system, and education for their children. Barbara Ransby has written that oppressed people, "whatever their level of formal education, have the ability to understand and interpret the world around them, to see the world for what it was and to move to transform it."[36] The participation of poor people in the planning phases of the campaign in their home communities and during the journeys to Washington, and their engagement with each other on the caravans and in Resurrection City, proved to be empowering for many and validated their cause to end poverty in America.

The role played by learning is crucial for understanding the PPC. For perhaps the first time in the history of the United States, poor people of different races and backgrounds came together in a shared space, organized around formal and informal learning, and laid the groundwork for future activism. They learned skills and crossed cultural boundaries.[37] Looking back on the campaign, Lafayette stated that one of his greatest regrets is that citizenship schools, so prominent in the 1960s movement and in the PPC, did not continue. A

Black Lives Matter activist concurs with Lafayette. He has asserted that in the twenty-first century, education is the most powerful weapon there is and that education can assist people to become active citizens and powerful people.[38] Activist Katherine Shannon maintained that people had changed by the time they left Resurrection City. They "got educated," and everyone "was touched" by the experience. She argued that they built something together and learned about oppressive authority and how to deal with it.[39] This insight reflects Citizenship Education Program leader Dorothy Cotton's view that the personal transformation that results from learning is fundamental to realizing the promise of democracy.[40]

People working to end poverty today owe a huge debt to Dr. King and to those who took up his call in 1968. The Poor People's Campaign has more relevance than ever before. King's vision for a more equitable society speaks to the contemporary world where the rich get richer and the poor get poorer. The initiative was ahead of its time and was a precursor of the modern Occupy Wall Street movement.[41] In New York's Zuccotti Park in 2012, for example, Occupy protesters created many of the infrastructures that were in evidence at Resurrection City, including mail service, sanitation crews, and, most significantly, educational activities. The Reverend Jesse Jackson alerted some Occupy protesters to the legacy of the King campaign: very few listening to him had ever heard of those who had gone before them.

People who became aware of the PPC after 1968 were inspired to try to follow King's example in tackling the issue of poverty and all its manifestations. Resurrection City 2 was launched in 1972 and brought black and white people together again. In 2003, a tent city named Bushville and the Poor People's Economic Human Rights Campaign re-created a PPC march. In 2011, the Rainbow Push Coalition built replicas of the tent structures from 1968.[42] In 2018, the year of the fiftieth anniversary of the campaign and King's death, a group of faith leaders tried to restart a moral agenda in America with a revival of the PPC. They called for a repeal of tax cuts and an increase in federal and state minimum wages. They described their program as "a national call for moral revival in uniting thousands of people across the country to challenge the evils of systematic racism, poverty, the war economy, ecological devastation, and the nation's distorted morality."[43] Dr. King could have written this statement himself.

King's vision of a "beloved community," including his demands in 1968 for a reallocation of resources and a restructuring of society, have never seemed more relevant than in 2020. In an echo of the Chicago Freedom Movement campaign of 1966, the use of force and power by the police in black communities came under scrutiny with the death of George Floyd. And yet again, the demand for economic justice became part of the national narrative in 2020. Minority groups, including the poorest and most vulnerable in society, have been disproportionately affected by COVID-19 and by the economic meltdown that followed. In a global response to these tumultuous events, millions of supporters of the Black Lives Matter movement protested to highlight systematic racism and the unpaid debts owed to black people. Although there was some violence, just as during the hot summers of the 1960s, the majority of protesters adhered to nonviolent protest. They were the latest wave in the movement inspired by Martin Luther King Jr.

A nonviolence trainer with Black Lives Matter has observed that King's methods remain relevant and may yet address the triple evils of poverty, racism, and militarism.[44] The demands and agendas of the PPC resonate in the current context in which many are denied employment, a livable wage, decent housing, and effective access to education and healthcare. Scholars have observed that what is lacking in the twenty-first-century movements against poverty is an "overarching ideology or mind-set," which can offer guidance on what can be done and how to do it.[45] The same criticism cannot be made of the PPC. Dr. King articulated a clear justification for the campaign and set out strategies and methodologies to take the initiative forward. We can only guess as to what the outcomes of the campaign might have been had he lived to accompany the poor to Washington, D.C. John Rutherford, administrative coordinator at Resurrection City, speculated that King understood that the PPC was a starting point only; by its nature, it would not change society completely, but it was revolutionary in intent. He argued that King was preparing people for the confrontation to come.[46]

In conclusion, threats to his life and his reputation hung over Martin Luther King Jr. as he made plans for the Poor People's Campaign. In fusing the costs of the war economy with the issues of poverty and racism, he attracted further derision, animosity, and hatred. But he refused to let up in his efforts to win over the poor and nonpoor of all races to his vision for a more equitable and just America. His compassion and deep sense of social justice found expression in the PPC. Not afraid to show his emotions, he occasionally wept in despair at the condition of poor people who had literally nothing. He did not compromise on his demand for universal economic rights. Many of the impoverished people who came to Washington, D.C., in May and June 1968 to dramatize the issue of poverty came because he had inspired them and their leaders and because they did not want to let him down. Dr. King's expansive global vision for economic justice positioned the Poor People's Campaign as an opportunity for the government to unite with its people and open a new age for the United States. His message continues to resonate in the current social and political climate.

NOTES

INTRODUCTION

1. Edelman, *Lanterns*, 103.
2. Hampton and Fayer, *Voices of Freedom*, 453.
3. Marian Wright Edelman, JFK, MLK, RFK, second session, 1960–1968, October 23, 2005, 8, Kennedy Presidential Library Forums.
4. Ibid..
5. Edelman, *Lanterns*, 103.
6. Ibid., 25.
7. SCLC Papers, box 177, 1, 1, King Library and Archives, King Center (hereafter King Center).
8. Young, *An Easy Burden*, 437; King, *My Life*, 153.
9. Edelman, *Lanterns*, 109.
10. Ibid.
11. Ibid.
12. King, *My Life*, 153.
13. Gollin, "Poor People's Campaign," 5.
14. SCLC Papers, Southwest Delegation, PPC, Mexican Americans, May–June 1968, box 179, 9, King Center.
15. Gollin, "Poor People's Campaign," 7.
16. McKnight, *Last Crusade*, 107.
17. Frady, *Jesse*, 242.
18. Lentz, *Symbols*, 335.
19. Martinez, "Where Was the Color in Seattle?," 19.
20. Wiebenson, "Planning and Using Resurrection City," 411.
21. Comfort interview, 2.
22. SCLC, "Who Are the Poor," Jack Ellwanger, May 1968, Schomburg Center for Research in Black Culture, New York (hereafter Schomburg).
23. SCLC Papers, Mexican Americans, Demands, Crusade for Justice, Denver, Colorado, May–June 1968, box 179, 9, 1, King Center.
24. Ibid.
25. SCLC (National Office), PPC Photographic Journal, ser. 6, box 2, 19, June 1968, Hosea Williams Collection.
26. "Resurrection City Looks Different from Inside," *Sunday Star*, May 19, 1968.

27. Le Blanc and Yates, *Freedom Budget*, 237.

28. Gandhi Memorial Lecture, November 1966, 14, King Center.

29. McKnight, *Last Crusade*.

30. Branch, *At Canaan's Edge*, 745.

31. Honey, *All Labor Has Dignity*, xiv.

32. Le Blanc and Yates, *Freedom Budget*, 15.

33. Ibid., 44.

34. Heltzel, *Resurrection City*, 106.

35. Eaves, *Morehouse Mystique*, 61.

36. Carson, *Autobiography*, 14.

37. D'Emilio, *Lost Prophet*, 231.

38. Hodgson, *Martin Luther King*, 54.

39. Honey, *To the Promised Land*, 44.

40. Eaves, *Morehouse Mystique*, 65.

41. "Crisis and the Church," *Council Quarterly* 11 (October 1, 1961): 6.

42. King, *Stride toward Freedom*, 78.

43. Washington, *Testament of Hope*, 38.

44. "Negroes Are Not Moving Too Fast," *Saturday Evening Post*, November 7, 1964, 8–10.

45. Ibid.

46. Nadasen, *Rethinking the Welfare Rights Movement*, 22.

47. Hampton and Fayer, *Voices of Freedom*, 450.

48. Kotz, *Judgment Days*; Updegrove, *Indomitable Will*.

49. Sugrue, *Sweet Land of Liberty*, 357.

50. Laurent, *King and the Other America*, 111.

51. Jackson, *From Civil Rights to Human Rights*.

52. Quoted in Washington, *Testament of Hope*, 58.

53. Ibid.

54. Washington, *Testament of Hope*, 635.

55. Carson, *Autobiography*, 337.

56. "To Charter Our Course for the Future," address to the SCLC conference, Penn Center, Frogmore, S.C., May 1967, King Center.

57. Wohl, *Father, Son, and Constitution*, 339.

58. Ibid., 332.

59. King, telegram to President Lyndon Johnson, July 25, 1967, in Mantler, *Power to the Poor*, 92.

60. Washington, *Testament of Hope*, 556.

61. Quoted ibid., 586.

62. Ibid., 556.

63. Ibid., 607.

64. Ibid., 557.

65. Ibid., 586.

66. Ibid., 557.

67. "To Charter Our Course for the Future," address to the SCLC conference, Penn Center, Frogmore, S.C., May 1967, King Center.

68. SCLC Papers, "You and the Poor," 1968, 3, King Center.

69. Chase, *Class Resurrection*; Kotz, *Judgment Days*.

70. Patterson, *Great Expectations*, 639.

71. Mayer, "Nixon Rides the Backlash."

72. Hodgson, *Martin Luther King*, 200.

73. Laurent, *King and the Other America*, 97.

74. Ibid., 98.

75. Chase, *Class Resurrection*, 24.

76. Jackson, "Resurrection City," 67.

CHAPTER 1. THE CHICAGO CAMPAIGN

1. Laurent, *King and the Other America*, 2.

2. Patterson, *Great Expectations*, 534.

3. Honey, *To the Promised Land*, 101.

4. Lentz, *Symbols*, 184.

5. King, statement to the press, Watts, August 20, 1965, King Center.

6. Dallek, *Lyndon B. Johnson*, 280.

7. Milton Viorst, "MLK Intends to Tie the City in Knots This Spring," *Washingtonian*, February 1968, 52.

8. Dallek, *Lyndon B. Johnson*, 167–69.

9. Ibid., 173.

10. Ibid., 183.

11. Ibid., 539.

12. Davies, *American Quarter Century*, 12.

13. Ibid., 13.

14. Ibid., 535.

15. Sugrue, *Sweet Land of Liberty*, 366.

16. Laurent, *King and the Other America*, 99.

17. Ibid., 103.

18. Ibid., 112.

19. Young, *An Easy Burden*, 380.

20. Frady, *Martin Luther King Jr.*, 168.

21. Jackson, *From Civil Rights to Human Rights*, 20.

22. Sugrue, *Sweet Land of Liberty*, xiii.

23. Ibid.

24. Ibid., xv.

25. Martin Luther King Jr. Papers, box 11, 2, August 18, 1962, 2, Howard Gotlieb Archival Research Center at Boston University (hereafter Gotlieb Center).

26. Carson, *Autobiography*, 312.

27. Chicago Plan, January 7, 1966, King Center.

28. Ibid.

29. Laurent, *King and the Other America*, 125.

30. Lentz, *Symbols*, 198.

31. Chicago Plan, January 7, 1966.

32. Abernathy, *And the Walls*, 368.

33. King, *Stride toward Freedom*, 84.

34. Hampton and Fayer, *Voices of Freedom*, 299.

35. Young, *An Easy Burden*, 381.

36. Ibid., 384.

37. Cornfield et al., "Labor and the Chicago Freedom Movement," 374.

38. Bernstein, "Longest March," 6.

39. Ibid., 7.

40. Cohen and Taylor, *American Pharaoh*, 337.

41. Ibid., 338.

42. Ralph and Finley, "In Their Own Voices," 13.

43. Young, *An Easy Burden*, 406.

44. Lemann, *Promised Land*, 6.

45. Ibid., 70.

46. Hampton and Fayer, *Voices of Freedom*, 299.

47. Cohen and Taylor, *American Pharaoh*, 347.

48. Abernathy, *And the Walls*, 364.

49. Cohen and Taylor, *American Pharaoh*, 347.

50. Honey, *To the Promised Land*, 105.

51. Ralph and Finley, "In Their Own Voices," 24.

52. See https://www.youtube.com/watch?v=lgEPcevoGxQ.

53. Bernstein, "Longest March," 9.

54. Arsenault, Afterword, 151.

55. Interview of Bernard Lafayette by author, May 4, 2017.

56. Ralph and Finley, "In Their Own Voices," 25.

57. Lafayette, "Nonviolence," 389.

58. Barnes, *Centennial History*, 234.

59. Carson, *Autobiography*, 298.

60. Cornfield et al., "Labor and the Chicago Freedom Movement," 374.

61. Chicago Plan, January 7, 1966, King Center.

62. Ibid.

63. Kamin, *Dangerous Friendship*, 206.

64. Chicago Plan, January 7, 1966, King Center.

65. Ralph and Finley, "In Their Own Voices," 33–34.

66. Lentz, *Symbols*, 198–99.

67. Young, *An Easy Burden*, 405.

68. Abernathy, *And the Walls*, 373.

69. Ibid., 372.

70. Young, *An Easy Burden*, 392.

71. Bernstein, "Longest March," 9.

72. Garrow, *Bearing the Cross*, 465.

73. SCLC (National Office), Annual Report: Chicago Project, Stoney Cooks, box 2, 2, 3, Hosea Williams Collection.

74. Carson, *Autobiography*, 300.

75. Abernathy, *And the Walls*, 377.

76. Cotton, *If Your Back's Not Bent*, 212.

77. Ibid., 213.

78. Abernathy, *And the Walls*, 376.

79. Ralph and Finley, "In Their Own Voices," 30.

80. Ibid., 31.

81. Smith, "Youth and Nonviolence," 302.

82. Marian Wright Edelman, JFK, MLK, RFK, second session, 1960–1968, October 23, 2005, 18, Kennedy Presidential Library Forums.

83. Ralph and Finley, "In Their Own Voices," 31.

84. Mantler, *Power to the Poor*, 54.

85. Ibid., 55.

86. Kotz, *Judgment Days*, 366.

87. Carson, *Autobiography*, 300.

88. Lafayette and Johnson, *In Peace and Freedom*, 98.

89. Smith, "Youth and Nonviolence," 299.

90. Lafayette and Johnson, *In Peace and Freedom*, 96.

91. Smith, "Youth and Nonviolence," 302.

92. Mantler, *Power to the Poor*, 57.

93. Lentz, *Symbols*, 220.

94. Mantler, *Power to the Poor*, 59., 287.

95. Bernstein, "Longest March," 11.

96. Smith, "Youth and Nonviolence," 302..

97. Updegrove, *Indomitable Will*, 215.

98. Jackson, *From Civil Rights to Human Rights*, 287.

99. Bernstein, "Longest March," 12.

100. Ibid.

101. Interview of Bernard Lafayette by author, May 4, 2017.

102. Young, *An Easy Burden*, 442.

103. Ibid., 443.

104. Hampton and Fayer, *Voices of Freedom*, 312.

105. Abernathy, *And the Walls*, 390.

106. Dorrien, *Breaking White Supremacy*, 401.

107. Bernstein, "Longest March," 15.

108. Abernathy, *And the Walls*, 395.

109. Kotz, *Judgment Days*, 367–68.

110. Sugrue, *Sweet Land of Liberty*, 359.

111. Updegrove, *Indomitable Will*, 276.

CHAPTER 2. A YEAR OF EDUCATION FOR DR. KING

1. Hampton and Fayer, *Voices of Freedom*, 299.

2. Jackson, *From Civil Rights to Human Rights*, 21.

3. Young, *An Easy Burden*, 421.

4. Kotz, *Judgment Days*, 370.

5. King, *My Life*, 152.

6. Mantler, *Power to the Poor*, 54.

7. SCLC Organizational Records, "You and the PPC," March 1968, Martin Luther King Jr. Collection, Atlanta University Center, Robert W. Woodruff Library, Morehouse College, Atlanta, Ga. (hereafter Morehouse King Collection).

8. Ralph and Finley, "In Their Own Voices," 71.

9. Ibid.

10. Poor People's Campaign, A Biographical Note on Mr. Anthony R. Henry, 1968, Schomburg.

11. Ralph and Finley, "In Their Own Voices," 37.

12. Chicago Plan, January 7, 1966, 5, King Center.

13. Frady, *Jesse*, 240.

14. Rutherford interview.

15. Ralph and Finley, "In Their Own Voices."

16. Carson, *Autobiography*, 299.

17. Conference of Religious Leaders under the Sponsorship of the President's Committee on Government Contracts, Sheraton Park Hotel, Washington, D.C., May 11, 1959, box 23, 4, Speeches, 1959 January–August, Gotlieb Center.

18. Mantler, *Power to the Poor*, 55.

19. Smith, "Youth and Nonviolence," 299.

20. Ibid., 300.

21. SCLC Papers, King, "The Crisis in America's Cities," Atlanta, August 15, 1966, 4, King Center.

22. Garrow, *Bearing the Cross*, 533.

23. Ibid., 535.

24. Gandhi Memorial Lecture, 1966, 6, King Center.

25. Ibid., 9.

26. Ibid.

27. Ibid., 11.

28. Ibid., 13.

29. Ibid., 14.

30. Ibid., 6.

31. Frogmore Address, November 14, 1966, King Center.

32. Joseph, *Stokely*, 101.

33. Ibid., 102; Edelman, *Lanterns*, 102.

34. Joseph, *Stokely*, 105.

35. Edelman, *Lanterns*, 101.

36. Sugrue, *Sweet Land of Liberty*, 336.

37. Ibid., 337.

38. Garrow, *Bearing the Cross*, 533.

39. D'Emilio, *Lost Prophet*, 428.

40. Frogmore Address, November 14, 1966, 13, King Center.

41. Ibid.

42. Ibid., 30.

43. Ibid., 27.

44. Ibid., 14.

45. Pastor Vernon Charles Lyons, "King Program Not Christian," *Ashburn Baptist News*, June 1967, 2, Morehouse King Collection.

46. Kamin, *Dangerous Friendship*, 71.

47. King, *Stride toward Freedom*, 79.

48. Ibid.

49. Laurent, *King and the Other America*, 15.

50. Kotz, *Judgment Days*, 237.

51. Frogmore Address, November 14, 1966, 19, King Center.

52. Ibid., 20.

53. *Freedom Budget for All Americans*; Le Blanc and Yates, *Freedom Budget*, 243–50.

54. Sugrue, *Sweet Land of Liberty*, 376.

55. Schmitt, "Appalachian Thread," 376.

56. Text of remarks of Senator Robert F. Kennedy, U.S. Congressional Record, 90th Cong., 1st sess., December 10, 1966, 5.

57. "Soaring Star," *Sunday Times*, August 28, 1966.

58. Frogmore Address, November 14, 1966, King Center.

59. Garrow, *Bearing the Cross*, 539.

60. Ribicoff Committee, December 1966, 2967, King Center.

61. Carson, *Autobiography*, 336.

62. Garrow, *Bearing the Cross*, 539.

63. Carson, *Autobiography*, 345.

64. Garrow, *Bearing the Cross*, 540.

65. Ibid., 539.

66. Ibid., 540.

67. Schmitt, *President of the Other America*, 172.

68. Patterson, *Great Expectations*, 649.

69. Updegrove, *Indomitable Will*, 237.

70. Washington, *Testament of Hope*, 58.

71. Garrow, *Bearing the Cross*, 538.

CHAPTER 3. THE WAR AT HOME AND ABROAD

1. Dallek, *Lyndon B. Johnson*, 239.

2. Ibid., 279.

3. Patterson, *Great Expectations*, 651.

4. Cannon, *Governor Reagan*, 124.

5. Ibid., 132.

6. Dallek, *Lyndon B. Johnson*, 199.

7. Cannon, *Governor Reagan*, 126.

8. Dorrien, *Breaking White Supremacy*, 406.

9. Cannon, *Governor Reagan*, 5.

10. Ibid., 144.

11. Updegrove, *Indomitable Will*, 214.

12. Ibid.

13. Dorrien, *Breaking White Supremacy*, 409.

14. Updegrove, *Indomitable Will*, 187.

15. Ibid., 206.

16. Hamilton Lytle, *America's Uncivil Wars*, 217.

17. Updegrove, *Indomitable Will*, 217.

18. Branch, *Pillar of Fire*, 542.

19. Kamin, *Dangerous Friendship*, 207.

20. Kotz, *Judgment Days*, 372.

21. Hampton and Fayer, *Voices of Freedom*, 335.

22. Updegrove, *Indomitable Will*, 189.

23. Wright, "Civil Rights Unfinished Business," 141.

24. Updegrove, *Indomitable Will*, 202.

25. Lentz, *Symbols*, 176.

26. Kamin, *Dangerous Friendship*, 207.

27. McKnight, *Last Crusade*, 12.

28. Clark, "Tribute," 442.

29. Edelman, *Lanterns*, 104.

30. Dionisopoulos et al., "Martin Luther King," 99.

31. Frogmore Address, November 14, 1966, 29, King Center.

32. King and Ruley, *New and Unsettling Force*, 8.

33. King, "The Casualties of the War in Vietnam," February 25, 1967, King Center.

34. "Equality Now," *Nation*, February 4, 1961, 4.

35. King, "My Talk with Ben Bella," *Amsterdam News*, October 27, 1962.

36. Honey, *Going Down Jericho Road*, 175.

37. King, "The Casualties of the War in Vietnam," February 25, 1967, 6, King Center.

38. Ibid.

39. Garrow, *Bearing the Cross*, 549–50.

40. Ibid., 552.

41. Ibid.

42. Kotz, *Judgment Days*, 371.

43. Clark, "Tribute," 433.

44. Ibid., 434.

45. Washington, *Testament of Hope*, 236.

46. Statement by King, March 4, 1968, 4, Morehouse King Collection.

47. Interview of Bernard Lafayette by author, April 1, 2014.

48. McKnight, *Last Crusade*, 15.

49. Kotz, *Judgment Days*, 387.

50. Clark, "Tribute," 442.

51. Kotz, *Judgment Days*, 378.

52. Clark, "Tribute," 442.

53. SCLC, "Does MLK Have the Right, the Qualifications, the Duty to Speak Out on Peace," April 1967, Schomburg.

54. Joseph, *Stokely*, 184.

55. SCLC Papers, *Meet the Press* transcript, August 21, 1966, 29, Morehouse King Collection.

56. Joseph, *Stokely*, 184.

57. Kotz, *Judgment Days*, 377–78.

58. SCLC Papers, Writings by Others, King interview, *Playboy*, 1967, 43, Morehouse King Collection.

59. Garrow, *Bearing the Cross*, 563.

60. Carson, *Autobiography*, 346.

61. Garrow, *Bearing the Cross*, 564.

62. Ibid.

63. SCLC Papers, King interview, *Playboy*, 4.

64. Updegrove, *Indomitable Will*, 237.

65. Ibid., 238.

66. Schmitt, *President of the Other America*, 175.

67. Edelman, *Searching for America's Heart*, 50.

68. Mills, "This Little Light of Mine," 192–93.

69. SCLC, "Eastland Is on Welfare," *Soul Force*, June 19, 1968, 12, Schomburg.

70. Edelman, *Searching for America's Heart*, 51.

71. Schmitt, *President of the Other America*, 178.

72. DeShazo et al., "Unwilling Partnership," 121.

73. Stein, *American Journey*, 124.

74. DeShazo et al., "Unwilling Partnership," 121.

75. Edelman, *Lanterns*, 109.

76. Hampton and Fayer, *Voices of Freedom*, 453.

77. DeShazo et al., "Unwilling Partnership," 124–25.

78. King, "Crisis in American Cities," August 1967, 4, King Center.

79. Garrow, *Bearing the Cross*, 568.

80. Mantler, *Power to the Poor*, 92.

81. King, "Crisis in American Cities," 1.

82. Patterson, *Great Expectations*, 667.

83. Ibid., 669.

84. King, "Crisis in American Cities," 5.

85. Ibid.

86. SCLC Organizational Records, Tenth Anniversary Convention, draft resolution regarding the War on Poverty, August 14–17, 1967, 1, Morehouse King Collection.

87. McKnight, *Last Crusade*, 20.

88. Hampton and Fayer, *Voices of Freedom*, 455.

89. Ibid., 454.

90. SCLC Papers, memorandum from Donna Allen to SCLC staff, "A Proposal regarding the Demands of the PPC," January 1968, box 179, 5, King Center.

91. Garrow, *Bearing the Cross*, 593.

92. Young, *An Easy Burden*, 444.

93. Frady, *Jesse*, 215.

94. Interview of Bernard Lafayette by author, May 4, 2017.

CHAPTER 4. PLANNING THE POOR PEOPLE'S CAMPAIGN

1. SCLC Records, statement by King, December 4, 1967, Morehouse King Collection.

2. Young, *An Easy Burden*, 443.

3. Barber, *Marching on Washington*, 2.

4. Frady, *Jesse*, 214.

5. Horton, *Long Haul*, 119–20.

6. Barber, *Marching on Washington*, 104.

7. Statement by King, December 4, 1967, 4.

8. Ibid., 1.

9. Ibid., 2.

10. Ibid., 3.

11. Frady, *Jesse*, 214.

12. McKnight, *Last Crusade*, 9.

13. Interview of Bernard Lafayette by author, April 1, 2014.

14. Martin Luther King Jr. Papers, box 23, 4: Speeches January–August 1959, May 11, 1959, 6–7, Gotlieb Center.

15. King, "Equality Now," *Nation*, February 4, 1961, 1.

16. Martin Luther King Jr. Papers, box 11, 1, 2; box 11, 1, 1–2 (February 4, 1961), Gotlieb Center.

17. PPC and the March on Washington: Mobilization for Collective Protest, 1968, Schomburg.

18. King, "I Have a Dream," August 1963, King Center.

19. McKnight, *Last Crusade*, 21.

20. Chester et al., *American Melodrama*, 515–16.

21. Statement by King, December 4, 1967, 1.

22. Honey, *Going Down Jericho Road*, 184.

23. Joseph, *Stokely*, 237.

24. Transcript, WBTV, Charlotte, N.C., February 19, 1968, Morehouse King Collection.

25. Mantler, "Press Did You In," 37.

26. Joseph, *Stokely*, 238.

27. Almena Lomax, "Blacks Turning against Dr. King, New Lomax Poll Shows," *Washington Post*, December 27, 1967.

28. Jackson, *From Civil Rights to Human Rights*, 16.

29. Carson, Foreword, x.

30. Honey, *To the Promised Land*, 50.

31. Garrow, *FBI and Martin Luther King*; McKnight, *Last Crusade*.

32. McKnight, *Last Crusade*, 24.

33. Harley, "We Are Poor, Not Stupid," 3.

34. Young, *An Easy Burden*, 446.

35. King, *My Life*, 155.

36. Patterson, *Great Expectations*, 639.

37. Johnson, State of the Union address, January 17, 1968.

38. Wright, "Civil Rights Unfinished Business," 159.

39. Kotz, *Judgment Days*, 395.

40. Wohl, *Father, Son, and Constitution*, 355.

41. Kennedy, *True Compass*, 263.

42. Bradshaw, "Comparative Study," 98.

43. Ambrose, *Nixon*, 144.

44. Ibid., 154.

45. Ibid., 178.

46. Ibid., 165.

47. SCLC Organizational Records, memorandum from Rutherford to SCLC staff members, special staff retreat, January 14–16, 1968, Morehouse King Collection.

48. Honey, *Going Down Jericho Road*, 180.

49. McKnight, *Last Crusade*, 24.

50. Ibid., 24.

51. Garrow, *Bearing the Cross*, 595–96.

52. Ibid., 590.

53. SCLC (National Office), "Questions and Answers about the Washington Campaign," ser. 6, box 2, 12, January 1968, Hosea Williams Collection.

54. Ibid., 1.

55. Ibid., 4.

56. Ibid., 10.

57. SCLC Papers, "You and the Poor," 1968, 3, King Center.

58. Milton Viorst, "MLK Intends to Tie the City in Knots This Spring," *Washingtonian*, February 1968, 52.

59. King, *Stride toward Freedom*, 85.

60. SCLC Organizational Records, Tenth Anniversary Convention, "The Philosophy of Nonviolence and the Tactics of Nonviolent Resistance," August 1967, 1–2, Morehouse King Collection.

61. SCLC Papers, box 180, 10, 4, King Center.

62. Gollin, "Poor People's Campaign," 6.

63. Garrow, *Bearing the Cross*, 591.

64. Frady, *Jesse*, 216.

65. Levine, *Bayard Rustin*, 216.

66. Long, *I Must Resist*, 343.

67. D'Emilio, *Lost Prophet*, 460.

68. Long, *I Must Resist*, 342.

69. Le Blanc and Yates, *Freedom Budget*, 9.

70. D'Emilio, *Lost Prophet*, 460.

71. Garrow, *Bearing the Cross*, 591.

72. SCLC (National Office), "Questions and Answers about the Washington Campaign."

73. National Association of Social Workers, "Some Common Questions about Poverty and Some Possible Answers," 1968, Schomburg.

74. Ibid., 2.

75. Beaudin interview, 1.

76. SCLC Organizational Records, PPC program: Committee for Nassau County, King address, January 1968, Morehouse King Collection.

77. Buskirk interview, 7.

78. SCLC Papers, box 180, 10, 2, King Center.

79. SCLC Papers, PPC Statement of Purpose, 1968, box 180, 10, King Center.

80. Reynolds, *Fight for Freedom*, 116.

81. SCLC Papers, box 180, 10, 2, King Center.

82. SCLC Papers, April 28, 1968, 8, 6, King Center.

83. Gollin, "Poor People's Campaign," 6.

84. PPC National Area Offices, April 29, 1968, King Center.

85. McKnight, *Last Crusade*, 24.

86. Branch, *Pillar of Fire*, 24; Brinkley, *Rosa Parks*.

87. Gollin, "Poor People's Campaign," 5.

88. Mantler, *Power to the Poor*, 99.

89. Ibid.

90. Interview of Bernard Lafayette by author, April 1, 2014.

91. SCLC Papers, memorandum from Arthur I. Waskow to Tony Henry and Bill Moyer, PPC, March 1, 1968, 2, King Center.

92. Houk interview, 8.

93. SCLC Papers, A Partial List of Sponsoring Organizations for the PPC, April 26, 1968, King Center.

94. Payne interview, 2.

95. Shabazz interview, 1.

96. Robinson interview, 2.

97. SCLC Organizational Records, PPC, National Committee of Black Churchmen, April 1968, 2, Morehouse King Collection.

98. SCLC Papers, Field Reports, New York, letter to Hosea Williams from Reverend Frederick Douglas Kirkpatrick and Jimmy Collier, March 21, 1968, King Center.

99. Givens interview, 6.

100. Honey, *Going Down Jericho Road*, 189.

101. SCLC Papers, box 177, 38, 1, King Center.

102. Educational Task Force, 1968, 1, Schomburg.

103. Ibid.

104. SCLC Speakers Bureau, "What Is Poverty," May 3, 1968, Schomburg.

105. Ibid.

106. SCLC Papers, Field Report, North Carolina, March 25, 1968, box 181, 2, King Center.

107. SCLC Papers, Field Report, Georgia, February–March 1968, box 178, 2, King Center.

108. SCLC Papers, Field Report, Illinois, March–May 1968, box 178, 5, King Center.

109. Wright, "Civil Rights Unfinished Business," 159.

110. SCLC Papers, Progress Report, Albert Turner to Hosea Williams, March 2, 1968, King Center.

111. SCLC Papers, memorandum from Albert Turner to Hosea Williams, Recruits, April 3, 1968, King Center.

112. SCLC Papers, staff meeting minutes, Department of Voter Registration and Political Education, Atlanta, March 26, 1968, box 180, 8, King Center.

113. SCLC papers, memo to all project directors from Dr. David Carter, April 22, 1968, box 178, 12, King Center.

114. Hamilton, "The Mule Train," 52.

115. SCLC Papers, progress report from Hilbert Perry and Mike Bibler to Reverend Bernard Lafayette, Mobilization for Washington, March 1, 1968, 1–4, King Center.

116. SCLC Papers, progress report to Bernard Lafayette, William Rutherford, and Reverend Andrew Young from Hilbert Perry and Mike Bibler, March 23, 1968, King Center.

117. SCLC Papers, memorandum on handling funds from Hosea L. Williams to all project leaders and field staff involved in mobilization of "field troops" for the Washington PPC, March 5, 1968, King Center.

118. SCLC Papers, letter to Hosea Williams, March 17, 1968, box 178, 5, Illinois, March–May 1968, King Center.

119. SCLC Papers, letter from Herbert V. Coulton to Hosea Williams, March 20, 1968, King Center.

120. SCLC Papers, Newark, New Jersey, Queen of Angels Parish, box 178, 13, King Center.

121. SCLC Organizational Records, memorandum from William Rutherford to Bernard Lafayette, re: Support for Washington Campaign Publicity Support, January 10, 1968, Morehouse King Collection.

122. Stations carrying *MLK Speaks*, 1968, Schomburg.

123. SCLC Papers, Mercer County, N.J., June 21, 1968, King Center.

124. McKnight, *Last Crusade*, 25.

125. Mantler, "Partners in Justice and Peace," 4.

126. SCLC Organizational Records, memorandum from Bernard Lafayette to executive staff: discussion with Brady Tyson, March 8, 1968, 1, Morehouse King Collection.

127. Barnes, *Centennial History*, 231.

128. Ibid.

129. Ibid., 236.

130. Mantler, "Partners in Justice and Peace," 5.

131. Barnes, *Centennial History*, 246.

132. Mantler, "Partners in Justice and Peace," 6.

133. Nadasen, *Rethinking the Welfare Rights Movement*, 143.

134. Honey, *Going Down Jericho Road*, 183.

135. SCLC Organizational Records, letter from George A. Wiley, Poverty Rights Action Center, to Reverend Andrew Young, March 25, 1968, Morehouse King Collection.

136. Honey, *Going Down Jericho Road*, 183; Jackson, *From Civil Rights to Human Rights*, 345.

137. SCLC Papers, memorandum from Arthur I. Waskow to Tony Henry and Bill Moyer, PPC, March 1, 1968, 2, King Center.

CHAPTER 5. THE MEMPHIS CAMPAIGN

1. Gollin, *Demography of Protest*, 7.

2. Ibid., 7.

3. SCLC Papers, box 180, 10, 1, King Center.

4. King and Ruley, *New and Unsettling Force*, 13.

5. Mantler, *Power to the Poor*.

6. King, *My Life*, 154.

7. Ibid.

8. Ibid., 155.

9. Mantler, *Power to the Poor*, 109.

10. Cobb, *Native Activism*, 149–50.

11. Houk interview.

12. Walker interview.

13. Wright, "Civil Rights Unfinished Business," 59.

14. Niermann, *American Indian Chicago Conference*.

15. Cobb, *Native Activism*, 149.

16. Ibid., 160.

17. Ibid., 156.

18. Ibid., 160–61.

19. Ibid., 154.

20. Mantler, *Power to the Poor*, 109.

21. Hamilton Lytle, *America's Uncivil Wars*, 301.

22. Oropeza, "Becoming Indo-Hispano," 180.

23. Ibid., 195.

24. SCLC Organizational Records, PPC, civil rights organizers, April 1968, Morehouse King Collection.

25. Tijerina, *King Tiger*, 101.

26. Oropeza, "Becoming Indo-Hispano," 201.

27. Ibid.

28. Mantler, *Power to the Poor*, 91.

29. Tijerina, *King Tiger*, 103.

30. Houk interview, 18.

31. Ibid.

32. Mantler, *Power to the Poor*, 190–91.

33. Pawel, *Crusades of Cesar Chavez*, 118.

34. Ibid., 157.

35. King, *My Life*, 155; SCLC Organizational Records, PPC, press release: Black and White Together, March 15, 1968, 1, Morehouse King Collection.

36. Pawel, *Crusades of Cesar Chavez*, 168.

37. Ibid., 370.

38. Laurent, *King and the Other America*, 161.

39. Houk interview, 16.

40. SCLC Organizational Records, "Black and White Together," press release, March 15, 1968, 1, Morehouse King Collection.

41. SCLC Organizational Records, PPC, civil rights organizers, April 1968, Morehouse King Collection.

42. Laurent, *King and the Other America*, 131.

43. Hamilton Lytle, *America's Uncivil Wars*, 180.

44. Houk interview, 19.

45. Ibid.

46. SCLC Organizational Records, Black and White Together, 2.

47. Austin interview.

48. Cobb, *Native Activism*, 172.

49. Horton, *Long Haul*, 118.

50. *Report of the National Advisory Commission on Civil Disorders* (Washington, D.C.: U.S. Government Printing Office, 1968), 1.

51. Updegrove, *Indomitable Will*, 276.

52. Sugrue, *Sweet Land of Liberty*, 328.

53. SCLC Organizational Records, PPC, Statement on the National Advisory Commission on Civil Disorders, March 1968, Morehouse King Collection.

54. Statement by King, March 4, 1968, 4, Morehouse King Collection.

55. Ibid.

56. McKnight, *Last Crusade*, 86.

57. Dallek, *Lyndon B. Johnson*, 334.

58. Statement by King, March 4, 1968, 2.

59. Ibid., 5.

60. SCLC Organizational Records, PPC, press release: Dr. King Touring Nation, March 17, 1968, Morehouse King Collection.

61. SCLC Papers, Timetable for the PPC, April 1968, box 178, 10, 1, King Center.

62. SCLC Organizational Records, Dr. King Touring Nation.

63. Garrow, *Bearing the Cross*, 601.

64. Memorandum from Hosea Williams to SCLC staff, Weekly Report and Dr. King's People to People Tours, March 8, 1968, Morehouse King Collection.

65. SCLC Papers, box 179, 4, 3, King Center.

66. Memorandum from Hosea Williams, March 8, 1968.

67. SCLC Organizational Records, Tentative Schedule, 1968, Morehouse King Collection.

68. Garrow, *Bearing the Cross*, 606.

69. SCLC Organizational Records, March 17, 1968, Morehouse King Collection.

70. Memorandum from Hosea Williams, March 8, 1968, 3.

71. Ibid.

72. King address at mass meeting in Eutaw, Ala., March 20, 1968, 6, King Center.

73. SCLC Organizational Records, PPC, memorandum from King to Action Committee, March 22, 1968, Morehouse King Collection.

74. Honey, *Going Down Jericho Road*, 13.

75. Ibid., xvii.

76. Mantler, *Power to the Poor*, 117.

77. Kamin, *Dangerous Friendship*, 215.

78. Frady, *Jesse*, 224.

79. Jackson, *From Civil Rights to Human Rights*, 22.

80. Honey, *To the Promised Land*, 55.

81. Honey, *Going Down Jericho Road*, 183.

82. King, "We Shall Overcome," *Industrial Union Department Digest*, 1961, 1.

83. Martin Luther King Jr. Papers, box 11, 1, AFL-CIO, December 11, 1961, 2–3, Gotlieb Center.

84. Jackson, *From Civil Rights to Human Rights*, 17.

85. Martin Luther King Jr. Papers, box 11, 1, Gotlieb Center.

86. King, *Stride toward Freedom*, 197.

87. Washington, *Testament of Hope*, 602.

88. Honey, *Going Down Jericho Road*, 185.

89. Chase, *Class Resurrection*, 135.

90. Ibid., 135–36.

91. Mantler, *Power to the Poor*, 106.

92. Honey, *Going Down Jericho Road*, 302.

93. Ibid., 302–3.

94. Carson, *Autobiography*, 352.

95. Interview of Bernard Lafayette by author, April 1, 2014.

96. Honey, *To the Promised Land*, 6.

97. Honey, *Going Down Jericho Road*, 417.

98. Mantler, "Press Did You In," 38.

99. Ibid., 39.

100. King, *My Life*, 157.

101. Abernathy, *And the Walls*, 425.

102. Frady, *Jesse*, 224.

103. McKnight, *Last Crusade*, 64.

104. Kotz, *Judgment Days*, 412.

105. SCLC (National Office), *New York Times Magazine*, ser. 6, box 2, 12, July 7, 1968, 3, Hosea Williams Collection.

106. Abernathy, *And the Walls*, 415.

107. Kotz, *Judgment Days*, 406.

108. Frady, *Jesse*, 224.

109. Kamin, *Dangerous Friendship*, 215.

110. Frady, *Jesse*, 225.

111. Abernathy, *And the Walls*, 497.

112. Interview of Bernard Lafayette by author, May 4, 2017.

113. Ibid.

114. Washington, *Testament of Hope*, 274.

115. Frady, *Jesse*, 226.

116. Interview of Charles Lewis Jr. by author, May 4, 2017.

117. Clark, "Tribute," 436.

118. Stein, *American Journey*, 253.

119. McKnight, *Last Crusade*, 84.

120. Ambrose, *Nixon*, 150.

121. Kotz, *Judgment Days*, 121.

122. Updegrove, *Indomitable Will*, 277.

123. Patterson, *Great Expectations*, 65.

124. Hamilton Lytle, *America's Uncivil Wars*, 237.

125. Joseph, *Stokely*, 258.

126. Sellers, *River of No Return*, 234.

127. Long, *I Must Resist*, 344.

128. Ibid.

129. Ralph and Finley, "In Their Own Voices," 72.

130. SCLC Papers, Field Reports, North Carolina, box 178, 16, February–March 1968, King Center.

131. Frady, *Jesse*, 234.

132. Austin interview.

133. Hamilton Lytle, *America's Uncivil Wars*, 252.

134. Freeman, *Mule Train*, 116.

135. Interview of Tyrone Brooks by author, April 2, 2014.

136. Long, *I Must Resist*, 344.

CHAPTER 6. THE MULE TRAIN

1. SCLC Papers, PPC flyer, April 1968, King Center.

2. Reef, *Ralph David Abernathy*, 18.

3. Abernathy, *And the Walls*, 494.

4. Ibid., 499.

5. Fager, *Uncertain Resurrection*, 12.

6. Reef, *Ralph David Abernathy*, 137.

7. McKnight, *Last Crusade*, 84.

8. Abernathy, *And the Walls*, 501.

9. Ibid.

10. *America*, May 18, 1968, 656, Schomburg.

11. King, *My Life*, 154.

12. King and Ruley, *New and Unsettling Force*, 38.

13. Freeman, *Mule Train*, 89.

14. Interview of Bernard Lafayette by author, April 1, 2014.

15. Ibid.

16. Freeman, *Mule Train*, 121.

17. U.S. Census Bureau, 1960, www.census.gov/data/tables/time-series/demo/income -poverty/historical-poverty-people.html.

18. Lackey, *Marks, Martin, and the Mule Train*, 23.

19. "Still Confederate," *West Side Torch* (Chicago), May 10–24, 1968.

20. Lackey, *Marks, Martin, and the Mule Train*, 27.

21. Edelman, *Lanterns*, 110.

22. Lackey, *Marks, Martin, and the Mule Train*, 26.

23. Ibid., 25.

24. King and Ruley, *New and Unsettling Force*, 39.

25. SCLC Papers, box 178, 9, 8, King Center.

26. Ibid., 2.

27. Approved Itinerary for Dr. King's Poor People's Tour, March 19–23, 1968, Morehouse King Collection.

28. Lackey, *Marks, Martin, and the Mule Train*, 21.

29. Branch, *At Canaan's Edge*, 721.

30. Kotz, *Judgment Days*, 399.

31. Freeman, *Mule Train*, 116.

32. Sampson interview, 16–17.

33. SCLC Papers, memorandum from Leon Hall to Hosea Williams, meetings and recruitment for PPC to Washington, February 21, 1968, King Center.

34. SCLC Papers, memorandum from Leon Hall to Hosea Williams, recruitment for PPC to Washington, February 19, 1968, King Center.

35. SCLC Papers, memorandum from Hall to Williams, February 19, 1968.

36. Ibid., 2–4.

37. SCLC Organizational Records, memorandum from Hosea Williams to PPC field staff, March 4, 1968, Morehouse King Collection.

38. Ibid., 3.

39. SCLC Papers, box 178, 9, March 1968, King Center.

40. Dittmer, *Local People*, 419.

41. SCLC Papers, box 178, 9, 1, King Center.

42. Lackey, *Marks, Martin, and the Mule Train*, 58.

43. SCLC Papers, staff meeting minutes, Department of Voter Registration and Political Education, March 26, 1968, box 180, 8, 5, King Center.

44. SCLC Papers, box 178, 12, King Center.

45. SCLC Papers, R. B. Cottonreader, letter to Hosea Williams, March 14, 1968, box 12, King Center.

46. Lackey, *Marks, Martin, and the Mule Train*, 36.

47. Ibid., 13.

48. Freeman, *Mule Train*, 130.

49. Ibid.

50. SCLC Papers, registration document, box 180, 22, King Center.

51. SCLC Papers, registration document, box 186, 6, King Center.

52. SCLC Papers, box 180, 21, King Center.

53. SCLC Papers, box 186, 7, March 1968, King Center.

54. SCLC Papers, box 180, 21, King Center.

55. SCLC Papers, registration document, box 180, 22, King Center.

56. SCLC Papers, registration document, Mississippi, box 181, 86, King Center.

57. SCLC Papers, registration document, box 181, 4, March 1968, King Center.

58. SCLC Papers, PPC pledges, box 180, 2, King Center.

59. SCLC Papers, box 155, 26, 2, King Center.

60. Freeman, *Mule Train*, 119.

61. Ibid.

62. SCLC Papers, box 177, 8, 1, King Center.

63. Interview of Bernard Lafayette by author, April 1, 2014.

64. "We're on Our Way," *Newsweek*, May 1968, 32, Schomburg.

65. Interview of Bernard Lafayette by author, April 1, 2014.

66. SCLC Papers, box 178, 9, 2–3, King Center.

67. SCLC Papers, box 181, 5, King Center.

68. Ibid., 6.

69. Interview of Bernard Lafayette by author, April 1, 2014.

70. Robnett, *How Long?*, 90.

71. "Still Confederate," *West Side Torch* (Chicago), May 10–24, 1968, 3, 17.

72. Ibid.

73. Lackey, *Marks, Martin, and the Mule Train*, 38.

74. "We're on Our Way," 32.

75. "Still Confederate," 3, 17.

76. Robnett, *How Long?*, 90.

77. E.g., Holst, *Social Movements*.

78. SCLC Papers, box 155, 23, 3, King Center.

79. SCLC Papers, box 151, 30, 1, King Center.

80. SCLC Papers, box 151, 8, November 1965, King Center.

81. SCLC Papers, box 178, 12, 1, March 1968, King Center.

82. SCLC Papers, box 177, 38, 2–3, May 1968, King Center.

83. SCLC Papers, box 177, 8, 2, King Center.

84. Freeman, *Mule Train*, 125–26.

85. Payne, *I've Got the Light of Freedom*.

86. Bell et al., *We Make the Road*, 156.

87. Freire, *Pedagogy in Process*, 8.

88. SCLC Papers, box 179, 5, 3, King Center.

89. SCLC Papers, box 179, 19, 2, King Center.

90. Freeman, *Mule Train*, 114.

91. Cotton, *If Your Back's Not Bent*, 221.

92. Freire, *Pedagogy in Process*, 14.

93. Ibid.

94. Wright, "1968 Poor People's Campaign," 112.

95. SCLC Papers, registration document, box 181, 2, March 1968, King Center.

96. SCLC Papers, box 181, 6, King Center.

97. Quoted in Freeman, *Mule Train*, 99.

98. SCLC Papers, box 181, 6, March 1968, King Center.

99. SCLC Papers, box 177, 10, June 1968, King Center.

100. SCLC Papers, box 180, 8, 4–5, King Center.

101. Freeman, *Mule Train*, 119.

102. Abernathy, *And the Walls*, 507.

103. Ibid.

104. SCLC Papers, Final Plans for D.C., April 22, 1968, King Center.

105. Freeman, *Mule Train*, 126.

106. SCLC Papers, box 177, 8, 4, King Center.

107. Freeman, *Mule Train*, 38.

108. Green, "Challenging the Civil Rights Narrative," 72.

109. Jackson, *From Civil Rights to Human Rights*, 347.

110. Wright, "1968 Poor People's Campaign," 124–25.

111. SCLC Papers, box 177, 8, 7, King Center.

112. Ibid., 4.

113. Abernathy, *And the Walls*, 508.

114. SCLC Papers, box 178, 9, 1–2, King Center.

115. SCLC Papers, box 180, 21, King Center.

116. SCLC Papers, box 181, 5, King Center.

117. Freeman, *Mule Train*, 129.

118. SCLC Papers, box 177, 8, 8, King Center.

119. Lackey, *Marks, Martin, and the Mule Train*, 86.

120. Wright, "1968 Poor People's Campaign," 125.

121. Lackey, *Marks, Martin, and the Mule Train*, 84.

122. Freeman, *Mule Train*, 53.

123. Quoted in Lackey, *Marks, Martin, and the Mule Train*, 86.

124. McKnight, *Last Crusade*, 96.

125. Ibid., 97.

126. Sampson interview.

127. Wright, "1968 Poor People's Campaign," 112.

128. Lackey, *Marks, Martin, and the Mule Train*, 107.

129. Ibid.

130. Lisa Land Cooper, "The Mule Train: A Different Kind of Stubborn," *Every Now and Then*, February 9, 2013, 3, http://douglascountyhistory.blogspot.com/2013/02/the-mule-train-different-kind-of.html.

131. Ibid., 5.

132. Ibid., 6.

133. Freeman, *Mule Train*, 96.

134. Interview of Tyrone Brooks by author, April 2, 2014.

135. Hill, "Activism as Practice," 93.

136. Cooper, "The Mule Train," 7.

137. Freeman, *Mule Train*, 127.

138. Ibid., 40.

139. Ibid., 121.

140. "Rickety Mule Train Plods in to Wait for March," *Washington Post*, June 19, 1968.

141. "Buses, Mule Train Arrive for Big Rally," *Evening Star*, June 18, 1968.

142. "Rickety Mule Train Plods in to Wait for March."

143. Ibid.

144. Ibid.

145. "Mule Train Misses Taking Part in Rally," *Daily News*, June 20, 1968.

CHAPTER 7. THE COMMITTEE OF 100

1. Statement of Demands for Rights of the Poor Presented to the U.S. Government by the SCLC and Its Committee of 100, PPC, Spring 1968, Schomburg.

2. SCLC Organizational Records, Final Plans For the Washington PPC, April 22, 1968, Morehouse King Collection.

3. Committee of 100, 1968, 50–54, Schomburg.

4. SCLC Papers, Abernathy statements, Department of Agriculture, box 177, 1, 1, May 1968, King Center.

5. Gollin, "Poor People's Campaign," 5.

6. "Rustin in Call for Mass Rally," *New York Times*, June 3, 1968, 2.

7. Austin interview.

8. SCLC Organizational Records, PPC Goals, April 1968, Morehouse King Collection.

9. SCLC Organizational Records, memorandum from Harry H. Wachtel to Research Committee members, March 1968, 8, Morehouse King Collection.

10. Statement of Demands for Rights of the Poor, 1.

11. Offenburger interview, 37.

12. SCLC (National Office), PPC Photographic Journal, ser. 6, box 2, 19, June 1968, Hosea Williams Collection.

13. The Poor People's Campaign Speaks to U.S. Department of Health, Education and Welfare, Wilbur Cohen, April 30, 1968, 39, Schomburg.

14. Statement of Demands for Rights of the Poor, 13.

15. Ibid., 3.

16. Poor People's Campaign Speaks, Wilbur Cohen, 32.

17. Declaration Committee, Senate Subcommittee on Employment, Manpower and Poverty, box 177, 134, 1, King Center.

18. Statement of the Reverend Dr. Ralph David Abernathy, Senate Subcommittee on Employment, Manpower and Poverty, April 30, 1968, 19, Schomburg.

19. Ibid., 7.

20. Ibid.

21. Declaration Committee, Senate Subcommittee on Employment, Manpower and Poverty, box 177, 134, 2, King Center.

22. Statement of Abernathy, Senate Subcommittee on Employment, Manpower and Poverty, 19.

23. SCLC Papers, Demands of the Indo Hispano to the Federal Government, Mexican Americans, box 179, 9, 1, May–June 1968, King Center.

24. Ibid.

25. Mantler, "Press Did You In," 40.

26. SCLC Papers, Demands of the Indo Hispano to the Federal Government, 1.

27. Cobb, *Native Activism*, 163.

28. Ibid.

29. The Poor People's Campaign Speaks to U.S. Department of the Interior, Stewart Udall, May 1, 1968, 45, Schomburg.

30. Cobb, *Native Activism*, 167.

31. Poor People's Campaign to Stewart Udall, 45.

32. Cobb, *Native Activism*, 168.

33. SCLC (National Office), PPC Photographic Journal, ser. 6, box 2, 19, June 1968, Hosea Williams Collection.

34. Cobb, *Native Activism*, 165–66.

35. SCLC Papers, Demands of the Indo Hispano to the Federal Government, 1.

36. SCLC Papers, Southwest Delegation PPC, Indians Denied Their Fishing Rights, Mexican Americans, May–June 1968, box 179, 9, King Center.

37. Ibid.

38. SCLC Papers, "Dr. Ralph Abernathy Speaks: Progress in Resurrection City," *Soul Force*, June 2, 1968, King Center.

39. The Poor People's Campaign Speaks to U.S. Department of Housing and Development, Robert C. Weaver, April 30, 1968, 30, Schomburg.

40. Sugrue, *Sweet Land of Liberty*, 374.

41. Cobb, *Native Activism*, 169.

42. Offenburger interview, 37.

43. Mantler, "Press Did You In," 40.

44. Lentz, *Symbols*, 313.

45. "We're on Our Way," *Newsweek*, May 1968, 32.

46. Ibid.

47. Ibid.

48. "The Poor People's March: Its Demands and Prospects," *U.S. News and World Report*, May 13, 1968, 44.

49. "We're on Our Way," 32.

50. "The Poor People's March: Its Demands and Prospects," 44.

51. Hamilton Lytle, *America's Uncivil Wars*, 254.

52. Patterson, *Great Expectations*, 686.

53. Branch, *At Canaan's Edge*, 745.

54. "Focus Turns to Tent City as Drive of Poor Opens," *Evening Star*, May 13, 1968, 2.

55. Fager, *Uncertain Resurrection*, 15.

56. "Poor Stake Out Their City Here," *Washington Daily News*, May 13, 1968, 1.

57. Fager, *Uncertain Resurrection*, 14.

58. "The Poor Close In on Washington," *Business Week*, May 18, 1968, 35.

59. Quoted in "Focus Turns to Tent City as Drive of Poor Opens," 2.

60. Wohl, *Father, Son, and Constitution*, 330.

61. McKnight, *Last Crusade*, 111.

62. "200 More Policemen Put on the Streets," *Washington Post*, May 8, 1968, 2.

63. SCLC, Suggestions for Groups Who Wish to Support the PPC, box 8, 2, Schomburg.

64. "The Poor People's March: Its Demands and Prospects," 43.

CHAPTER 8. THE POOR ARRIVE IN WASHINGTON

1. King and Ruley, *New and Unsettling Force*, 25.

2. SCLC (National Office), PPC Photographic Journal, ser. 6, box 2, 19, June 1968, Hosea Williams Collection.

3. McKnight, *Last Crusade*, 84.

4. Chase, *Class Resurrection*, 49–50.

5. Austin interview.

6. Mantler, "Press Did You In," 41.

7. Ibid.

8. Ibid.

9. "Abernathy Starts Caravan on Way from New Mexico," *Sunday Star*, May 19, 1968, 6.

10. Tijerina, *King Tiger*, 106.

11. Cobb, *Native Activism*, 174.

12. SCLC Papers, Western PPC, box 178, 21, May 1968, King Center.

13. Cobb, *Native Activism*, 175.

14. "Poor Start for Washington," *West Side Torch* (Chicago), May 10–24, 1968.

15. "Marchers Hailed at Trenton Rally," *New York Times*, May 14, 1968, 27.

16. "Poor Build a 'City' of Plastic, Plywood," *Washington Post*, May 14, 1968, 2.

17. SCLC Papers, Caravan Chronicle, box 177, 8, 1, April–May 1968, King Center.

18. "The Poor Move toward Capital," *New York Times*, May 16, 1968, 28.

19. "Marchers in Philadelphia," *New York Times*, May 16, 1968, 17.

20. "Caravan Frolics in Baltimore," *Star*, May 17, 1968, 2.

21. Ibid.

22. SCLC Papers, box 177, 8, 3, King Center.

23. Lentz, *Symbols*, 311.

24. "Challenging the Pharaoh," *Time*, May 17, 1968, 35.

25. SCLC Papers, box 177, 8, 3, King Center.

26. "Chicago Poor Start for Washington," *West Side Torch*, May 10–24, 1968.

27. "Delays Plague Midwesterners," *Sunday Star*, May 19, 1968, 6.

28. SCLC Papers, Caravan Chronicle.

29. "Detroit Mayor Apologizes to Poor People's Marchers for Police Clash," *New York Times*, May 15, 1968, 17.

30. SCLC Papers, Gollin, box 16, 7, 6, King Center.

31. Key People, Local Coordinators, 1968, Schomburg.

32. SCLC Papers, press releases, box 179, 30, March 4, 1968, King Center.

33. SCLC Papers, staff meeting minutes, Department of Voter Registration and Political Education, box 180, 8, 5, March 26, 1968, King Center.

34. Abernathy, *And the Walls*, 501.

35. Wiebenson, "Planning and Using Resurrection City," 406.

36. Henry interview, 18.

37. SCLC Papers, Mike Finkelstein, memorandum to Al Gollin, City Plan, 1969, King Center.

38. SCLC Papers, press releases, PPC Committees, 1968, box 179, 30, 2, King Center.

39. SCLC, Who's Who in the PPC, May 25, 1968, 6, Schomburg.

40. "Leader in March Denies a Report of Funds Crisis," *New York Times*, May 19, 1968, 1.

41. Mantler, "Press Did You In," 41.

42. See www.hollywoodreporter.com/news/hollywood-flashback-barbra-streisand-sang-898675.

43. Lee and Vale, "Resurrection City, Washington, D.C., 1968," 113.

44. SCLC Papers, Shelters and Site Committee, box 179, 35, March 10, 1968, King Center.

45. Lee and Vale, "Resurrection City, Washington, D.C., 1968," 114.

46. Congressional Quarterly Weekly Report, Lobbying Activities: Poor People's Campaign, May 17, 1968, 1131, Schomburg.

47. "Leader in March Denies a Report of Funds Crisis," 38.

48. Lee and Vale, "Resurrection City, Washington, D.C., 1968," 114.

49. SCLC Papers, Finkelstein to Gollin, City Plan.

50. SCLC Papers, Community Services, 1968, box 177, 15, 1, King Center.

51. Ibid., 2.

52. J. Edward Haycraft, "Poor People's Government," *Soul Force*, June 19, 1968, 3, King Center.

53. SCLC Papers, box 180, 4, 2, *Soul Force*, 1968, King Center.

54. Henry interview, 25.

55. SCLC, Registration Plans for Participants in the Poor People's Campaign, May 4, 1968, 1, Schomburg.

56. Albert E. Gollin, PPC, "The First Four Thousand: A Brief Statistical Profile," 1968, box 14, 10, 1, Schomburg.

57. "Streams of Volunteers Help First Marchers," *Evening Star*, May 13, 1968, 1.

58. "Hammer Beats 'Freedom, Freedom,'" *Washington Afro-American*, May 14, 1968, 1, Schomburg.

59. "Streams of Volunteers Help First Marchers," 1.

60. SCLC, Registration Plans for Participants, 2.

61. Ibid.

62. SCLC, Registration in Danville, April 11, 1968, 1, Schomburg.

63. SCLC Papers, PPC: What Can Students Do?, 1968, King Center.

64. Ibid.

65. Arsenault, *Freedom Riders*; Halberstam, *Children*.

66. SCLC Papers, box 16, 7, King Center; Gollin, *Demography of Protest*.

67. SCLC (National Office), Faith Berry, *New York Times Magazine*, ser. 6, box 2, 12, July 7, 1968, 3, Hosea Williams Collection.

68. "March Problems Spur an Emergency Meeting," *Washington Post*, May 16, 1968, 2.

69. Mantler, "Press Did You In," 42.

70. "500 New Marchers Set for Greenbelt," *Daily News*, May 17, 1968, 3.

71. "SCLC Appeals for Funds as Poor Pour into Capital," *Washington Afro-American*, May 18, 1968, 3.

72. "Poor Come, but Go, Too," *Washington Daily News*, May 16, 1968, 5.

73. SCLC Papers, box 16, 7, King Center; Gollin, *Demography of Protest*.

74. Ibid.

75. Gollin, "The First Four Thousand," 2.

76. SCLC Papers, box 16, 7, King Center; Gollin, *Demography of Protest*.

77. "Resurrection City: Metaphors," *New Yorker*, June 1968, 73.

78. SCLC Papers, box 16, 7, King Center; Gollin, *Demography of Protest*.

79. SCLC (National Office), PPC Photographic Journal, ser. 6, box 2, 19, June 1968, Hosea Williams Collection.

80. "Focus Turns to Tent City as Drive of Poor Opens," *Evening Star*, May 13, 1968, 2.

81. "Welcome to My Country: The First Bus Load Arrives," *Washington Afro-American*, May 14, 1968, 2.

82. "Poor's Drive Open."

83. "Fresh Arrivals Overtax Space at Poor Camp," *Star*, May 15, 1968, 1.

84. "Leader in March Denies a Funding Crisis," *New York Times*, May 19, 1968, 39.

85. "March Problems Spur an Emergency Meeting," *Washington Post*, May 16, 1968, 2.

86. "Leader in March Denies a Report of Funds Crisis," 38.

87. "Second Campsite Sought as 2 Caravans Near D.C.," *Sunday Star*, May 19, 1968.

88. "Second Campsite Is Sought for the Poor," *Sunday Star*, May 19, 1968, 6.

89. SCLC Organizational Records, memorandum from Bernard Lafayette to executive staff, Discussion with Brady Tyson, March 8, 1968, Morehouse King Collection.

CHAPTER 9. BUILDING RESURRECTION CITY

1. Cheng interview, July 11, 1968, 59.

2. "Young Builders Get Sobering Advice," *Washington Star*, May 13, 1968,

3. "Poor People Seek Support for Big Rally," *Washington Post*, June 11, 1968, 2.

4. "Mother's Day Opens 'Campaign of Conscience,'" *Washington Daily News*, May 13, 1968.

5. Ibid.

6. Ibid.

7. "Welcome to My Country: The First Bus Load Arrives," *Washington Afro-American*, May 14, 1968, 2.

8. "The Birth of the Poor People's Resurrection City," *Washington Afro-American*, May 18, 1968, 22.

9. "Campaign Gets Off to Low-Key Start," *Evening Star*, May 13, 1968, 1.

10. King, *My Life*, 28.

11. Ibid., 29.

12. Honey, *To the Promised Land*, 110.

13. King, *My Life*, 38.

14. "Mrs. King Blames Congress for Poverty," *Washington Afro-American*, May 14, 1968, 2.

15. "Mrs. King Sets The Tone: Campaign of Conscience," *Evening Star*, May 13, 1968.

16. "Focus Turns to Tent City as Drive of Poor Opens," *Evening Star*, May 13, 1968, 2.

17. "Poverty: We're on Our Way," *Newsweek*, May 1968, 32.

18. "Welcome to My Country, Indian Chief Tells Poor," *Washington Afro-American*, May 14, 1968, 2.

19. "Mrs. Ralph Abernathy: Her Goal: Marshalling Multicolored Womanpower," *Washington Post*, May 15, 1968, D2.

20. "I Welcome You," *Washington Afro-American*, May 14, 1968, 5.

21. "Poverty: We're on Our Way," 32.

22. "Focus Turns to Tent City as Drive of Poor Opens," *Evening Star*, May 13, 1968, 1.

23. "A Living History, Poor People's Campaign," produced by Arthur Alexander, WBAI broadcast, June 21, 1968, BB3128, Pacifica Radio Archives, https://www.pacificaradio archives.org/.

24. "City of Huts Started near Mall: Leaders Vow a Long Camp-In," *Washington Post*, May 14, 1968, 1.

25. "Work Pushed on Shelters for Marchers," *Evening Star*, May 14, 1968, 1.

26. "A Living History, Poor People's Campaign."

27. "City of the Poor Is Dedicated in Washington by Abernathy," *New York Times*, May 14, 1968, 2.

28. "The Birth of Poor People's Resurrection City," *Washington Afro-American*, May 18, 1968, 22.

29. "The Mood Is Humid: Oppressed Are Oppressing," *Evening Star*, May 14, 1968, 1.

30. Ibid.

31. "Resurrection City: Metaphors," *New Yorker*, June 1968, 73.

32. "Stokely Makes Music at the 'City,'" *Washington Daily News*, May 15, 1968, 7.

33. Memorandum from Mike Finkelstein to Al Gollin, City Plan, Security System, February 19, 1969, Schomburg.

34. SCLC (National Office), *New York Times Magazine*, ser. 6, box 2, 12, July 7, 1968, Hosea Williams Collection.

35. Ibid.

36. Sampson interview, 16.

37. SCLC (National Office), *New York Times Magazine*, ser. 6, box 2, 12, July 7, 1968, Hosea Williams Collection.

38. Ibid.

39. McKnight, *Last Crusade*, 112.

40. "Tent City Awaits Its First Dwellers," *Evening Star*, May 14, 1968, 4.

41. "Poor Build a 'City' of Plastic, Plywood," *Washington Post*, May 14, 1968, 2.

42. Abernathy, *And the Walls*, 514.

43. "March Problems Spur an Emergency Meeting," *Washington Post*, May 16, 1968, 2.

44. "Mayor's Plea to Hill: Halt Attacks, Rebuild," *Washington Post*, May 14, 1968, 2.

45. "Work Pushed on Shelters for Marchers," *Evening Star*, May 14, 1968, 1.

46. "Marchers Move into Shelters," *Washington Post*, May 15, 1968, 2.

47. "The Poor People's March: Its Demands and Prospects," *U.S. News and World Report*, May 13, 1968, 44, Schomburg.

48. Congressional Quarterly Weekly Report, Lobbying Activities: Poor People's Campaign, May 17, 1968, 1131, Schomburg.

49. "The Poor Close In on Washington," *Business Week*, May 18, 1968, 34–35.

50. "A Time of Questions but No Answers," *Sunday Star*, May 19, 1968, 1.

51. Ibid.

52. Henry interview, 12.

53. Lee and Vale, "Resurrection City, Washington, D.C., 1968."

54. Ibid.

55. "City of the Poor Is Dedicated in Washington by Abernathy," *New York Times*, May 14, 1968, 2.

56. Wiebenson, "Planning and Using Resurrection City," 406.

57. "Caravan Frolics in Baltimore," *Star*, May 17, 1968, 2.

58. Cobb, *Native Activism*, 175.

59. "Poor Build a 'City' of Plastic, Plywood," 2.

60. "City of the Poor Develops Style All Its Own," *New York Times*, May 24, 1968, 30.

61. Ibid.

62. Cobb, *Native Activism*, 177.

63. Abernathy, *And the Walls*, 512.

64. Peterson interview, 35.

65. "Focus Turns to Tent City as Drive of Poor Opens," *Evening Star*, May 13, 1968, 1.

66. "Second Campsite Is Sought for the Poor," *Sunday Star*, May 19, 1968, 6.

67. "Second Campsite Sought as 2 Caravans Near D.C.," *Sunday Star*, May 19, 1968.

68. "Tent City Awaits Its First Dwellers," *Evening Star*, May 14, 1968, 4.

69. "Construction of Resurrection City Under Way," *Evening Star*, May 13, 1968, 1.

70. Wiebenson, "Planning and Using Resurrection City," 407.

71. Memorandum from Mike Finkelstein to Al Gollin, City Plan, Information System, Supplies, February 19, 1969, Schomburg.

72. Wiebenson, "Planning and Using Resurrection City," 410.

73. Ibid., 408.

74. "Focus Turns to Tent City as Drive of Poor Opens," *Evening Star*, May 13, 1968, 1.

75. "Souvenir Hucksters Tent-In Too," *Washington Daily News*, May 14, 1968, 5.

76. "'Resurrection City' Is Growing," *Washington Post*, May 14, 1968, 5.

77. "The Mood Is Humid: Oppressed Are Oppressing," *Evening Star*, May 14, 1968, 1.

78. "Two Views of the PPC," *Evening Star*, May 14, 1968, 4.

79. "The Mood Is Humid: Oppressed Are Oppressing," 1.

80. Mantler, "Press Did You In," 42.

81. SCLC (National Office), PPC Photographic Journal, ser. 6, box 2, 19, June 1968, Hosea Williams Collection.

82. "For and about Women, Poor Approve 'City,'" *Washington Post*, May 16, 1968, 1–2.

83. Ibid.

84. "Marchers Move into Shelters," *Washington Post*, May 15, 1968, 2.

85. "Poor Build a 'City' of Plastic, Plywood," 2.

86. "Second Campsite Is Sought for the Poor," 7.

87. Billings, "Health Care," 1697.

88. Wright, "Civil Rights Unfinished Business," 405.

89. "City of the Poor Develops Style All Its Own," 30.

90. Billings, "Health Care," 1698.

91. Ibid., 1696.

92. Ibid.

93. Afield and Gibson, *Children of Resurrection City*, 11.

94. Ibid., 18.

95. Ibid., 29–30.

96. Ibid., 33–34.

97. Rutherford interview, 34–36.

98. "Movie Industry to Aid Campaign," *Washington Afro-American*, May 14, 1968, 2.

99. "City of the Poor Develops Style All Its Own," 30.

100. SCLC Papers, "Food in Resurrection City," *Soul Force*, box 180, 4, King Center.

101. Ibid.

102. Ibid.

103. "City of the Poor Develops Style All Its Own," 30.

104. J. Edward Haycraft, "Poor People's Government," *Soul Force*, June 19, 1968, 3, King Center.

105. "Marchers Move into Shelters," *Washington Post*, May 15, 1968, 2.

106. "City of the Poor Develops Style All Its Own," 30.

107. "Stokely Makes Music at the 'City,'" *Washington Daily News*, May 15, 1968, 7.

108. "Marchers Move into Shelters," 2.

CHAPTER 10. POOR PEOPLE GET DOWN TO WORK

1. The Memorial and Dedicatory Litany for Martin Luther King Jr., May 1968, Schomburg.

2. "Challenging the Pharaoh," *Time*, May 17, 1968, 35.

3. SCLC Papers, "Let's Have a Revolution, a Real Revolution," Action Center, box 177, 3, May 1968, King Center.

4. Ibid.

5. "Focus Turns to Tent City as Drive of Poor Opens," *Evening Star*, May 13, 1968, 2.

6. Interview of Bernard Lafayette, May 4, 2017.

7. Gollin, "Poor People's Campaign," 5.

8. Heltzel, *Resurrection City*, 113.

9. "Marchers Move into Shelters, Hint They're Here for a Long Stay," *Washington Post*, May 15, 1968, 2.

10. McKnight, *Last Crusade*, 92.

11. "The Poor People's March: Its Demands and Prospects," *U.S. News and World Report*, May 13, 1968, 44.

12. "Delays Plague Midwesterners," *Sunday Star*, May 19, 1968, 6.

13. "The Poor Close In on Washington," *Business Week*, May 18, 1968, 35.

14. "The Poor People's March: Its Demands, the Prospects," *U.S. News and World Report*, May 13, 1968, 44.

15. Fager, *Uncertain Resurrection*, 15.

16. "Rights Expert Says That Liberals Failed Blacks," *New York Times*, May 17, 1968, 31.

17. "A Guaranteed Income: Idea Gains Ground among Leaders, but to Many People It's a Handout," *New York Times*, May 28, 1968, 8.

18. "That Guaranteed Income Deal," *Daily News*, May 15, 1968, 31.

19. "Nixon Warns about Yielding to Marchers," *Washington Post*, May 15, 1968, 2.

20. "Nixon Evades Poverty Issue, Young Charges," *Washington Post*, July 7, 1968, 2.

21. Maddison and Sclamer, *Activist Wisdom*.

22. Green, *Taking History to Heart*.

23. McKnight, *Last Crusade*, 118.

24. "Abernathy and 72 Congressmen Confer on Poor People's Goals," *New York Times*, May 16, 1968, 29.

25. "Senate Ambush by Campaign 'Truth Squad,'" *Washington Daily News*, May 16, 1968, 5.

26. "The Poor Close In on Washington," 34.

27. "March Is Getting to Target," *Sunday Star*, May 19, 1968, 6.

28. "Poor to Disrupt Washington as Last Resort," *Philadelphia Inquirer*, May 16, 1968, 5.

29. "The Poor Close In on Washington," 35.

30. SCLC, Congressional Reaction, box 177, 34, King Center.

31. Ibid.

32. "The Poor Close In on Washington," 34.

33. "18 Are Arrested in March of Poor," *New York Times*, May 24, 1968, 30.

34. "Court Clears Last 2 of Capitol Marchers," *Washington Post*, July 9, 1968, 2.

35. "18 Are Arrested in March of Poor," 30.

36. Frady, *Jesse*, 243.

37. "18 Are Arrested in March of Poor," 30.

38. Freeman interview, 12.

39. "Poor Marchers Stage Agriculture Department Protest," *Washington Post*, May 29, 1968, 2.

40. Freeman interview, 12.

41. Ibid., 13.

42. SEDFRE, Background Information, April 1968, Schomburg.

43. Ibid.

44. Ibid.

45. "More Militancy Pledged for Poor," *New York Times*, June 3, 1968, 2.

46. Lee and Vale, "Resurrection City, Washington, D.C., 1968," 114.

47. "Poor Cautions U.S. in Ousting Them by Force," *Washington Post*, June 1, 1968, 4.

48. "Poor People Plan More Militancy," *Washington Post*, June 3, 1968, 2.

49. McKnight, *Last Crusade*, 131.

50. Ibid., 132.

51. Freedman, *Old News*, 59.

52. Ibid., 59–60.

53. "400 Marchers Balked at Justice Department," *Washington Post*, June 3, 1968, 2.

54. Mantler, "Press Did You In," 43.

55. "Resurrection City: Metaphors," *New Yorker*, June 1968, 73.

56. Cobb, *Native Activism*, 178.

57. "Poor Marchers Stage Agriculture Department Protest," *Washington Post*, May 29, 1968, 2.

58. Tijerina, *King Tiger*, 109.

59. Oropeza, "Becoming Indo-Hispano," 201.

60. Cobb, *Native Activism*, 179.

61. Ibid., 181.

62. "Violence against the Court," *Washington Post*, May 31, 1968, 20.

63. Tijerina, *King Tiger*, 111.

64. Cheng interview, June 6, 1970, 57.

65. Meek, "Propaganda," 169.

66. "Abernathy Says Poor Will Stay in Capital until Goals Are Met," *New York Times*, June 11, 1968.

67. Ibid.

68. Moyer interview, 19.

69. Senate Subcommittee on Employment, Manpower and Poverty, May 23 and 29, June 12 and 14, 1968, 66–67.

70. "SCLC'S 'Portia' Besieges the Hill," *Daily Star*, July 7, 1968, 3.

71. Senate Subcommittee on Employment, Manpower and Poverty, 95.

72. Ibid.

73. Ibid., 105.

74. Ibid.

75. Ibid., 108–9.

76. Ibid., 109.

77. Ibid., 112.

78. Ibid., 113.

79. Ibid.

80. Ibid., 114.

81. Ibid., 115.

82. Ibid., 116.

83. Ibid., 117.

84. Ibid., 121.

85. Ibid., 122.

86. Ibid., 124.

87. Ibid., 126.

88. Buskirk interview, 14.

CHAPTER 11. LEARNING IN RESURRECTION CITY

1. E.g., McKnight, *Last Crusade.*

2. E.g., Cunningham, "Social Dimension"; Crowther et al., *Popular Education*; Holst, *Social Movements*; Walter, "Adult Learning"; Langdon, "Democracy Re-Examined"; Hall et al., *Learning and Education.*

3. E.g., Adams and Horton, *Unearthing Seeds of Fire*; Bell et al., *We Make the Road*; Rachal, "We'll Never Turn Back."

4. "I Welcome You," *Washington Afro-American*, May 14, 1968, 5.

5. "Poverty: We're on Our Way," *Newsweek*, May 1968, 32.

6. SCLC Papers, "Workers Wanted! Space Needed!! for Continuing Education," Septima Clark, 1962, box 155, 23, 5, King Center.

7. Lackey, *Marks, Martin, and the Mule Train*, 41.

8. Crawford et al., *Women in the Civil Rights Movement*; Robnett, *How Long?*

9. Crawford et al., *Women in the Civil Rights Movement.*

10. Harding, Introduction, xvii.

11. Robnett, *How Long?*, 88.

12. E.g., Burns, *Daybreak of Freedom.*

13. Bell et al., Editors' Introduction, xxxvii.

14. Bell et al., *We Make the Road*, 93.

15. Honey, *To the Promised Land*, 58.

16. Harding, Introduction, xvii.

17. Robnett, *How Long?*, 91.

18. SCLC Papers, box 151, 8, King Center.

19. SCLC Organizational Records, Tenth Anniversary Convention, CEP Report, Dorothy Cotton and Septima Clark, 1967, 3, Morehouse King Collection.

20. Cotton, *If Your Back's Not Bent*, 214.

21. Jackson, *From Civil Rights to Human Rights*, 17.

22. Rachal, "We'll Never Turn Back."

23. Bell et al., *We Make the Road*, 72.

24. Rachal, "We'll Never Turn Back," 169.

25. SCLC Papers, Proposal, 1965, box 151, 24, King Center.

26. Cheng interview, July 11, 1968, 2.

27. "A Living History, Poor People's Campaign," produced by Arthur Alexander, WBAI broadcast, June 21, 1968, BB3128, Pacifica Radio Archives, https://www.pacificaradio archives.org.

28. Freedman, *Old News*, 4.

29. "A Living History, Poor People's Campaign."

30. Sampson interview.

31. Bell et al., *We Make the Road*, 79.

32. SCLC, Registration in Danville, April 11, 1968, 2, Schomburg.

33. SCLC Papers, PPU, Statement of the Purpose and Objectives, 1968, King Center.

34. SCLC Papers, box 179, 28, King Center.

35. Cooks interview, 8.

36. Ibid., 9.

37. Ibid., 14.

38. Gollin interview.

39. SCLC Papers, J. Edward Haycraft, "Nourishing Our Minds," *Soul Force*, June 19, 1968, 6, King Center.

40. "Area Teachers Pledge Support for Campaign," *Washington Afro-American*, May 14, 1968, 11.

41. "Poor People's University Planned to Specialize in Study of Poverty," *Washington Post*, May 14, 1968, 2.

42. SCLC Papers, Poor People's University, box 179, 23, May 1968, King Center.

43. "Some 5,000 Collegians Expected to Join March," *Evening Star*, May 14, 1968, A4.

44. SCLC Papers, Poor People's University, box 179, 23, May 1968, King Center.

45. Gollin interview, 1.

46. Statement of the Purpose and Objectives.

47. Haycraft, "Nourishing Our Minds," 6.

48. SCLC Papers, press release, June 1968, King Center.

49. Hamilton, "Did the Dream End There?"

50. SCLC Papers, Freedom University Schedule, June 9–15, 1968, King Center.

51. SCLC Papers, June 20–21, 1968, King Center.

52. Holst, "Frameworks," 125.

53. Cooks interview, 21.

54. SCLC Papers, Freedom University Schedule, June 1968, King Center.

55. Shannon interview.

56. SCLC Papers, *Soul Force*, 1968, King Center.

57. Haycraft, "Nourishing Our Minds," 6.

58. SCLC Papers, PPU press release, June 1968, King Center.

59. SCLC Papers, PPC Information Center, June 3, 1968, King Center.

60. R. M. Moore, Scholarship, Education, and Defense Fund for Racial Equality (SED-FRE) in Resurrection City, June 5, 1968, 8, Schomburg.

61. Walker interview, 35.

62. Statement of the Purpose and Objectives, 1.

63. Cooks interview, 17–18.

64. "Poor People's University: A Convocation," *Washington Post*, June 11, 1968.

65. Ibid.

66. Ibid.

67. Henry interview, 24.

68. SCLC Papers, "Take a Look at Tom," Action Center, box 177, 23, May 1968, King Center.

69. "Some 5,000 Collegians Expected to Join March," A4.

70. Cheng interview, June 6, 1970, 61.

71. "Freedom Schools Open: No Philosophy and No Pencils," *Daily News*, May 18, 1968, 1.

72. Ibid.

73. Rachal, "We'll Never Turn Back."

74. SCLC Papers, A Living Philosophy to Guide the Freedom School during the PPC Campaign, 1968, 1–2, King Center.

75. Cheng interview, July 11, 1968, 1.

76. Cheng interview, June 6, 1970, 56–57.

77. A Living Philosophy to Guide the Freedom School, 1–2.

78. Cheng interview, June 6, 1970, 60.

79. Cheng interview, July 11, 1968, 2.

80. SEDFRE, Background Information, April 1968, Schomburg.

81. SCLC Papers, R. M. Moore, Scholarship, Education, and Defense Fund for Racial Equality (SEDFRE) in Resurrection City, June 5, 1968, King Center.

82. SEDFRE, Ronnie M. Moore, "My Views of the PPC," June 5, 1968, 5–8, Schomburg.

83. Newman, *Teaching Defiance*, 50.

84. SEDFRE, Report from Spiver Gordon to Ronnie Moore: Activities Report, June 1, 1968, 3, Schomburg.

85. Rachal, "We'll Never Turn Back," 182.

86. Hamilton, "Did the Dream End There?," 19.

87. Thomas, "Review," 287–88.

88. A Living Philosophy to Guide the Freedom School during the PPC Campaign.

89. Jackson, "Resurrection City," 67.

90. Moore, Scholarship, Education, and Defense Fund for Racial Equality in Resurrection City.

91. Speech by "Jimmy," July 12, 1968.

92. Jackson, Foreword, 17.

93. Meek, "Propaganda," 173.

94. Entwistle, *Antonio Gramsci*, 12.

95. Williams, "Base and Superstructure."

96. Coben, "Revisiting Gramsci."

97. Coben, "Revisiting Gramsci"; Meek, "Propaganda."

98. Entwistle, *Antonio Gramsci*, 111.

99. Wright, "Civil Rights Unfinished Business," 416.

100. Austin interview, 24.

101. Langdon, "Democracy Re-Examined," 148.

102. Larrabure et al., "New Cooperativism," 194.

103. Shannon interview, 36.

CHAPTER 12. A CITY LIKE ANY OTHER

1. SCLC (National Office), *New York Times Magazine*, ser. 6, box 2, 2, July 7, 1968, Hosea Williams Collection.

2. SCLC Papers, box 16, 7, 9, King Center.

3. "Poor Marchers Stage Agriculture Department Protest," *Washington Post*, May 29, 1968, 2.

4. "How It Was in Resurrection City: I'm Poor and Black Myself, I Had to Be a Witness," *Boston Globe*, July 1, 1968, 11.

5. "Poor People Plan More Militancy," *Washington Post*, June 3, 1968, 20.

6. "Poor Marchers Stage Agriculture Department Protest," 2.

7. SCLC (National Office), *Black Liberator*, ser. 6, box 2, 19, June 1968, Hosea Williams Collection.

8. Frady, *Jesse*, 242.

9. McKnight, *Last Crusade*, 119.

10. Bretz, "Poor People's Campaign," 19.

11. SCLC Papers, Ken Mann, Resurrection City and the Media, September 4, 1968, 4, King Center.

12. Peterson interview, 34.

13. Jackson, "Resurrection City," 66.

14. M. Finkelstein, Department of Transportation Route Slip to Mr. Al Gollin, February 19, 1969, Schomburg.

15. Harris interview, 2.

16. Eaton interview.

17. Freedman, *Old News*, 18.

18. Givens interview, 23.

19. "More Militancy Pledged for Poor," *New York Times*, June 3, 1968, 20.

20. SCLC, R. M. Moore, Scholarship, Education, and Defense Fund for Racial Equality (SEDFRE) in Resurrection City, June 5, 1968, Schomburg.

21. Sampson interview, 19.

22. Shannon interview, 45.

23. Austin interview.

24. Ibid.

25. "18 Poor Marchers Arrested at Capitol," *Washington Post*, July 10, 1968, 21.

26. Tijerina, *King Tiger*, 107.

27. "Resurrection City: Metaphors," *New Yorker*, June 1968, 73.

28. Shannon interview, 46.

29. "Poor People Seek Support for Big Rally," *Washington Post*, June 11, 1968, 2.

30. Cobb, *Native Activism*, 176.

31. Ibid.

32. Houk interview, 38.

33. Mantler, "Press Did You In," 43.

34. SCLC (National Office), Faith Berry, *New York Times Magazine*, ser. 6, box 2, 12, July 7, 1968, Hosea Williams Collection.

35. Ibid.

36. Cobb, *Native Activism*, 185.

37. Ibid., 185.

38. Ibid.

39. Abernathy, *And the Walls*, 498.

40. Mantler, "Black, Brown, and Poor," 255.

41. Baker interview, 37.

42. Walker interview, 10.

43. Walker interview.

44. Ibid., 35.

45. Cheng interview, June 6, 1970, 58.

46. Jackson, "Resurrection City," 66.

47. Cobb, *Native Activism*, 188.

48. SCLC (National Office), *New York Times Magazine*, ser. 6, box 2, 12, July 7, 1968, Hosea Williams Collection.

49. Tijerina, *King Tiger*, 114.

50. Ibid.

51. Reynolds, *Fight for Freedom*, 137.

52. SCLC Papers, box 179, 34, King Center.

53. Mantler, *Black, Brown, and Poor*, 273.

54. Givens interview, 24.

55. "How It Was in Resurrection City," 11.

56. SCLC Papers, *Soul Force*, 1968, box 180, 4, 1, King Center.

57. Grayson, "Organising, Educating and Training," 209.

58. SCLC Papers, *Soul Force*, 1968, 4, King Center.

59. Mantler, *Black, Brown, and Poor*, 279.

60. Freedman, *Old News*, 126.

61. SCLC Papers, The Many Races Soul Center, 1968, 4, King Center.

62. SCLC Papers, Mariette Wicks, Cultural Program for the PPC, box 180, 4, May 30, 1968, King Center.

63. Ibid.

64. SCLC Papers, *Soul Force*, box 180, 4, King Center.

65. Mariette Wicks, Cultural Program for the PPC.

66. Ibid.

67. Ibid.

68. Ibid.

69. Ibid.

70. SCLC Papers, *Soul Force*, box 177, 14, King Center.

71. SCLC Papers, *Soul Force*, box 155, 26, 2, King Center.

72. SCLC Papers, *Soul Force*, box 180, 3, King Center.

73. SCLC Papers, box 180, 3, 10, King Center.

74. Howard McConnell, "Why We Are Here," *Soul Force*, June 19, 1968, 10, Schomburg.

75. Offenburger interview, 46.

76. *True Unity News* of Resurrection City, June 5, 1968, 2, Schomburg.

77. SCLC Papers, J. Edward Haycraft, "Poor People's Government," *Soul Force*, June 19, 1968, 6, King Center.

78. "Songs of the Poor," *Soul Force*, June 19, 1968, 11, Schomburg.

79. SCLC Papers, J. Edward Haycraft in Resurrection City, box 178, 270, King Center.

80. "Resurrection City Offers Hope to Man," *Soul Force*, June 19, 1968, 7, Schomburg.

81. Free Man, "A Curse on the Men of Washington," *Soul Force*, June 19, 1968, 8, Schomburg.

82. "How It Was in Resurrection City," 11.

83. Ibid.

84. Ibid.

85. Ibid.

86. Ibid.

87. "Resurrection City Looks Different from Inside," *Sunday Star*, May 19, 1968, 6.

88. Ibid.

89. Ibid.

90. Ibid.

91. "City of the Poor Develops Style All of Its Own," *New York Times*, May 24, 1968, 30.

92. Ibid.

93. SCLC, National Office, *New York Times Magazine*, Faith Berry, ser. 6, box 2, 12. July 7, 1968, 3.

94. Abernathy, *And the Walls*, 503.

95. Jackson, "Resurrection City," 66.

96. Rutherford interview, 9.

97. Ibid.

98. "How It Was in Resurrection City," 11.

99. Peterson interview, 5.

100. SCLC Papers, box 179, 31, 3, King Center.

101. Grace et al., "Art as Anti-Oppression," 75.

102. Lee and Vale, "Resurrection City," 113.

103. Frady, *Jesse*, 242.

104. Fager, *Uncertain Resurrection*, viii.

105. "A Living History, Poor People's Campaign," produced by Arthur Alexander, WBAI broadcast, June 21, 1968, BB3128, Pacifica Radio Archives, https://www.pacificaradio archives.org/.

106. "Resurrection City Offers Hope to Man," 7.

107. Peterson interview, 41–42.

108. Lee and Vale, "Resurrection City, Washington, D.C., 1968," 120.

109. "City of the Poor Develops Style All of Its Own," 30.

110. Young, *An Easy Burden*, 488.

CHAPTER 13. THE FINAL DAYS OF THE POOR PEOPLE'S CAMPAIGN

1. Thomas, *Robert Kennedy*, 126.

2. Marian Wright Edelman, JFK, MLK, RFK, second session, 1960–1968, October 23, 2005, 11, Kennedy Presidential Library Forums.

3. "FBI Files Suggest MLK Was More Complicated than His Myth," *Economist*, June 8, 2019, 1–2.

4. Edelman, JFK, MLK, RFK, second session, 11.

5. Young, *An Easy Burden*, 380.

6. Edelman, *Lanterns*, 111.

7. Clarke, *Last Campaign*; Schmitt, *President of the Other America*.

8. Schmitt, "Appalachian Thread," 371.

9. Ibid., 372.

10. Schmitt, *President of the Other America*, 213.

11. Edelman, JFK, MLK, RFK, second session, 24.

12. SCLC Papers, Ralph Abernathy Statements, box 177, 1, June 6, 1968, 1–2, King Center.

13. Schmitt, *President of the Other America*, 308.

14. SCLC Papers, News Dispatches, June 9, 1968, 1, King Center.

15. Ibid., 2.

16. Laurent, *King and the Other America*, 161.

17. Shannon interview, 55.

18. SCLC, Proposal for a Grant to Plan the Development of a Poor People's Embassy, July 12–14, 1968, 1–2, Schomburg.

19. D'Emilio, *Lost Prophet*, 464.

20. King and Ruley, *New and Unsettling Force*, 28.

21. Mantler, *Power to the Poor*, 43.

22. Romero interview, 8.

23. Mantler, "Press Did You In," 44.

24. Bretz, "Poor People's Campaign," 19.

25. McKnight, *Last Crusade*, 127.

26. "18 Poor Marchers Arrested at Capitol," *Washington Post*, July 10, 1968, 21.

27. "SCLC'S 'Portia' Besieges the Hill," *Daily Star*, July 7, 1968, 3.

28. "Police Force Bolstered to 4,300 for Big March," *Star*, June 18, 1968, A1.

29. SCLC Papers, "Dr. Ralph Abernathy Speaks: Progress in Resurrection City," *Soul Force*, June 19, 1968, 2, King Center.

30. Ibid.

31. "All Were in the March," *Washington Post*, June 20, 1968, B5

32. "For Demonstrators, a Chance to Do Their Thing," *New York Times*, June 20, 1968, 30.

33. "People of the March: Weary but Wanting to Do Their Part," *Washington Post*, June 20, 1968, 6.

34. "Religious Leaders United in Solidarity with the Poor," *Washington Afro-American*, June 19, 1968, 6.

35. U.S. National Student Association, press release, June 7, 1968, Schomburg.

36. "For Demonstrators, a Chance to Do Their Thing," 30.

37. "Woman Power Major Factor in Solidarity Day Activities," *Washington Afro-American*, June 22, 1968, 1.

38. "Crowds Far Greater than Expected," *Evening Star*, June 20, 1968, 6.

39. "Suburbanites Hike in to Help Poor," *Washington Post*, June 20, 1968, 4.

40. "Women Voters Head Tells Why She's Marching," *Washington Post*, June 19, 1968, 3.

41. "800 Baltimoreans March in Solidarity Day Trek," *Washington Afro-American*, June 22, 1968, 22.

42. "Suburbanites Hike in to Help Poor," 4.

43. "In the Slums, It Was a Slow Hopeful Day," *Washington Post*, June 20, 1968, C1.

44. "Solidarity Day Over: What Next," *Washington Examiner*, June 20–22, 1968, 2.

45. "People of the March," 6.

46. "Mood of the Marchers: Patience Worn Thin," *New York Times*, June 20, 1968, 31.

47. "Suburbanites Hike in to Help Poor," 4.

48. "For Demonstrators, a Chance to Do Their Thing," 30.

49. "The March 5 Years Later: Frustration Replaces Hope," *Washington Post*, June 20, 1968, 9.

50. SCLC, Solidarity Day, box 180, 2, June 15, 1968, King Center.

51. "Police Force Bolstered to 4,300," A1.

52. "Solidarity Day Over," 2.

53. Ibid., 3.

54. "Eartha Kitt's Song for Today: Putting Our Hands Together," *Washington Post*, June 19, 1968, C2.

55. "Seating Problems Caused Confusion in VIP Section," *Washington Afro-American*, June 22, 1968, 23.

56. "Brando: Hunger Obscene," *Washington Post*, June 20, 1968, 2.

57. "Lawmakers 'March' in Cool Comfort," *Washington Daily News*, June 20, 1968, 12.

58. "Solidarity Day Over," 2.

59. SCLC Papers, *Soul Force*, June 19, 1968, 2, Schomburg.

60. "Solidarity Day Over," 2.

61. Abernathy, *And the Walls*, 528.

62. "Coretta Seeks Womanpower," *Washington Daily News*, June 20, 1968, 18.

63. "Care Power Was the Message," *Washington Post*, June 20, 1968, 25.

64. "Solidarity Day Over," 2.

65. "Highlights from Speeches at 'Solidarity' Rally," *Washington Post*, June 20, 1968, 6.

66. "The March 5 Years Later," 9.

67. "Power of the Poor," *Washington Daily News*, June 24, 1968, 21.

68. "Solidarity Day Over," 3.

69. Mantler, "Press Did You In," 44.

70. "Solidarity Day 1968," *Washington Post*, June 20, 1968, 19.

71. "A Gratifying March," *Washington Afro-American*, June 22, 1968, 4, Schomburg.

72. Dorr interview.

73. "Tension Prevails at Mud-Spattered Resurrection City," *Washington Post*, June 20, 1968, 9.

74. Cobb, *Native Activism*, 188.

75. *True Unity News* of Resurrection City, June 1968, 4, Schomburg.

76. Ibid.

77. Freedman, *Old News*, 126.

78. Frady, *Jesse*, 244.

79. SCLC (National Office), *New York Times Magazine*, ser. 6, box 2, 12, July 7, 1968, Hosea Williams Collection.

80. Cobb, *Native Activism*, 191–92.

81. SCLC (National Office), *New York Times Magazine*.

82. Reynolds, *Fight for Freedom*, 146–47.

83. Cobb, *Native Activism*, 192.

84. "Thurmond Puts Cost of March at $1 Million," *New York Times*, July 14, 1968.

85. PBS, "The Promised Land," episode 10 of *Eyes on the Prize*, 1990.

86. Wright, "Civil Rights Unfinished Business," 414–15.

87. Abernathy, *And the Walls*, 539.

88. Rutherford interview, 8.

89. Gollin, *Demography of Protest*, 7.

90. Freedman, *Old News*, 31.

91. Ibid.

92. SCLC Papers, "Dr. Ralph Abernathy Speaks: Progress in Resurrection City," *Soul Force*, June 19, 1968, 2, King Center.

93. SCLC Papers, Ralph Abernathy Statements, June–July 1968, box 177, 2, 1, King Center.

94. SCLC (National Office), Faith Berry, *New York Times Magazine*, ser. 6, box 2, 12, July 7, 1968, Hosea Williams Collection.

95. Ibid.

96. Shannon interview, 20.

97. "Vigil to Mark Release of Abernathy," *Evening Star*, July 11, 1968, 70.

98. "More Poor Jailed, Action Goes On," *Washington Afro-American*, July 9, 1968, 13.

99. Ibid.

100. Ibid.

101. "17 of the Poor Held on Capitol Grounds," *New York Times*, July 10, 1968, 20.

102. "18 Poor Marchers Arrested at Capitol," 20.

103. "They're Still Here," *Washington Examiner*, July 11, 1968, 13.

104. "18 Poor Marchers Arrested at Capitol," 20.

105. "New Protests Set at Capitol: 18 Seized after Warning," *Evening Star*, July 10, 1968, 13.

106. "Poor Plan District Jail Vigil," *Washington Post*, July 11, 1968, 13.

107. "Vigil to Mark Abernathy's Release," *Daily News*, July 11, 1968, 13.

108. "Demonstrator Given 90 Days, $250 Fine," *Daily News*, July 13, 1968, 13.

109. SCLC, draft, PPC Legal Redress Committee, June 1968, Schomburg.

110. SCLC, PPC, Information Bulletin, July 7, 1968, 2, Schomburg.

111. "New Protests Set at Capitol: 18 Seized after Warning," 13.

112. Letter from Ralph Abernathy to clergymen, June 25, 1968, 1, Schomburg.

113. Ibid., 2.

114. "Freed Abernathy Talks of New Plans," *Washington Post*, July 14, 1968, 8.

115. "Abernathy Leaves D.C. Jail, Revisits Site of Tent City," *Evening Star*, July 14, 1968, 2.

116. Ibid., 8.

117. SCLC, Proposal for a Grant to Plan the Development of a Poor People's Embassy, July 12–14, 1968, Schomburg.

118. "Abernathy Leaves D.C. Jail, Revisits Site of Tent City," 2.

119. "Abernathy Sends Poor Home to Push Campaign," *Washington Post*, July 17, 1968.

120. "150 Poor Marchers Protest Again at the Capitol," *Washington Post*, July 22, 1968.

121. SCLC Papers, Ralph Abernathy Statements, June–July 1968, box 177, 2, 1, King Center.

122. "Freed Abernathy Talks of New Plans," 8.

123. "Abernathy Leaves D.C. Jail, Revisits Site of Tent City," 2.

CONCLUSION

1. Jackson, "Resurrection City," 74.

2. Chester et al., *American Melodrama*, 498–99.

3. Quoted in Patterson, *Great Expectations*, 701.

4. Ibid.

5. Ambrose, *Nixon*, 163.

6. Chester et al., *American Melodrama*, 491.

7. Ibid., 492.

8. "Agnew Meets Nixon in New York then Criticizes Campaign of Poor," *Washington Post*, June 21, 1968, B1.

9. Mantler, *Power to the Poor*, 215.

10. Chester et al., *American Melodrama*, 491, 517.

11. Updegrove, *Indomitable Will*, 297.

12. Chester et al., *American Melodrama*, 517.

13. Reynolds, *Fight for Freedom*, 145.

14. SCLC Papers, Note to Editors, Congressional Quarterly Service press release, Government Meets Half of Poor People's Campaign Demands, November 8, 1968, 2, King Center.

15. Ibid.

16. Barnes, *Centennial History*, 247.

17. Marian Wright Edelman, JFK, MLK, RFK, second session, 1960–1968, October 23, 2005, 24, Kennedy Presidential Library Forums.

18. Holst, "Frameworks," 118.

19. Eaklor, "Learning from History."

20. Walter, "Adult Learning," 259.

21. Grace et al., "Art as Anti-Oppression," 77.

22. Shannon interview, 21.

23. SCLC Papers, box 180, 10, 4, King Center.

24. Freeman, *Mule Train*, 117.

25. Ibid.

26. SCLC, Appalachian people's meeting, May 25, 1968, 2, King Center.

27. Ibid., 1.

28. Interview of Tyrone Brooks by author, April 2, 2014.

29. Grace et al., "Art as Anti-Oppression," 72.

30. Peterson interview, 35.

31. Jackson, "Resurrection City," 74.

32. Ibid.

33. Givens interview, 6.

34. Walker interview, 40.

35. Cobb, *Native Activism*, 149.

36. Quoted in Green, "Challenging the Civil Rights Narrative," 58.

37. Honey, *To the Promised Land*, 187.

38. Lewis, Epilogue, 440.

39. Shannon interview, 76–77.

40. Cotton, *If Your Back's Not Bent*, 240.

41. Sidy, "Poor People's Campaign."

42. Hamilton, "Did the Dream End There?," 22.

43. H. Sherwood, "'Our Faith Compels Us': Christian Resistance to Trump Gathers Steam," *Guardian*, October 26, 2018.

44. Lewis, Epilogue, 440.

45. Le Blanc and Yates, *Freedom Budget*, 236.

46. Rutherford interview, 22.

BIBLIOGRAPHY

ARCHIVES

Albert E. Gollin Collection, Schomburg Center for Research in Black Culture, New York.

Catherine Clarke Civil Rights Collection, Schomburg Center for Research in Black Culture, New York.

Civil Rights Documentation Project: Ralph J. Bunche Oral History Collection, Moorland-Spingarn Research Center, Manuscript Division, Howard University, Washington, D.C.

Dr. Martin Luther King Jr. Papers, Howard Gotlieb Archival Research Center, Boston University, Mass.

Hosea Williams Collection, Auburn Avenue Research Library on African American Culture and History, Atlanta, Ga.

King Library and Archives, King Center, Atlanta, Ga.

Martin Luther King Jr. Collection, Atlanta University Center, Robert W. Woodruff Library, Morehouse College, Atlanta, Ga.

President John F. Kennedy Presidential Library Forums, Boston, Mass., https://www.jfklibrary.org/events-and-awards/forums.

ORAL TESTIMONIES AND INTERVIEWS

Austin, E. July 9, 1968. Interview by Katherine Shannon. Civil Rights Documentation Project: Ralph J. Bunche Oral History Collection, RJB 264. Washington, D.C.: Howard University.

Baker, Ella. June 19, 1968. Civil Rights Documentation Project: Ralph J. Bunche Oral History Collection, RJB 203. Washington, D.C.: Howard University.

Beaudin, Bruce. July 2, 1968. Interview by Tony Newkirk. New York: Schomburg Center for Research in Black Culture.

Buskirk, P. June 12, 1968. Civil Rights Documentation Project: Ralph J. Bunche Oral History Collection, RJB 381. Washington, D.C.: Howard University.

Cheng, C. July 11, 1968. New York: Schomburg Center for Research in Black Culture.

———. June 6, 1970. Civil Rights Documentation Project: Ralph J. Bunche Oral History Collection, RJB 558. Washington, D.C.: Howard University.

Comfort, M. November 16, 1968. Civil Rights Documentation Project: Ralph J. Bunche Oral History Collection, RJB 338. Washington, D.C.: Howard University.

Cooks, S. July 12, 1968. Interview by Katherine Shannon. Civil Rights Documentation
    Project: Ralph J. Bunche Oral History Collection, RJB 260. Washington, D.C.: Howard
    University.
Dorr, Robin. July 2, 1968. Interview by Tony Newkirk. New York: Schomburg Center for
    Research in Black Culture.
Eaton, D. June 25, 1968. New York: Schomburg Center for Research in Black Culture.
Freeman, Orville. January 14, 1969. Civil Rights Documentation Project: Ralph J. Bunche
    Oral History Collection. Washington, D.C.: Howard University.
Givens, C. July 7, 1968. Interview by Katherine Shannon. Civil Rights Documentation
    Project: Ralph J. Bunche Oral History Collection, RJB 223. Washington, D.C.: Howard
    University.
Gollin, Gillian. July 15, 1968. Interview by Tony Newkirk. New York: Schomburg Center
    for Research in Black Culture.
Harris, Ruth Bates. July 1, 1968. New York: Schomburg Center for Research in Black
    Culture.
Henry, A. July 15, 1968. Civil Rights Documentation Project: Ralph J. Bunche Oral History
    Collection, RJB 225. Washington, D.C.: Howard University.
Houk, Thomas. July 10, 1968. Interview by Katherine Shannon. Civil Rights Documen-
    tation Project: Ralph J. Bunche Oral History Collection, RJB 230. Washington, D.C.:
    Howard University.
"Jimmy." July 12, 1968. Speech at HEW auditorium. New York: Schomburg Center for
    Research in Black Culture.
Jones, C. July 7, 1968. New York: Schomburg Center for Research in Black Culture.
Lynch, G. June 27, 1968. New York: Schomburg Center for Research in Black Culture.
Moyer, William H. July 7, 1968. Civil Rights Documentation Project: Ralph J. Bunche Oral
    History Collection, RJB 228. Washington, D.C.: Howard University.
Offenburger, T. E. July 2, 1968. Civil Rights Documentation Project: Ralph J. Bunche Oral
    History Collection, RJB 227. Washington, D.C.: Howard University.
Payne, T. June 17, 1968. Metropolitan Citizens Advisory Council. New York: Schomburg
    Center for Research in Black Culture.
Peterson, J. E. July 3, 1968. Civil Rights Documentation Project: Ralph J. Bunche Oral His-
    tory Collection, RJB 224. Washington, D.C.: Howard University.
Robinson, U. June 17, 1968. Phoenix Society, Washington, D.C. New York: Schomburg
    Center for Research in Black Culture.
Romero, R. June 11, 1968. Civil Rights Documentation Project: Ralph J. Bunche Oral His-
    tory Collection, RJB 193. Washington, D.C.: Howard University.
Rutherford, J. July 4, 1968. Civil Rights Documentation Project: Ralph J. Bunche Oral His-
    tory Collection, RJB 226. Washington, D.C.: Howard University.
Sampson, A. R. July 8, 1968. Interview by Katherine Shannon. Civil Rights Documen-
    tation Project: Ralph J. Bunche Oral History Collection, RJB 229. Washington, D.C.:
    Howard University.
Shabazz, L. June 28, 1968. Black Muslims of the Lost-Found Nation of Islam. New York:
    Schomburg Center for Research in Black Culture.
Shannon, K. August 12, 1968. Interview by Claudia Rawles. Civil Rights Documentation
    Project: Ralph J. Bunche Oral History Collection, RJB 297. Washington, D.C.: Howard
    University.
Walker, T. July 1968. Interview by Katherine Shannon. Civil Rights Documentation Proj-
    ect: Ralph J. Bunche Oral History Collection, RJB 231. Washington, D.C.: Howard
    University.

INTERVIEWS BY THE AUTHOR

Brooks, Tyrone. Poor People's Campaign activist. April 2, 2014.

Lafayette, Bernard. Poor People's Campaign national director. April 1, 2014, and May 4, 2017.

Lewis, Charles, Jr. Southern Christian Leadership Conference president. May 4, 2017.

PUBLISHED SOURCES

Abernathy, R. D. *And the Walls Came Tumbling Down*. New York: Harper and Row, 1989.

Adams, F., and M. Horton. *Unearthing Seeds of Fire: The Idea of Highlander*. Winston-Salem, N.C.: John F. Blair, 1975.

Afield, W. B., and A. B. Gibson. *Children of Resurrection City*. Washington, D.C.: Association for Childhood Education International, 1970.

Ambrose, S. *Nixon: The Triumph of a Politician, 1962–1972*. London: Simon and Schuster, 1989.

Arsenault, R. Afterword. In *In Peace and Freedom: My Journey in Selma*, edited by B. Lafayette and K. L. Johnson, 149–51. Lexington: University Press of Kentucky, 2013.

———. *Freedom Riders: 1961 and the Struggle for Racial Justice*. Oxford: Oxford University Press, 2006.

Barber, L. G. *Marching on Washington: The Forging of an American Tradition*. Berkeley: University of California Press, 2002.

Barnes, G. A. *A Centennial History of the American Friends Service Committee*. New York: Friends Press, 2016.

Bell, B., J. Gaventa, and J. Peters. Editors' Introduction. In *We Make the Road by Walking: Conversations on Education and Social Change: Myles Horton and Paulo Freire*, edited by B. Bell, J. Gaventa, and J. Peters, xv–xxxvii. Philadelphia, Pa.: Temple University Press, 1990.

Bell, B., J. Gaventa, and J. Peters, eds. *We Make the Road by Walking: Conversations on Education and Social Change: Myles Horton and Paulo Freire*. Philadelphia, Pa.: Temple University Press, 1990.

Bernstein, D. "The Longest March." *Chicago Magazine*, July 24, 2016, 1–20.

Billings, G. "Health Care in Resurrection City." *American Journal of Nursing* 68, no. 8 (1968): 1695–98.

Bradshaw, C. "A Comparative Study of the Presidential Primary Campaigns of the Kennedy Brothers (1960, 1968, and 1980)." PhD thesis, University of the West of Scotland, 2016.

Branch, T. *At Canaan's Edge: America in the King Years, 1965–1968*. New York: Simon and Schuster, 2006.

———. *Pillar of Fire: America in the King Years, 1963–1965*. New York: Simon and Schuster, 1998.

Bretz, B. "The Poor People's Campaign: An Evolution of the Civil Rights Movement." *Sociological Viewpoints* (Spring 2010): 19–25.

Brinkley, D. J. *Rosa Parks: A Life*. London: Penguin, 2000.

Burns, S. *Daybreak of Freedom: The Montgomery Bus Boycott*. Chapel Hill: University of North Carolina Press, 1997.

Cannon, L. *Governor Reagan: His Rise to Power*. New York: Public Affairs, 2003.

Carson, C., ed. *The Autobiography of Martin Luther King Jr.* London: Abacus, 2000.

———. Foreword. In *The Chicago Freedom Movement: Martin Luther King Jr. and Civil Rights*

Activism in the North, edited by M. L. Finley, B. Lafayette Jr., J. R. Ralph Jr., and P. Smith, ix–xii. Lexington: University Press of Kentucky, 2016.

Charron, K. M. *Freedom's Teacher: The Life of Septima Clark*. Chapel Hill: University of North Carolina Press, 2009.

Chase, R. T. *Class Resurrection: The Poor People's Campaign of 1968 and Resurrection City*. Charlottesville: Corcoran Department of History, University of Virginia, 1998.

Chester, L., G. Hodgson, and B. Page. *An American Melodrama: The Presidential Campaign of 1968*. London: Literary Guild, 1969.

Clark, L. D. "A Tribute to Dr. Martin Luther King Jr.: A Man of Peace and Wisdom." *Widener Journal of Public Law* 2, no. 2 (1993): 431–46.

Clarke, T. *The Last Campaign: Robert Kennedy and 82 Days That Inspired America*. New York: Holt, 2008.

Cobb, D. M. *Native Activism in Cold War America: The Struggle for Sovereignty*. Lawrence: University Press of Kansas, 2008.

Coben, D. "Revisiting Gramsci." *Studies in the Education of Adults* 27, no. 1 (1995): 36–51.

Cohen, A., and E. Taylor. *American Pharaoh: Mayor Richard J. Daley and His Battle for Chicago and the Nation*. Boston: Back Bay Books, 2000.

Cornfield, G., M. Heaps, and N. Hill. "Labor and the Chicago Freedom Movement." In *The Chicago Freedom Movement: Martin Luther King Jr. and Civil Rights Activism in the North*, edited by M. L. Finley, B. Lafayette Jr., J. R. Ralph Jr., and P. Smith, 373–86. Lexington: University Press of Kentucky, 2016.

Cotton, D. F. *If Your Back's Not Bent: The Role of the Citizenship Education Program in the Civil Rights Movement*. New York: Atria, 2012.

Crawford, V. L., J. A. Rouse, and B. Woods. *Women in the Civil Rights Movement: Trailblazers and Torchbearers, 1941–1965*. Bloomington: Indiana University Press, 1990.

Crowther, J., I. Martin, and M. Shaw, eds. *Popular Education and Social Movements in Scotland Today*. Leicester, England: NIACE, 1999.

Cunningham, P. M. "The Social Dimension of Transformative Learning." *PAACE Journal of Lifelong Learning* 7 (1998): 15–28.

Dallek, R. *Lyndon B. Johnson: Portrait of a President*. London: Penguin, 2005.

Davies, Philip John. *An American Quarter Century: U.S. Politics from Vietnam to Clinton*. Manchester, England: Manchester University Press, 1995.

D'Emilio, J. *Lost Prophet: The Life and Times of Bayard Rustin*. Chicago: University of Chicago Press, 2003.

DeShazo, R., R. Smith, W. F. Minor, and L. B. Skipwort. "An Unwilling Partnership with the Great Society. Part II: Physicians Discover Malnutrition, Hunger and the Politics of Hunger." *American Journal of the Medical Sciences* 352, no. 1 (July 2016): 120–27.

Dionisopoulos, G. N., V. J. Gallagher, S. R. Goldzwig, and D. Zarefsky. "Martin Luther King, the American Dream, and Vietnam: A Collision of Rhetorical Trajectories." *Western Journal of Communication* 56, no. 2 (1992): 91–107.

Dittmer, J. *Local People: The Struggle for Civil Rights in Mississippi*. Chicago: University of Illinois Press, 1994.

Dorrien, G. *Breaking White Supremacy: Martin Luther King Jr. and the Black Social Gospel*. New Haven, Conn.: Yale University Press, 2018.

Eaklor, V. L. "Learning from History: A Queer Problem." *International Journal of Sexuality and Gender Studies* 3 (1998): 195–211.

Eaves, J. H. *The Morehouse Mystique: Lessons to Develop Black Men*. Atlanta, Ga.: African American Images, 2009.

Edelman, M. W. *Lanterns: A Memoir of Mentors*. Boston: Beacon, 1999.

Edelman, P. *Searching for America's Heart: RFK and the Renewal of Hope*. Washington, D.C.: Georgetown University Press, 2003.

Entwistle, H. *Antonio Gramsci: Conservative Schooling for Radical Politics*. London: Routledge and Kegan Paul, 1979.

Fager, C. *Uncertain Resurrection: Dr. King's Poor People's Campaign*. 50th anniversary ed. Durham, N.C.: Kimo, 2017.

Frady, M. *Jesse: The Life and Pilgrimage of Jesse Jackson*. New York: Random House, 1996.

———. *Martin Luther King Jr.: A Life*. London: Penguin, 2002.

Freedman, J. *Old News: Resurrection City*. New York: Grossman, 1970.

A Freedom Budget for All Americans: Budgeting Our Resources, 1966-1975 to Achieve Freedom from Want. Rev. ed. New York: A. Philip Randolph Institute, 1966.

Freeman, R. L. *The Mule Train: A Journey of Hope Remembered*. Nashville, Tenn.: Rutledge Hill, 1998.

Freire, P. *Education for Critical Consciousness*. New York: Seabury, 1973.

———. *Pedagogy in Process: The Letters to Guinea-Bissau*. New York: Seabury, 1978.

Galbraith, John Kenneth. *The Affluent Society*. New York: Houghton Mifflin, 1958.

Garrow, D. J. *Bearing the Cross: Martin Luther King Jr. and the Southern Christian Leadership Conference*. London: Vintage, 1993.

———. *The FBI and Martin Luther King Jr.* London: Penguin, 1983.

Gibson Robinson, J. A. *The Montgomery Bus Boycott and the Women Who Started It: The Memoir of Jo Ann Gibson Robinson*. Edited by D. Garrow. Knoxville: University of Tennessee Press, 1987.

Goldwater, Barry. *The Conscience of a Conservative*. Shepardsville, Ky.: Victor, 1960.

Gollin, A. E. *The Demography of Protest: A Statistical Profile of Participants in the Poor People's Campaign: Report to Southern Christian Leadership Conference*. Atlanta, Ga.: Southern Christian Leadership Conference, 1968.

———. "The Poor People's Campaign and the March on Washington: Mobilization for Collective Protest." Paper presented at the 24th annual conference of the American Association for Public Opinion Research, May 16–19, 1969, Lake George, N.Y.

Grace, A. P., R. J. Hill, and K. Wells. "Art as Anti-Oppression Adult Education: Creating a Pedagogy of Presence and Place." In *Adult and Higher Education in Queer Contexts: Power, Politics and Pedagogy*, edited by R. J. Hill and A. P. Grace and Associates, 69–86. Chicago: Discovery Association Publishing House, 2009.

Grayson, J. "Organizing, Educating and Training: Varieties of Activist Learning in Left Socialist Movements in Sheffield (UK)." *Studies in the Education of Adults* 43, no. 2 (2011): 197–215.

Green, J. *Taking History to Heart: The Power of the Past in Building Social Movements*. Amherst: University of Massachusetts Press, 2000.

Green, L. B. "Challenging the Civil Rights Narrative: Women, Gender and the 'Politics of Protection.'" In *Civil Rights History from the Ground Up: Local Struggles, a National Movement*, edited by E. Crosby, 52–80. Athens: University of Georgia Press, 2011.

Halberstam, D. *The Children*. New York: Fawcett, 1998.

Hall, B. L., D. E. Clover, J. Crowther, and E. Scandrett, eds. *Learning and Education for a Better World: The Role of Social Movements*. Rotterdam, Netherlands: Sense, 2013.

Hamilton, R. "Did the Dream End There? Adult Education and Resurrection City, 1968." *Studies in the Education of Adults* 45, no. 1 (2013): 4–26.

———. "The Mule Train: Adult Learning and the Poor People's Campaign, 1968." *Studies in the Education of Adults* 48, no. 1 (2016): 38–64.

Hamilton Lytle, M. *America's Uncivil Wars: The Sixties Era from Elvis to the Fall of Richard Nixon*. New York: Oxford University Press, 2006.

Hampton, H., and S. Fayer. *Voices of Freedom: An Oral History of the Civil Rights Movement from the 1950s through the 1980s*. London: Vintage, 1995.

Harding, V. Introduction. In *If Your Back's Not Bent: The Role of the Citizenship Education Program in the Civil Rights Movement*, edited by D. F. Cotton, xv–xxi. New York: Atria, 2012.

Harley, A. "'We Are Poor, Not Stupid': Learning from Autonomous Grassroots Social Movements in South Africa." In *Learning and Education for a Better World: The Role of Social Movements*, edited by B. L. Hall, D. E. Clover, J. Crowther, and E. Scandrett, 3–32. Rotterdam, Netherlands: Sense, 2012.

Harrington, Michael. *The Other America: Poverty in the United States*. New York: Macmillan, 1962.

Heltzel, P. J. *Resurrection City: A Theory of Improvisation*. Grand Rapids, Mich.: Eerdmans, 2012.

Hill, R. J. "Activism as Practice: Some Queer Considerations." In *Promoting Critical Practice in Adult Education*, edited by R. St. Clair and J. A. Sandlin, 85–94. San Francisco, Calif.: Wiley, 2004.

Hodgson, G. *Martin Luther King*. London: Quercus, 2009.

Holst, J. D. "Frameworks for Understanding the Politics of Social Movements." *Studies in the Education of Adults* 43, no. 2 (2011): 117–26.

———. *Social Movements, Civil Society, and Radical Adult Education*. Westport, Conn.: Bergin and Garvey, 2002.

Honey, M. K. *Going Down Jericho Road: The Memphis Strike, Martin Luther King's Last Campaign*. New York: Norton, 2007.

———. *To the Promised Land: Martin Luther King and the Fight for Economic Justice*. New York: Norton, 2018.

———, ed. *All Labor Has Dignity*. Boston: Beacon, 2011.

Horton, M., with J. Kohl and H. Kohl. *The Long Haul: An Autobiography*. New York: Teachers College Press, 1998.

Horton, M., and P. Freire. "Educational Practice." In *We Make the Road by Walking: Conversations on Education and Social Change*, edited by M. Horton and P. Freire, 145–98. Philadelphia, Pa.: Temple University Press, 1990.

———. Introduction. In *We Make the Road by Walking: Conversations on Education and Social Change*, edited by M. Horton and P. Freire, xv–xxxvii. Philadelphia, Pa.: Temple University Press, 1990.

Jackson, J. "Resurrection City." *Ebony Magazine*, October 1968, 65–75.

Jackson, K. Foreword. In *Adult Education for a Change*, edited by J. Thompson, 9–18. London: Hutchinson, 1980.

Jackson, T. F. *From Civil Rights to Human Rights: Martin Luther King Jr. and the Struggle for Economic Justice*. Philadelphia: University of Pennsylvania Press, 2007.

Joseph, P. E. *Stokely: A Life*. New York: Basic Civitas, 2014.

Kamin, B. *Dangerous Friendship: Stanley Levison, Martin Luther King Jr., and the Kennedy Brothers*. East Lansing: Michigan State University Press, 2014.

Kennedy, E. M. *True Compass: A Memoir*. Boston: Little, Brown, 2009.

King, A., and C. Ruley. *A New and Unsettling Force: Reigniting Rev. Dr. Martin Luther King Jr.'s Poor People's Campaign*. New York: Union Theological Seminary, 2012.

King, C. S. *My Life, My Love, My Legacy*. New York: Holt, 2017.

King, M. L., Jr. *Stride toward Freedom: The Montgomery Story*. London: Souvenir, 2011.

———. *Where Do We Go from Here: Chaos or Community?* 1967. Reprint, New York: Beacon, 2010.

Kotz, N. *Judgment Days: Lyndon Baines Johnson, Martin Luther King Jr., and the Laws That Changed America*. Boston: Houghton Mifflin, 2005.

Lackey, H. L. *Marks, Martin, and the Mule Train*. Bloomington, Ind.: Xlibris, 2014.

Lafayette, B. "Nonviolence and the Chicago Freedom Movement." In *The Chicago Freedom Movement: Martin Luther King Jr. and Civil Rights Activism in the North*, edited by M. L. Finley, B. Lafayette Jr., J. R. Ralph Jr., and P. Smith, 389–406. Lexington: University Press of Kentucky, 2016.

Lafayette, B., and K. L. Johnson. *In Peace and Freedom: My Journey in Selma*. Lexington: University Press of Kentucky, 2013.

Lampinen, L. G. "The Poor People's Campaign." *International Socialism* 34 (1968): 8–10.

Lang, J. M. "Notes towards a Pedagogy of Presence." James M. Lang blog, November 4, 2014. http://www.jamesmlang.com/2014/11/notes-toward-pedagogy-of-presence.html.

Langdon, J. "Democracy Re-Examined: Ghanaian Social Movement Learning and the Re-Articulation of Learning in Struggle." *Studies in the Education of Adults* 43, no. 2 (2011): 147–62.

Larrabure, M., M. Vieta, and D. Schugurensky. "The 'New Cooperativism' in Latin America: Worker-Recuperated Enterprises and Socialist Production Units." *Studies in the Education of Adults* 43, no. 2 (2011): 181–95.

Laurent, S. *King and the Other America: The Poor People's Campaign and the Quest for Economic Equality*. Berkeley: University of California Press, 2019.

Le Blanc, P., and M. D. Yates. *A Freedom Budget for All Americans: Recapturing the Promise of the Civil Rights Movement in the Struggle for Economic Justice Today*. New York: Monthly Review Press, 2013.

Lee, Tunney, and Laurence Vale. "Resurrection City, Washington, D.C., 1968." *Thresholds* 41 (Spring 2013): 112–21.

Lemann, N. *The Promised Land: The Great Black Migration and How It Changed America*. New York: Knopf, 1991.

Lentz, R. *Symbols, the News Magazines, and Martin Luther King*. Baton Rouge: Louisiana State University, 1990.

Levine, D. *Bayard Rustin and the Civil Rights Movement*. New Brunswick, N.J.: Rutgers University Press, 2000.

Levingston, S. *Kennedy and King: The President, the Pastor, and the Battle over Civil Rights*. New York: Hachette, 2017.

Lewis, J. "Epilogue: Nonviolence Remix and Today's Millennials." In *The Chicago Freedom Movement: Martin Luther King Jr. and Civil Rights Activism in the North*, edited by M. L. Finley, B. Lafayette Jr., J. R. Ralph Jr., and P. Smith, 435–41. Lexington: University Press of Kentucky, 2016.

Lippmann, Walter. *An Inquiry into the Principles of the Good Society*. Boston: Little, Brown, 1937.

Long, M. G., ed. *I Must Resist: Bayard Rustin's Life in Letters*. San Francisco, Calif.: City Lights, 2012.

Maddison, S., and S. Sclamer. *Activist Wisdom: Practical Knowledge and Creative Tension in Social Movements*. Sydney, Australia: University of New South Wales Press, 2006.

Mantler, G. K. "Black, Brown, and Poor: Martin Luther King Jr. and the Poor People's Campaign and Its Legacies." PhD diss., Duke University, 2008.

———. "Partners in Justice and Peace: AFSC and the Poor People's Campaign of 1968." May 17, 2017. https://www.afsc.org/sites/default/files/documents/2017_Gordon_K._Mantler_AFSC_Paper.pdf.

———. *Power to the Poor: Black-Brown Coalition and the Fight for Economic Justice, 1960–1974*. Chapel Hill: University of North Carolina Press, 2013.

———. "'The Press Did You In': The Poor People's Campaign and the Mass Media." *Sixties: A Journal of History, Politics and Culture* 3, no. 1 (2010): 33–54.

Martinez, E. B. "Where Was the Color in Seattle? Looking for Reasons Why the Great Battle Was So White." *ColorLines* 3, no. 1 (2000). https://www.colorlines.com/articles/where-was-color-seattlelooking-reasons-why-great-battle-was-so-white.

Mayer, J. D. "Nixon Rides the Backlash to Victory: Racial Politics in the 1968 Presidential Campaign." *Historian* 64, no. 2 (2002): 351–66.

McKnight, G. D. *The Last Crusade: Martin Luther King Jr., the FBI, and the Poor People's Campaign.* Boulder, Colo.: Westview, 1998.

McLemee, S. "'A Freedom Budget for All': Interview with P. Le Blanc." *Inside Higher Ed* (August 21, 2013): 1–6.

Meek, D. "Propaganda, Collective Participation and the War of Position in the Brazilian Landless Workers' Movement." *Studies in the Education of Adults* 43, no. 2 (2011): 164–80.

Mills, K. "This Little Light of Mine: The Life of Fannie Lou Hamer." In *The Chicago Freedom Movement: Martin Luther King Jr. and Civil Rights Activism in the North,* edited by M. L. Finley, B. Lafayette Jr., J. R. Ralph Jr., and P. Smith, 192–93. Lexington: University Press of Kentucky, 2016.

Moynihan, Daniel P. *The Negro Family: The Case for National Action.* Washington, D.C.: U.S. Government Printing Office, 1965.

Nadasen, P. *Rethinking the Welfare Rights Movement.* London: Routledge, 2012.

Newman, M. *Teaching Defiance: Stories and Strategies for Activist Educators: A Book Written in Wartime.* San Francisco, Calif.: Jossey-Bass, 2006.

Niermann, T. A. *The American Indian Chicago Conference, 1961: A Native Response to Government Policy and the Birth of Indian Self-Determination.* Lawrence: University Press of Kansas, 2006.

Oropeza, L. "Becoming Indo-Hispano: Reies Lopez Tijerina and the New Mexican Land Grant Movement." In *Formations of United States Colonialism,* edited by A. Goldstein, 180–206. Durham, N.C.: Duke University Press, 2014.

Patterson, J. T. *Great Expectations: The United States, 1945–1974.* New York: Oxford University Press, 1997.

Pawel, M. *The Crusades of Cesar Chavez.* London: Bloomsbury, 2014.

Payne, C. M. *I've Got the Light of Freedom: The Organizing Tradition and the Mississippi Freedom Struggle.* Berkeley: University of California Press, 1995.

Rachal, J. R. "We'll Never Turn Back: Adult Education and the Struggle for Citizenship in Mississippi's Freedom Summer." *Adult Education Quarterly* 50, no. 3 (2000): 166–95.

Ralph, J. R., Jr., and M. L. Finley. "In Their Own Voices: The Story of the Movement as Told by the Participants." In *The Chicago Freedom Movement: Martin Luther King Jr. and Civil Rights Activism in the North,* edited by M. L. Finley, B. Lafayette Jr., J. R. Ralph Jr., and P. Smith, 13–79. Lexington: University Press of Kentucky, 2016.

Reef, C. *Ralph David Abernathy.* Parsippany, N.J.: Dillon Press, 1995.

Reynolds, J. *The Fight for Freedom: A Memoir of My Years in the Civil Rights Movement.* Bloomington, Ind.: Authorhouse, 2012.

Robnett, R. *How Long? How Long?* New York: Oxford University Press, 1997.

Schmitt, E. R. "The Appalachian Thread in the Antipoverty Politics of Robert F. Kennedy." *Register of the Kentucky Historical Society* 107, no. 3 (2009): 371–400.

———. *President of the Other America: Robert Kennedy and the Politics of Poverty.* Amherst: University of Massachusetts Press, 2010.

Sellers, C., with R. Terrell. *The River of No Return: The Autobiography of a Black Militant and the Life and Death of SNCC.* Jackson: University Press of Mississippi, 1990.

Sidy, R. "The Poor People's Campaign 43 Years Later through the Lens of Occupy Wall

Street." *Seeking New Solutions* 10, no. 10 (November 2011) : 1–4. www.snspress.com/pages /Vol.10_no10.htm.

Smith, P. "Youth and Nonviolence: Then and Now." In *The Chicago Freedom Movement: Martin Luther King Jr. and Civil Rights Activism in the North*, edited by M. L. Finley, B. Lafayette Jr., J. R. Ralph Jr., and P. Smith, 292–324. Lexington: University Press of Kentucky, 2016.

Stein, J. *American Journey: The Times of Robert Kennedy*. Edited by G. Plimpton. New York: Harcourt Brace Jovanovich, 1970.

Sugrue, T. J. *Sweet Land of Liberty: The Forgotten Struggle for Civil Rights in the North*. New York: Random House, 2008.

Thomas, E. *Robert Kennedy: His Life*. London: Simon and Schuster, 2000.

Thomas, J. E. "Review of Youngman, F., *Adult Education and Socialist Pedagogy*." *Adult Education* 59, no. 3 (December 1986): 112–13.

Tijerina, R. *They Called Me "King Tiger": My Struggle for the Land and Our Rights*. Houston, Tex.: Arte Publico Press, 2000.

Updegrove, M. K. *Indomitable Will: LBJ in the Presidency*. New York: Crown, 2012.

Walter, P. "Adult Learning in New Social Movements: Environmental Protest and the Struggle for the Clayaquot Sound Rainforest." *Adult Education Quarterly* 57, no. 3 (2007): 248–63.

Washington, J. M., ed. *A Testament of Hope: The Essential Writings of Martin Luther King Jr.* San Francisco, Calif.: Harper and Row, 1986.

Wiebenson, J. "Planning and Using Resurrection City." *Journal of American Planning Association* 35, no. 6 (1969): 405–11.

Williams, R. "Base and Superstructure in Marxist Cultural Theory." *New Left Review* 1, no. 82 (November–December 1973). https://newleftreview.org/issues/I82/articles /raymond-williams-base-and-superstructure-in-marxist-cultural-theory.

Wohl, A. *Father, Son, and Constitution: How Justice Tom Clark and Attorney General Ramsey Clark Shaped American Democracy*. Lawrence: University Press of Kansas, 2013.

Wright, A. N. "The 1968 Poor People's Campaign, Marks, Mississippi, and the Mule Train: Fighting Poverty Locally, Representing Poverty Nationally." In *Civil Rights History from the Ground Up: Local Struggles, a National Movement*, edited by E. Crosby, 109–43. Athens: University of Georgia Press, 2011.

———. "Civil Rights 'Unfinished Business': Poverty, Race, and the 1968 Poor People's Campaign." PhD diss., University of Texas, Austin, 2007.

Young, A. *An Easy Burden: The Civil Rights Movement and the Transformation of America*. New York: HarperCollins, 1996.

Youngman, F. *Adult Education and Socialist Pedagogy*. London: Croom Helm, 1986.

INDEX

CPSIA information can be obtained
at www.ICGtesting.com
Printed in the USA
LVHW031806300321
682972LV00009B/567

9 780820 358277